Eleventh Edition

Thomas W. Bean | John E. Readence | Judith Dunkerly-Bean
Old Dominion University | University of Nevada Las Vegas | Old Dominion University

Content Area Literacy
An Integrated Approach

Kendall Hunt
publishing company

Book Team

Chairman and Chief Executive Officer   Mark C. Falb
President and Chief Operating Officer   Chad M. Chandlee
Vice President, Higher Education   David L. Tart
Director of Publishing Partnerships   Paul B. Carty
Senior Developmental Coordinator   Angela Willenbring
Vice President, Operations   Timothy J. Beitzel
Permissions Editor Carla Kipper
Cover Designer Faith Walker

www.kendallhunt.com
Send all inquiries to:
4050 Westmark Drive
Dubuque, IA 52004-1840

Copyright © 1981, 1985, 1989, 1992, 1995, 1998, 2001, 2004, 2008, 2011, 2017 by Kendall Hunt Publishing
Company

Textbook alone ISBN: 978-1-5249-1589-6
Textbook with Website ISBN: 978-1-5249-9986-5

Published in the United States of America

Brief Contents

Contents

12   Studying and Preparing for Examinations, 331

Preface

The eleventh edition focuses on developing 21st century learners who are adept at reading and critiquing multiple texts in print and online forms. In the spirit of moving content area literacy forward, this edition includes the following features:

- Theory and related discipline-specific learning strategies designed to assist middle and secondary students in reading and learning through 21st century literacy practices

- A multimedia approach that integrates the book with additional resources on the related website that includes chapter activities as well as hotlinks to other literacy and content area websites

- A discussion of current literacy issues

- The presentation of new teaching and learning strategies

This edition consists of two parts: Part 1: Learning with Text and Technology and Part 2: Teaching and Learning Strategies.

Part 1 includes five chapters that introduce content area literacy:

- Chapter 1 provides a rationale and knowledge base for content area and disciplinary literacy as well as a discussion of multiple literacies.

- Chapter 2 explores the ever-expanding world of technology and its relationship to content area literacy.

- Chapter 3 follows with an examination of the reading/writing process and a discussion of sociocultural and linguistic variables that influence print and online literacy.

- Chapter 4 introduces readers to the sociopolitical nature of textbooks and then focuses on quantitative and qualitative procedures for evaluating and introducing textbooks and multimedia materials.

- Chapter 5 concludes this section of the book with a discussion of naturalistic and standards-based assessment.

Part 2 consists of seven chapters of strategies for teaching and learning in the content areas:

- Chapter 6 gives suggestions for unit and lesson planning.

- Chapter 7 explores young adult and global literature.

- Chapter 8 provides principles for effective vocabulary instruction.

- Chapter 9 addresses principles of comprehension as well as integrated teaching and learning approaches.

- Chapter 10 looks specifically at strategies for prereading, reading, and post-reading.

- Chapter 11 is about using writing as a vehicle to learn in the content areas.

- Chapter 12 concludes Part 2 by introducing study strategies and test preparation tactics for state reading assessments.

Features of the Eleventh Edition

Through the use of several different features, we present a model that reinforces our beliefs and demonstrates that our techniques DO work for teaching in the content areas. Preservice and in-service teachers will refer to this book often when constructing lesson plans and applying strategies in their classrooms.

The page format has been redesigned to provide teachers quick and easy access to the myriad concepts, ideas, and strategies presented in this eleventh edition of *Content Area Literacy*.

IN-TEXT LEARNING AIDS

Technology

A long-time leader in the content area discipline, this new edition carries on that tradition by providing a complete learning package including an expanded companion website.

Website

The reader may go to the *Content Area Literacy* website to access additional information. The *Content Area Literacy* website: https://www.grtep.com, supplements the textbook with the following:

- Internet activities that expand chapter content by demonstrating how to access current and relevant information for teaching art, literature, science, and other content areas;

- Hotlinks to websites such as professional organizations, trade book locations, and other sources to provide valuable and current information relevant to literacy issues and special interests of subject area specialists.

CHAPTER OPENERS

Anticipation Guide (Part 1)

Anticipation Guides open each chapter in PART 1: LEARNING WITH TEXT AND TECHNOLOGY. These guides present a series of statements that correlate with the content and facilitate discussion of literacy issues presented in each chapter.

Directions: Before reading the chapter, read each statement. Decide whether you agree or disagree with the statement and place a check in the appropriate column. Be prepared to explain your choices.

Vignette (Part 2)

Vignettes open each chapter in PART 2: TEACHING AND LEARNING STRATEGIES. These short vignettes present a classroom scenario that sets the tone of the chapter lesson.

Directions: Before reading the chapter, read and react to the short vignette. Answer the questions that follow and be prepared to justify your responses. Your instructor may ask you to work in pairs or small groups.

Rationale

The Rationale section provides background and explains the purpose of the chapter.

Learning Objectives

This section focuses on the major literacy issues discussed in each chapter.

Graphic Organizer

The Graphic Organizer provides a preview of new vocabulary and concepts.

Chapter Features

- Applications—many chapters include practical application exercises to help students gain a concrete understanding of chapter concepts.

- Consider This—this feature gives examples of material being discussed in the chapter.

- Glimpse into the Classroom—this feature demonstrates how chapter concepts translate into real-life classroom situations.

- Summary—the summary at the end of each chapter reinforces key concepts.

END OF CHAPTER AIDS

Reaction Guides/Vignettes

These activities reinforce the Anticipation Guides and Vignettes from the beginning of the chapter and confirm the big picture presented in the chapter.

Directions for Reaction Guides (Part 1)—Reconsider your responses to the statements at the beginning of the chapters.

- If the chapter content supports your original choice, place a ✓ in the Confirmed column. Then write what the text says in your own words under Column A—Why is my choice confirmed?

- If the chapter content does not support your choice, place a ✓ in the Disconfirmed column. Then write in your own words what the text says in Column B—Why is my choice not confirmed?

Directions for Vignettes (Part 2)—Reread the instructional vignette at the beginning of the chapter. React to the questions posed.

Mini Projects

This section gives you an opportunity to apply information from the chapter.

Website Activity

At the end of each chapter, there is a reference to the *Content Area Literacy* web page for the exercises relating to the chapter content.

END OF TEXT AIDS

Glossary

The Glossary serves as a ready reference for *italicized* vocabulary terms encountered in each chapter.

Bibliography

Recommended readings are identified by chapter in the Bibliography and are given as additional readings to extend and refine the information presented. References are also identified by chapter and listed in the Bibliography, thus providing a comprehensive list of references in one section.

Indexes

Both an Author and a Subject Index are provided for quick page reference for important terms and individuals cited in the text.

About the Authors

THOMAS W. BEAN is the Rosanne Keeley Norris Endowed Professor of Reading/Literacy in the Darden College of Education, Department of Teaching and Learning at Old Dominion University Norfolk, VA. Tom's teaching and research interests center on civic engagement projects aimed at increasing adolescent and child literacy development and possible futures. Along with Dr. Judith Dunkerly-Bean, Tom conducts qualitative studies of literacy projects at the crossroads of social justice and literacy development in the Tidewater, Virginia area. Tom's hobbies include kayaking, stand up paddle boarding, creating guitar YouTube clips, and crafting pyrography wind chimes, mobiles, and collages from recycled materials.

JOHN E. READENCE is an Emeritus Professor in the College of Education and former Dean of the University College at the University of Nevada, Las Vegas. His professional interests include research and practice in content area literacy and teacher education. John's personal interests include traveling, hiking, collecting art, movies, and music.

JUDITH M. DUNKERLY-BEAN is an Assistant Professor of Literacy in the Department of Teaching and Learning at Old Dominion University. Her work has been published in the *Journal of Adolescent and Adult Literacy*, the *Journal of Literacy Research*, *Comparative Issues in Education*, and the *Australian Journal of Language and Literacy*, as well as several edited volumes and research handbooks on gender and literacy and mobile learning. Along with Tom Bean, she is the coauthor of *Teaching Young Adult Literature: Developing Students as World Citizens*. Judith's research explores the intersection of critical literacy, social justice, and human rights, especially for marginalized youth. When she is not teaching and writing, Judith trail rides her quarter horse "Cloud," peddle boats with family, and reads novels.

PART 1
Learning with Text and Technology

© bikeriderlondon/Shutterstock.com

PART 1: Learning with Text and Technology

Content Area Literacy:
Developing Contemporary Learners

ANTICIPATION GUIDE

	Agree	Disagree

1. Upon leaving elementary school, students should have mastered the skills necessary for content area literacy across the disciplines.   _____   _____

2. Reading content area material is more demanding than in the past and many careers now require increasingly high levels of literacy.   _____   _____

3. Standardized tests measure the reading achievement needed for contemporary life.   _____   _____

4. Instructional strategies should fit the unique discourse features of the various content disciplines.   _____   _____

5. We live in a global society that calls for a citizenry able to evaluate and critique print and digital texts.   _____   _____

RATIONALE

The History Channel's popular series, *Pawn Stars*, is set in Las Vegas, Nevada where Rick Harrison's knowledge of arcane facts about jewelry and a host of other items customers bring in to sell or pawn creates a highly engaging show. In *License to Pawn* (2011), Rick's autobiography, we learn why books and reading were so important in his youth. As a child, Rick suffered from *grand mal* epileptic seizures that often came on at night and resulted in his missing school for 10 days at a time.

He recalls, "I didn't have a television in my room. Video games and iPads hadn't been invented. I was left to my own devises. So I read books. A lot of books" (p. 8).

Rick read a series of books entitled *The Great Brain* about a 10-year-old boy who, much like the Pawn Star star, was highly skilled at making money.

> *He was a generous schemer, a con artist with a big heart. He'd do things like build a roller coaster in his backyard and charge to let people ride it, but there was always some twist at the end that caused him to have a crisis of conscience and give all the money back. (p. 8)*

Rick Harrison credits reading and books for a pawn shop career that produced a show with historical content and a heart amid the rough and tumble streets of Las Vegas. In many ways, Rick Harrison, his dad, and the family are self-taught, making a living initially in a much smaller jewelry venue off the strip near the old Binion's casino. While this is a story of a family with a strong work ethic, a willingness to take risks, and a loyal viewer following, how will careers look in the future and what are the implications for our students and content area literacy?

The *Pew Research Center Report* (2014) notes that by 2025 jobs that are repetitive, rote, and easily automated are likely to disappear. The following are a few of these jobs:

- Meter readers
- Butchers and meat cutters
- Bank tellers
- File clerks
- Cashiers
- Bookkeepers and accounting clerks
- Secretaries and stenographers

In contrast, careers that involve significant educational preparation and the capacity to navigate and use digital technology include the following:

- Teachers
- Foresters and conservation scientists
- Engineers
- Software designers
- Artists
- Archivists and curators
- Airline pilots and navigators
- Actors, directors, and producers

These are positions that call for creativity and problem-solving skills. However, amid that idyllic view, teachers wrestle with policy mandates that include Common Core State Standards Initiative (2010) and high-stakes testing. Indeed, the widespread media portrayal of our schools is usually based on high-stakes test scores (Noddings, 2013). Is this the model we want to embrace as we plan content area lessons and units?

Fortunately, the Common Core State Standards are open-ended enough to allow for an emphasis on student attainment of increasingly complex content area and disciplinary reading skills across content areas. These skills include the ability to read and integrate multiple texts on a topic, as well as being able to comprehend and critique multiple interpretations of literary works and events in history. In addition, digital literacy capitalizes on formats that are often less predictable than traditional linear print and related text structures (e.g., pro–con arguments). Specifically, digital media are nonlinear and fluid, visual embellishments are common, and critical media literacy aimed at evaluating who has voice and who is silenced in the media becomes important for contemporary learners (Bean, 2016). Across the various content areas, each discipline has its own unique discourse, academic vocabulary, and ways of knowing (Bean & Dunkerly-Bean, 2015). For example, historians value determining the accuracy of sources used in tracing historical accounts. Scientists seek verification in accounts of experimental validity. Learning to think like an "insider" in a discipline is yet another element of content area literacy that contemporary learners need.

Eminent educational philosopher Nel Noddings (2013) argues that we live in a global community where collaboration, dialogue, interdependence, and creativity should be paramount in our classrooms. In addition, our students represent this global diversity. For example, the number of international migrants to the United States grew from 154 million in 1990 to 232 million in 2013 (Banks, 2015). By 2021, it is estimated that students of color will comprise 52% of the nation's school-age youth. These migration patterns exist in other countries too.

For teachers and public schools, this challenge is defined by a host of policy mandates, including Common Core Standards Initiative (2010), which specify student attainment of increasingly complex reading skills across content areas. These skills include the ability to read and integrate multiple texts on a topic, as well as being able to comprehend and critique multiple interpretations of literary works and events in history. The standards acknowledge the changing nature of what counts as "text" to include multimodal texts combining visual media and meaningful images. Thus, advanced levels of comprehension and critical media literacy are part and parcel of the standards across disciplines. Can we move content area literacy out of the Dark Ages of narrow high-stakes testing and into an era where it is possible to develop advanced reading comprehension across content areas?

This text is based on the conviction that these literacy dilemmas are ultimately solvable and that each and every teacher can play a role in the resolution. In fact, we believe that programs in which reading is the subject matter are inferior to programs in which each content teacher is committed to making students literate with respect to the specific source materials that make up their unique discipline and curriculum.

This chapter discusses the educational and social meaning of literacy, presents a rationale for incorporating particular literacy strategies that mesh with the unique discourse features of various content area classrooms, describes some of the standard misconceptions about content area literacy, and investigates why subject matter specialists need to accept responsibility for developing students' advanced reading processes necessary for contemporary citizenship.

 ## LEARNING OBJECTIVES

- o Define content area literacy from historical and social perspectives.
- o Refute common misconceptions about literacy instruction.
- o State the instructional recommendations that are integrated into the literacy strategies recommended in this text.

 ## GRAPHIC ORGANIZER

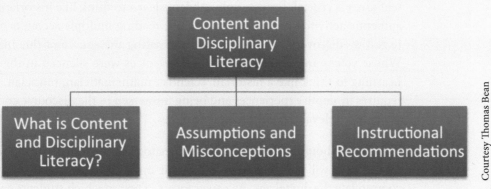

Courtesy Thomas Bean

WHAT IS CONTENT AREA LITERACY AND DISCIPLINARY LITERACY?

Literate is derived from the Latin *litterae* (i.e., letters). The standard dictionary definition of literate is to be able to read and write. That seems straightforward except that people aren't simply literate or illiterate: they are literate or illiterate to some degree, which is defined by historical and social contexts. Beginning in 1840, the United States Census Bureau began assessing literacy by asking individuals if they could read and write simple messages in any language. People who answered "Yes" were classified as literate. By this definition, 20% of the US population considered themselves illiterate in 1870 as opposed to less than 1% in 1979 (Kaestle, 1991). By the standards of 100 years ago, virtually all Americans are literate today. But literacy is relative to societal demands, and reading and writing skills that were sufficient in 1670 or 1870 are clearly inadequate in today's world of credit cards, mass advertising, computers, big business, and income tax forms.

In the not-so-distant past, it was widely believed that the ability to read and comprehend the bulk of a daily newspaper was a measure of functional literacy (i.e., how well one needs to read to get by on a day-to-day basis). This might be good enough to meet the job demands of a lumberjack, but probably not the daily reading and writing tasks of a contemporary corporate lawyer. Thus, the issue of literacy in content areas must be contextualized and defined in terms of the reading and writing demands of specific classrooms and disciplines. For example, students in a 10th-grade biology class are literate to the extent that they can learn with and react appropriately to the written materials (textbooks, lab directions, websites, magazines, etc.) used in the class. Hence, *content area literacy* is defined as the level of reading and writing skill necessary to read, comprehend, and react to appropriate instructional materials in a given subject area. The fundamental purpose of this text is to communicate knowledge and strategies that you can use to help your students become more literate in your subject area, with particular attention to its nuances in terms of how knowledge is structured and acquired. That said, there are no magic bullets or strategies that are uniformly appropriate across content areas. Rather, careful attention to the uniqueness of particular content areas is crucial. For example, students learn to think like historians by doing authentic activities in history that include reading multiple accounts of an event (e.g., the "discovery" of Hawaii) and evaluating the source of this information. Whose voices are represented and whose voices were silenced in the accounts? Learning to think like a historian, scientist, mathematician, musician, and so on requires in-depth experiences and being immersed in the discourse communities of practice relevant to particular disciplines.

Finally, we should also mention that questions of just what constitutes content area literacy will continue to evolve as our instructional materials change to accommodate the digital age. As newer forms of text in which students engage (e.g., the Internet, pop culture, teen magazines, music, media sources, young adult novels) mix with traditional forms of text, our strategies for helping students learn will need to evolve also. However, this does not decrease the importance of students' general competence with traditional forms of print, as they still form the basis for students in their dealings with newer literacies (e.g., the Internet) as well as with the standardized tests we use to measure students' abilities.

ASSUMPTIONS AND MISCONCEPTIONS

Teachers in science, history, and other content areas are frequently reluctant to accept an instructional emphasis that fuses reading with content. In part this is because many content teachers have false assumptions about reading instruction and the reading abilities of students when they arrive in subject matter classrooms (see Table 1.1).

Belief in these assumptions presupposes that students have mastered the processes necessary to enable them to glean essential information from reading, regardless of writing style and content. It also presupposes that students can meaningfully blend new information with prior knowledge and efficiently utilize textbook and digital aids designed to refine and extend important concepts. A close examination of these assumptions reveals how wrong they are.

Reading instruction has been the traditional interest of the elementary school, the assumption being that normal students in normal programs *should* enter subject matter classrooms knowing how to read. But consider this:

o If reading is defined in terms of elementary tasks, e.g., basic decoding skills, the assumption is reasonable.

o In contrast, the assumption is pure fantasy if reading is defined in terms of subject matter tasks, e.g., expanded homework and independent reading assignments, required note taking in class, and vastly increased dependence upon technology and textbooks, and online reading assignments with varied and complex organizational patterns.

It does not make sense to assume that students will automatically modify elementary reading skills to suit subject matter reading demands.

TABLE 1.1

False Assumptions of Content Teachers

1. Students have learned to read in elementary schools.
2. Students have sufficient prior knowledge to cope effectively with important information in content textbooks.
3. The processes involved in reading and comprehending efficiently in content textbooks and online texts are identical to those utilized in reading from basal readers in elementary school.
4. Content reading means teaching phonics and other skills not directly related to subject areas.
5. Teachers are information dispensers.

APPLICATION 1.1

Read the following paragraph and summarize it in your own words from recall:

We are completely in agreement with him on this point: That symbolization is constitutive of symbolic consciousness will trouble no one who believes in the absolute value of the Cartesian cogito. But it must be understood that if symbolization is constitutive of consciousness, it is permissible to perceive that there is an immanent bond of comprehension between the symbolization and the symbol. (Sartre, 1948, p. 65)

Did you have difficulty reading the passage from Sartre? If you were familiar with existential philosophy and Sartre, you might have breezed right through it. However, if this material was foreign to your own personal experiences, adequate comprehension probably proved elusive. In addition, the burden of many new terms and concepts may have caused the passage to seem obscure.

In order to read this passage with full understanding, you would need background knowledge in the subject area, and an introduction to the unusual vocabulary and new concepts in the passage. Even then the long, complicated sentences could prove tedious and confusing.

After reading the paragraph from Sartre, you should have some sensitivity for the demands placed on young students in reading their subject matter materials. Students usually lack experiential background, and are unfamiliar with the academic vocabulary and concepts in social studies, science, or any other content areas. It is presumptuous, and possibly damaging, to expect students to perform well automatically with subject matter texts. In addition, teachers with Arts and Sciences majors often develop a mind-set to convey a body of information to students, view reading as a simple mechanism for dispensing information, and see no reason to provide instruction in reading and learning with text.

Perhaps a final complication to utilizing content literacy in subject matter classrooms is the well-intended, but detrimental, slogan that "every teacher is a teacher of reading." Tell social studies teachers, for instance, that they are teachers of reading and you may understand how receptive they are to the concept. If apoplexy does not occur, their certain retort will be that they are teachers of social studies, not reading! The reading model that content teachers usually witness, emphasizing the previously mentioned elementary level skill characteristics, will not encourage them to attend to the reading needs of their classes. Moreover, their resolve that they are subject matter specialists first is a valid one.

Reexamining the Roles of Teachers and Texts

When subject matter teachers are surveyed concerning their attitude toward teaching reading in the content areas, they typically give a less than enthusiastic response toward the slogan that "every teacher is a teacher of reading." Ask this same set of teachers their opinion about the statement that "every teacher teaches students to learn with texts," and you will usually hear a favorable response. This latter statement connotes a model of reading instruction that focuses on aiding students in learning with text rather than learning isolated skills.

We agree with this reemphasis. Content literacy has too many prior associations with learning to read and skills instruction. Under this reemphasis, content teachers are considered catalysts for learning, whose responsibility it is to aid students in reading and learning with multiple text forms encompassing print and non-print materials. The focus of content literacy instruction is on reading to learn, not on learning to read.

Let us examine in depth the roles of the teacher, the reader, and texts, broadly defined as each relates to success in learning. First, if texts were meant to be read in isolation, there would be little, if any, need for a teacher. Similarly, if texts are so easy to read that a reader needs little or no help to learn the material, a teacher, again, would be superfluous. Yet, as the Sartre quotation illustrated, this is not normally the case with text materials. Texts are usually challenging, and present students with a myriad of problems.

Second, it makes sense to describe content reading as a means of improving communication. There is a sort of long-distance communication that materializes between the author of a text and a reader attempting to comprehend it. The reader is, in effect, trying to communicate with the authors of texts by constructing meaning with their words and thoughts. Given, then, the goal of the reader and the difficulty of texts, a facilitator is needed to promote this interaction between reader and text. Indeed, this should be the role of the teacher.

If teachers consider themselves to be information dispensers, then there is no need for texts. Teachers who make text reading assignments and then go over in class exactly what is in the text not only make class boring but also encourage students to neglect reading their assignments. This type of teacher does not encourage the development of independent readers who can take their place as 21st century citizens and lifelong learners in our society. A teacher who focuses only on content ignores the processes needed by students to comprehend the content in immediate and future reading situations.

The teacher's role is to encourage the thinking processes essential to understanding, that is, to facilitate learning with texts. Teachers, then, can promote this interaction if they conceive of themselves as facilitators of the learning process, because they have inherent advantages over textbooks or any other information-dispensing device. For instance, teachers have knowledge of at least four skills and processes they can exercise in their teaching that a text cannot—tailoring the message, activating prior knowledge, focusing attention, and monitoring comprehension.

1. **Teachers tailor the message** by adapting their presentations to the needs, abilities, and experiential backgrounds of their students. They already know what students know and do not know and can interact with them during their presentations.

2. **Teachers activate prior knowledge** by reminding students of what they know and how it relates to what they are expected to learn.

3. **Teachers focus attention** by increasing students' interest and motivation to learn new material, and by directing them to pay attention to selected pieces of the text.

4. **Teachers monitor comprehension** by checking to see if students understand important parts of a text presentation.

Clearly, texts cannot accomplish any of these tasks. Nevertheless, it is also true that texts are not designed to do this. They are designed to present information. **Materials don't do the teaching; teachers, by definition, do the teaching,** and this teaching includes helping students acquire the processes necessary for successful learning in content areas.

WHAT MAKES THIS TEXTBOOK INTEGRATED?

We have adopted the following set of instructional recommendations, which are integrated into the strategies you encounter throughout the book.

TABLE 1.2

Instructional Recommendations
1. Present content and processes concurrently.
2. Provide guidance in all aspects of the instructional lesson—before, during, and after reading.
3. Use all language processes to help students learn with texts.
4. Use small groups to enhance learning.
5. Use technology to promote learning with text.

1. **Present content and processes concurrently.** There are several possible approaches to learning with text: (a) presenting isolated skills; (b) aiming toward content; and, (c) presenting content and processes concurrently.

   a. *Presenting isolated skills* consists of the direct teaching of skills, with no consideration for content. Students use special materials unrelated to the texts that they are assigned to learn in their regular classes. This approach, like most skill-centered remedial programs, fails because students also need to be taught how to transfer skills from one material to another. More importantly, they fail to see any purpose in learning skills divorced from content.

   b. *Aiming toward content* focuses on what content to acquire rather than on how to acquire that content. In other words, the teacher sets purposes for reading, and during a follow-up discussion checks to see if the purposes were met. This method is unsuccessful because there is no instruction in how to extract the information from the text. Students are told what to do but not how to do it; this is not synonymous with instruction and is not sufficient to improve their reading abilities.

   c. Students learn best and acquire content most successfully when they focus their attention directly on the material to be learned. *Presenting content and processes concurrently* provides direct instruction in the processes necessary to acquire content and points out what content is to be acquired. For example, if the content to be learned is organized into a cause–effect format, the teacher might first present a lesson on organizing content according to that format before giving students the actual content in which they would use their knowledge of that process. Thus, text information is stressed alongside the processes needed to attain it. Specifying what should be attained, without specifying how to do it, is pointless. Taking process into account as well as content acknowledges that (1) reading is indispensable to the successful learning of all academic subjects, and (2) content as specified in a text is only one part of the dynamic interaction among reader, text, and teacher in classroom learning situations. As a consequence, the learning of content and the teaching of processes to help learn it become integrated within a total lesson framework.

2. **Provide guidance in all aspects of the instructional lesson—before, during, and after reading.** Learning content is not simply reading the assigned pages, answering the end-of-chapter questions, and listening to the teacher present what has already been read. Generally, students need to be prepared to read a text, need guidance in reading for selected ideas, and need reinforcement to retain the material learned.

More specifically, before reading, students need to be aware that using their prior knowledge, and having purposes for reading, aids the comprehension process. In addition, teachers can explicitly demonstrate how to learn with text through *modeling*. In this technique, teachers become role models by explaining how they comprehended something, that is, a reporting of the mental operations involved in their comprehension of a particular text. Students can then repeat the process in order to comprehend on their own.

During reading, students are searching for information to satisfy the purposes set by the teacher and/or themselves. The teacher may use some adjunct material to guide the students' search. After reading, teachers check to see if preset purposes have been attained.

One useful way to give feedback to students is to have a *debriefing* session, which includes self-reports, introspection, and hindsight by students. Debriefing does not cover content alone, but also entails checking out the processes students used to comprehend the text in relation to what was modeled for them. As students become more adept, the demonstration and guidance that teachers provide should be faded, or withdrawn, so that they can move toward independence in their reading and learning. Thus, helping students learn content is integrated throughout all phases of the instructional lesson.

3. **Use all language processes to help students learn with text.** We believe that all language processes, not just reading, can be utilized to approach learning with text. While reading will undoubtedly remain the major means of dealing with text, other language processes can play key roles in helping students learn content. Indeed, it is suggested that all teachers become language educators and consider using all language processes to enhance students' ability

to cope successfully with subject matter materials. Reading and writing are interconnected, and reading should be viewed as a composing process. In effect, writing, listening, and speaking become additional tools to teach more content.

We believe that the receptive language processes of reading and listening should be integrated with the expressive processes of writing and speaking to promote thinking and learning with content materials. The integrative aspects of reading and the other language processes are shown in Figure 1.1. In a system such as this, content reading takes on the larger notions of content communication or content literacy by emphasizing those teaching practices that integrate language processes and thinking as one learns content.

4. **Use small groups to enhance learning.** While the lecture method is the dominant means of instruction in our classrooms, one of the most effective is small group instruction. Encouraging students to work collaboratively, rather than competitively, with peers, enhances productivity and achievement. We realize that the lecture method is prevalent in teaching, yet many of the strategies advocated in this text are best used with, or even require, small group instruction. We recommend such strategies because they promote active learning situations and emphasize peer interaction.

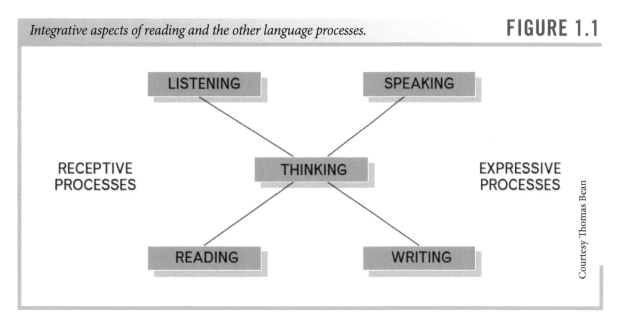

Integrative aspects of reading and the other language processes.   **FIGURE 1.1**

LISTENING   SPEAKING

RECEPTIVE PROCESSES   THINKING   EXPRESSIVE PROCESSES

READING   WRITING

Courtesy Thomas Bean

Initial attempts at small group instruction may be chaotic and create management problems; however, this is simply part of learning to interact within a group for both the students and the teacher. Once both are accustomed to such instruction, this method will pave the way for greater output in learning content, both in depth of understanding and in breadth of cognitive and affective experiences. Thus, teachers become cost-efficient when they integrate small groups into their teaching (i.e., they enhance the learning environment through good teaching practices which, in turn, create more knowledgeable students).

5. **Use technology to promote learning with text.** Teachers need to be aware of new technologies as well as how their application in the classroom will promote students' learning. In particular, instruction with computers and Smart Boards seems most promising as an educational innovation that provides new methods of presenting information, new ways of structuring and organizing instruction, and new ways to motivate students to learn. As schools provide students at all levels with access to technology, it is incumbent upon teachers to integrate the use of technology, especially computers, with text and video sources to enhance students' learning in content classrooms.

STRATEGY IMPLEMENTATION AND REALITY CHECKS

The chapters that follow contain various strategies for improving content area and disciplinary literacy, and we trust that you will have an opportunity to experiment with them in real classrooms. As we noted earlier, the particular way in which your content area structures knowledge needs to be a central consideration in the application of any instructional strategy. For example, Venn diagrams make sense in comparing and contrasting ideas like philosophical positions but may not be useful at all in delineating structure and function relationships in biology. So, be patient.

Our advocacy of content literacy instruction is based on the belief that it can better equip preservice and in-service teachers with the knowledge and processes to facilitate students' learning with a variety of text forms. As you read and apply ideas in the subsequent chapters, we encourage you to discover for yourself what works best for you and your students in your particular content area.

To get a better feel for the philosophy behind this text, examine the list of practices in Application 1.2. These practices are detailed in later chapters. For any immediate clarification of terminology used in the list, consult the glossary.

APPLICATION 1.2

These practices are recommended for enhancing reading and learning in the content areas. If you are an in-service teacher, check the appropriate number showing how much you do each of these. If you are a preservice teacher, observe a content area teacher to see which practices are used.

1—Almost always   2—Most of the time   3—Sometimes   4—Seldom   5—Never

Recommended Practices for Teaching in Content Areas

	1	2	3	4	5
1. The teacher utilizes all language processes to enhance students' learning with text.					
2. The reading levels of the students are known by the teacher.					
3. Lessons capitalize on the cultural backgrounds of students.					
4. The teacher has evaluated texts for the presence or absence of characteristics that support or impede comprehension.					
5. Materials for instruction, including the textbook, are chosen to match the reading levels of the students.					
6. Books and other materials are available for students who read below and above the readability level of the text.					
7. Textbook aids, such as illustrations, maps, and graphs, are explained or called to the attention of the students.					
8. Class time is spent discussing how to read the text effectively.					
9. The teacher presents the academic vocabulary and concepts introduced in the text materials assigned for reading in the context of a well-planned lesson.					
10. Prior knowledge of the text concepts is activated before reading the text.					
11. Purpose is provided for each reading assignment.					
12. Assignments are stated clearly and concisely.					
13. The teacher adapts instruction to suit the ability and language levels of students.					
14. The teacher asks questions designed to promote thinking at all levels of comprehension.					
15. The teacher provides some form of study guide, listening guide, or outline to aid in comprehension.					
16. The course content requires reading more than a single textbook.					
17. A variety of reference materials and software is made available.					
18. Students are taught to use appropriate reference materials.					
19. Students are encouraged to do wide reading of materials related to the text.					
20. Small group instruction is used where appropriate.					

REACTION GUIDE

		Confirmed	Disconfirmed
1.	Upon leaving elementary school, students should have mastered the skills necessary for content area literacy across disciplines.	_____	_____
2.	Reading content area material is more demanding than in the past and careers now require increasingly high levels of literacy.	_____	_____
3.	Standardized tests measure the reading achievement needed for contemporary life.	_____	_____
4.	Instructional strategies should fit the unique discourse features of the various content disciplines.	_____	_____
5.	We live in a global society that calls for a citizenry able to evaluate and critique print and digital texts.	_____	_____

A	B
Why my choice is confirmed.	Why my choice is not confirmed.
1. _____	_____
2. _____	_____
3. _____	_____
4. _____	_____
5. _____	_____

MINI PROJECTS

1. Write a sentence or paragraph using the technical academic vocabulary from your own content field. Exchange this with a class member from a different subject matter area. Can you understand each other's passage? Why or why not? What might help you increase your understanding?

2. Reflect on your literacy experiences by writing about them from your earliest memory of being read to, through elementary school, middle school, and high school, to the present. Comment on what you read, your feelings associated with reading or being read to, key people who influenced your feelings about reading, and places where you acquired books. How are your experiences different from or similar to the generation of students you are teaching?

RECOMMENDED WEBSITE

All About Adolescent Literacy: www.adlit.org

WEBSITE ACTIVITY

Go to the website for Chapter 5 activities.

Technology and Changing Literacies

CHAPTER 2

ANTICIPATION GUIDE

	Agree	Disagree
1. Technology has had a greater impact on social networking than on school achievement.	_____	_____
2. It is impossible to make the Internet safe for children.	_____	_____
3. Computers and the Internet have replaced textbooks as the dominant instructional tools in public education.	_____	_____
4. The computer is morally neutral.	_____	_____
5. Virtual worlds and avatars are a passing fad.	_____	_____

RATIONALE

In the middle of the last century, automobiles all had manual transmissions and no air conditioning. There were no cellular phones, and there were no convenient ATMs to drive up to for fast cash. Passenger planes were propeller driven only. There were also no televisions, automatic dishwashers, digital clocks, or hundreds of other technological conveniences that are now taken for granted in most American homes. The raging revolution in technology should change the fundamentals of classroom instruction and that revolution is well underway. This chapter examines the impact of technology on content literacy. Indeed, whenever we attempt to pin this dynamic topic down for a moment it shifts shape in an instant. With that caveat, we examine the impact of technology and offer some resources that should be very helpful in your teaching.

© Monkey Business Images/Shutterstock.com

LEARNING OBJECTIVES

- o Explain how the meaning of literacy continues to shift in the light of technology.
- o State several appropriate uses of technology in the classroom.
- o Define the terms multimedia, wiki, blog, virtual world, and social media.
- o State several current and potential misuses of the Internet.

 GRAPHIC ORGANIZER

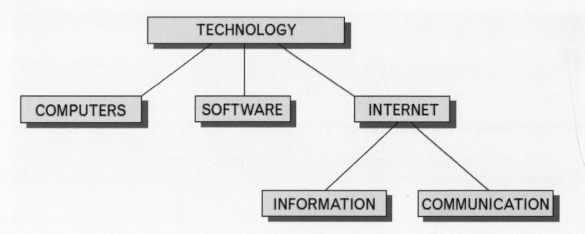

Courtesy Thomas Bean

TECHNOLOGY: REVIEWING THE PAST AND IMAGINING OUR FUTURE

As some of the Anticipation Guide statements suggest, even great minds can fail to divine the future or see the potential in technological innovations that in retrospect are obvious. It is easy to chuckle knowingly over the flawed technology predictions of the past (e.g., *teachers will be replaced by robots*). We can examine this claim through the eyes of Dr. Machio Kaku (Kaku, 2014), a professor of theoretical physics at the City University of New York and a cofounder of string theory. In his quest to understand a variety of topics including artificial intelligence, he interviewed over 200 prominent scientists including Nobel laureates from the United States and abroad about the influence of computers and robots. They agreed that the growth of computer power based on Moore's law shows that this technological power doubles every two years. To put that finding in perspective, our cell phones today have more computer power than all of NASA with its 1969 launch to put two astronauts on the moon.

While that is the upside of technology, the future use of robots is a bit more sobering. Robots lack human consciousness, and, while adept at performing precise, rule-governed tasks like playing chess, they fail miserably at crossing a busy city street safely (Kaku, 2014). The effort to produce driverless cars is a good example of the degree to which each and every condition must be thought out to program computers to take us to work and home safely.

It is much more difficult to predict the future. At the close of the stock market each day there are thousands of analysts and reporters who will tell you with certainty why the market went up or down, but most of them won't even hazard a guess about what the stock market will do the next day. Predicting what technology will do for—or to—the world in the next 50 or 20 or even 5 years is even more difficult. We believe it is safe to say that technology is here to stay and that it is a tsunami of change that will not stop. Populist politics are being fueled by social networks such as Facebook and Twitter. Technology is changing world politics. Is it changing the functionality of the American classroom?

Smaller, Faster, and Stronger

The ENIAC (Electronic Numerical Integrator and Computer) was the first modern computer built in 1946 after scientists realized that information could be represented by the absence or presence of electrical current (pluses and minuses). It weighed 30 tons, filled a large room, required a staff of engineers to keep it running, and operated with thousands of bulky vacuum tubes.

Today, there are computers a million times more powerful than the ENIAC and small enough to fit into the palm of your hand. The portability of cell phones, notebook computers, wireless connectivity, and various tablets make it possible for us to communicate and to store and retrieve information almost anywhere. In just the past few years, the word *app* has entered the languages of the world. *App*, short for application, refers to hundreds of programs for handheld communication devices that allow the user to store and retrieve information as well as solve problems and manage daily activities. For example, carb counters help with diets, step apps chronicle our exercise patterns, and shark apps show where in the surfing world shark attacks have occurred on a daily basis. Jump drives the size of a stick of gum can store huge amounts of data. Technological changes are occurring so rapidly that it is almost impossible to predict even the near future. This is particularly true with respect to the storage of information.

The Technology Revolution in American Schools

 View the website video clip on the Future of Technology in Education.

Computers and Smartboards are now ubiquitous in schools, with increasingly rare exceptions. It is readily apparent that high school students know more about digital technologies than the students of a quarter century ago. Most students use computers and cellular devices for word processing, conducting Internet searches, and participating in electronic social media such as *YouTube, MySpace*, *Facebook*, *Twitter*, and texting. Far less clear are the contributions of digital technologies to school achievement. Can high school graduates today read and comprehend better than their peers of 25 years ago? Are their mathematical skills superior? Do they know more about biology, economics, history, or any other subject area? One might expect some measurable improvements in achievement after so many years of technology in the classroom. Unfortunately, we are unaware of any systematic research that demonstrates this. Why might it be true that technology has yet to influence academic achievement?

Historically, innovative instructional technology tools such as computers, film, radio, and television have consistently met with resistance from teachers and educators at large. This failure of instructional technologies to be integrated into the classroom has been clearly demonstrated by Larry Cuban (1986) in his book, *Teachers and Machines: The Classroom Use of Technology Since 1920*. According to Cuban, instructional technology has consistently failed to bring about the revolutionary changes predicted by its advocates (Cuban, 2003, 2010). Beginning with an examination of the introduction of motion pictures in the schools nearly a century ago, and continuing with the introduction of new forms of media such as radio and television, Cuban provides a convincing historical demonstration of how new educational technologies meet with only limited use by teachers in the classroom. For example, during the 1950s and 1960s a variety of mechanical teaching machines were introduced to public schools (Cook, 1962), a decade or more before the invention of microprocessors and digital calculators. At that time there were many educators who believed that teaching machines would change the fundamental character of education—or even replace teachers altogether. But even before microcomputers entered their first classroom, teaching machines had proven to be little more than a curious fad. Will computers in the classroom suffer the same fate?

Unfortunately, computers in the classroom may be used primarily to support low-end applications, such as word processing, that mirror rather than alter and improve existing teaching practices. Placing computers in the classroom will make no difference in achievement unless the technology is accompanied by teachers and students changing their assumptions about teaching and learning. A teacher-centered curriculum with an emphasis on narrowly defined standards and rote memorization combined with an assembly line mentality will render the best of technology impotent.

Other critics of the technology revolution in public schools argue that there is little evidence to support the benefits of classroom computer applications and that technology is a distraction in the classroom and may actually impair intellectual development, writing skills, and problem-solving abilities (Oppenheimer 1997, 2003; Postman, 1999). Given limited school financing and available time for the total curriculum, critics argue that music, art, and other subjects are systematically squeezed out of the curriculum as more instructional time and resources are being devoted to the support of technology. American political and business leaders seem to embrace the notion that technology is good and more of it is better. Only time will reveal the true value of technologically sophisticated classrooms and the unforeseen consequences of technology interventions. There is one certainty; by the time you read this chapter our presentation on technology will already be out of date.

LITERACY IN THE NEW MILLENNIUM

In Chapter 1 we defined content area literacy as the level of reading and writing skill necessary to read, comprehend, and react to appropriate instructional materials in a given subject area. Years ago this definition would have been limited to conventional print mediums such as road signs, newspapers, and textbooks, but now students must also become facile in the use of computers, the Internet, cell phones, software, iPads, and other technologies directly or indirectly related to reading and writing. Being literate in today's world requires the application of conventional reading and writing skills to software applications and the complicated universe of cyberspace.

Basic and advanced reading skills including word recognition, spelling, vocabulary, prior knowledge, comprehension strategies, and critical literacy are essential in using the Internet for academic purposes (Bean, 2016). Clearly, technology cannot replace conventional reading and writing skills because students who have difficulty spelling, read slowly, and have a limited understanding of the world outside their immediate community are unlikely to be able to acquire multiple literacies.

Software, Multimedia, and eBooks

Software refers to applications that run on computers, which include everything from encyclopedias and word processing programs to games and academic programs that support the full range of content areas. *Multimedia* refers to combinations of audio, text, graphics, and animation. Multimedia software refers to computer-based programs that combine two or more multimedia elements.

Software allows students to participate in adventure games or to design their own programs. Many programs allow students to participate in sophisticated simulations, construct new worlds, and experience historical events as virtual participants.

Another example of problem-solving software is *Clues in Crime: The Role of Forensic Science in Criminal Investigations* (Duke University). This multimedia introduction to forensic science includes video lessons, lab demonstrations, actual case files, and a true-to-life crime scene investigation that allows students to exercise their problem-solving abilities.

In addition to using professionally prepared multimedia products, high school students are creating their own sophisticated products using digital video cameras, scanners, and multimedia software such as *iMovie, Macromedia*, and *MovieWorks*. Content area literacy is being redefined by multimedia applications.

Some software programs are free and some are expensive: some are junk and some offer extraordinary opportunities for enhancing classroom learning.

Electronic books (eBooks) are a computerized alternative to traditional forms of printed text (Dobler, 2015). They include digital tools that support literacy in ways not possible with traditional books— adjustable print size and touch screen dictionaries, for example. These electronic books can be downloaded immediately by customers and at lower prices than printed books. The Kindle, marketed by Amazon.com, is an eBook reader with a huge array of books or other documents, each of which can be downloaded from the Internet within seconds.

INTERNET

The *Internet* is a complex set of interlinking computer networks that began as a project in the U.S. Defense Department's Advanced Research Projects Agency (ARPA) as part of a military strategy in the United States to maintain communications in the event of a nuclear war. The network went operational in 1969 and was initially called the ARPANET. By 1984 there were 1,000 computers connected by the Internet. Today there are hundreds of millions of computers sending tens of billions of emails and doing tens of billions in business transactions on the Internet every day.

Speed, currency, and breadth of information are among the many attributes that make the Internet so dynamic. Email is rapidly replacing regular (snail) mail, and texting is rapidly replacing email for electronic social communications. Correspondence that formerly took three days takes three seconds, and it is now possible to send legal signatures via Internet. Another advantage of the Internet is its capacity for constant updating. As a reference source, the Internet is far more current than conventional paper documents such as textbooks or even newspapers. It also possesses extraordinary subject breadth, and hundreds of online libraries such as EBSCOhost and ProQuest offer media centers and college libraries full-text, searchable databases of thousands of magazines, professional journals, books, and documents whose pages number in the billions. Websites are readily available to address almost every need and interest from buying airplane tickets to finding a local chess club. Some of the applications available on the Internet are nothing short of fantastic. For example, Google Earth (http://earth.google.com) combines satellite imagery with maps and the Google search engine to allow the viewer to search the entire surface of the Earth as though one were flying in from space to zero in on the Grand Canyon, the Eiffel Tower in Paris, or even the viewer's own home.

World Wide Web

A critical component of the Internet is the *World Wide Web* (WWW, or, simply, the Web), which was introduced in 1989. The Web is an extensive, continually expanding collection of interlinked documents, images, sounds, and other resources that one accesses electronically through the Internet. The development of popular tools that enable people to design three-dimensional virtual environments on the Web, and to interact with content posted on the Web, has irreversibly altered the nature of the Web itself. Initially, single parties (e.g., businesses, agencies, individuals) used the Web to post information in digital form for other interested parties to access. The Web was the information superhighway. As users became intrigued with the technology and interested in participating themselves, the Web evolved into a massive platform of applications that enables people not only to share information, but also to interact with data posted by others.

Various web applications allow users to render their websites interactive, such that viewers may respond (typically in electronic text format) to what the author has expressed. This interactivity led to the development of broad-based social networks, groups of individuals who share a particular interest and interact with each other electronically. Early Internet-based social networks included electronic bulletin boards and network discussion groups. Advances in technology and the apparently unquenchable human need to congregate and communicate with each other have led to such popular multimedia social network sites, which allow more varied means of sharing and interacting. Most students now entering college have spent much of their lives interacting with others in this way.

Virtual Worlds

You are standing on a white beach at sunset looking at the rapidly changing play of red and purple light on the clouds in the distance. You can hear the waves and soft cries of gulls overhead. You lift your arms above your head and soar into the sky like Superman. You hover for a moment at a thousand feet, then fly across a verdant island to land in a magnificent tree house where some of your colleagues have already gathered. You communicate by voice in real time as the wind brushes through the trees and the stars begin to twinkle. You are avatars in a virtual world. The psychological projection is subtle, but you almost feel as though you are really there.

Cyber platforms known as *virtual worlds* offer an even higher level of interactive applications. Many different labels have been applied to virtual worlds, including collaborative virtual environments (CVEs), multi-user virtual environments (MUVEs), and massively multiplayer online games (MMOs). There are many different types of virtual worlds, but all share a fundamental characteristic: participants in virtual worlds interact with each other in the form of avatars—graphic representation of themselves, which, because the development of these platforms has been greatly influenced by the gaming industry, may be reality-based or fantastical—in specially designed internet-based simulated environments. Although the medium has historically been associated with online role-playing games for adolescents and young adults (e.g., *World of Warcraft*), many virtual worlds have been designed to attract a broader audience. The technology has been adopted by a growing number of businesses to allow for greater interactions with potential customers, and by educators to enhance the learning experiences of their increasingly computer-savvy students.

Second Life

Second Life, which opened to the public in June 2003, is a robust, highly successful virtual world that is owned and operated by Linden Lab of Linden Research in San Francisco.

Second Life is comprised of thousands of islands (server space actually) owned or rented by people with avatars. Although basic membership in Second Life is free, as are many services and materials, a thriving economy exists inworld. Subscribers can open an account and purchase Linden Dollars (280 Lindens = 1 US dollar) for the purpose of buying such commodities as land (which may also be rented), structures, clothing, and scripted programs such as avatar animations. Much of Second Life has great educational value.

Cybraries

Cybrary, a blend of the words cyber and library, is a collection of websites accessible from a single site and dedicated to a specific subject area. For example, Remember. org is a cybrary of the Holocaust and shares powerful stories of survival through art, photography, painting, and remembrance (http://www.remember.org). Another example is Global Access to Educational Sources: A Cybrary for Middle School and Beyond (http://www.geocities.com/Athens/Academy/6617?200629). It is a comprehensive link to collections of websites for academic areas such as art, mathematics, and science. This cybrary also includes links to websites dedicated to internet resources, new and current events, reference sources, and teacher resources.

Other cybraries are huge compendiums of websites that have been evaluated by educators and deemed safe for student use. For example, Nettrekker (http://www. nettrekker.com) is a collection of 180,000 educator-selected websites, 600 periodicals, 3,000 domestic and international newspapers, and its own search engine. Nettrekker supports specific state standards by providing teachers with online resources, lesson plans, and student activities once the teacher has requested support for a particular standard. The Pennsylvania Department of Education has recently purchased access to Nettrekker for every public school student in the state.

Wikis and Blogs

Wiki is derived from the Hawaiian word for fast and refers to software that supports an open editing environment. This means that anyone can go to a wiki website and edit the text. A wiki is a quick way to collaboratively edit documents, and serves as a perpetual collective work of many authors. However, it also means that the validity of the information on the site is always in question because anyone can alter the content for any reason at any time. The most famous wiki is Wikipedia (http://en.wikipedia.org), a free online encyclopedia that boasts one and a half million pages of information. An internet search for a definition will frequently identify Wikipedia as a resource. The information may be interesting but should be digested with skepticism because the content may change at the whim of anyone who visits the site. Another example of a wiki is eBaywiki (http://ebay.about.com/od/ebaylifestyle/a/el_wiki.htm), a forum for eBay members to discuss best practices and strategies for buying and selling on eBay.

Blog is short for weblog and is similar in nature to a wiki except that the original material cannot be edited except by the individual who established the blog. Individuals respond to the material published on the blog and to each other. Blogs allow individuals to express their opinions and beliefs on any subject without necessarily identifying themselves. The first blogs began in 2001, and as of this writing there are more than 57 million. There is even a blog search engine called Technorati (http://www.technorati.com), which finds blogs on almost every subject. Adult bloggers are typically interested in information networking rather than self-expression. In contrast, teenage bloggers are primarily concerned with self-expression and social interactions. For instance, a typical profile in LiveJournal (http://www.livejournal.com), a teen blog, usually focuses on personal interests, lists of friends, and group memberships.

INSTRUCTIONAL PRACTICES USING THE INTERNET

WebQuests and Internet Workshops

WebQuest is an inquiry-oriented activity in which some or all of the information acquired from the activity comes directly from the student's interaction with the Internet. It is also an instructional paradigm for integrating the Internet into content area classrooms. The term *Internet Workshop* (Leu & Leu, 2000) is sometimes used when the purpose of the lesson is to teach students how to use the Internet (e.g., navigate, search, document information, avoid dangerous sites, and ask good questions). WebQuests are usually tied directly to the science, social studies, or language arts curriculum. There is no one correct way to conduct WebQuests and Internet Workshops, but they usually have the following steps:

1. Provide students with direct instruction in the use of internet search strategies and safety precautions.

2. Locate an appropriate internet site and provide students with the URL (web address) or bookmark for location.

3. Create an activity that will require students to use the site.

4. Assign the activity allowing enough time for all students to access the site.

5. Encourage students to share their explorations, frustrations, and accomplishments during the workshop session.

An appropriate site is one that is well organized, well documented, and suitable to the age group. Activities may be simple, controlled tasks such as finding a single piece of information, or they may be complex and open-ended, depending on the age and technological sophistication of the students. The following are good websites for teachers interested in WebQuests:

1. **Kathy Schrock's Guide for Educators**
   http://school.discovery.com/schrockguide/webquest/webquest.html

2. **The WebQuest Page at San Diego State University**
   http://webquest.sdsu.edu

3. **WebQuest News**
   www.webquest.com

4. **New York Public Media**
   (http://www.thirteen.org/edonline/concept2class/webquests/index.html).

Sample WebQuest for Grade 8 General Science

Froguts (http://www.froguts.com/flash_content/index.html) is a commercial website that offers schools virtual laboratory experiences. Visit the site and select "Demo."

A. Go to the link called "Froguts." This site will allow you to dissect animals using the computer. Select an animal; dissect it; and answer these questions:

   What animal did you dissect? _____

Circle the word that best describes how you felt about this activity:

interested   disgusted   bored   excited

Name one advantage of digital dissections. _____

If you were given a real (dead) animal, do you think you could dissect it based on what you learned from Froguts? Why or why not?

B. Other "cool" science sites are available from the Science Learning Network (http:// www.sln.org). Go to the Science Learning Network and select a cool site. Name the site and be prepared to share three things about the site that make it cool.

Site Name: _____

Fact #1: _____

Fact #2: _____

Fact #3: _____

Online Literature Circles

Literature circles are a collaborative approach to instruction that integrates the reading of a book with discussions of themes and related background information. Small groups of students at any grade level work together, and each individual selects an aspect of the book for which he or she will provide leadership in research and discussion. For example, if a class were reading *The Diary of Anne Frank*, members of a literature circle might select topics such as World War II, the Holocaust, the history of Warsaw, or ethnic prejudice. These topics would be researched on the Internet with appropriate guidance from the teacher.

The Dark Side of the Net

Dad: Son, what did you learn in your first year of college?

Son: Well, Dad, I learned that the only substance you can eat or drink in unlimited quantities without dying from it is water.

Dad: That's interesting, what else?

Son: I learned how to make a fertilizer bomb using the Internet.

As enthusiastic as we are about the Internet and the general use of technology to enhance education, we would be remiss if we failed to mention the downside of technology. The Internet is the Wild West of communications. Laws that were designed to protect children, copyrights, and personal privacy are different or entirely inapplicable to the Internet. In addition to good information, the Internet carries enormous amounts of bad information and outright danger. The intellectual scum of society are online and prepared to turn the information superhighway into an alleyway for predatory sex, business scams, misinformation, and pathologic mayhem. (What purpose is served by the creation of computer viruses?) You can buy illegal drugs and child pornography on the Internet just as easily as sporting goods equipment or antiques; we all seem doomed to receive ridiculous amounts of *spam*, internet junk mail from the bottom feeders of cyberspace. We are all getting tired of opening our email accounts only to find dozens of brazen titles such as, MAKE MONEY FAST, CHEAP DRUGS, and NEW ADULT WEBSITE WITH HOT LINKS. For these reasons and many more it is vital that students ask good questions whenever they view a website:

o Do the authors of the website identify themselves? What are their credentials?

o Why should I believe the information on this website?

o Are the authors informing me for my benefit, or are they biased?

o Is the website trying to sell me something or change my beliefs?

o Do the authors of the website want information from me, and should I provide it?

o Is there any potential danger to me or to others from the website?

Cyberbullying

In yet another aspect of the Internet, cyberbullying has invaded homes and schools with dire consequences for the psychosocial well-being of students (Jacobs, 2010). While First Amendment rights apply to the Internet, not all entries are protected, nor should they be. For example, the following categories of discourse do not enjoy free speech protection:

o Lewd and obscene speech

o Speech that is profane

o Libelous speech

o Insulting or fighting words that intend to injure or incite

Another form of cyberbullying refers to being "publicly shamed" on the Internet (Ronson, 2015). The only entity benefitting from this practice, especially if the shaming goes viral, are search engines that glean extra advertising power from this dark side of the internet posts.

Schools and local law enforcement generally take cyberbullying and public shaming very seriously and practice zero tolerance to create a safe and sane learning environment.

Additional information on internet safety is available through iSafe (http://www.isafe.org), a nonprofit foundation dedicated to protecting the online experiences of youth everywhere. Online protection practices are also available from the American Library Association's *The Librarians' Guide to Great Websites for Kids* (http://www.ala.org/ala/pio/availablepiomat/librariansguide.htm).

Thoughtful, critical literacy has never been more important, and no other technological or intellectual tool will serve the young Internet reader as much as the right question asked at the right time in the right way.

CONCLUSIONS

We believe that the promise of technology is real but also that it will not be realized until there is a universal commitment to integrate technology into the curriculum (Williamson, 2013). In addition, the curriculum in most schools is driven by textbooks in print or online form, which are frequently misused to ensure that all students are exposed to the same content and progress through the curriculum at the same pace. Contrast this with the individualistic nature of cyber exploration and blogging. Perhaps the time has come for our profession to question the necessity of all students acquiring the same knowledge base. This might require tossing out the textbooks—or at least making them supplemental—and elevating the Internet, interactive multimedia programs, and original source documents as the primary tools for learning in schools of the future. It might also mean taking creativity and problem-based learning in schools seriously, engaging students in civic action projects and efforts to solve environmental issues like local water quality (Bean & Dunkerly-Bean, 2016).

Teachers in content areas need to understand the value of integrating the Internet, multimedia software, and electronic databases into their respective subject areas. Problem solving and the multidimensional exploration of art, history, literature, mathematics, music, and the physical sciences are all possible through multimedia software. What are the advantages of such systems? How will they change the process of learning? Will they significantly affect the traditional role of the teacher? These are just a few of the important questions teachers like you will need to address in the near future.

Computer instruction, when combined with video and text sources, promises to be an exciting technological and educational innovation. New methods of presenting traditional information, new methods of problem solving, new ways of organizing and structuring large databases, and new ways of providing personalized instruction are just a few of the opportunities available. Schools must provide students at all levels access to the new technology and ensure equal access to resources whatever their socioeconomic background, race, or gender. At the same time, we must make sure that the new technologies do not limit or impede our capacity to be humane and critical interpreters of the world in which we live and work.

REACTION GUIDE

		Confirmed	Disconfirmed
1.	Technology has had a greater impact on social networking than on school achievement.	_____	_____
2.	It is impossible to make the Internet safe for children.	_____	_____
3.	Computers and the Internet have replaced textbooks as the dominant instructional tools in public education.	_____	_____
4.	The computer is morally neutral.	_____	_____
5.	Virtual worlds and avatars are a passing fad.	_____	_____

	A Why my choice is confirmed.		B Why my choice is not confirmed.
1.	_____		_____
2.	_____		_____
3.	_____		_____
4.	_____		_____
5.	_____		_____

MINI PROJECTS

1. This chapter contrasts current societal expectations for computers and related technology with the failed expectations of the teaching machines of the 1950s and 1960s. Read the article, *The Automatization of Socrates*, by Desmond Cook on the website. Were the purposes of the old teaching machines the same as today's educational technology? Do you believe that today's computers and software will succeed where the machines of 40 years ago failed? Why or why not?

2. Discuss the advantages and disadvantages of a multimedia encyclopedia over a traditional printed one.

3. Compare and contrast the ENIAC with modern computers that have multimedia capabilities.

4. Explain how the computer revolution might contribute to the social evils of gender bias, stereotyping, and physical violence.

5. American educators have in large part embraced the notion that the use of computers in schools is inevitable and even desirable. In many respects, the increasingly widespread use of computers in our culture and schools parallels the introduction of the automobile at the beginning of the previous century. Although the automobile made rapid and convenient travel possible, it also engendered highway construction, air pollution, and frequent accidental deaths. Both from a personal and an educational point of view, what might be some of the hidden costs of introducing computers into our schools? Can these problems be avoided, or are they inevitable?

RECOMMENDED WEBSITES

Teaching for Creativity

o   TEDed: http://ed.ted.com

o   Teaching Channel: https//teachingchannel.org

o   Quicktime: http://quicktime-download.org (Make your own instructional videos; upload to YouTube)

o   Blendspace: http://blendspace.com (One of our favorites for lesson development with video clips)

WEBSITE ACTIVITY

Go to the website for Chapter 5 activities.

Language and Diversity in the Disciplines

CHAPTER 3

ANTICIPATION GUIDE

	Agree	Disagree
1. Addressing students' culture and language diversity is preferable but not necessary.	_____	_____
2. Strategies for English as Additional Language (EAL) are not helpful for other students.	_____	_____
3. Comprehending print and digital texts are unrelated processes.	_____	_____
4. Student learning depends mostly on the teacher's content knowledge.	_____	_____
5. Whole class discussion discourages wide student participation.	_____	_____

RATIONALE

© bikeriderlondon/Shutterstock.com

Language and literacy are uniquely and inextricably connected; so are literacy and power. In the young adult book, *From Slave to Abolitionist: The Life of William Wells Brown* (Warner, 1993), African-American William Wells Brown provides a harsh, realistic account of his flight from 20 years of slavery and the tearing apart of his family. His autobiography, first published in 1847, reveals the powerful role literacy played in his flight to freedom. Through great personal danger and dedication, William Wells Brown learned to read and write, giving him the voice needed to fight slavery and prejudice for 22 years as a lecturer and author. In 1834, on the run to Canada and freedom, he traded candy for lessons in reading at an abolitionist's home in Ohio. He progressed to a stage where he could read complex texts and, ultimately, contribute to the antislavery movement.

Soon I bought an arithmetic book and a grammar and studied them equally hard. Next I bought other, general books and in leisure moments, I read them to improve my skills—and my knowledge. This reading of books whenever possible became my lifelong practice. Wherever I might be, there will always be with me a volume of grammar, mathematics, history, or literature. (p. 92)

While modern day students in the Global North may often view content area textbooks as overwhelming and at times dull, for William Wells Brown they represented a route to learning and a voice in the political struggle for freedom. In the early 1830s, teaching an enslaved African-American to read was a severely punishable crime. Denied literacy as a slave, William Wells Brown knew reading and writing were keys to fighting a system that was brutal and unjust. Similarly, for the millions of illiterate people worldwide, reading is truly the difference between social, political, and economic freedom or not.

More recently, scholars have argued that in order to participate as informed citizens in an increasingly diverse, cosmopolitan global society, students need opportunities to wrestle with problem-based political issues (Beck & Sznaider, 2010). Empirical research is documenting students' literate lives, revealing how a world youth culture is developing, how global migration is impacting youth, how global capitalism is changing their economic and vocational futures, how instant computer-mediated communication with the world is changing literacy needs and identities of local/global 21st century students (Bean & Dunkerly-Bean, 2015). Critical literacy offers a particularly powerful frame of reference to examine geopolitical problems in a variety of content areas, and we consider these ideas as they relate to language and diversity (Harper & Bean, 2007; Stevens & Bean, 2007).

Many immigrant populations continue the struggle to adapt to unfamiliar surroundings in the United States after fleeing conditions of war, poverty, and persecution in their native lands. Indeed, issues surrounding immigrants and refugees dominate conversation at the local, national, and global levels. In many ways, schools are on the "frontline" of these discussions. The United States Census Bureau projects that nearly 90% of the population that is expected to increase between 2000 and 2050 will be children of immigrants with a concomitant need for English language instruction (Bean & Harper, 2011).

Culture and language differences can help or hinder student progress in content literacy, depending on the knowledge and strategies you, as the teacher, have at your disposal. Students can flourish or flounder in content area classrooms based on what is known about diverse cultures, and how lessons are conducted that capitalize on this knowledge. Are multicultural features incorporated in lessons, or are teachers merely maintaining the mainstream European American traditions of individual competition and assimilation?

Digital literacies and access to digital texts are another critical dimension of content area literacy. Print based or "traditional" literacies are rapidly shifting in complexity in the digital age. The skills and strategies involved in assisting students to be savvy consumers and producers of online and digital texts are also addressed in this chapter. Similarly, we also explore issues related to access and equity in digital literacies, most notably around the "digital divide" and the affordances and challenges of mobile learning (Dunkerly-Bean & Crompton, 2016).

In this chapter, we also explore the related dimensions of language and diversity in print and digital with an eye toward some activities and strategies that will situate student learning in real-world contexts and intercultural literacies. Subsequent chapters expand on specific strategies in the areas of lesson and unit design, young adult literature, vocabulary, comprehension, writing, studying, and other content area literacy approaches.

LEARNING OBJECTIVES

o   State the linguistic and diverse learner factors that influence reading comprehension and subject area learning.
o   State the cognitive and text-based factors that influence reading comprehension and subject area learning.

GRAPHIC ORGANIZER

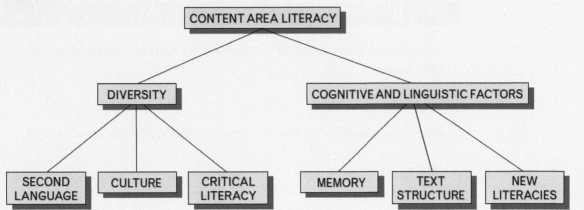

Courtesy Thomas Bean

One of the major challenges for EAL students reading content area material is *academic language* (Cummins, 2009; Kieffer & Lesaux, 2010). Academic language includes words like "cause and effect," and "analysis" commonly found in print and online expository texts. Coupled with each content area's particular technical vocabulary, these language features pose special challenges for both native and nonnative speakers of English.

CONSIDER THIS!

Grace, a Filipino immigrant employed at a rural flower farm in Hawaii, wrote the following query to her employer:

Claudia,

I have a ? Do you know what is a Bombay. Some one order that but I don't know what is it.

Thanks,
Grace

Grace formatted her query about the Bombay like a letter but used grammatical structures familiar to her. Nevertheless, she got her message across. As it turned out, Claudia did not know what a "Bombay" was either. At this point in her use of English as a second language, Grace would benefit from a small amount of explicit instruction. She would then have a model to use in future queries.

Researcher Allison Skerrett (2015) reminds us that, "Language and literacy are inextricably connected. A sociocultural perspective of literacy views literacy as a constellation of multimodal and multilingual tools and practices situated across multiple social contexts and activities." (p.22) This means that, as teachers, we need to attend to the linguistic knowledge, tools, practices, and beliefs of our students in order to value their language while increasing their proficiency in English. It is also important to relate student learning to themes or issues that are important to them in order to make the learning relevant. Integrating students' experiences, culture, and language in unit and lesson planning can contribute to their understanding. For example, in a social studies unit on immigration, including short stories from *First Crossing: Stories About Teen Immigrants* (Gallo, 2007) would be a powerful way of illuminating expository content on this topic.

Programs designed for second language (L2) learning vary according to the emphasis on immersion in the target language (Nieto, 2004). Generally, programs may be characterized as follows:

a) Immersion bilingual education;

b) English as a second language;

c) Transitional bilingual education;

d) Developmental bilingual education;

e) Two-way bilingual education.

- o *Immersion bilingual education* is termed "submersion" by Nieto because it parallels her demoralizing experiences as a native speaker of Spanish expected to abruptly shift to English as the dominant language of instruction.

- o *English as a Second Language,* or ESL, provides structured lessons in English while the student may choose to maintain facility in the native language. The goal is to learn English through a structured program of lessons.

- o *Transitional bilingual education* consists of content area instruction in the native language while the student engages in ESL instruction with the proviso that the native language will be phased out in three years.

- o *Developmental bilingual education,* in contrast, does not have a time limit for phasing out the native language.

- o *Two-way bilingual education* may be the most attractive, because both native English and nonnative English speakers learn each other's language while they do the bulk of their content learning in the strong native language.

Two-way bilingual learning, and classrooms where nonnative English speakers find their native language is valued and used in content learning, have a number of benefits. Since language and culture are inextricably linked, a teacher who demonstrates respect and enthusiasm for language and cultural diversity advances students' self-esteem and identity. Such aA classroom can help reduce the high dropout rates of nonnative speakers. Even more importantly, valuing a student's native language helps students from diverse cultures maintain the often close family relationships with parents, siblings, grandparents, and extended family members. In instances where students are immersed in English and denied the use of their native language, the whole network and culture a student knows is treated as if it is less important than mainstream culture. This assimilation model results in real resentment and detachment from one's family. Many successful middle-aged immigrants abandoned their native identities to survive in America, and recall these experiences with a good deal of pain.

In essence, once EAL students are engaged in content area learning in history, science, mathematics, and English, they need extra teacher support to cope with academic language (Kieffer & Lesaux, 2010; Nagy & Townsend, 2012). Nagy and Townsend (2012) define academic language as "the specialized language both oral and written, of academic settings that facilitates communication and thinking about academic content." (p. 92) Technical vocabulary and the unique expository text structures that students encounter in the content areas require additional teacher guidance in the form of visuals, gestures, demonstrations, and activity-based hands-on inquiry learning where students have a chance to practice English language elements. Dianna Townsend (2015) draws from the work of Zwiers (2008) in looking at the purposes of academic language in the disciplines (p. 378):

TABLE 3.1

Content Area	Purposes of Academic Language
ELA	• Interpretation of messages and meaning in text • Persuasion of others to take a side on an issue • Exploration of cause and effect
Math	• Interpretation/translation of words and symbols • Problem solving by analyzing and organizing information
Science	• Description of scientific data inquiry • Exploration of cause and effect relating to scientific phenomena • Interpretation of observation and data • Comparisons based on close observation and data
Social Studies	• Cause and effect of historical events • Interpretation of events to infer and construct meanings • Perspective taking to participate in the lives of others, and in some cases, to empathize

As you can observe from Table 3.1, proficiency in academic language is imperative for engaging with content area knowledge and, even more importantly, for engagement in the wider world. Teacher modeling, guided practice in questioning, summarizing text concepts, and using high-level strategies that link students' prior knowledge to text concepts will go a long way toward fostering optimal content learning (Garcia & Godina, 2004). Using literature that connects to EAL students' life experiences and offering opportunities for creative and analytical writing connected to their prior knowledge from diverse contexts will also advance English language development while respecting and supporting students' native language and dialects. The wealth of multicultural literature now available, including novels that feature English and Spanish discourse as well as novels set in international contexts, expands content area learning in social studies and other subject areas.

Today, there is a renaissance of multicultural literature, poetry, and music (Bean, 2008). The following poem, written in Hawaiian Islands Dialect or pidgin, treats a universal topic. Hawaiian poet Leomi L. Bergknut (1997) used unique linguistic structure, intonation, and deep cultural understanding to show how it feels when you are walking across campus and someone gives you "stink eye."

STINK EYE*

You ever give
Sombody one stink eye?
If, you wen do em
Den you know
Wat I stay writen about.
Da udda day wen
I wuz cruizin to class,
I wen feel
Sombody givin me

Da stink eye.
So, I turn around
And I know wuz you!
So, I give
Da stink eye back to you!
Da stink eye!

And den you
Wen stay laugh at me
And den you tell me
"Wat?
Wat you like?"
I know,
Cuz I could
Feel em at
Da back
Of my neck.

And da moe I walk,
Da moe I catch
Dat feelin dat make me wonda—
Who stay givin me
Da stink eye?

Stupidhead!
No give me
Da stink eye
Cuz you just might
Not live to regret it!

Reprinted with permission of Leomi L. Bergknut (1997) and Kanilehua.

View the website video clip and listen to the author of
Stink Eye recite her poem in its original dialect.

Kathy Au (2006) and her colleagues (Au & Kaomea, 2009) have done a substantial amount of curriculum design work focusing on students who speak Hawaiian dialect. She regards reading and writing in Hawaiian dialect as a solid foundation for learning. Thus, she recommends having students answer questions using some of their native language as they move toward proficiency in the target language. Hudelson's (2001) extensive work with Spanish-speaking students led her to the conclusion that a good foundation in the native language provides a framework for subsequent language learning. Furthermore, she argues that there is no single best way to enhance second language literacy development for second language learners. However, there are a number of approaches and strategies you can use in your content area to value diverse students' existing knowledge and build on this base.

Strategies and Resources for Supporting Language Learners

The most important strategy is to consciously make your classroom an inviting place for all students, especially for students from diverse cultural and linguistic backgrounds.

FIRST LANGUAGE FIRST. Encourage your EAL students to brainstorm or draft responses in their first language first. This will support their ability to process the material presented before having to communicate it in a second language.

INTERACTIVE ONLINE GAMES. Many engaging and informative games to support EAL students are readily available. The International Literacy Association (ILA) website www.readwritethink.org has lessons that incorporate interactive components such as story generators, vocabulary games, etc. More games specific to vocabulary, grammar, and word knowledge may be found at http://www.eal-teaching-strategies.com/learning-games-online.html

IMAGES. It is now very easy to access images via Google or other search engines to supplement text for students. Consider utilizing images to enhance your instruction, especially when the material is complex.

MODEL SPEAKING AND LISTENING. Use strategies such as "goldfish bowl" to model speaking and listening exchanges. This can be done with students or another adult. This strategy showcases the importance of active listening. Be sure to walk students through the process by incorporating a think-aloud into the process.

LABELS. Using labels for items in class that include both English and other languages known to students in the classroom helps expand second language students' technical vocabulary in science, math, social studies, and other content fields.

PRE-HIGHLIGHT. When possible, make extra copies of text or handouts with key vocabulary or passages already highlighted.

TRANSNATIONAL AND COMMUNITY LITERACIES. *Transnationalism* refers to written language practices that move beyond national borders, often via the Internet (Jimenez, Smith, & Teague, 2009). Your students may live in neighborhood communities where multiple languages are represented in advertisements for local markets, ads for transferring money overseas, and so on. Students can photograph these native language artifacts and translate these "texts" to the target language (e.g., English).

In addition to the above strategies, numerous visual and digital texts are available to support bilingualism and biliteracy in the classroom (Ward, 2015). These resources provide teachers with a way to support English language learning while also honoring and valuing students' first languages:

o **The International Children's Digital Library (ICDL) (en.childrenslibrary. org).** This site offers hundreds of digitized books (some bilingual) in various languages, such as, Farsi, Mongolian, French, Spanish, and Arabic. It exponentially expands any teacher's library to be inclusive of many readers. The mission of the ICDL is to nurture and promote cultural understanding and respect for all members of the global community.

o **Words Without Borders (wordswithoutborders.org).** If you are struggling to find books or other materials that will interest your students, this is a great site to visit. Similar to the ICDL, Words Without Borders is designed to encourage and facilitate global tolerance and understanding through reading works of international authors. The site offers translations and publications of international literature, typically at a rate of 12 a month, with more than 1,700 currently available.

o **Scribjab (www.scribjab.com).** This site is a project of Simon Fraser University. It is an app that allows the creation of digital stories using any two languages. In addition to writing bilingual texts, users have the ability to read from a collection of books written by other Scribjab users. Another great feature is that a one can record audio for the story in addition to or instead of print text. Students who may not be able to read or write in their second or even first language yet can still author their own works.

These are just a few of the online resources available. We encourage you to take advantage of the global nature of the digital world to find more ways to explore the world with both your monolingual and bilingual students.

APPLICATION 3.1

Take a moment to write a short response (quick write) to the following prompt. Break into small groups and share your thoughts.

What do you see as the benefit of students speaking two or more languages? In what ways do you see educators, textbooks, assignments, etc., including or excluding different language and literacy knowledge that students bring to school?

In addition to digital resources, print resources—especially young adult literature and graphic novels—should not be overlooked as powerful means of supporting language learners while also valuing their home cultures, beliefs, and practices. Chapter 7 deals with literature, with a particular focus on young adult and multicultural young adult literature. These books offer a powerful vehicle for the exploration of language and teen interaction. For example, Gary Soto's books are often infused with Spanish language phrases intermingling with English narration. This inclusion of second language phrases offers a bridge from the native language to English as a second language.

LANGUAGE AND CULTURE

Language becomes the surface manifestation of a more subtle and invisible culture. Skerrett (2015) also points to the various repertoires of practice and resources that students constantly engage in. Moreover, she points to research by Paris (2011) and others that shows the richness and complexity of languages such as "African American English and the new shared language practices diverse youth create from engaging together in communities of language and literacy practices like schools." (p.22) In our increasingly diverse classrooms, students speak multiple languages and bring their cultural beliefs and social practices to the process of content area learning (Murillo & Smith, 2008). Nieto (2004) points to a number of potential gaps in mainstream and divergent cultures that manifest themselves in classrooms. For example, she states that textbooks often emphasize a European American perspective while stereotyping, ignoring, or misrepresenting African and Native American contributions. Sociocultural values of various groups may run counter to mainstream classroom values if the teacher fails to be inclusive.

For example, Native-American students who value respect, harmony, and cooperation may have problems in a competition-oriented classroom. Some cultures disapprove of spotlighting a single student in front of the whole class (Au, 2000). Including more culturally compatible strategies like cooperative-learning groups can help you achieve an inclusive, culturally responsive teaching style that appeals to many students. Given the range of cultural diversity in classrooms, you may find some students view your style as too informal. Some students may regard your classroom as completely disconnected from their community. You can avoid this cultural gap through some labor-intensive effort to learn about students' cultures, and then design lessons accordingly. Content lessons should, as often as possible, connect the classroom to the problems and diverse values represented by your students. Urban, rural, and suburban communities all have unique contributions to make to instruction.

Instructional Design

The way in which teachers interact with students of diverse cultures may result in students seeing little connection between their native culture and the mainstream classroom value system of individual survival and competition. Unless culturally diverse students see some connection between your teaching and their unique sociocultural experiences, they are likely to just go through the motions in completing text reading assignments, project completion, and other classroom activities. A culturally sustaining pedagogic (Paris, 2011, 2015) approach means that teachers engage students in critical research around cultural issues. This involves creating very direct links between students' community life outside the classroom and the lessons they experience in the classroom (Morrell, 2009). For example, when students are allowed to bring in their contemporary music as a vehicle for studying conventions of poetry, they are more likely to experience success in reading this genre and they are more likely to tackle more challenging Shakespearean sonnets. In addition, by using music from their respective cultures such as rap, hip-hop, reggae, and Hawaiian, students see their respective cultural identities honored and respected. When parents of students visit as scholars-in-residence to discuss their jobs, their presence clearly demonstrates a direct link between the classroom and community. Without that connection, school is seen as distant and unrelated to day-to-day life for too many adolescents.

Critical Literacy and Culturally Conscious Curriculum

Another important aspect of a culturally conscious pedagogy involves infusing the classroom with a high level of critical literacy. *Critical literacy* is crucial in any content area lesson design, but it is too often absent. Critical literacy, first of all, is not the same as critical thinking (Cervetti, Damico, & Pardeles, 2001; Stevens & Bean, 2007). Critical thinking has been a part of curriculum design in the United States for many years, generally in the form of helping students distinguish facts from opinions, instances of propaganda, and so on. Critical literacy, on the other hand, aims at looking behind the text to determine whose agenda is served by the text message, what groups are silenced, and how a text could be rewritten to disrupt these conditions. When we take up the topic of reading comprehension, we explore in more detail ways to infuse critical literacy in content area classrooms. Critical literacy encourages readers to consider issues of social justice when they encounter a variety of texts that may have obvious or unstated agendas.

By engaging students as critical researchers to investigate and critique popular culture from a social justice stance, disenfranchised and marginalized adolescents are more likely to embrace academic literacy (Morrell, 2009; Pitre, 2007). For example, Ernest Morrell worked with African-American high school students in Los Angeles where they created hip-hop documentaries to protest a racist video game. Students wrote daily journal entries on their laptops and participated in a seminar that treated them as coresearchers. Morrell viewed this curriculum design as culturally conscious and likely to contribute to the development of critical citizens in a collective democracy.

You can increase student motivation in your content classroom by using activities and participation structures that ask critical literacy questions within a multicultural framework (Dunkerly-Bean, Bean & Alnajjar, 2014; Janks, 2014) such as the following:

o Who benefits from the way gender, race, and culture are portrayed?

o What identities (global and local) are possible in this text?

o How does this text position self to other?

o How would this text change if it was situated within a different context or culture?

o What is my responsibility to others in this text?

Another multicultural activity we have used in classes involves having students bring in two artifacts that represent their cultures (Maaka, 2001). For example, a student from India brought in a small replica of the Taj Mahal; another student who lost a significant amount of weight and became interested in riding motorcycles explained his various tattoos. Tom, raised in Hawaii, brought in a can of Spam° and a surf club T-shirt. The point is, the artifacts in our lives offer a window on our unique cultures.

Student Names

Students' names are special and each has a unique history as well as a wealth of associations. Throughout our history, names have been shaped by the power relationships of the time. You can use the importance and cultural interest of students' names to get to know their unique contributions to your class. Application 3.2 is a good icebreaker.

As a teacher, you can devote a section of the bulletin board in your classroom to a name history profile of your students. For example, in one content area class, a student with the last name "Kamalani" in Hawaiian, explained its meaning and significance. "Kama" means child and "lani" means heavenly. Thus, this student's name meant "heavenly child." Another student from Japan had the last name "Ohsuga." Her name denoted a young rice plant with great potential for growth and success. She shared the "kanji" or ideographic symbol for her name, which is 禾.

This simple activity of pairing, sharing, and discussing student names helps develop a sense of multicultural community in a classroom, and it focuses on an important element of language, one's name. The goal of activities like name sharing is to enable learners from different cultures and perspectives to develop some understanding of another student's world view. This movement toward a multicultural appreciation and related competency is vital for understanding text readings in history, science, music, art, English, economics, and other content areas. This brief name sharing activity can be extended through peer interviewing, video recording of these profiles, and subsequent reading and discussion in a class in social studies or English. Application 3.3 is such an extension.

Community Projects

In addition to interviewing and developing student profiles of cultural norms, you can institute other projects in your content area that link the school, classroom, and community. In science, students can connect with the community through projects in tree planting and beautification through playground cleanup at a local elementary school. A math or economics class can help an elementary school establish an in-school store for supplies or food.

Hobbies, food, and music offer additional areas where unique language and cultural differences can contribute to learning. For example, the African-American lyrical patterns found in blues and rap can be used to develop songs to study topics ranging from cell structure in biology to the stages of a revolution in history.

Cooperative-learning strategies encompassing small group work with students of diverse cultures and abilities offer yet another means of linking students' sociocultural learning styles and the classroom. For example, Hawaiian students enjoy a participation structure called "talk story" where group performance in a free-flowing discussion of current events, family activities, and community concerns is common. Indeed, the flow of information in "high context" cultures is dominated by oral language networks that rely on talk story exchanges to accomplish the day-to-day business of the community. In contrast, "low context" cultures like many urban, European American communities rely heavily on a paper trail to do business. A profusion of memos, position papers, policy statements, and legal documents characterize the flow of information in a low context culture.

Pair up with another class member and use the following survey questions to interview him or her about his or her ethnic and cultural biography and values (Kinney, 1993). This information can be used to introduce class members, assign small groups, and design lessons that build on student diversity.

1. Where did your ancestors come from? (Country, region, city)

2. Why did they come to _____ (our state, country, etc.)?

3. Where does most of your cultural community live?

4. What are the more popular jobs for your community?

5. What are the popular unique terms and gestures used by your community?

6. Do families stay close geographically as they grow up?

7. Do multiple generations live in the same household?

8. Who are the decision makers in the family?

9. How does the decision-making process happen?

10. How are elders treated in the family and community?

11. How is respect shown?

12. Do family members have certain cultural names? What are the popular names?

13. Who are married children influenced by the most in their decision making? Prioritize.

    _____ Children   _____ Grandparents   _____ Cultural leaders

    _____ Parents   _____ Nieces/nephews _____ Spiritual leaders

    _____ Siblings   _____ Neighbors   _____ Other

14. What are some special values and beliefs your culture upholds?

15. Is your community focused more on the individual or the group? Please state examples.

16. What are some ways a teacher can act that are culturally appropriate in your community?

In rural Hawaiian communities, talk story as a high context form of "coconut wireless" is still quite common. It saves trees, and works remarkably well. Talk story as a cooperative teaching strategy is directly related to the Hawaiian cultural values of "laulima" (cooperation), "ohana" (family), and "lokahi" (unity). Hawaiians and many other Pacific Island and Asian cultures revere their "kupuna," or elders, for their ability to teach culturally appropriate actions. Indeed, much of the cultural lore that needs to be shared with younger generations is not written down but must be passed along in chants and stories.

Teachers sensitive to the special values of a culture like the Hawaiians or Native Americans design content lessons that place students in small groups to discuss content text readings, react to reading guides, develop projects, and study for exams. Cooperative learning is discussed in greater detail in subsequent chapters where we demonstrate specific teaching strategies in vocabulary, comprehension, and writing. Cooperative learning has been recommended as a culturally appropriate strategy for students from high context cultures like Native American, African-American, and Hawaiian. However, cooperative learning groups mirror the problem-solving approaches used in many low-context settings in business and community groups across many cultures. Thus, learning to organize participation structures like cooperative learning will enhance teaching for most of the students in your content area classes.

In addition to the important sociocultural dimensions that influence content area learning, a number of cognitive and linguistic factors operate as students read and study content area texts and materials. Given the changing nature of what counts as "text," we differentiate the demands of reading traditional, linear print texts from the more idiosyncratic demands of online reading. We take this up later in this chapter under the title "new literacies."

COGNITIVE AND LINGUISTIC FACTORS IN PRINT TEXT COMPREHENSION

A student's prior knowledge is the vehicle for comprehending new information in a text. This constructivist view of learning argues that knowledge is constructed from experience. A student builds a body of prior knowledge through the accumulation of experiences, and this uniquely personal body of knowledge guides comprehension of subsequent text reading.

Read the following sentence and see if you can figure out what it refers to.

> The phoscheck dropped left of the cat.

If you lived in a canyon in Southern California where the early fall Santa Ana winds fan wildfires that regularly destroy homes and forests, the term "phoscheck" would be very familiar from numerous news reports and personal experience. In firefighting operations, phoscheck, a fire retardant, is dropped from helicopters. The term "cat" refers to a Caterpillar tractor cutting a fire line near where the chemical fire retardant is being dropped.

Prior knowledge, then, is constructed from experience and stored in memory. Understanding how information is organized in memory helps appreciate individual differences in reading comprehension.

ORGANIZATION OF PRIOR KNOWLEDGE IN MEMORY

Cognitive structure is a term used to describe the way in which an individual stores experiences and concepts. In such structuring, each individual forms a system of categories based largely on common cultural and experiential patterns. For example, the Eskimo culture specifies a rich category system for the quality of snow, which is virtually nonexistent in the Hawaiian culture. Such categories serve to aid an individual in organizing and understanding experiences by promoting an efficient memory search of prior experiences during problem-solving tasks. Figure 3.1 depicts a portion of a possible category system for classifying various kinds of mammals.

FIGURE 3.1

Possible Category System for Mammals

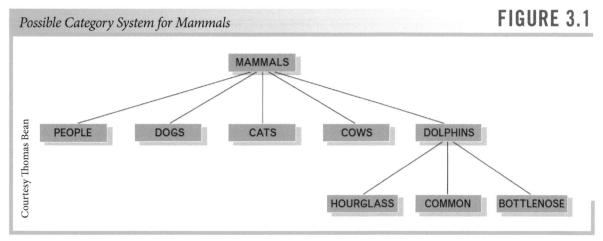

Courtesy Thomas Bean

Such a category system functions as a representation of knowledge in memory that can be searched to make sense of the surrounding environment. In general, information located at a high level (e.g., mammals) in our cognitive structure is more easily retrieved than lower-level details such as the category of hourglass or bottlenose dolphins. For example, although the category "dolphin" is readily accessible when we see a dolphin or a picture of one, the more than 50 types of dolphins would be much harder to recall. The accessibility of subsets of a category is highly dependent on individual differences with respect to one's past experience, culture, and interests. A student who was raised near the sea and has a strong interest in marine biology may have a readily accessible and highly detailed cognitive structure for the category dolphins, whereas the general population of students possesses a much less elaborate network for this category.

Most studies of student learning demonstrate the positive effects of prior knowledge as an aid to learning new concepts. Thus, content teachers should help students activate their prior knowledge before they begin a textbook or other reading assignment. Prior knowledge, however, is a double-edged sword, and existing knowledge can hinder new learning when students have misconceptions to which they cling. For example, students may believe that all dolphins are the same. Thus, understanding students' prior knowledge for a content topic, and how this knowledge is represented and organized, is important.

As a student moves into the secondary grades, an ever-expanding wealth of prior knowledge is available to cope with the flood of new information introduced in the content areas. While the concept of cognitive structure explains how this prior knowledge is organized in memory, *schema theory*, patterned after Jean Piaget's formulation, provides a more detailed explanation of comprehension. A person's schema or knowledge structure can be regarded as the central guidance system in the comprehension process. An individual searches existing schemata to make sense of incoming information from the text. The degree to which this incoming information is consistent with the expectations generated from existing schemata determines the presence or absence of comprehension.

While the cognitive structure dimension of schema theory has been a mainstay in comprehension research in reading for many years, others have argued that sociocultural elements need to be included if schema theory is to be useful in classrooms (Pearson, 2009). Teachers are crucial in guiding students' knowledge acquisition, particularly in complex content area domains. Thus, in addition to the cognitive demands of any text, other sociocultural elements, including race, class, gender, and sex, also influence students' interactions with content area material.

Concept Learning in Content Areas

CONSIDER THIS!

Take a moment and consider each of the following statements:

1. All bees sting.

2. If you are bitten by a tarantula in the hills of southern California, you might as well be dead.

3. The earth is flat.

Each of these statements comprise erroneous knowledge structures or misconceptions that students sometimes stubbornly cling to, despite a teacher's best efforts to convince them otherwise. Indeed, the first two misconceptions may be consistent with your schema for bees and tarantulas. Yet a male bee does not have a stinger; you can hold a male bee in your hand without any fear of injury. And, although tarantulas are poisonous and even deadly in South America, the southern California variety is not deadly. Finally, at the secondary and college levels, students generally know that the earth is not flat.

APPLICATION 3.4

In your content area (science, art, math, etc.) you learn a number of concepts (e.g., Newton's second law of motion) that defy common sense or conventional wisdom. Identify two such concepts from your content area and write a statement for each that is the commonly held belief by people who have not studied your field. Share these statements with another class member from a different field. Did they agree or disagree with the two statements. Why? What were their reasons?

Despite potential problems with misconceptions, linking new concepts to some familiar, existing concept remains a powerful strategy we can use to advantage in content teaching. Teachers routinely resort to verbal analogies when they see students looking perplexed. Sometimes these analogies are successful but at times they fail to connect with students' experiences, especially if the students are approaching English as a second language. As a content teacher, you need to identify students' existing knowledge and provide experiences in reading, listening, speaking, and writing that help them progress smoothly through tuning and restructuring knowledge. Activities such as the anticipation guide and brainstorming, especially reflective brainstorming written in a dialogue journal, provide us with some sense of students' prior knowledge. We can then anticipate misconceptions that may arise as students read and take measures to help them modify existing information that is naive or in error. In later chapters we introduce specific strategies aimed at exploring students' concept development through reading and writing.

Prior Knowledge of a Topic and Reader Interest

Contemporary models of the reading process present comprehension as a complex interaction of reader knowledge, text variables, reader interest, and the quality of teaching that assists text comprehension. Despite the obvious power of a close match between students' expressed interest and a text that matches those interests, you as the teacher also have a profound impact on interest. As a teacher, you help students establish a purpose and a particular frame of reference or schema for reading text assignments. Because content area assignments often entail reading expository material that may depart from a student's preferred interests, you need to carefully guide students' understanding of text. Building prior knowledge and generating topic interest through purpose-setting activities like anticipation-reaction guides can make a difference. In later chapters we introduce systematic procedures for discovering students' reading preferences. More importantly, we introduce techniques a content teacher can employ to insure that students become lifelong readers.

Motivation to Learn with Content Texts

When students are confronted with expository textbooks that hold little intrinsic appeal, their motivation for reading and learning may sink. Without adequate teacher guidance and ingenuity, students in content fields such as science and social science may sluggishly go through the motions of learning, dispensing only minimal effort. If you lecture, assign text reading, and ask students only low-level factual questions that encourage memorization and forgetting, students are likely to lapse into a reluctant, sluggish mode of participation. If you want to encourage students to actively link new knowledge to their existing background knowledge, to critically evaluate ideas advanced in your class texts and discussions, and to value their growing concept knowledge, the following general principles are important.

You need to provide a supportive, well-structured classroom environment and assignments that are challenging but not frustrating. Your learning objectives should be problem-centered issues worth pursuing, rather than busy work that merely encourages memorizing facts and copying text-based definitions. For example, if you are studying a unit on the Constitution with a focus on the Bill of Rights, you might engage students in a discussion of student rights as a prelude to their text reading.

Slicing the complexity of lengthy tasks into manageable increments that students can accomplish in a short period of time helps reduce that feeling of helplessness and inertia associated with tasks students perceive to be beyond their capacity. Similarly, teaching students to set their own realistic learning goals may help reduce frustration. These goals may be in the form of reading a small section of a chapter or answering a specific, reasonable portion of the chapter questions. Along with reducing the scope of a task, providing immediate feedback and rewarding success through pleasurable activities, points, or simple praise will go a long way toward helping student motivation and interest in your content area.

Opportunities for active student responses to text concepts are crucial to enthusiasm for content learning. Projects, experiments, discussions, debates, role-playing, computer simulations, and student-created multimedia productions all contribute to student interest in learning content that could otherwise be potentially dull. Classroom activities that place students in cooperative learning dyads and triads with their peers, especially if they are engaged in solving problems or grappling with higher-order questions, also enhance motivation. In addition, providing immediate feedback on how they are succeeding or experiencing difficulty will help them see the value in their efforts.

Finally, when students have opportunities to complete projects, whether in the form of essays, reports, multimedia productions, models, a play, artwork, or a gourmet meal, they have a vivid and tangible record of their efforts. We can all remember, possibly in some detail, those learning situations in which we produced something of intrinsic value. You need to strive for lessons that capture these principles. In subsequent chapters we introduce specific strategies designed to involve students actively in content learning. Additionally, we consider those students for whom content learning is especially challenging because of a persistent cycle of failure. We offer strategies for coping with the wide-ranging individual differences typical of our content classrooms.

GUIDELINES TO HELP STUDENTS ACTIVELY LINK NEW KNOWLEDGE TO EXISTING KNOWLEDGE

1. Provide a supportive, well-structured classroom environment.
2. Give assignments that are challenging but not frustrating.
3. Break up complex, lengthy tasks into manageable increments.
4. Teach students to set realistic goals.
5. Provide immediate feedback.
6. Reward success.
7. Provide opportunities for active student responses to text.

Memory

This section introduces some important concepts concerning human memory. Since a student's prior knowledge is represented in memory, it is essential to understand how memory aids or disrupts the efficient use of prior knowledge in the comprehension process.

Cognitive psychologists typically differentiate two aspects of memory—short-term memory and long-term memory. In reality, these terms represent hypothetical constructs about memory rather than particular locations in the brain. Figure 3.2 illustrates the flow of information as it is processed by our memory system.

FIGURE 3.2

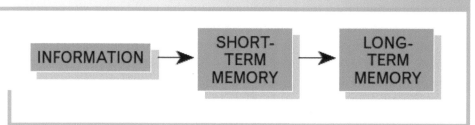

Courtesy Thomas Bean

Short-Term Memory

Short-term memory is often called working memory because it holds information on a temporary basis until the information is either processed into long-term memory or erased to accept more incoming information. Short-term memory contains traces of the most recent information we are attending to at any given moment.

The single most important feature of short-term memory is its limited capacity for storing information. The short-term storage capacity for individual chunks of information is four. Your struggle to retain a new friend's phone number is a concrete example of this principle in operation. Including the area code, a phone number such as 618-296-9149 exceeds the storage capacity of short-term memory. Fortunately, there is a way to circumvent this capacity limitation. Using a chunking strategy, the phone number 618-296-9149 can be held in short-term memory as three, rather than 10, discrete items (i.e., [618] [296] [9149]). However, short-term memory has a second limitation that even chunking cannot overcome.

The second important feature of short-term memory is its fleeting nature. Information such as a new friend's phone number must be constantly rehearsed if it is to remain available in short-term memory for longer than a few seconds. If attention is diverted for even a moment to something else, the limited storage capacity of short-term memory will be overloaded and the phone number erased to accept the new, incoming information. Both the fleeting duration of short-term memory and its limited storage capacity have important implications for the reading process in general and content teaching in particular.

EFFECTS OF SHORT-TERM MEMORY ON LITERACY. In terms of the reading process in general, if a student plods along in print attempting to sound out every unfamiliar word, short-term memory will be overburdened. The result of this word-by-word reading is that students can forget the beginning of a sentence before they get to the end. They must learn to read text material, including unfamiliar words, in the most efficient way possible to overcome the limits of short-term memory. Chapter 8 introduces decoding strategies that encourage fluent reading.

In the content areas, some modes of presenting unfamiliar material may inadvertently impose excessive demands on students' short-term memories. The oral presentation of a large amount of new information in social studies or science may exceed the capacity of their short-term memories. Problem-solving tasks in mathematics present similar problems. Word problems, which involve temporary storage of one part of the problem while the student simultaneously processes additional information, place excessive demands on the limited storage capacity of short-term memory. Finally, the processing limitations of short-term memory suggest that rote memorization of content material is likely to be an ineffective study strategy, and these should be kept in mind when a teacher plans or analyzes content teaching and learning tasks.

Long-Term Memory

Long-term memory, or permanent memory, plays an important role in compensating for the limitations of short-term or working memory. In contrast to short-term memory, long-term memory seems to have an infinite capacity for storing information. It is the storage system for all our prior knowledge. It comprises our individually complex schema of the world, shaped by cultural experiences and beliefs. As such, long-term memory is a highly organized system. Indeed, the ease with which we can retrieve information from long-term memory is directly related to how well the information was organized at the time of initial processing from short-term memory.

One of the most powerful ways to encode information in long-term memory is through writing. Increasingly, writing is seen as a learning strategy that teachers should integrate across content areas. Chapter 11 offers a number of specific writing-to-learn approaches you can weave into your own teaching repertoire to enhance students' comprehension and long-term retention of concepts.

Long-term memory's one limitation is that the rate at which information can be processed into it is relatively slow. However, the ease with which this happens depends largely on how meaningful the information is in terms of the student's prior knowledge. The more meaningful the information, the more easily it will be processed.

Figure 3.3 summarizes the two major aspects of memory treated in this section. In general, content teachers should acknowledge the importance of prior knowledge and meaningful organization in long-term memory information processing in their teaching. Students will be able to comprehend new information in a content area if you take time to demonstrate how the new information builds upon and extends what they already know about the topic. They will be able to retrieve information from long-term memory if you model and encourage meaningful organization of new information when it is first presented to the class.

FIGURE 3.3

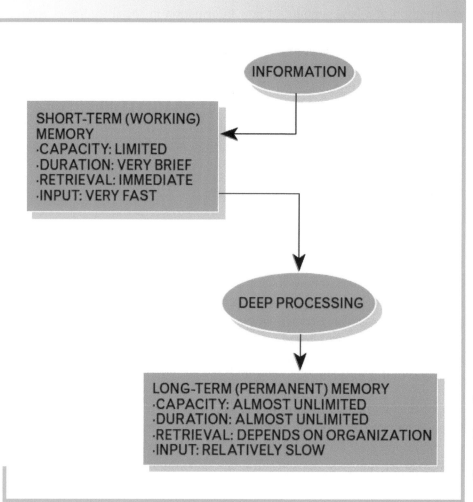

Courtesy Thomas Bean

Although cognitive factors play a major role in reading comprehension, linguistic factors also influence the reading process. This section describes and demonstrates specific linguistic aspects of written language that interact with cognitive factors to aid or inhibit reading comprehension.

Language of Text

Authors of stories and even challenging scientific print-based texts use predictable organization patterns or *text structures.* For example, stories usually begin with a setting and one or more characters. The reader follows the main character's attempts to solve a problem or achieve a goal. This familiar text structure makes it relatively easy for a reader to make predictions about story events. Even more difficult, expository texts in science have an identifiable pattern of organization. For example, biology texts usually inform the reader about properties and functions of a topic such as carbohydrates or enzymes.

Students who are made aware of the overall structure of a particular text can use this knowledge to comprehend, study, and discuss key concepts. Moreover, a text that provides a discernible organizational pattern places fewer demands on the limitations of short-term memory than poorly structured text. Chapter 9 discusses text structure in detail and introduces comprehension strategies that capitalize on this important linguistic aspect of text.

Contemporary views of what constitutes a text are changing rapidly, and we need to consider the multiple texts students typically use. Texts come in many shapes and forms, including internet texts, radio and film media, electronic mail, instant messages, and hosts of other forms. It may be helpful to think of texts as cultural tools for constructing knowledge rather than encyclopedic collections of information upon which to be tested (Moje, 2008).

Becoming grounded in the unique discourse features of a discipline requires acting on content in fields, including mathematics, science, social science, and English (Moje, 2008). In essence, learning the particular discourse of a discipline is best accomplished by acting like a neophyte scholar in the field. For example, when students conduct water quality studies in science by testing water samples in their community, they are engaging fully in the scientific method and discourse related to data collection and analysis. In history, when students evaluate competing accounts of grand narratives of discovery (e.g., Captain Cooke "discovered" Hawaii versus the presence of Hawaiians at his landfall), they are engaging in the steps historians take to evaluate warrants and claims for any account of an event. "Part of learning in the subject areas, then, is coming to understand the norms of practice for producing and communicating knowledge in the disciplines" (Moje,

2008, p. 100). These scenarios contrast sharply with transmission teaching models where students read and recount information in a test. Indeed, contemporary students are already engaged in creating and producing knowledge via social media. Engaging them in an inquiry stance in your content area is a natural extension of their lives, assuming they have access to some technology in the school context.

Helping students manage a wide array of multiple texts in broad-based thematic units undoubtedly builds on the multitasking to which they are accustomed and best prepares them to become independent learners. While the single-textbook approach may continue to be found in content area classrooms, students need to learn how to manage a wider array of text forms, including WebQuests and other multimedia or internet-based text formats (Walker, Bean, & Dillard, 2010).

Language of Students

In addition to features of texts that make them friendly or unfriendly, our earlier discussion of second language learners suggests that students' language facility plays a powerful role in comprehension. If the texts students must read are very distant from their native language, these students may have difficulty forming the mental pictures necessary for learning concepts.

CONSIDER THIS!

The following sentence, adapted from Laird and Jossen (1983, p. 10), illustrates the frustration a second language learner may experience in text material containing vocabulary that is largely unfamiliar:

> "Oh! Dakine mea'ai stay so ono," said Wili Wai Kula.

If readers must translate every word of a text with a dictionary or a laborious search through memory, they will have little attention left for comprehension. Moreover, integration of ideas across words and sentences becomes impossible.

Contrast the above example with Laird and Jossen's (1983) original text, *Wili Wai Kula and the Three Mongooses*, a Hawaiian version of the familiar *Goldilocks and the Three Bears*.

> "Oh! The mea'ai smells so ono," said a hungry Wili Wai Kula. She tasted the rice and sausage on the biggest plate. It was too hot. Next, she tasted the rice and sausage on the medium-sized plate. It was too cold.

In this instance, some of the vocabulary is unfamiliar. However, your prior knowledge of the original fable, combined with some vocabulary knowledge, and context clues should help you comprehend "mea'ai," a Hawaiian word for meal, and "ono," which means good.

Texts for second language learners should strike a delicate balance between familiar and unfamiliar vocabulary. Visual aids and prereading guides that help students see how their prior knowledge is related to concepts in the text help them use semantic cues. Otherwise, there is a real tendency for these students to read in a word-by-word fashion or to decode accurately without really comprehending what they have read. Notice that once you see a bridge between the familiar Goldilocks story and the Hawaiian version you can comprehend the selection despite not knowing all the vocabulary. In content areas, students' background knowledge is not likely to be quite this direct. But you can try to select texts that capitalize on familiar topics while adding new information to students' concept learning.

Visual representation of content area concepts helps second language learners connect the new to the known (Bean, 2010). For example, if students are studying fish in science, the ancient Japanese art of origami will help them develop a hands-on grasp of fish anatomy through paper-cutting, painting, and labeling key parts. Moreover, this form of hands-on activity usually generates many opportunities for language interaction. In addition, the guide material discussed in Part 2 of this text can go a long way toward unlocking text concepts in the target language.

Digital Literacies and Text Structure

Digital literacies refer to the skills and strategies needed by readers to effectively navigate, interpret, manage, and share a growing variety of texts. The need for proficiency in digital literacies emerges from research into the ways in which individuals navigate newer technologies that have changed the ways in which we read (Bean, 2010; Kist, 2010). The reason these newer forms of text are important is because they demonstrate a shift in the methods one uses to read them (Hartman, Morsink, & Zheng, 2010). For example, to a great extent, the linear and somewhat predictable text structures mentioned earlier (e.g., cell structure and function in a biology textbook) shift when students are reading and navigating internet-based texts. Indeed, Kress (2003) observed that reading paths in internet texts vary across multiple sites and call for fairly sophisticated search strategies. Hartman et al. (2010) note that, "Online comprehension is more complicated" (p. 131).

In traditional print-based textbooks, students work with fairly predictable, established text structures (e.g., problem solution; simple listing of ideas; cause–effect relationships in science). In contrast, online text is characterized by chunks of information organized multi-sequentially, requiring readers to create their own navigational pathways and structures. In essence, these more unpredictable and varying online text pathways require more teacher guidance, particularly for struggling readers. "Seductive details, images, ads, titles, videos, and the sort reshape the focus or redirect the goal at any click along the way" (Hartman et al., 2010). Without your careful guidance, students are likely to do cursory searches for information, accept ideas without critique, and produce projects and papers that reflect little thought. Thus, in our view, the increasing use of online texts, while powerful from an information standpoint, is a double-edged sword: there is as much fallacious information out there as there is valid. An example of this may be found at the website, http://martinlutherking.org. Although students may assume that the ".org" ending legitimizes the website, it is in fact a page dedicated to desecrating and demeaning the life and work of Dr. Martin Luther King, Jr. Thus, many of the strategies aimed at guiding students' understanding of vocabulary and key ideas in content areas become even more crucial as text structures blur and morph into collections of information organized in a wide-ranging panoply of forms on the Internet.

When you engage students in reading multiple texts in your content area, coupled with careful guidance and support to help them make connections across texts, you prepare them to manage the vast array of information available on the Internet. As we consider vocabulary and comprehension issues in subsequent chapters, we expand on this changing nature of text, and examine strategies that will help students across traditional and newer forms of text.

The Classroom Social Context

In addition to cognitive and linguistic factors, the social context of a classroom has its own linguistic conventions and features. A number of studies, stemming from the anthropologic tradition of intensive participant observation, provide us with an emerging picture of teacher–student and student–student interaction that belies a simplistic view of content teaching. The goal of intensive observational study is to uncover the social patterns that influence teacher and student success in constructing meaning. Social context is as powerful as the following true Glimpse into the Classroom suggests.

Glimpse into the Classroom

In my first year as a ninth-grade English teacher, I had one class of 28 boys and no girls. These young men were the reputed dregs of the school: low achievers, truants, and troublemakers—one was sent to youth detention for robbing the blind man at the post office. I will always remember the day I handed out spelling books with a big number 3 on the front. Most of the boys were reading at a primary school level, and I wanted to have them working with materials at their instructional level. I explained to the class that learning to spell wasn't so difficult and that these spelling books would help them earn better grades in school. They said nothing;

but when class was over, 28 copies of Fun With Spelling went into the wastebasket in the back of the room. I never forgot the lesson.

The teacher in this story may have known a lot about English spelling, and he may have had an appropriate instructional strategy in mind, but he failed to consider the social context in which the instruction had to take place. Those ninth-grade boys were not about to walk around a tough, urban school advertising to their peers the fact that they were using third-grade books. Getting kicked out of school or failing English for the year would no doubt have been preferable to them.

Schools are institutions with rules and agendas that tend to reflect the values of adults and the dominant culture, and not the social and cultural values of adolescent readers and writers. Within the school is a variety of subcultures with their own unique beliefs and goals, frequently in conflict with each other. Adults, children, European Americans, Hispanics, African-Americans, Haitians, fundamentalist Christians, and many other groups will view the school, its curricula, and your teaching in different ways, because these events are filtered through alternative cultural realities (O'Brien & Stewart, 2007). For example, classroom interaction patterns are, at least on the surface, usually orchestrated by the teacher and based on an intuitive or conscious theory of learning. Thus, teachers instruct, question, praise, and monitor students' comprehension in observable patterns that reveal their particular view of reading comprehension. This may range from simply assigning text reading, questioning students orally, and giving a test, to the more carefully guided approach we advocate.

In a classroom that follows our model of content teaching, an observer would expect to see various forms of prereading strategies in use (e.g., Anticipation Guides), small group discussion of text concepts using the guides, and postreading Reaction Guide discussion. In addition, online reading would be scaffolded where needed and, in other cases, would depend more on students using these teacher models to develop their own comprehension monitoring strategies for gathering information from the Internet. Yet even with this guided approach, the classroom remains a social environment with its own hidden curriculum that is shaped by social as well as academic factors. Peer-status rankings strongly influence whose voice gets heard and who is silenced, even in small groups (Moje & Dillon, 2006).

Classroom reading and discussion patterns often contain the following dimensions. Students are required only to reproduce text, merely reiterating text content. Amid such low-level discussions, they become skilled at procedural display—looking as if they are doing the work and participating, while simultaneously carrying on other, more personally interesting and rewarding activities.

Thus, a teacher-dominated discussion of text concepts produces an overly passive style of student thinking and participation. In our view, a classroom content lesson coexists with the larger context of the school and the sociolinguistic context of students' lives. A content lesson competes for students' attention amid other, often more compelling, interests. It is likely to compete successfully if most students have adequate opportunities to participate.

One of the more recent, dominant themes in adolescent literacy now informing our teaching in various content areas is the degree to which classrooms and texts influence students' identity construction. Simplistic, stereotypical views of adolescents have been heavily challenged, arguing for a much more complex portrayal of youth (Lesko, 2001). Older developmental stage theories of adolescence have been deconstructed and replaced with more contemporary views of youth. "Youth are simultaneously young and old, learning and learned, working and in school." (Lesko, 2001, p. 197) Thus, adolescents are not at some static plateau where they are waiting to evolve into adults. Rather, they are active individuals with a multitude of interests and identities that shift with varying social contexts. They need to be considered active, critical participants in content learning. We have much to learn from youth as students.

Much of this recent effort to reconceptualize adolescents shows a disconnection between the out-of-school literacy lives of students and the tasks they perform to succeed in school. For example, a student viewed as only a marginal achiever in school core content areas may write about athletic performance in a running diary when not in school. Although marginalized in terms of literacy performance in school, this same student writes and reflects on running performance eloquently when at home or with peers on the cross-country team. The disparity between school and out-of-school identity has been well documented (Moje, 2002). What is truly important in this work is to consciously find ways to incorporate, acknowledge, and build on students' interests as a bridge to content area concepts. For example, running involves the mathematic elements of time, biologic elements of cell structure, geography, weather, and attention to attire to maximize performance, among other things. McCarthey and Dressman (2000) recommended developing a curriculum that truly represents students' diversity by focusing on local, situational literacies. "Students would read and critique texts created from multimedia and written from a variety of points of view that reflected the diversity of their racial, social, cultural, and linguistic backgrounds" (p. 548). We agree that capitalizing on students' interests in curriculum design in the content areas is advantageous. For example, students in a biology class who are interested in running might examine and evaluate the truth claims of various high-energy, fluid replacement drinks. Thus, their day-to-day interests from local, situational contexts are connected to issues of health and nutrition, as well as concepts of cellular energy storage.

A number of studies show that transmission of information teaching has changed little over the years. However, if a teacher takes a participatory approach to learning, and students have the opportunity to interact with others, more learning is likely to take place (Moje, 2008). A traditional transmission approach to teaching concepts from a single textbook disempowers and disenfranchises students, particularly students from diverse cultural and linguistic groups. Since students have multiple identities in and out of school, it behooves the content teacher to help them bridge text concepts with their individual interests and identities whenever possible. For example, a student who wants to be a paramedic is positioned to gain from biology and health sciences, especially if the teachers in these areas are aware of this related interest. Magazines, internet material, first-aid pamphlets, and other forms of text would be naturals to help engage this student in content learning. In addition to knowing something about students' outside-of-school lives, cultural dimensions play a profound role in how students respond to the classroom context. Moje et al. (2000) urged content teachers to ask themselves, "How will my choices of texts and literacy activities reflect and expand the cultural backgrounds of my learners?" (p. 178) Chapter 7 introduces an array of multicultural young adult novels that expand on content area concepts and connect with students' lives.

APPLICATION 3.5

John Ogbu (2007) provides powerful anthropologic insights into academic problems commonly experienced by minority children. Obgu also proposes a theory that explains why some ethnic minorities have more success in public schools than others. Read Professor Ogbu's article and write a 1–2 page essay explaining how his research and theories do or do not seem to explain patterns of minority achievement with which you yourself are familiar.

Teacher–student interaction patterns influence students' comprehension and attitude toward the content being studied. Collaborative, small group discussion using pre- and postreading strategies, such as Anticipation-Reaction Guides, are a good alternative to teacher-centered discussion. We are not suggesting that there is anything wrong with whole group lectures and discussions. But we do believe that small, problem-solving groups can afford greater opportunities for student participation if they are focused on an important topic with clear task guidelines.

Part 2 of this text considers comprehension strategies that you may wish to adopt to enhance students' critical reading and discussion. Reflective writing can also form a basis for student-centered sharing and discussion of ideas and issues. These elements of content literacy are elaborated upon in subsequent chapters.

REACTION GUIDE

		Confirmed	Disconfirmed
1.	Addressing students' culture and language diversity is preferable but not necessary.	_____	_____
2.	Strategies for EAL are not helpful for other students.	_____	_____
3.	Comprehending print and digital texts are unrelated processes.	_____	_____
4.	Student learning depends mostly on the teacher's content knowledge.	_____	_____
5.	Whole class discussion discourages wide student participation.	_____	_____

	A Why my choice is confirmed.	B Why my choice is not confirmed.
1.	_____	_____
2.	_____	_____
3.	_____	_____
4.	_____	_____
5.	_____	_____

MINI PROJECTS

1. Visit a classroom in your content area and interview the teacher to determine how the issues in the first part of the chapter on language and diversity are handled. Before the interview, develop a few questions to stimulate discussions that focus on sociocultural and linguistic diversity as well as mainstreaming. Share your results with another class member in a discussion.

2. List at least one method you currently use, or plan to use, to assist second language learners' comprehension of concepts in your content area.

3. List at least three methods you currently use, or plan to use, to mobilize students' existing knowledge of topics in your particular content area. Compare your compilation with listings produced by other class members.

4. Visit a classroom in your content area. Based on your observation notes, analyze the interaction pattern that occurs and determine the level of comprehension emphasized.

RECOMMENDED WEBSITES

Go to the website for Chapter 5 activities.
- o   www.readwritethink.org
- o   http://en.childrenslibrary.org
- o   http://www.eal-teaching-strategies.com
- o   www.tolerance.org

Selecting Textbooks and Multimedia Materials

CHAPTER 4

ANTICIPATION GUIDE

	Agree	Disagree
1. Censorship is both bad and unnecessary.	_____	_____
2. Government regulations require that tenth-grade books be written on a tenth-grade reading level.	_____	_____
3. It is safe to assume that high school students know how to use a textbook index.	_____	_____
4. The content of subject area textbooks is politically influenced.	_____	_____

RATIONALE

© wavebreakmedia/Shutterstock.com

What is a textbook? Broadly speaking, a textbook could be any book that is used in formal study. This might include, for example, novels, reference books, or other works of non-fiction that may or may not have been designed exclusively for schools. More commonly, textbooks refer to books written specifically for school use and designed to summarize a body of knowledge or to present the fundamental principles of a discipline. The American history tomes, literature anthologies, and other textbooks to which you are accustomed vary tremendously in their quality. Some offer excellent presentations whereas others are too difficult for their intended audiences or are poorly organized. In addition, as we demonstrate, the personal values of authors and the agendas of special-interest groups cause textbooks that cover the same content to differ in terms of how they represent the truth.

From the primary grades through college, textbooks are a pervasive element of education in the United States. Assuming that the average student spends five hours per school day using textbooks, the number of hours spent with textbooks exceeds 10,000 by the end of high school ($5 \times 180 \times 12$). Clearly, how we select those books and what we ask students to do with them will have an enormous impact on how well students learn, what they learn, what they believe, and how well they think.

In this chapter we examine issues related to the selection and appropriate use of textbooks, first from social and political perspectives and then from an instructional viewpoint. Additionally, we discuss the appropriate selection of multimedia materials. Finally, we demonstrate a strategy for introducing students to an unfamiliar text.

LEARNING OBJECTIVES

o   Discuss the political and social dilemmas associated with textbook adoption processes.
o   Understand what close reading entails and know to create a multimodal text set.
o   State which quantitative and qualitative factors make a text more or less easy to understand.
o   Employ a checklist of quantitative and qualitative factors to evaluate a textbook and/or multimedia materials for use in your classroom.
o   Conduct a textbook preview to acquaint students with the essential learning aids in a text.

GRAPHIC ORGANIZER

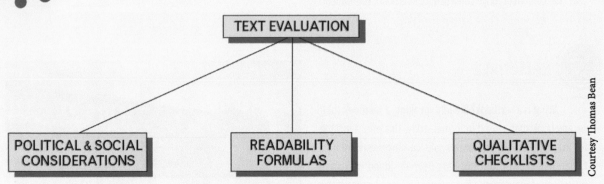

Courtesy Thomas Bean

POLITICS AND TEXTBOOKS

We customarily associate the word "politics" with government. However, politics has the broader meaning of any social or cultural arrangement in which people make decisions that have consequences for other people. There are political dimensions to marriage, bridge clubs, and team sports. Public education is no exception.

School systems wrestle with political matters every day, and most of them are outside the interest or beyond the control of most classroom teachers. However, there is one political issue that must be of critical concern to every subject area specialist—the selection and interpretation of textbooks. Ultimately, content area teachers are responsible for the accuracy, truth, and representativeness of the textbooks they use. Which stories and essays should be included in literature anthologies, for instance? Because it is impossible to include everything in an anthology, something must be excluded. What stays, what goes, and who makes the decision? Should the biblical version of creation be included in biology texts along with theories that espouse evolution? How explicit should health texts be on subjects of human sexuality, AIDS, and abortion? How these issues are resolved fluctuates over time. Textbooks are not almanac-like tomes of facts. Instead, they are books written and published by human beings whose cultural biases can slant, bend, or bury someone else's interpretation of the truth.

CONSIDER THIS!

Historical truth is slippery. It is possible, for example, to portray American westward expansion in a variety of ways. One account would describe fanatical, materialistic malcontents who out of greed organized a bloody rebellion against lawfully constituted authority and then murdered or expelled those who remained loyal to the legitimate regime. It would be the tale of a people who institutionalized genocide against American Indians and slavery of African peoples by invoking scriptural revelations of their god. *Bury My Heart at Wounded Knee* by Dee Brown has a graphic description of the treatment of American Indians. If you ever get a chance to read the book, it will not be difficult for you to view European Americans as the bad guys.

In the more traditional account of westward expansion, the nation's past is presented as a triumphant celebration of freedom, social progress, human rights, and individual fulfillment. Starting with the flight of a few enterprising and courageous souls from religious persecution, and continuing with a just and glorious revolution against the oppression of a tyrannical monarch, this would be the tale of virtue, both civic and cultural. This version of American history would portray a happy, freedom-loving people, the product of rugged individualism and hard work. It would be the story of manifest destiny with a people resolved to reclaim the wilderness, to civilize the savages, and to spread the principles of democracy across the virgin continent.

It has been suggested that although both Brown's version and the typical textbook version are extreme, both versions are also true to some degree. Yet one is the approved version that appears in US history textbooks. The latter, familiar version is taught almost universally in American schools as the truth, while the former version seldom finds its way into American history books. Many of the brutal truths of American history are presented by James Loewen (2007) in his provocative book, *Lies My Teacher Told Me: Everything Your American History Textbook Got Wrong.*

Close Reading

Contemporary thinking about curriculum design in the content areas emphasizes the use of multiple texts and engaging students in comparing ideas across multiple print and nonprint texts (Hinchman & Moore, 2013). Students are expected to read, write, and discuss ideas using digital literacy resources to explore and inquire about a host of content area topics (e.g., climate change). The complex demands of connecting, comparing and contrasting, and critically evaluating ideas across this multiple-text terrain also calls for multiple readings. Sometimes referred to as a "close reading," these practices involve making intertextual connections. Intertextuality is a term that encompasses reading, listening, and viewing across a range of texts related to a central theme (Bean, Dunkerly-Bean, & Harper, 2014). This more complex arena may pose challenges for students. For example, Hinchman and Moore note, "English learners, striving readers, and students with special needs are especially vulnerable—particularly if their intervention reading has focused on decoding and low-level comprehension tasks" (p. 445). It will be helpful to keep this caveat in mind as we explore the use of multimodal materials.

One way to accommodate an array of student needs with respect to close reading is to create multimodal text sets (Dunkerly-Bean, & Bean, 2015). These are defined as collections of print and nonprint texts that are related to a central theme or topic. They include a mix of multigenre, multimodal texts that may be digital texts, podcasts, videos, news footage, live feeds, social media, photographs, artistic works and performances, in addition to traditional print-based texts. In science, a theme like climate change might well encompass all of these forms of texts in a multimodal text set aimed at fostering close reading practices and scaffolded to accommodate various students' needs.

Materials may include print texts, multimedia (e.g., YouTube clips), artwork, movies, hip-hop, news satires, and a host of other multimedia. Indeed, publishers are paying attention to our more complex standards and expectations when they develop new materials that align with close reading practices (Hinchman & Moore, 2013). And, the disciplinary differences in close reading also matter. For example, sourcing and evaluating historical documents in history, close reading in mathematics to solve a problem, following directions carefully in laboratory experiments, and a host of other forms of close reading that are specific to the disciplines matter. As we consider ways to evaluate our instructional materials, it will be helpful to think of how your discipline conceptualizes close reading, intertextuality, reading multiple times, and scaffolding learners' comprehension. In addition to these elements, the political and sociocultural dimensions loom large as we consider material for adoption.

Censorship

In early Rome there were magistrates known as censors. Their job was to take an accounting of the people and also to look after public morals. From their former duty we have acquired the word *census*. From their latter commission we have inherited *censor* and *censorship*. A censor today is someone who indirectly supervises morality by regulating films, books, music, or other information to which people may have access. The people who assign ratings of G, PG, PG-13, R, and X to movies are censors. Parents are censors when they do not let their children watch a television show because they believe the show is too crude or too violent. A librarian who decides that a book should not be in the school library is a censor. For example, the Harry Potter books have been some of the most banned books in America because they promote witchcraft. When publishers decide not to put a story into a literature anthology, they are censors—if they exclude the story because they are afraid of reprisals from the National Rifle Association, the American Civil Liberties Union, animal rights activists, or a fundamentalist Christian organization in California.

Censorship issues involving children and schools are not the same as adult censorship issues. With adults the issue usually is constitutional:

> *Congress shall make no law respecting an establishment of religion, or prohibiting the free exercise thereof; or abridging the freedom of speech, or of the press; or the right of the people to assemble, and to petition the Government for a redress of grievances.*
>
> FIRST AMENDMENT TO THE CONSTITUTION

Presumably, the First Amendment gives adults the right to read whatever they want. However, censorship issues with students are more complex because students, especially young children, are assumed not to have the ability to make sound choices. Someone else decides for them: what movies they may watch, what establishments they may enter, what books they may read, what content they will find in their subject area textbooks. Either restriction is censorship. When accused of censorship, school officials invariably respond that it is not a matter of censorship but rather a matter of selecting appropriate reading materials for children. They have a point. Censorship in this sense is a fact of life in public education. Books will be chosen for children by someone. The real question revolves around who the someone is that decides: teachers, administrators, church groups, parents, publishers, or special-interest groups in another state.

Textbook Censorship

One of the mightiest—and most hidden—powers in our society rests with those who are in a position to control the meanings of words and the distribution of concepts. Nowhere else in our culture is this power less obvious to the public or more critical to our collective future than in the development of school textbooks.

Textbooks are typically developed as a collaboration between teachers/college professors and an editorial staff within a publishing house. As a rule, the lower the grade level the more the final product is the work of professional editors. In contrast, the content of high school and college texts is more likely to reflect the thinking and writing of teachers/professors.

Publishers are businesses that sell books for money. Their primary responsibility is to shareholders and employees, and not to the abstractions of accuracy and truth. Compared with the profit motive, all other concerns are secondary. In this respect the publishing business is the same as the oil industry, retail furniture stores, and the hotdog stand at the beach. To make a profit the publishers must meet a market demand. If schools will buy more history books because the covers are more attractive, the publisher will make more attractive covers. If schools will buy more history books if they are made to contain fewer references to Ulysses S. Grant and more references to Robert E. Lee, then you can bet that Grant will wane while Lee rises.

This is not intended to be an indictment of textbook publishers. Most of them are sincere in their efforts to publish quality books for children, but they are under tremendous pressure from schools and special-interest groups to censor social science, literature, and physical science textbooks.

If you peruse a secondary literature anthology you will probably find that the anthology has been censored so that some or all of the following are absent from every selection:

o Potentially offensive words such as "hell" or "crap"

o References to any drugs—even aspirin

o References to any junk foods like potato chips

o Any reference—even indirect—to the theory of evolution

o Pejorative comments about any minority groups

o References to witchcraft

o Any sexist language

o Any reference to human sexuality

o Any discussion of religion

o Any story in which children question the values or moral reasoning of their parents.

While reading this list, you probably feel some of the censored material would not be objectionable to you. Why do all of these aspects of literature have to be removed? The answer is that the most efficient way for publishers to eliminate potential objections from various censors is to self-censor *anything* that *anyone* might find offensive. A fundamental principle of censorship is that censors are sensitive to what is in the text that should not be there. They are seldom worried about what is not there that should be. Therefore, a special-interest group that wants to suppress references to junk foods will not notice that essays about dangerous drugs, information about human sexuality, and pertinent dramas about teenage value systems bit the dust along with the Twinkies. The result is a carefully homogenized and bland anthology that no longer reflects the adolescent literature it is supposed to represent.

You might imagine that publishers could avoid overcensoring by developing multiple textbooks to suit the needs of individual schools that are more or less progressive, located in different geographic areas, or have different ethnic representations. The problem with this solution is that books are so expensive to develop that the costs of multiple versions are prohibitive. The approximate cost of developing a new literature series, for example, may be 10 million dollars—or more.

Textbook Adoption Policies

Another cause of publisher overcensoring is state textbook adoption policies. When a tenth-grade biology textbook is adopted by a school system, it means that high schools within the school system are permitted to order the book for use in grade 10 biology classes. If the textbook has not been adopted, the book cannot be ordered. There are several reasons for book adoptions. One is that publishers give significant discounts when textbooks are purchased in large quantities. It is less expensive to buy 10,000 copies from one publisher than to buy 1,000 copies from 10 different publishers. A second reason for system-wide adoption is that it provides for quality control. A school system will usually have a textbook adoption committee composed of content area specialists, administrators, and in some cases community leaders or parents. Their task is to evaluate textbooks on the market and choose the one that is most suitable for their school system given the variables of price, text difficulty, methodologic approach, and general philosophy. In principle, adoptions can take place at the level of the individual teacher, school, school system, or at the level of the state.

There are now many states that have state textbook adoption programs, and they include three of the most populous states in the country: California, Florida, and Texas. States have adoptions for the same reasons that school systems do: control of costs and curriculum quality. Procedures vary from state to state and subject area to subject area. Typically, a state will cycle through the various subject areas every 5–7 years. Publishers submit textbooks to the appropriate committee, which receives recommendations from individual school systems and special-interest groups. The number of books adopted at one time in one subject area varies from 10% to 80%, depending on circumstances. When they buy new textbooks, public schools must choose from among those on the state-adopted list. Once a textbook has been adopted, the tractor trailers roll to book depositories throughout the adoption state. The book depositories are big warehouses that store state-adopted books for shipment to nearby schools.

California submits its criteria to publishers years in advance of an adoption decision to let them know what the state expects in the way of format and content. If the state of California says it does not want a literature anthology to contain references to junk food, a publisher can tell its editors and authors to censor any and all references to cheeseburgers and fries or risk having its literature series fail the adoption. Failing to make an adoption in California, for instance, means that the publisher cannot sell the textbook or series to public schools in that state until the next cycle of textbook adoptions.

It is not hard to understand why publishers sweat blood over textbook adoptions. The adoption of a textbook in California or Texas may provide enough revenue to pay for the entire cost of developing the book. This is why they cave in to the demands of state adoption committees, many of which are heavily influenced by special-interest groups. For the last 30 years textbook adoption committees, especially in California and Texas, have been strongly influenced by special-interest groups such as Educational Research Analysts in Longview, Texas, and Citizens for Excellence in Education. Over the years, such groups have caused history textbooks, literature anthologies, science books, and even dictionaries to be modified, removed from classrooms, or stricken from the lists of state-approved books. Publishers have become so sensitive to the issues involved that they increasingly censor their own work to avoid the prospect of failing an adoption.

The problem is not the special-interest groups themselves. Peaceful political activism is a constitutional right that is guaranteed to all individuals and organizations, including those concerned with the format and content of textbooks and parent empowerment in the education process. The real problem is that the states with the highest levels of coordinated censorship become the common denominator for textbooks across the country. In other words, students in states such as Pennsylvania and Iowa, which do not have state-level adoptions, end up using the same textbooks that have been heavily censored to suit the religious, social, or political groups in other states. The truth is that a few people in California exercise considerable control over what students in Pennsylvania are permitted to read.

As you can see, textbooks are not neutral sources of information. They are, in fact, highly politicized. The textbooks you hand to students on the first day of class have been authored by people who have agreed that the publisher is the final authority for what gets written. The textbook has probably been massaged and censored to meet a market demand and to suit the various lobbies that might threaten sales. You cannot afford to assume that a textbook developed for public school consumption is truly representative of any body of knowledge, free of intentional bias, or even factually accurate. Just knowing this makes you a political agent in the instructional process, and the decisions you make about how to use textbooks constitute a significant political stance.

Tips for filling the void left by textbooks:

1. Supplement textbooks with trade literature and primary sources of information, such as newspapers, professional magazines, unabridged novels, nonfiction single-author books, oral histories, and multimodal text sets. (See Chapter 7 for additional information.)

2. Teach your students how—and then encourage them—to use the library and the Internet. Do not allow the textbook to become the entire curriculum.

3. Encourage students to read their textbooks critically. The textbook is not always correct, and there must be room for competing points of view.

Politics aside, there are a number of other instructional issues related to the selection and appropriate use of textbooks. One of the most important of these involves determining the difficulty level of books.

For many years educators have had an interest in predicting the approximate difficulty of instructional materials. This is commonly referred to as *readability,* a measure of the extent to which a reader finds a given text comprehensible. Ideally, the level of text material can be matched to the appropriate reading level of students. In reality, though, the selection of a core text has been largely based on teacher intuition. Usually, content area teachers choose text materials based primarily on an analysis of the text content. While the content of a core text is certainly important and should reflect a teacher's instructional objectives, there are additional features of the text that merit careful consideration.

Lexile measures based on standardized test scores provide teachers with a means to match student reading levels with appropriate materials that are leveled by lexiles. Based on word frequency and sentence length, a lexile score of 200L would indicate a beginning reader, and a lexile score of 1,700L, an advanced reader.

The evaluation of printed material can be a highly refined and systematic process given our current understanding of those features that make textbooks understandable and useful as learning tools. Indeed, some striking features of textbooks do increase or diminish the likelihood of student understanding. Therefore, in order to match the difficulty level of the text to the reading level of students, both quantitative and qualitative factors of text material must be evaluated.

Quantitative factors include such language variables as word and sentence length. These factors can be counted and measured with a formula to estimate the grade level designation of text difficulty. *Qualitative factors* are more difficult to determine and include such elements as prior knowledge of the reader, organization of the text, and student interest.

Quantitative Factors in Readability Measurement

There are a number of different approaches designed to help the content area teacher estimate the difficulty level of text material. Each approach has inherent advantages and limitations. For example, a teacher can simply guess the grade level of a text. Unfortunately, this approach, while attractive in its speed and simplicity, has not proven to be very reliable.

A second, more reliable, approach to an estimate of text difficulty involves the administration of one or two informal tests based on a portion of the text. These procedures are described in detail in Chapter 5. In this section we explore a third approach to predict the difficulty of text material, the use of readability formulas.

Readability formulas are mathematically derived indices of text difficulty based on an analysis of language variables. Over 30 different readability formulas and graphs have been developed, including specialized formulas for appraising foreign language texts. Although none of the formulas is an absolute measure, they all share some common features used to obtain a rough estimate of a textbook's readability.

The two most common language variables accounted for in most readability formulas are sophistication of vocabulary and grammatical complexity. These two variables are never actually measured by readability formulas. Instead, the formulas attempt to estimate them based on word length or syllable counts in the case of vocabulary sophistication and sentence length in the case of grammatical complexity.

Raygor Readability Estimate

The *Raygor Readability Estimate* (Raygor, 1977) is both simple to use and reliable because it eliminates a common source of error found in many readability formulas. While counting sentences in a text sample presents little difficulty, formulas that combine this measure with a syllable count (e.g., the Fry Readability Graph) introduce a moderate potential for error. Two or more evaluators are likely to arrive at divergent answers for the number of syllables in the same text sample. The individual dialects of evaluators and the inherent difficulty in defining exactly what a syllable is contribute to unreliable syllable counts among evaluators. For example, when you say the words as you would in normal speech, do *little* and *title* have one syllable or two? A good alternative to a syllable count is a determination of the proportion of words with six or more letters in a 100-word text sample.

Following are the directions and the accompanying graph for the Raygor Readability Estimate. Application 4.1 will give you some initial, guided experience with this formula.

Directions for completing the Raygor Readability Estimate:

1. Count out three 100-word passages at the beginning, middle, and end of a textbook selection. Count proper nouns, but not numbers.

2. Count the number of sentences in each 100-word passage, estimating to the nearest tenth for partial sentences.

3. Count the number of words with six or more letters.

4. Average the sentence length and word length measures over the three samples and plot the average on the graph. The grade level nearest the spot marked is the best estimate of the difficulty of the selection.

Keep in mind that passage difficulty will fluctuate within the same text. Therefore, the more 100-word samples you evaluate, the more likely you are to arrive at a valid grade level designation. Never use a readability formula to estimate the grade level difficulty of a single sentence or paragraph because the outcome will be highly unreliable. Using the Raygor Readability Estimate as directed provides readability estimates that are accurate within a range of plus or minus one year. In this way you will have a realistic idea of the difficulty level of the text and can begin to judge how readable it will be for your students.

APPLICATION 4.1

Directions: In order to gain practice using the Raygor Readability Estimate, evaluate a text in your discipline.

Remember to average the three estimates before plotting them on the graph.

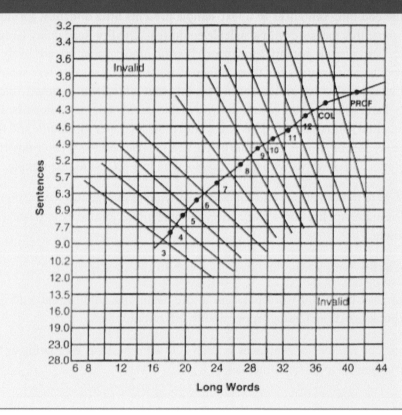

QUALITATIVE FACTORS IN TEXTBOOK EVALUATION

Although readability formulas are a useful component in the analysis of text material for adoption, they do have some inherent limitations. They provide an estimate of the linguistic features of print that influence text difficulty, vocabulary, and grammar. Unfortunately, the variables used to estimate the real linguistic factors do a poor job of estimating the readability of poetry or the symbolic discourse of such disciplines as mathematics and chemistry. Additional factors need to be considered in evaluating the readability of a text.

First, it must be remembered that, generally speaking, attractive, aesthetically pleasing things seem to work better for people, that is, their attractiveness produces more positive emotions, more creative responses, and a greater tolerance for minor difficulties (Norman, 2004). This same aspect of human nature applies to your students also and their reaction to the text materials that they are given to read and learn.

More specifically, the quality of the writing style needs to be carefully considered. For example, scrambling the word order of a selection would not alter the grade level rating established by a readability formula, but it would absolutely destroy the readability of the passage. Readability formulas are universally insensitive to writing style.

APPLICATION 4.2

Directions: Using the Raygor Graph, determine the readabilities of the following two paragraphs. What do you conclude from your findings?

Paragraph A
The beer truck slid on the black ice and rolled onto the grassy median. Unfortunately, a truck carrying fresh pretzels, heading in the opposite direction, slipped on the same icy terrain and mashed into the beer truck. Beer bottles and pretzels went flying in every direction and would have gone to waste if not for the hundreds of cars that stopped to help the drivers, neither of whom was injured. When the police arrived, the festivities were in full swing. Many partiers were arrested that evening, but the video clips made a terrific commercial at the next Super Bowl.

Paragraph B
The truck beer slid the black on ice and rolled grassy onto the median. Unfortunately, a truck carrying fresh opposite pretzels was heading in on the direction, slipped icy on the mashed same terrain and into the beer truck. Beer pretzels went flying in bottles and every direction and have would gone to if not for the waste hundreds of that stopped to whom help the drivers, neither cars of was injured. When the arrived, in the festivities police were full swing. Many but partiers were the arrested that evening, video next clips made a terrific super commercial at the bowl.

Readability formulas imply that short sentences are easier to understand than longer sentences. This is certainly not the case, since grammatical structures can aid or disrupt important semantic relations. In the following illustration, example one would be easier to understand than example two, yet readability formulas that use sentence length as an index of difficulty would rate the second example as the less difficult structure.

1. Tim slept late because he was lazy.

2. Tim slept late. He was lazy.

Sentence one is easier to comprehend because the causal relation in the sentence is made explicit by the use of the word *because*. Conversely, example two disrupts the causal relation, requiring the reader to infer in order to establish the implied connection between the two events.

The criticism of short sentences may also be applied to short words. For instance, in the sentence, "The dog the cat bit died," not only is the sentence short but also the words are short. Yet, the sentence will provide some difficulty for students because of the unusual grammatical structure. Therefore, the length of words is not necessarily an indicator of easier understanding.

Other text-centered factors deserve careful consideration in the text evaluation process. The abstract concepts and technical vocabulary an author uses are often complex, particularly in content areas such as science. The explanations of complex concepts, such as the process of photosynthesis, may require longer sentences in order to preserve important meaning relationships. Furthermore, since concept load and technical vocabulary are closely related in the content areas, reducing the use of technical terms would dilute important concepts essential to a discipline. One indication of conceptual difficulty in a text is the degree to which technical terms can be translated to more commonly occurring synonyms. For example, the word *compression* is easily substituted using the more familiar term, *squeezed*. In contrast, a highly specific technical term, like the word, *photosynthesis*, will undoubtedly require a good deal of teacher explanation if students are to cope with this concept in their reading.

Although readability formulas have been used to rewrite text material, the practice of mechanically reducing sentence and word length in a selection is not recommended. Although the rewritten version may be easier to read on a surface level than the original, important meaning relationships may be disrupted, making the rewritten version more difficult to comprehend. Readability formulas make no distinction between conceptually important information and trivial ideas. Nor do they differentiate between coherent writing that flows logically from one idea to the next and incoherent, disorganized prose.

For example, rewritten versions of text often disrupt explicit connections among ideas in the original sentences. At the sentence level, a modest amount of incoherence rarely presents much difficulty. However, if this incoherence extends across sentences, the text may present comprehension problems.

CONSIDER THIS!

Reggie wanted to sleep late, but John woke him up early for their trip to the north shore. Just as they were ready to leave, Reggie's girlfriend June arrived. She wanted to go shopping. THEY took the Toyota.

Now answer the following questions:

1. Who went shopping?

2. Who took the Toyota?

Pronouns are notorious for the potential comprehension problems they can cause when antecedents are unclear. However, readability formulas are not intended to measure these more subtle features of a text.

On the other hand, readability formulas do provide an estimate of vocabulary difficulty. Vocabulary difficulty undeniably influences student comprehension, even when the writing is coherent.

CONSIDER THIS!

Nadine perused the grocery shelves, carefully scrutinizing each jar of peanut butter as if it was a rare, prehistoric bone. She systematically ignored the organic products in favor of the more familiar brands. Her ARACHIBUTYROPHOBIA had been getting worse lately. She finally chose a jar of creamy style peanut butter, knowing it would never be opened once she got it home.

If the main idea of this passage is at all obscure it is because of the technical, polysyllabic word *arachibutyrophobia*. This word may look like it should be fear of spiders, but it actually means fear of getting peanut butter stuck on the roof of the mouth! Notice that a single, precise term like arachibutyrophobia is extremely economic for a writer, in this case encompassing 12 short words.

Readers often rely on an author's organizational structure in their attempts to recall important information. Moreover, some organizational patterns such as comparison–contrast seem more conducive to long-term recall than less cohesive patterns such as simple listing. Readability formulas are not sophisticated enough to account for the influence of these higher-level features of text on student comprehension. For these reasons, readability formulas must be used in combination with other qualitative considerations in order to develop a comprehensive approach to the evaluation of instructional materials.

Readability formulas like the Raygor can only hint at potential problems in text. As you examine texts in your content area, consider how well the author weaves ideas together within and across sentence and paragraph boundaries. Also examine technical vocabulary that may present potential problems.

Contemporary texts supply an abundance of student aids designed to enhance comprehension. These include visual aids such as photographs, line drawings, graphs, tables, and diagrams. Other aids might include pre- and post-questions or questions interspersed within a chapter. Some authors also use *metadiscourse*, or text intrusions in which the author talks directly to the reader about the information in the text, to aid student comprehension. In addition, a glossary can be valuable in helping students cope with difficult technical vocabulary. Some contemporary texts also include supplemental films, multimedia, and planned interactions with the Internet.

All of these devices can be valuable aids to student understanding; however, none is a substitute for carefully guided instruction. Indeed, the very nature of content learning and content texts implies knowledge to be acquired in conjunction with a course of study. Thus, teacher-centered factors are likely to influence student comprehension more than all the text-centered factors combined. Content texts are simply not designed to be read and comprehended in isolation, independent of a carefully guided course of instruction. The degree to which a teacher provides a bridge between what the students currently know about a topic and new conceptual information is undoubtedly the essential ingredient in the teaching and learning process. The amount of instructional guidance you provide before, during, and after reading text assignments will significantly affect student comprehension of even the least challenging text. In the chapters that follow, a number of teaching strategies are introduced to help you improve students' understanding of text concepts.

Finally, student-centered factors also play a prominent role in content area learning. Two important student-centered factors are the prospective readers' prior knowledge and interest in a course topic. Students generally have a preconceived notion about particular courses and books. Therefore, it is good practice to have students representing various levels of subject interest and reading achievement directly involved in the text evaluation process. Their opinions and recommendations often provide an alternative perspective that you might find difficult to achieve since your prior knowledge and interest are extensive.

TEXTBOOK AND MULTIMEDIA EVALUATION GUIDELINES AND CHECKLISTS

In general, students profit from text that adheres to classic principles of good writing. They can best comprehend authors who use frequent examples and graphic aids while avoiding unnecessary jargon. The following procedure for evaluating text material is designed to combine a quantitative measure of readability with additional qualitative factors, including student-centered information.

A number of different guidelines and related checklists for evaluating text material have been advanced (e.g., Leonard & Penick, 1993; Singer, 2007). While all of these guidelines and checklists are intuitively derived and informal in nature, they comprise the best currently available approach to text evaluation. The 18-item checklist in Figure 4.1 has been adapted from these sources, with some additional factors that are essential to text comprehension.

This Text Evaluation Checklist and Decision Guide are based on the typical layout of most nonfiction text material. Hence, you may need to adjust the criteria somewhat if you are evaluating fictional material presented in a literary anthology format. The checklist should not be interpreted as a device for categorically accepting or rejecting text material. Rather, the more ways the textbook meets the given criteria, the better and more useful it will be for your students. Additionally, the criteria are broad enough to allow for the exclusion of some items that are simply not present in a particular text. For example, item number 8 would not be included in an evaluation of the text you are reading right now since pictures are not needed to understand the content. Simply code such items as not applicable (N/A) and continue. Application 4.2 is designed to give you some practice in using the text evaluation checklist on the present text.

FIGURE 4.1

Text Evaluation Checklist

Directions: Enter the intended grade level of the text. Compute an estimate of text readability using the Raygor Readability Estimate. Complete the 18-item checklist to determine the acceptability of the text for your students.

Title of textbook: _____

Author(s): _____

Publisher: _____

Copyright date: _____

Cost: _____

Evaluated by: _____

A. Readability

1. Intended grade level of text: _____. Readability estimate: _____. Is the computed reading level realistic for the students who will be using the text?

B. Format

2. The book is recently copyrighted and the contents genuinely up to date.
3. The text is suitable for achieving the stated course objectives.
4. The text contains a table of contents, an index, and a glossary.
5. The table of contents indicates a logical development of the subject matter.
6. When the text refers to a graph, table, or diagram, that aid is situated close to the textual reference.
7. Captions over graphs, tables, and diagrams are clearly written.
8. Pictures are in color and are contemporary, not dated by dress unless author's intention is to portray a certain period.
9. Various ethnic groups and male and female characters are depicted authentically in the text.
10. The text suggests out-of-class readings and projects to stimulate additional student interest.

C. Organization

11. The main idea(s) or purpose(s) for reading a chapter are stated at the beginning.
12. Difficult new vocabulary words are highlighted, italicized, or underlined.
13. Context clues and synonyms for difficult vocabulary words are used in the text.
14. The writing is coherent in that ideas are clearly developed and related to each other, within and across sentence and paragraph boundaries.
15. New concepts are introduced by relating them to previously learned concepts so that the volume of new information does not frustrate students.
16. The text refers to practical, real-life situations and multicultural contexts to which students can relate and are interested in.
17. The text includes references to, and quotations from, other sources and authorities to support its statements.
18. When there are questions and activities at the end of a chapter, they elicit different levels of thinking, ranging from text explicit to experience-based, problem-solving tasks.
19. The text provides multimodal resources including relevant websites and URLs.
20. The text is easy to navigate to locate key information in a discipline.

Decision

_____ **Appropriate**   _____ **Marginally Appropriate**   _____ **Unacceptable**

Chapter 2 introduced multimedia materials as an essential component of content literacy. Therefore, we have also included a checklist for multimedia software (Figure 4.2). Again, the determination of the appropriateness, pedagogic utility, and value of the software relative to other instructional alternatives is ultimately a matter of professional judgment. In the end one must decide if the benefits of the software are worth the price.

APPLICATION 4.3

Directions: Using the Text Evaluation Checklist, rate the textbook materials from the chapter, *Matter and Energy in the Web of Life*, on the website as to its acceptability for a high school level classroom.

OR

Find a multimedia software program that is designed primarily for education. Evaluate the software using the Multimedia Evaluation Checklist.

INTRODUCING THE TEXTBOOK TO STUDENTS

It is unlikely that any single content area text will be the most appropriate for all students in a course. The wide range in students' prior knowledge and subject interests practically insures that your text will be frustrating for some students and too easy for others. Assuming that your particular content area text survives the evaluation checklist and your own informed observations, there is something you can do to help students perceive the text as a familiar learning aid rather than as a threatening obstacle.

You can conduct a preview of the text early in the term to acquaint students with the text they will be using, which will go a long way toward making students feel they can use the text effectively. Undoubtedly, many of us have discovered by sheer chance, often halfway through the term, that our text contained a glossary of difficult vocabulary. The preview is designed to guide students to this and other text aids early in the term.

Conducting a Preview of the Text

The following activity should be conducted as a group task. Using Figure 4.3 as a guide, the teacher reads each item on the preview and indicates its location. The guide will help you conduct a preview of the text in your content area.

FIGURE 4.2

Text Evaluation Checklist

Title of software: _____

Content area: _____

Instructional objective(s): _____

Prerequisite skills: _____

Publisher: _____

Copyright date: _____

Cost: _____

Evaluated by: _____

A. Configuration Requirements
- _____ PC
- _____ Macintosh
- _____ Other

B. Software Friendliness
- _____ 1. Readability of directions and other text is appropriate.
- _____ 2. Directions are easy to follow.
- _____ 3. Feedback to students is clear.
- _____ 4. Video, audio, text, and graphics are well integrated.
- _____ 5. Students can exit the program at any time.
- _____ 6. Students can reenter the program at the point of previous exit.
- _____ 7. The program is resistant to disruption from random keystrokes.
- _____ 8. The program maintains student interest.

C. Teacher Features
- _____ 9. The software manual is readable, logical, and comprehensive.
- _____ 10. The program includes an assessment component.
- _____ 11. The program is applicable to a variety of skill/grade/age levels.
- _____ 12. The user level advances automatically.
- _____ 13. Graphics are clearly related to the purpose of the software.
- _____ 14. The software comes with toll-free technical support.

D. Recommendation
- _____ **Highly Appropriate—Purchase immediately**
- _____ **Appropriate—Purchase if budget permits**
- _____ **Inappropriate—Do not purchase**

FIGURE 4.3

Previewing Your Text

Name of subject: _____

Title of textbook: _____

Author(s): _____

Author(s) qualifications (e.g., job experience, university degrees): _____

_____

Copyright date: _____

Has the book been revised (brought up to date)?: _____

_____

1. *Preface, Foreword,* and *Introduction* contain essentially the same information. These lead-in comments give the author(s) a chance to talk about why the book was written and how it is organized. Often, a suggestion about how to read the book is provided.

    Read the Preface, Foreword, or Introduction. In the space below, use your own words to explain what the *Preface* told you about your text.

    _____
    _____
    _____
    _____

2. The *Table of Contents* provides an early road map of the whole text. It gives a good indication of the learning aids that are provided in the text. Answer the following questions in your own words by referring to the Table of Contents.

    (1) Does the organization of topics in the book appear logical and easy to follow?

    _____
    _____

    (2) How many total pages are there in your text?

    _____

    (3) How complete do you think the treatment of the subject is in your book (i.e., very complete or only deals with a few aspects of the subject)?

    _____
    _____

    (4) Using the Table of Contents, see if your text contains each of the following learning aids. Answer yes if you find it, no if you don't.

    Glossary _____   Appendix _____   Bibliography _____   Index _____

3. The Glossary gives definitions of difficult technical terms used in the text and helps understand the vocabulary of a difficult subject. If your text has a Glossary, locate at least one difficult word supplied by your teacher and write the definition here.

    _____
    _____
    _____

4. The *Appendix* provides additional information about a topic. An Appendix is located at the end of the book and contains information that supports and expands a chapter topic. If your text has an Appendix (or *Appendices*), write a list of some of the items you find there.

_____

_____

_____

_____

_____

5. A *Bibliography* gives specific information about authors and books that were consulted during the writing of the text. Some of these books may be recommended as additional reading. The Bibliography is usually located at the end of the book (see the Table of Contents for its exact location), but it may follow each chapter. Locate the Bibliography in your text and write down three books you might want to read in addition to your text.

_____

_____

_____

_____

_____

6. The **Index** provides the fastest means for locating topic information referred to in the text. Locate the Index in your book. Study it and list two or three kinds of information found there.

_____

_____

_____

_____

7. Many other textual aids, in addition to the Preface, Table of Contents, Glossary, Appendix, Bibliography, and Index, are included in most texts. See if you can locate each of the following text aids (write yes if it is there; no if it is not) and indicate in writing how each of these aids might help you understand the subject.

(1) Questions at the beginning of the chapters

_____

(2) Objectives at the beginning of the chapters

_____

(3) Figures

_____

(4) Illustrations or diagrams

_____

(5) Graphs

_____

(6) Maps

_____

(7) Words in italics, bold-faced words, large guide words

_____

(8) Pronunciation guide [e.g., paradigm (para dime)]

_____

(9) Footnotes

_____

(10) Headings

_____

(11) Marginal notes

_____

(12) Questions at the end of chapters

_____

(13) Practice exercises

_____

(14) Interface with textbook-affiliated technology

_____

(15) Other

_____

APPLICATION 4.4

Directions: Using this text as an example, conduct a preview. Did you discover anything which you were not aware of previously?

In some cases, a teacher may feel it necessary to determine the extent of the students' knowledge about basic textbook elements before conducting a preview. The exercise in Figure 4.4 can also reinforce students' understanding of textbook learning aids. It can be used as a model to develop a similar activity in your own content area.

FIGURE 4.4

Directions: In column B you will find a brief description of the information contained in a particular textbook learning aid (listed in column A). See if you can match each textbook aid (column A) with its description (column B). Place the letter of the description on the line in front of the textbook aid to which it refers.

A.	**B.**
____ 1. Index	A. Author discusses why the book was written and how to read it.
____ 2. Table of Contents	B. The easiest place to locate topic information quickly
____ 3. Bibliography	C. Provides additional information about a topic
____ 4. Appendix	D. A road map of how the text is organized
____ 5. Preface	E. Provides definitions of difficult technical terms
____ 6. Copyright Date	F. Indicates when the book was published
____ 7. Glossary	G. A listing of what books were consulted in writing the text [end figure]

Courtesy Thomas Bean

If your text should prove unacceptable for some students in your content class, there are a number of alternative approaches you can employ. For example, you might consider adopting multiple texts at varying levels of difficulty. Or you can use newspapers, resource speakers, demonstrations, simulations, and discussion groups. Finally, increasing the amount of guidance you provide students before, during, and after reading assignments should go a long way toward making the core text more understandable. Future chapters advance a variety of methods for helping students cope with difficult text material. Such methods range from providing additional guidance in vocabulary development and comprehension to individualizing assignments for some students.

REACTION GUIDE

		Confirmed	Disconfirmed
1.	Censorship is bad and unnecessary.	_____	_____
2.	Government regulations require that tenth-grade books be written on a tenth-grade reading level.	_____	_____
3.	It is safe to assume that high school students know how to use a textbook index.	_____	_____
4.	The content of subject area textbooks is politically influenced.	_____	_____

	A Why my choice is confirmed.	B Why my choice is not confirmed.
1.	_____	_____
2.	_____	_____
3.	_____	_____
4.	_____	_____
5.	_____	_____

MINI PROJECTS

1. Apply the Raygor Readability Estimate to a commonly used text in your content area.

2. Complete the Text Evaluation Checklist for the same text you used in mini-project number one. Is the text appropriate for its intended grade level?

RECOMMENDED WEBSITES

o National Council of Teachers of English Anti-Censorship Center: www.ncte.org/action/anti-censorship
o Dealing with Censorship of Multimedia Materials: www.ncte.org/position/statements/censorshipofnonprint
o Understanding Lexiles: www.lexiles.com

WEBSITE ACTIVITY

Go to the website for Chapter 5 activities.

Assessment

CHAPTER 5

ANTICIPATION GUIDE

	Agree	Disagree

1. Assessment should occur naturally as part of teaching and learning.

2. Most state reading assessments are valid measures of reading.

3. Standardized tests provide teachers with enough information concerning students' abilities to begin instruction.

4. The best reading tests to administer to students are those that compare them with other students across the nation.

5. Diagnosis is necessary for effective content area instruction.

RATIONALE

Instruction is the means by which teachers bridge the gap between what students already know and what they need to know. For instruction to be as effective as possible, teachers must be familiar with a variety of assessment techniques, because information about students' abilities and levels of achievement provides a foundation for selecting appropriate teaching strategies. Without assessment information, teachers are forced to make hazardous assumptions about what students do and do not know. In this chapter various types of assessment strategies are described and recommended for use by content teachers.

© Lisa F. Young/Shutterstock.com

LEARNING OBJECTIVES

o   Understand the need for assessment in the content classroom.
o   Describe the differences between formal and informal testing.
o   Utilize various types of assessment strategies.

GRAPHIC ORGANIZER

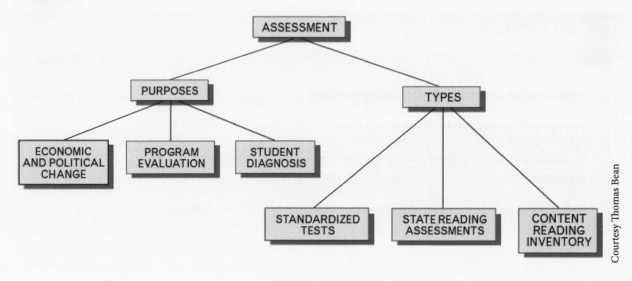

Courtesy Thomas Bean

PART 1: Learning with Text and Technology

Before you begin this chapter, your instructor may want to determine your familiarity with assessment terminology. Use the Knowledge Rating strategy (p. 110) and enter a 3, 2, or 1 rating for each technical term.

Knowledge Rating: Assessment Terminology

Directions: Rate your knowledge of each of the terms below.

WORD	3 CAN DEFINE/ USE IT	2 HEARD OF IT	1 DON'T KNOW
Norms			
Standard error of measurement			
Passage independence			
Raw score			
Percentile			
Stanine			
Norm-referenced test			
Criterion-referenced test			
Diagnostic test			
Multiple-choice test items			
Performance test items			
Rubric			
Mean			
Standardized test			
Reliability			
Validity			

PURPOSES FOR ASSESSMENT

Traditional purposes for assessment include program evaluation and student diagnosis. To these we must now add economic and political purposes, because high-stakes testing has changed the meaning of education and the curricula in public schools across the country. Indeed, the current backlash against allocating way too much instructional time to test preparation and administration is a direct consequence of an overemphasis on high-stakes testing. This chapter discusses the implications of high-stakes reading assessments and how the results are used to hold public schools accountable, with unfortunate consequences for 21st century life. In light of the limitations of narrow, high-stakes multiple-choice assessments, a number of critics are arguing for assessments that truly gauge students' abilities to apply knowledge to solve significant problems. Indeed, these 21st century skills are crucial. For example, Darling-Hammond (2010) notes,

> *Students in schools that organize most of their efforts around the kinds of low-level learning represented by most widely used tests are profoundly disadvantaged when they need to engage in the extensive writing, critical thinking, and problem solving required in college and the workplace. (p. 282)*

Other critics lament the path we have placed students on that contrasts markedly with 21st century skills and dispositions. For example, Wagner (2010), argues,

> *Our current accountability system primarily tests how much students have memorized and can recall at a given moment in time, and there are fifty different state standards for work, college, or citizenship in the twenty-first century. (p.125)*

Indeed, at present, narrow assessments have short-changed students in the United States who are not measuring up on international comparisons that tap higher-order thinking necessary for problem solving. When learning in the content areas is attached to high-stakes tests, creativity and problem solving suffer, not to mention the potential content learning time traded off to train students in taking high-stakes tests.

The end product of assessment in the content classroom, or any classroom for that matter, should be instructional decision making. *Performance assessments* that evaluate what students can actually do in a content area are a powerful alternative approach (Gillis & Van Wig, 2015). We say more about discipline-specific performance assessments later in this chapter.

In the past, various assessments of reading skills and levels of achievement were routinely administered for program evaluation and student diagnosis. If teachers and schools were free to conduct the business of education with the sole purpose of creating effective curricula for students, the presentations in this chapter could be limited to discussions of program evaluation and student diagnosis. Unfortunately, in recent years reading assessments have become increasingly tied to accountability in public education, and we must add economic/political to the list of purposes of assessment. It is essential that we discuss some of the politics of reading, because it will almost certainly influence what and how you teach.

Economic and Political Change

The constant bashing of K-12 public education in the mass media and by politicians at every level of American government appears to be part of a carefully crafted political agenda for public education. A market-based reform movement aimed at corporate takeovers of public schools, the erosion or elimination of teacher certification, reductions in the cost of labor (teachers' salaries), and the shifting of state resources from secular schools to private, faith-based schools drive this agenda. The primary mechanism of this reform movement is the imposition of unattainable standards so that K-12 public education can be conveniently labeled a failure.

The intensity of this antipublic school reform movement varies from state to state, but the phenomenon is national in scope. With the onset of Common Core Standards aimed at specifying needed content knowledge in the disciplines, this may change. During this transition, we are likely to see high-stakes assessments coexisting with a much needed shift to discipline-based performance standards that emphasize complex learning including inquiry and creative problem solving.

Program Evaluation

Program evaluation is usually conducted for accountability purposes, and formal tests are usually the devices used. Formal testing instruments, that is, standardized reading tests, are administered at regular yearly intervals, usually in the fall or spring of the school year to monitor student progress in reading. With the help of this assessment, school administrators are able to compare the reading levels of their students with those of other students across the nation at the same grade levels. Although such comparisons may help a particular school district justify its need for federal support for its instructional programs, they are virtually useless for instructional decision making by teachers with regard to the individual needs of students.

Formal testing may also be used to identify weaknesses in the instructional program. If students in school district A as a whole score low relative to the national average on a particular type of test such as vocabulary or comprehension, that district may decide to examine the emphasis placed on that portion of the reading program. Finally, formal testing may serve as a screening device for those students not performing up to reading program expectations. This should indicate to the school district the need for more intensive diagnostic testing to pinpoint areas of skill weakness in individual students. Unfortunately, the results of these tests may be inappropriately used to refer students to special programs, without the benefit of further testing.

We believe that it is important to know the intricacies of what standardized tests can, and cannot, do. As a content area teacher, you naturally have an array of assessments directly related to your discipline, but standardized tests remain a benchmark schools use to gauge their success in comparison with other schools and districts. Therefore, it is important to know how these tests contribute to an overall picture of students' learning.

Student Diagnosis

Another purpose for reading assessment is student diagnosis, which can provide teachers with information necessary to make instructional decisions. Informal assessment tools are usually utilized to gather such information (Gillis & Van Wig, 2015). Specifically, informal tests can be used to diagnose possible reading and learning problems of students related to the demands of different disciplines. For example, word problems in mathematics require close reading and deconstruction to eliminate extraneous details and isolate the key mathematical elements to solve a problem. Additionally, such tests can be used to determine the reading levels of students. Knowledge of students' reading and learning problems and reading levels provides a starting point for good teaching. This knowledge eliminates the need to presuppose any learning on the part of the students and provides the essential foundation for instructional decision making.

One of the more recent educational developments is the use of *standards* to realize these overall purposes for assessment. For example, professional organizations like the International Reading Association and National Council of Teacher of English regularly update and publish standards that reflect the changing nature of what counts as appropriate performance in literacy.

Thus, performance standards are not static documents. Rather, they change to meet the dynamic properties of "texts," which now include both print and online forms. Nevertheless, standardized tests still coexist with these more contemporary views of what counts as texts, and you need to know what these instruments offer, as well as their limitations.

View the video clip on the website on the consequences of high-stakes standardized testing.

DESCRIPTIVE TERMINOLOGY OF ASSESSMENT

Before launching into a discussion of the advantages and disadvantages of particular types of tests, we need to introduce several challenging statistical concepts.

Formal Tests

Formal tests are often referred to as standardized tests. A *standardized test* is one that is designed to be administered under the same conditions with each administration. For instance, all test-takers should receive identical directions; and if the test is timed, all the test takers should have exactly the same amount of time to complete the test. Most standardized tests are copyrighted and commercially published. Most standardized tests are also *norm-referenced*, which means that one can only interpret the meaning of a test score by comparing that score with the scores of others who have taken the same test. The scores of those others are called *norms*, and they represent the standard against which the performances of others may be compared.

For example, imagine that the norms established for sixth- and seventh-grade students, respectively, are 40 and 50 items correct on a particular standardized, norm-referenced reading achievement test. Tyrannosaurus Middle School administers this test to its seventh-grade students, and the result is an average of 40 items correct. One could conclude that the students in Tyrannosaurus Middle School achieved on a par with sixth-grade students in the norm group but that their performance was below the average for seventh graders.

Figure 5.1 examines the notion of standardized scores more closely. This is the normal curve, and all standardized scores are based on it. The *normal curve* is a bell-shaped distribution with scores distributed symmetrically around an average score called the *mean*. The number of scores above and below the mean is identical, and the number of individuals who earn the same score decreases with distance from the mean, which makes sense because most people are about average in any kind of assessment. The greatest number of scores (about 68%) occurs within one standard deviation (SD) of the mean—between points A and B in Figure 5.1. A SD is a statistic that tells how much variation there is in a group of scores. For instance, if the scores are close together, the SD will be small. If the scores are widely scattered from low to high, the SD will be large. Although it is possible, most teachers do not create standardized, norm-referenced tests because of the complex and expensive procedures involved.

Think of the bell-shaped curve as a narrow, three-dimensional glass container into which you could throw marbles. If you filled the container with marbles, most of them would be stacked up in the middle and only a few would be in the tails (sides). The numbers inside the curve above show the percentages of marbles that could fit into the area defined by the lines on either side of the number. Only 2.1% would fit in the area between +2 and +3 SD. A bit more than 68% of the marbles (test scores) would be stacked up in the area between –l and +1 SD.

FIGURE 5.1 *Normal Curve*

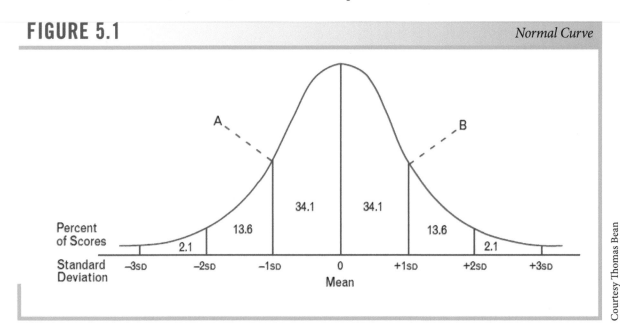

Courtesy Thomas Bean

The most commonly used scores in standardized testing are the raw score, the stanine, and the percentile rank. A *raw score* is simply the total number of correct items on a test. A *stanine* is the score converted to a standard 9-point scale with a mean of 5 and a SD of 2. A stanine score of 5 is average. Stanine 1 would be a very low score, and a stanine 9 score would be very high. Finally, the *percentile rank* represents the percentage of scores equal to and lower than a certain score. It is the position of a score within the entire group of scores. A percentile rank of 60 means the individual has scored as well as or better than 60% of the people who took the test. The percentile rank does not represent the percentage of correct answers.

Informal Tests

Informal assessment tools differ from standardized tests. *Informal tests*, or *criterion-referenced tests*, do not employ the use of norms as standards for comparison. Rather they employ a relative standard, or *criterion*, which implies adequate achievement for a given task or assignment. The score itself has meaning, even without reference to the performances of others. For instance, if the criterion has been set at 60% correct, a student must meet that figure to progress to another level of instruction; otherwise the student might need to work through the unit again and might require some special help to do so. Finally, informal tests are often teacher-made, though some are published. Thus, they can be designed to obtain information specifically related to an individual school's reading program. A second distinction used in describing tests involves survey and diagnostic tests.

Survey Tests

A survey test does what its name implies; it surveys global areas of achievement such as vocabulary and comprehension. *Survey tests* are usually standardized tests and therefore useful for group comparisons but not for individual instructional guidelines. No specifics with regard to the global areas of the survey are provided. That is, we are unable to determine what the specific areas of weaknesses in vocabulary and comprehension may be. That is what a diagnostic test endeavors to measure.

Diagnostic Tests

Scores from a *diagnostic test* can indicate strengths and weaknesses in specific skill areas. For example, diagnostic tests provide scores for recognizing main ideas, details, inferences, etc.,—the specifics of comprehension. Therefore, it might readily be seen that a standardized, survey-type instrument can be used as a screening device to tell a teacher, for instance, in which global areas a student might be experiencing difficulty. The teacher can then employ diagnostic tests to ascertain which specific areas are causing the difficulty.

Group and Individual Tests

Two other distinctions can be made in discussing testing instruments, neither of which requires a lengthy explanation. There are *group* and *individual* tests. As the names imply, tests may be group-administered or individually administered.

Silent and Oral Tests

The other distinction is between silent and oral tests. Again, as the names imply, tests may be silently or orally administered or may employ some combination of the two. Usually, standardized tests utilize a format that requires a group, silent administration. At the other end of the continuum are informal tests that are diagnostic in scope and are administered in an individual, oral format.

CAUTIONS CONCERNING STANDARDIZED TESTING

Standardized tests offer some advantages in a total reading assessment program. Because they are administered in a group setting, they do not take the great amount of time that individual testing requires. Since formal tests are administered silently instead of orally, confusion is also kept to a minimum. Additionally, the scores achieved by students allow school districts to compare the performance levels of their students with other students across the nation.

The ease of administration of standardized tests and their use of norms also present some disadvantages, which content teachers must be aware of. It is all too easy to obtain students' standardized test scores from their permanent files and make decisions about their abilities based on those scores.

1. What exactly does a score such as 7.0 on reading mean?

2. What exactly are standardized tests measuring?

3. How accurate a picture do I obtain about the reading ability of students from examining their test scores?

The following discussion of cautions concerning standardized tests will answer these questions and others you may have in mind.

1. *Inappropriate norms.* Even though great care is taken by test makers in standardizing a test, the norms established for comparison may be inappropriate for a particular class. The norms may be based on students with whom your students should not be compared.

2. *Extraneous factors.* It must be emphasized that the scores achieved by a student on a formal test are only a measure of that student's performance at that particular point in time. They may not necessarily be indicative of a student's true ability. An individual's performance may vary radically from day to day, depending on extraneous factors that can complicate matters. Factors as simple as the amount of sleep students had the night before, to factors as complex as the emotional stability of their homes, may interfere with students' daily performance in school as well as their performance in testing situations.

3. *Timed testing.* Most standardized tests employ a time limitation in their administration procedures. Thus, a premium is placed on speed in completing the test. We can all probably remember personal experiences with friends or students who may be categorized as slow, but accurate (i.e., students who lack speed in completing tasks, but thoroughly weigh alternatives before responding accurately). The slow but thorough reader may fail to complete the com-

prehension section of a test and thus get a low score when compared to the established norm. In reality, the student's comprehension could be excellent.

4. *Prior knowledge.* Since comprehension occurs when students are able to associate the unknown with the known, prior knowledge may be a factor in test performance. In fact, there is a question as to whether standardized instruments actually measure reading comprehension or prior knowledge. Test items that may be answered from prior knowledge without the aid of a reading selection are said to be *passage independent*. Items that require students to read a selection in order to answer them correctly are termed *passage dependent*. It may be virtually impossible to eliminate the effect of prior knowledge on test performance. However, depending on the degree to which prior knowledge is a factor in particular test questions, the resulting scores can yield an unfair comparison between individuals.

5. *Comprehension skills.* Standardized tests of reading comprehension, in many cases, emphasize factual recall of relatively insignificant facts. Is this the type of comprehension utilized in most reading situations? Such tests are at great variance in their demands versus the demands of reading in most school tasks and in everyday life. Factual recall is certainly important, but it is only one dimension of comprehension.

6. *Interest.* Everyone is aware of the effect of interest in reading. In fact, reading comprehension is better when the topic of a passage interests the reader. On the other hand, lack of interest may militate against the completion of a reading task. If the passages to be read on a standardized test are of little or no interest to students, it is bound to affect their ability to answer comprehension questions based on the passage.

7. *Guessing.* Most standardized tests employ a multiple-choice format for their questions to facilitate scoring by machines and for convenience. With such a limited format, guessing can unduly raise test scores. If four choices are offered, chances are one in four that a correct guess can be made. In any given test situation, two people with identical reading skills could get different test scores simply because one person happened to guess better that day. In fact, on most standardized tests, it is possible to receive grade-level equivalents, for example, fourth-grade level, by guessing, that is, by pure chance.

8. *Test floors and ceilings.* When formal tests are standardized through averaging scores of students at a particular grade level, limits are placed on the range of performance at that grade level. Students are not supposed to score below a certain grade-level norm or, for that matter, above a certain level in their performance. In effect, the use of *test floors* and *ceilings* may affect the validity of test scores. Specifically, the ceiling of the test may underestimate a more

competent student's performance, while the floor may overestimate a less competent student's ability. In effect, the ceiling may penalize better readers because tests cannot truly measure their ability, while the floor may place a poorer reader at a level where success cannot be achieved. Standardization is designed to predict average performance, not performance at the extremes.

9. *Standard error of measurement.* This term indicates the variation in test scores that one might expect if that test were administered repeatedly to an individual student. By adding or subtracting this built-in error to a student's obtained test score, one obtains a range of scores within which the student might actually score. For example, if the standard error of measurement is five months and a student's resulting score is 7.0, the range of scores within which the student might actually have scored is 6.5 to 7.5. Awareness of this built-in error is essential when examining scores on standardized tests.

10. *Fallacy of grade-level reporting.* So what does a score of 7.0 mean? First, it is an estimation of performance. Second, it really says little with regard to students' performance; yet it is commonplace to use such scores when discussing reading ability of students. Just because two students score 7.0 does not mean they are equivalent in reading ability. There are countless ways in which individuals may perform to attain a score of 7.0, yet each performance may be unique. Grade-level scores obscure differential performances of individuals with like scores in the same grade, or in different grades. Further analysis of each student's performance is necessary.

Content teachers must be cautious of these factors when examining standardized test scores or when provided information concerning them by other school personnel. Such scores provide the basis for comparing group performances and for program evaluation. Many of the factors that cause standardized tests to provide inaccurate scores for individuals (e.g., guessing and personal interests) balance out in group situations, thus making results far more accurate for groups than for individuals. However, they may not provide the kind of information necessary for making instructional decisions.

Recent efforts to make standardized tests more useful to classroom teachers include the development of *Lexile* measures mentioned in Chapter 4 on Text Selection and Evaluation. Lexile measures are reported as a numeric score (e.g., 800 L) that relates directly to a lexile readability score on various texts (http://lexile.com). Lexile scores range from below 200 L for beginning readers to over 1,700 L for advanced readers. Much like readability scores, lexile text difficulty scores are based on word frequency and sentence length. A number of contemporary standardized reading comprehension tests, such as the Iowa Test of Basic Skills and Scholastic Reading Inventory, now report lexile scores for students. Nevertheless, the limitations of standardized tests for gauging students' specific performance in content area classes remain.

Test Validity

An evaluation of test validity answers the question, "Does the test measure what it claims to measure?" In the case of reading tests, the assessments should measure reading ability and, to the extent possible, nothing else. There are, of course, no pure reading tests that can assess reading comprehension without also indirectly measuring prior knowledge and general intelligence. However, for the last 30 years, the authors of standardized reading tests have been scrupulous in their attempts to render standardized reading tests as pure as possible; but most of the current state assessments of reading include test items that make it unclear as to just exactly what is being measured by the "reading" tests. These items fall into two categories: performance items and passage-independent items.

PERFORMANCE ITEMS. *Performance items* are short essays that ask students to write, for example, a brief summary, an evaluation of the author's purpose, or a prediction of events that goes beyond the passage itself. Usually, the state has a rubric for scoring performance items. There is nothing at all wrong with assessing writing skills and encouraging writing across the curriculum. However, when an assessment that claims to test reading achievement includes performance items and does not provide separate scores for reading and writing, these two aspects of literacy are confounded, reducing the validity of the assessment. It is possible to be a good reader and not a good writer.

PASSAGE DEPENDENCE. As previously stated, a test item is passage independent if you can answer it without even reading the passage. If you have to read the passage to acquire the information to answer the question correctly, the test item is passage dependent. Reading tests become invalid when test items are passage independent because the questions can be answered based on prior knowledge and logic rather than on reading ability. To the extent that state assessments of reading contain passage-independent items, they are measures of general knowledge or achievement instead of reading. Assume, for example, that this question follows a passage on one of the state reading assessments:

Which of the following countries was a US ally in World War II?

A. England
B. Japan
C. Italy
D. Germany

In this hypothetical case, you would certainly be able to answer the question without having to read the passage. The question would, therefore, be passage independent for you and irrelevant or misleading in any assessment of your reading ability. Instead, the item would assess knowledge of American history. Obviously, a question can be passage independent for one person and passage dependent for another. When a reading test contains too many questions that are passage independent, the test is measuring something besides reading ability.

Some questions are answerable based on general knowledge. Others have formats that make the answer passage independent. For example, distinguishing fact from opinion is assessed in the following test item, but the question can be answered without reading the passage. Word clues such as *might* in option C occur frequently in reading assessments, which means that the answer is found in the question itself rather than the passage.

Which of the following statements expresses an opinion by the author?

A. The Civil War ended in 1865.
B. John Brown died leading a slave revolt.
C. The South might have won the war if Lee had prevailed at Gettysburg.
D. The North had more trains and factories than the South.

Questions about vocabulary are another common form of passage independence in many reading assessments. Multiple-choice items regularly include general vocabulary and technical terms taken from a passage. Typically, the words in the multiple-choice questions are not introduced in the passage as new vocabulary but are instead merely words that occur in the passage. The example here is an eighth-grade level item typical of a state assessment:

By using context clues, the reader can determine that the word *cower*, as in "cower behind me," means

E. jump repeatedly
F. hide fearfully
G. crawl slowly
H. rise quickly

Given the restrictions of time, it is unlikely that a student who did not already know the meaning of *cower* would be able to return to the passage, find the word, and then use context clues to decipher its meaning. This test item is, therefore, passage independent.

Many reading assessments for middle and secondary students are in reality assessments of reading ability, writing ability, and prior knowledge. This means that many of the tests are of questionable validity as reading assessments and are, in many ways, more like general achievement tests. However, it also means that a subject-oriented approach to reading to learn makes sense because art, English, foreign language, health, mathematics, music, science, and social studies teachers are the people who build the vocabulary and prior knowledge essential to improved scores on state reading assessments. The nature of the tests also makes it realistic for subject-area teachers to prepare students systematically for state assessments without sacrificing curriculum objectives. Test preparation is discussed in Chapter 12.

High-Stakes Assessment of Public Schools

Tests are administered under secure testing conditions, and the percentage of students reaching proficiency is calculated. If the percentages are too low, the school receives a warning or improvement notice or is scheduled for corrective action.

There are many potentially negative consequences of high-stakes testing. Here are just a few of them:

o Achievement and the value of education are being defined by performances on a few standardized tests in selected areas of the curriculum.

o Because proficiency in reading and mathematics is being defined by state assessments, schools are teaching to the test. Scores in reading and math may go up, but students may not read, calculate, or think any better than they did in the past.

o The consequences of failing the tests are so traumatic that schools have no choice but to convert instructional time to test preparation.

o Schools are curtailing art, music, physical education, and other content areas to increase instruction and test preparation in reading and math.

Common Core Standards

As an antidote to the confusion, chaos, and general instability of divergent state standards under No Child Left Behind (NCLB), the National Governors Association for Best Practices (NGA) and the Council of Chief State School Officers (CCS-SO) created and developed national *Common Core Standards* in 2010 (http://www. corestandards.org). These standards specify the knowledge and skills students should have across various content areas including English, social studies, and so on. The standards are aligned to college and workforce expectations with a particular emphasis on higher-order thinking (e.g., evaluation and critique), as well as the recognition that students will be living and working in a global economy. The assessment vision for these standards proposes that states collaborate to create a shared set of assessments that measure students' performance on the core standards.

There are alternatives to the limited information provided to content-area teachers by standardized tests or poorly constructed state tests. Indeed, the knowledge you need about your students' performance relates directly to the discourse and concepts relevant in your content area. The Content Reading Inventory offers a discipline-based assessment that helps you gauge what your students know as they begin study in your field.

CONTENT READING INVENTORY

The *Content Reading Inventory* is designed to obtain information about the ability of students to learn successfully with specific text material. Since it is an informal-group silent-diagnostic assessment, its numerous advantages far outweigh the disadvantage of the time it takes to prepare the instrument:

o   The content reading inventory is quick and easy to administer in a group setting.

o   The content reading inventory is textbook based. This makes the diagnostic information relevant since it is taken directly from the major source of instruction in the subject matter area.

o   Since it is teacher-made and textbook based, it provides for ease in scoring. Criteria for judging test answers are objective, eliminating subjectivity as a deterrent in effective scoring.

o   This instrument later may become the basis for teaching. Once the teacher has obtained essential diagnostic information, the test may become an instructional instrument with which the teacher can begin to acquaint students with the author's style and the organization of the textbook.

The content reading inventory consists of three major sections. The first section concerns knowledge of, and ability to utilize, the various aids within the textbook or supplemental to it. Specifically, the test covers book parts common to most textbooks, such as the table of contents, index, and pictorial aids. The students' ability to use resource aids that supplement the textbook, such as the encyclopedia, are also examined. The premise behind this section of the content reading inventory is that the ability to effectively utilize the internal and external aids of the text is critical to learning with it.

In the last two sections of this inventory, students are asked to read a short three- to four-page selection from the text. Section II then determines the ability to deal with the technical and specialized vocabulary encountered in the reading. Section III examines the ability to comprehend explicit and implicit information in the text as well as to grasp an author's text structure. A representative content reading inventory, therefore, should contain the following sections:

Section I: Textual Reading/Study Aids

A. Internal Aids
   1. Table of Contents
   2. Index
   3. Glossary
   4. Chapter Introduction/Summaries
   5. Pictorial Information
   6. Other Pertinent Aids
B. External Aids
   1. Electronic Databases
   2. Reader's Guide
   3. Encyclopedias
   4. Other Pertinent Aids

Section II: Vocabulary Knowledge

A. Recall
B. Contextual Meanings

Section III: Comprehension

A. Literal Information
B. Nonliteral Information
C. Text Structure

GUIDELINES TO CONSTRUCT, ADMINISTER, AND SCORE A CONTENT READING INVENTORY

1. Plan to construct approximately 20–25 questions. It is recommended that 8–10 questions be constructed for Section I, 4–6 for Section II, and 7–9 for Section III.
2. Choose a short 3–4 page selection for students to read.
3. Explain to the students the rationale for using the content reading inventory. Administer it in two sections, being careful to orally read each question to the students before they begin.
4. Section I is administered first, as the ability to use the various parts of the total text is examined.
5. Sections II and III are administered next. Ensure that students are appropriately ready to read the selection. Questions for these sections are based solely on the short selection, not the entire text.
6. The completed content reading inventory is scored using the following criteria:

% Correct	Text Difficulty
86–100	Too easy
64–85	Adequate for instruction
63	Too difficult

Complete the following example of a content reading inventory. It is designed just as you, as the content teacher, would construct and present a content reading inventory to your students. Your task, just as that of your students would be, is to answer the questions. Section I is based on the total text; sections II and III are based on Chapter 8.

Content Reading Inventory

Section I: Textual Reading/Study Aids

Directions: Using your textbook or your previous knowledge, answer each of the following questions:

A. Internal Aids

1. On what page does Chapter 4 begin? What is the title of the section of which it is a part?

   _____

2. On what page(s) would you find information regarding Critical Media Literacy?

   _____

3. Where would you look in the text to find the definition of "text explicit"?

   _____

4. Of what use is the section entitled Rationale at the beginning of Chapter 8?

   _____

5. Using the GWP checklist in Chapter 11, what recommendations would you make concerning the student's writing?

   _____

   _____

6. Where would you look to find out how this text is organized?

   _____

B. External Aids

7. What library guide would aid you in locating a book on attitudes and attitude development?

   _____

8. If you were to give an oral report in class about content area literacy and you knew that much of the information you needed would be in current periodicals, what guide would you use to help you find the information?

   _____

9. Name one set of encyclopedias. How are the topics in it arranged?

   _____

Directions: Read the sections in your text entitled Words and Vocabularies in Chapter 8. Based on what you have read, answer the questions in sections II and III.

Section II. Vocabulary Knowledge

10. Define the concept of "word" as used in this text.

    _____

11. Compare and contrast denotations and connotations. Provide an example.

_____

_____

12. Define the italicized word as it is used in this sentence: A vocabulary is a _corpus_ of many thousands of words and their associated meanings.

_____

_____

13. What term refers to the process by which new information is incorporated into existing schemata?

_____

14. Define the italicized word as used in this sentence: Technical vocabulary words present labels for unfamiliar concepts that must be accommodated by modifying _extant_ schemata.

_____

_____

Section III: Comprehension

15. Why do adult language users have little difficulty agreeing whether or not a particular sequence of sounds or symbols is a word?

_____

16. Learning new words (concepts) requires more than a simple explanation by the teacher. Why?

_____

17. What are the largest vocabularies for literate adults?

_____

18. Describe the differences between the words (concepts) "Cold War" and "crass."

_____

19. Describe the process involved with regard to the schemata of students when the word "secant" is presented to them.

_____

20. Explain the role of the school with regard to the development of the expressive and receptive vocabularies of students.

_____

21. How is the section entitled Vocabularies organized?

_____

Now that you have completed the content inventory, turn to the end of this chapter (Figure 5.6) for the answers. Classify your performance according to the criteria specified previously for the content reading inventory. Most individuals taking this test will find this text adequate for instruction. A few of you may score above or below that level. As can be seen, the content reading inventory can provide the teacher with information concerning the difficulty level of the text, as well as specific information concerning students' ability to effectively utilize the textbook. The checklist in Figure 5.2 provides a format for teachers to record the information gathered from the content reading inventory.

If the results of the content reading inventory indicate student deficiencies in certain areas, teachers may want to use the inventory as an instructional tool. Since the questions asked on the inventory are probably similar to those that teachers ask in the classroom, they can expect the students' responses to be similar to those they would make in class discussions. Therefore, the content reading inventory provides the framework for teachers to initiate a preview of the text, as described in Chapter 4. The premise behind this strategy is that the teacher will model the use of the various text parts and efficient use of the author's organizational structure and introduce the students to their textbook in a systematic manner. The preview offers students an introduction to proper utilization of the various reading/study aids authors incorporate into textbooks.

FIGURE 5.2 — *Content Reading Inventory Checklist*

Subject _____   Title of Text _____

Grade and Section _____   Teacher _____

Student Name	Table of Contents	Index	Glossary	Chapter Introduction/Summary	Pictorial Information	Other Internal Aids	Electronic Databases	Reader's Guide	Encyclopedia	Other External Aids	Vocabulary-Recall	Vocabulary-Context	Literal	Nonliteral	Text Structure
1. John Bead	✓		✓	✓	✓		✓		✓			✓	✓		
2. Tom Rean	✓	✓		✓			✓		✓		✓	✓	✓		✓
3. Scott Bee		✓	✓	✓			✓	✓	✓		✓		✓		✓
4.															
5.															
6.															
7.															

Courtesy Thomas Bean

Students are broken into small, cooperative groups and asked to reach consensus on the correct responses on the content reading inventory. Students struggling with various aspects of the textbook will have the opportunity to experience how others arrived at their conclusions. Again, teachers should follow these small group discussions with a whole group discussion, insuring an effective introduction to the textbook.

Cooperative groups may be utilized to provide additional practice in areas of need as indicated by an analysis of the summary information sheet with the results of the inventory. For instance, if the class as a whole seems to have difficulty processing text implicit information, the teacher can construct a series of questions emphasizing the use of this skill and assign them to the task groups. Through peer interaction and a follow-up whole group discussion, the teacher can let the students experience some of the processes necessary to enhance learning with text.

Knowledge of the students' ability to successfully cope with their text material is essential, and the diagnostic use of the textbook enables content teachers to initiate instruction in their classrooms on an informed basis. No assumptions are made about what is already known, and instruction is based on establishing the background necessary for effective comprehension of new material.

Since only a few items are assessed in each area, the content reading inventory is only a beginning—a point of departure—for assessing students' abilities. In essence, the results of this inventory allow teachers to begin the development of student *portfolios,* or systematic collections of students' work in the classroom. As teachers observe students interacting with texts in their daily reading and writing assignments, they will acquire additional information that will corroborate or refute the initial findings to add to the portfolios.

Online Reading Assessment

In addition to reading print texts, students increasingly explore multiple websites to gather information in social studies, science, geography, economics, and other content areas. There is a growing awareness that, for students who are struggling readers, the process of reading online material is onerous and more complex than traditional print texts with predictable text structures (e.g., comparison/contrast, cause/effect, time order). For example, in an analysis of online reading demands, Tierney (2009) noted the following five critical processes involved:

o Forward inferencing, where readers use prediction strategies to envision upcoming information at sites not yet visited;

o Evaluating relevance of sites listed to gauge which ones are more useful;

o Evaluating the source of the information to critically consider ideological or other hidden agendas permeating a site;

o Strategic searching to avoid becoming lost in a maze of misinformation;

o Making intertextual connections between sites where creating a chain of useful information entails evaluating multiple perspectives on a topic (e.g., immigration).

To assess your students' online reading for information in your content area, you can use a simple Online Content Inventory based on a topic you provide (e.g., power beverages in health class). Figure 5.3 will have some students selecting ads for power beverages that may be seductive and may include outrageous claims. Indeed, some power beverages have been banned in some college settings due their high alcohol and caffeine content.

The Online Content Inventory can be structured as an online form to be downloaded to students' laptops, smartphones, and a classroom smart board. Based on an examination of sites they select, you should be able to get a preliminary idea of potential online reading difficulties, including

o Getting lost trying to navigate sites online;

o Being taken in by seductive details in ads and other online material;

o Experiencing difficulty in creating intertextual links across sites.

FIGURE 5.3   *Online Content Inventory*

Directions: Conduct a key word search for "power beverages" and evaluate the trustworthiness of the sites you find. Bookmark sites so you can return to them later. For each site, answer the following questions:

1. Is this a reliable, trustworthy site?

   Yes:

   No:

   How do you know?

2. Does this site provide useful information?

   Yes:

   No:

   How do you know?

3. How does this site connect with the information in the other sites you visited?

4. List and summarize your final choices of 3–5 sites that provide information on power beverages.

Courtesy Thomas Bean

By all accounts, online reading poses significant difficulties for struggling readers and requires additional teacher scaffolding by way of structured WebQuests and other teacher-guided assignments (Bean, 2010).

An array of other approaches are available to help you assess your students' initial efforts to read and comprehend both print and online texts in your content area. These informal measures are relatively easy to create and administer, and they tap into students' prior knowledge, an important precursor for comprehension.

The attractiveness of *rubrics* for rating students' performance on these and other assessments you develop has been enhanced by the availability of websites with rubrics you can customize to fit your needs. For example, RubiStar features a site sponsored by the U.S. Department of Education that offers templates you can customize to create your own rubrics (http://rubistar.4teachers.org/index.php).

RUBRICS

Rubrics specify the criteria for success on a task linked to numeric ratings, often in a 3- or 4-point scale. For example, if your students created a counterpoint YouTube ad to challenge the health benefits of power beverages, this video production could be evaluated using a 3-point rubric that included the following elements:

DESIGN

3—Exemplary: Engaging content; smooth transitions; multimodal elements including music, texts, costumes, and props.
2—Good: Multiple techniques and includes two of the exemplary elements.
1—Below Average: Minimal content; talking head narrator; no transitions, music, or other multimodal elements.

VIDEO COMPOSITION AND COUNTERPOINT MESSAGE

3—Exemplary: Engaging storyline and pacing of scenes that highlight negative features of the product. Scenes carefully framed to make the product the center of viewer attention. Careful editing.
2—Good: Some scenes supporting the negative features of the product but need further development. Editing could produce a more cohesive clip.
1—Below Average: Few scenes that actually center on the product and its negative effects. Scenes seem chaotic and not well edited.

ASSESSING PRIOR KNOWLEDGE

Throughout this book we have stressed the importance of prior knowledge in reading and learning with text. In essence, the more knowledge students bring to the printed page, the more likely they will successfully comprehend the text, particularly if they or the teacher activate the appropriate prior knowledge. Conversely, if students lack, or fail to select, the appropriate prior knowledge, their comprehension may suffer. Therefore, teachers may wish to assess students' knowledge about a topic, making decisions about the quality and quantity of prereading instruction they provide students. If teachers know that students possess a vast store of prior knowledge about a topic under study, it is less necessary to spend great amounts of time in prereading. On the other hand, if students know little about a topic, it benefits teachers to spend time activating and building background knowledge.

In later chapters we suggest a number of prereading vocabulary and comprehension strategies, as well as some prewriting strategies that teachers can use to initiate instruction in the content areas. Though instructional in scope, each of those strategies can provide teachers with relevant knowledge about what students know and do not know about a topic. However, we would like to suggest some techniques for assessing prior knowledge that are easy to implement and can provide teachers with the information necessary for effective instructional planning and teaching.

Knowledge Rating

Knowledge rating (Blachowicz, 1991) is a simple strategy for establishing what students already know about a topic by having them rate how well they know the vocabulary. In planning for the lesson, teachers select the vocabulary words they think are needed to understand the concepts to be learned and develop a sheet that lists that vocabulary; they then ask students to rate themselves on how well they know the words. Using the example of the topic, Warts and Their Cures, the knowledge rating sheet might resemble the example in Figure 5.4.

Introduce this technique by telling students that in order to get them thinking about the text material they would start by assessing what they already know about the topic. After handing out the sheet, pronounce the words, so decoding is not a problem for students. Then ask them to rate their knowledge of each word

FIGURE 5.4   *Knowledge Rating: Warts and Their Cures*

Directions: Decide how well you know each of the words below.

WORD	3 CAN DEFINE/USE IT	2 HEARD IT	1 DON'T KNOW
Spunk water			
Pliny the Elder			
Caustic painting			
Electrocautery			
Folk treatments			
Polyoma virus			
Autosuggestion			
Nostrums			

Courtesy Thomas Bean

by checking the appropriate column. The first time this strategy is used, teachers may need to model for students exactly what is expected. For instance, students might have some idea of folk treatments and rate it a 2; others may even rate it a 3. On the other hand, students probably would not know nostrums and would give it a 1. After students complete the sheet, teachers tally how many students knew each word. Students' prior knowledge can be ascertained collectively as well as individually and teachers will have some information about it before making a judgment about the amount of prereading instruction to provide.

Prediction Guide

The *prediction guide* is a series of fact-based statements given to students before they encounter a text assignment. The students indicate whether each statement is true or false. For instance, a teacher about to cover the Cold War in American history might provide students with a series of prediction guide statements. By examining their response to each of the guide statements, the teacher can discover not only how much students know about the Cold War, but also what particular aspects about the topic are known or not known. Thus, the teacher can gain valuable information for instructional planning. Figure 5.5 is an example prediction guide for the topic of bats and the text from which the statements are drawn (adapted from Webster, 1984).

FIGURE 5.5   *Prediction Guide: Bats*

Directions: Before you read a text passage on bats, predict which of the statements that follow are true based on what you already know about them. Place a check (✓) on the line next to every true statement.

_____ 1. Bats are the second largest group of mammals.

_____ 2. Some bats are the size of a bumblebee.

_____ 3. Bats transmit disease.

_____ 4. Bats are about as intelligent as dogs.

Bats

Next to the 3,000-odd kinds of rodents, some 900 species of bats constitute the second largest order of mammals in the animal kingdom, both in number of species and, by estimation, of individuals alive at any one time. Bats belong to the order Chiroptera, meaning winged hand, and make up nearly one-fourth of all mammalian species.

They range in size from Kitti's hognosed bat, which is the size of a bumblebee and weighs about as much as a penny, to the large fruit-eating bats called flying foxes because of their foxlike faces and their size—they are almost as big as a small fox cub, weighing two pounds and having a wingspan of up to six feet.

Most bats' gargoyle-like noses, used for transmitting high-frequency bursts of sound, and their huge ears, used to pick up the echoes from the waves of sound, have contributed to the human perception of bats as eerie, even supernatural, creatures that are probably vicious, filthy, and likely to attack humans and transmit disease.

Recent studies, however, show that bats are gentle, keep themselves meticulously clean, rarely transmit rabies, have a measure of intelligence that scientists equate with that of dogs, can be easily trained, and, in rare cases with a knowledgeable owner, can even become pets.

Whether each statement is actually true and how many statements should be used in the guide are not at issue here. What matters is that the statements reflect information the teacher thinks is important for students to know after completing the assignment. In this way teachers will know in what areas to provide prereading instruction.

We would like to caution teachers that prediction guides are characterized as a series of fact-based statements that aid you in assessing students' prior knowledge. Please remember that prediction guides are separate and distinct from anticipation guides, which have opened each chapter of this text thus far and are experience-based statements used to activate students' prior knowledge before they read. Please read the section on anticipation guides in Chapter 10 if this distinction is unclear.

REACTION GUIDE

		Confirmed	Disconfirmed
1.	Assessment should occur naturally as part of teaching and learning.	_____	_____
2.	Most state reading assessments are valid measures of reading.	_____	_____
3.	Standardized tests provide teachers enough information concerning students' abilities to begin instruction.	_____	_____
4.	The best reading tests to administer to students are those that compare them with other students across the nation.	_____	_____
5.	Diagnosis is necessary for effective content area instruction.	_____	_____

	A Why my choice is confirmed.	B Why my choice is not confirmed.
1.	_____	_____
2.	_____	_____
3.	_____	_____
4.	_____	_____
5.	_____	_____

MINI PROJECTS

1. Interview a school principal, superintendent, or school board member to find out what they think of NCLB and the newer Common Core Standards.

2. Select one of the techniques for assessing prior knowledge and try it on a small group of students or your peers. Evaluate its effectiveness.

3. Examine a standardized reading test provided by your instructor. Evaluate each subtest of the instrument for the criteria listed below. Use the following classification system: 1 = Satisfactory; 2 = Unsatisfactory; 3 = Not Clear. Add any other evaluative criteria you deem necessary.

    A. Is the stated purpose of each subtest reflected in the test items?
    B. Are the directions clearly written?
    C. Are the test items always passage dependent?
    D. Does the test measure what it purports to measure?
    E. Does the test include performance items?
    F. Is adequate time allowed for the completion of each subtest?

4. Using a content text of your choice, design a content reading inventory. Utilize the procedures described earlier in the chapter. Administer the inventory, if possible, to three students to ascertain their ability to cope with the text. Evaluate the effectiveness of the content inventory as a device for gathering diagnostic information about students.

RECOMMENDED WEBSITES

Rubric Assessments:
o   RubiStar: http://rubistar.4teachers.org/

Teaching Channel Video Clips:
o   Daily assessment with tiered exit cards (6–12, 5 minutes)
o   Reading like a historian: Sourcing (9–12, 7 minutes)
o   Studying using stations to review for tests (7th grade, 6 minutes)

WEBSITE ACTIVITY

Go to the website for Chapter 5 activities.

FIGURE 5.6

Answers for Content Reading Inventory

Section I: Textual Reading/Study Aids

A. Internal Aids

    1. Page 63, Learning with Text and Technology (Table of Contents)

    2. Pages 231–232 (Index)

    3. The glossary

    4. It provides an overview of the chapter. (Chapter Introduction)

    5. The student needs help with supporting details, sentence length, and spelling. (Pictorial Information)

    6. The preface

B. External Aids

    7. Electronic databases

    8. The reader's guide

    9. Answer open; alphabetically (Encyclopedias)

Section II: Vocabulary Knowledge

    10. A word is a pattern of auditory or visual symbols that represent schemata. (Recall)

    11. A denotation of a word is its broad meaning, while a connotation of a word is defined by its subtle shades of meaning and its limiting grammatical and semantic conditions. Examples open. (Recall)

    12. A corpus is a body, or collection, of recorded utterances used as a basis for the descriptive analysis of a language. (Context)

    13. Assimilation is the process by which new information is incorporated into existing schemata. (Recall)

    14. Extant means existing. (Context)

Section III: Comprehension

    15. Adult language users have a common sensitivity to the concept of a word because they know speakers do not interrupt words with fillers such as "um" or "uh" during speech. (Literal)

    16. Learning new words requires more than a simple explanation because they are not just isolated bits of information. Rather, words are defined by the ways and the extent to which they are related to all other words. (Literal)

    17. The largest vocabularies for literate adults are the listening and reading vocabularies because the schemata required for recognizing word meanings in context are more fully developed. (Literal)

    18. Crass is a general vocabulary term not specifically associated with a teaching area. Cold War is a technical vocabulary term uniquely related to social studies. (Nonliteral)

    19. Secant is a technical vocabulary term that requires students to accommodate their schemata by modifying them or creating new ones to learn a novel word. (Nonliteral)

    20. Children enter school with developed listening and speaking vocabularies. Instruction in the school enables these children to be exposed to many new concepts. Eventually, this exposure enables the listening vocabulary to further expand and the reading vocabulary to overtake the expressive vocabularies. (Nonliteral)

    21. The Vocabularies section is organized around a pattern of comparison/contrast as the types of vocabularies are enumerated and discussed. (Author Organization)

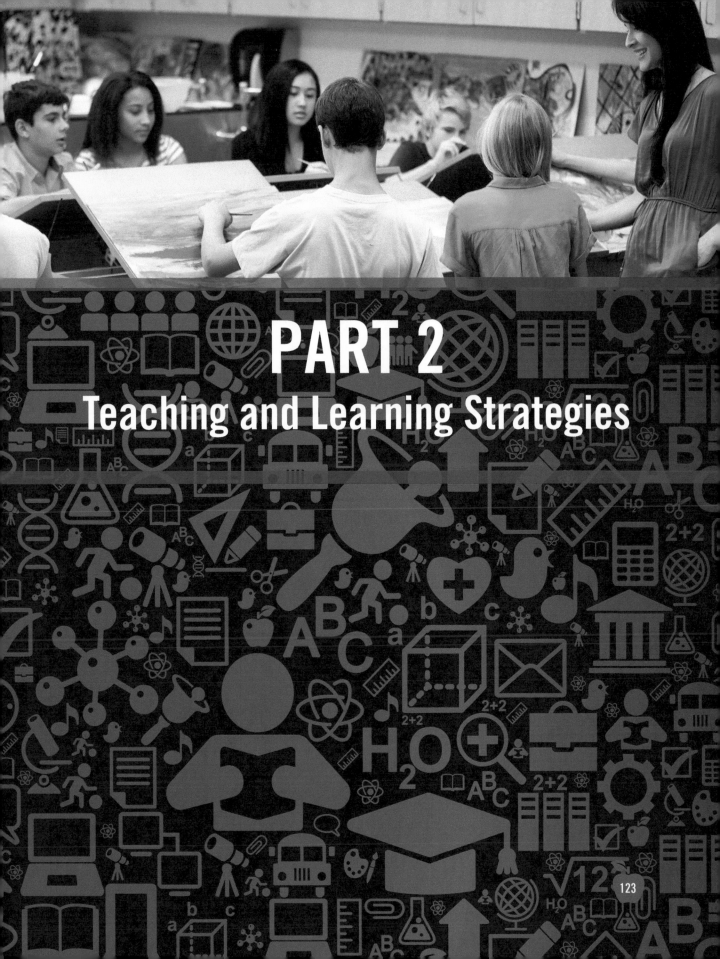

PART 2
Teaching and Learning Strategies

PART 2: Teaching and Learning Strategies

CHAPTER 6

Unit and Lesson Planning

 VIGNETTE

Setting

We are observing Shane Bintliff's ninth-grade US history class in a unit on the industrial revolution. Mr. Bintliff is a first-year teacher with an interest in technology as a way of engaging adolescents in learning history. His classroom has a smartboard, as well as tablets and laptops for student use. Although Mr. Bintliff is not well versed in creating WebQuests for his students, he believes that using the Internet to search for information on the industrial revolution will at least interest students in the topic. And, many of his students are reading at the fourth-grade level, so he assumes that computer-based texts will be easier to read

than the assigned textbook. He wants his students to understand how various machine inventions were influential in improving productivity and transportation. Mr. Bintliff's high school of 3,000 students is located in a high-density urban area of the Southwest, where language and ethnic differences abound. Significant numbers of students are struggling readers, reading two or more grades below the ninth-grade level.

The Lesson

We observe Mr. Bintliff and his students as they begin to explore the topic of machine inventions and their influence on productivity and industrialization. Mr. Bintliff tells his students to browse the Internet using the Google search engine, figuring they are well versed in this process. He provides a search prompt to guide their exploration of the Internet. The prompt students are advised to use to begin their search reads:

o   Machine inventions during the industrial revolution

Students type this in and get a number of sites, sequentially listed by this topic. We watch as Rhett, a struggling reader, selects the first site that pops up following his key word search. The site provides very traditional looking single-spaced text on the industrial revolution, organized by subheadings such as "The Newcomen and Watt Steam Engines." The vocabulary load in this text includes general terms like "ramifications" and "inefficient," as well as a wide array of technical vocabulary including "micrometer" and "atmospheric." Its Raygor Readability would yield a rating of 12th-grade level, making it well out of the range of Rhett's reading level. As a struggling reader, Rhett reads around the fourth-grade level, or five grade levels below this text. As a result, he briefly scans the text and exits the site. He then selects the next site in the list, but its homepage features a brain tickler puzzle that has nothing to do with the industrial revolution and a sidebar list of "signs of depression." Finally, Rhett locates a Wikipedia site that seems a bit friendlier but, by then, he is simply worn out and depressed about his reading. The period ends and he has zero information to take back to class to share with his cooperative learning group. Meanwhile, Mr. Bintliff is busy checking the latest travel deals on Expedia.com.

Now that you have considered this lesson, write down your thoughts on the following questions:

1. What are the good points about the lesson?

2. What are the weak points about the lesson?

3. What, if anything, would you change about the lesson?

 ## RATIONALE

In Chapter 3 we discussed the importance of social context in content area literacy. When you plan a *unit of instruction* that may span 3–6 weeks of individual lessons, the success of the unit depends on how well you develop connections between the content and your students' prior knowledge and experiences. Thus, having a clear sense of students' language, culture, and interests is crucial in designing and delivering successful lessons. Planning time is needed to consider instructional purposes and goals. In addition, students' prior knowledge, ability, and motivation should be considered at the planning stage. For example, in the vignette of Mr. Bintliff's introduction to his unit on the industrial revolution, students were let loose to conduct a topic search without much guidance, other than a prompt statement. In Chapter 2 we talked about ways that content teachers can develop a structure to guide students' search process. Given that Mr. Bintliff's class had a significant number of struggling readers, careful planning and guidance would have overcome some of the frustration experienced by students like Rhett in the vignette. An increasing array of online resources is available to help you create well-designed internet-based assignments (Bean, 2010; Kist, 2015), as well as more traditional print-based aids to lesson and unit planning. In addition, resources tapping into Web 2.0's creative potential for student productions (e.g., YouTube video clips) now abound (Kist, 2010). We include a short selection of these resources in the Recommended Readings at the close of the chapter. Task analysis of text characteristics such as vocabulary and important concepts should guide lesson planning. Finally, how much time will be available for delivering lessons and what grouping structures might be possible? Even if you do an outstanding job of planning a lesson, it will probably not be flawless the first time through. But planning can alleviate a number of problems related to student boredom, pacing, and evaluation.

As you plan lessons and units following the formats outlined in this chapter, you should keep a journal where you reflect on your teaching. Your professional development as a teacher hinges on constant reflection and efforts to improve lesson design and delivery. In essence, teaching is a process of constant transformation for both students and teachers (Britzman, 2003).

In this chapter, we introduce a format for unit and lesson planning with an emphasis on formulating clear goals and objectives, using exciting hooks or anticipatory set activities, and ensuring that a lesson takes advantage of students' experiences and interests. This framework should be helpful as you explore teaching and learning strategies in vocabulary, comprehension, writing, and studying approaches. In essence, this chapter provides the umbrella for all the individual teaching strategies that follow.

o   Use a unit blueprint to develop a 3–6 week unit of instruction in your content area.

o   Use a lesson-planning framework to write a lesson plan in your content area.

o   Write lesson objectives that encompass the main elements of expected performance, product, condition, and criteria, applicable to your state curriculum standards.

o   Deliver a 5-minute lesson to your peers based on a hobby or area of interest.

o   Deliver a 20-minute microteaching lesson to peers and field-experienced students in your content area.

 GRAPHIC ORGANIZER

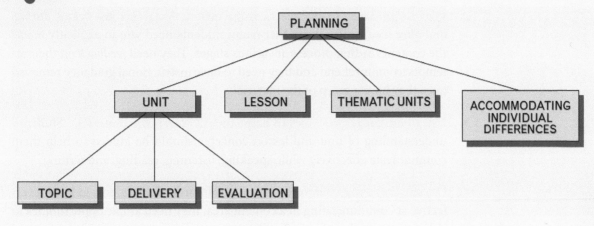

Courtesy Thomas Bean

PLANNING

In the early stages of planning, when you begin to collect materials, draft lessons, and think about what teaching strategies you will use, keep the following points in mind:

Tips for Lesson Planning

1. **Present content and processes concurrently.** The particular teaching strategies you select for an assignment should grow out of a careful content analysis of the material. What is the purpose of the assignment? What text structure does the author use to portray ideas? This analysis should suggest which vocabulary, comprehension, writing, and studying strategies are likely to be most helpful.

2. **Provide guidance in all aspects of the instructional lesson**—*before, during, and after reading.* Be aware that many students need you to explicitly *model* the content reading process at various stages. They need *feedback* on their attempts to comprehend and they need to have instructional guidance removed once they have a grasp of the material.

3. **Use all language processes to help students learn the material.** Students' understanding of unit and lesson concepts should be guided to help them communicate effectively while speaking, listening, reading, and writing.

4. **Use small groups to enhance learning.** In order for students to become effective at communicating in a content area, they need ample opportunities to risk expressing their ideas. Small group activities encourage risk-taking and expression.

5. **Be patient in new unit and lesson implementation.** It takes teachers and students time to become comfortable with new material. Give your new units and lessons enough trial runs with modifications so you can fully judge their effectiveness.

An additional point to keep in mind is the structure of an instructional unit and its related lessons. We conceive of a typical lesson structure as having three phases: prereading, reading, and postreading.

In the *prereading* **phase**, students apply what they know to what they are learning. Teachers can facilitate this process by appraising and, if need be, increasing students' knowledge of the topic under scrutiny before they begin reading text and course assignments.

In the *reading* phase, students are encouraged to think deeply about what they are learning. Teachers can guide this process by insuring that students adopt an active, questioning approach to the text through reasoning across a full range of levels of understanding. This involves students not only comprehending what the text explicitly states, but also understanding the text in relation to their own prior knowledge and experiences.

In the *postreading* **phase**, students refine and extend ideas; teachers can involve students in activities that encourage them to synthesize and organize information for long-term retention.

Bear in mind that these phases are just useful constructs for talking about teaching, learning, and instructional planning. They are not to be blindly adhered to regardless of the instructional situation. Now that we have provided some background, it would be interesting to read how some teachers use the textbook in their instructional lessons. Finally, before we introduce some of the details common to unit and lesson planning, please look up the following website offering a wealth of guidance for developing sound lesson and unit plans that are likely to maximize students' comprehension [http:// www.internet classrooms.com/lesson.htm]. We strongly recommend spending some time browsing this site to gain an understanding of the support being offered in lesson and unit planning across the key dimensions of vocabulary development, comprehension, and study strategies highlighted in Part 2 of our book.

Developing Units and Lessons

A unit may be as short as a single week of instruction, or may span three to six weeks. In most cases, developing a unit on a topic in your content area will entail using a unit blueprint that contains the following elements:

Unit Blueprint Categories

1. Topic

2. Goals and objectives

3. Content outline

4. Learning activities

5. Resources and materials

6. Evaluation plan

In order to understand the role each of these elements plays in planning, we follow a secondary natural science teacher at a Kauai, Hawaii high school as she designs a unit entitled Ocean Predators: The Shark. The teacher's name is Toni Avila.

Ms. Avila's unit on the topic, Ocean Predators: The Shark, spans three weeks with a focus on basic shark biology, shark species, and habits of sharks related to attacks reported in the islands. Many of Ms. Avila's students, and Ms. Avila, are avid watersports enthusiasts. She regularly windsurfs the outer reefs off Poipu Beach and many of her students surf, kayak, scuba dive, fish, and swim in the waters on the south and north sides of the island. Thus, in planning her unit, Ms. Avila thinks about her students' varied experiences in the nearby Hawaiian waters. She also consults district and state curriculum guideline materials and objectives to include this material in her planning process. And, she goes over all her resource material ranging from texts, trade books, videos, smart board Internet web pages, and a set of very large tiger shark jaws borrowed from a marine fisheries friend. In the early planning stages of the unit, she has all this material laid out on the living room floor of her apartment. In addition, she is aware of an upcoming exhibit on sharks at a local museum. Finally, the Internet features a number of useful sites about sharks.

Ms. Avila also thinks carefully about the range of students in her class. Her students are heterogeneously grouped, spanning a range of achievement levels and needs. As she reviews all this material, the following unit blueprint emerges over the span of a week.

Blueprint

Topic
Ocean Predators: The Shark

Goal and Objectives
Be able to identify biologic features of sharks, species, and know what shark habits influence attacks in Hawaiian waters and how to prevent their occurrence.

1. The students will be able to identify the biologic features of a tiger shark by labeling a shark drawing with its missing features with 100% accuracy.
2. The students will be able to distinguish dangerous sharks from harmless species by watching slides of various sharks and checking "dangerous" or "harmless" on a paper listing each slide number. They will also be asked to label the species next to each slide number, and the criterion for success at both tasks is 80% accuracy overall.
3. The students will develop shark education materials (posters, videos, pamphlets) to assist the state's effort to reduce shark attacks. These materials will be judged by a panel of science teachers, community members, and State

Fisheries biologists, using a scale that includes (a) accuracy of information on sharks; (b) artistic merit; and (c) potential impact on beach safety.

Content Outline

Ms. Avila goes to the library and checks out a number of resource books on sharks in addition to the class textbook. In order to develop a unit content outline that addresses the planned objectives, she also visits key Internet websites on sharks.

Because of the unusually large number of fatal shark attacks attributed to tiger sharks, Ms. Avila decides to focus on this shark as a basis for comparing and contrasting information about other sharks. Based on selectively reading and taking notes on these books, Ms. Avila created the following content outline:

I. Biologic Features of a Tiger Shark
   A. A kind of fish that has
      1. a vertebral column
      2. median fins
      3. gills
   B. Two groups of jawed fishes
      1. bony fishes
      2. cartilaginous fishes (sharks)
II. Misconceptions about Sharks
   A. Misconceptions:
      1. All sharks are the same.
      2. Sharks are color blind.
      3. Sharks must turn on their backs to bite.
      4. They have simple brains.
   B. Facts and characteristics:
      1. 350 species and much diversity
      2. Characteristics:
         a) Good vision
         b) Sensitivity to vibrations
            (1) Lateral line organs
            (2) Ampullae of Lorenzini (jelly-filled pores of nerve endings on snout and head to sense electrical impulses in hunting)
         c) No gas bladder like fish to control buoyancy–they must swim to avoid sinking.
         d) Five to seven gill openings
         e) Eyelid protection–nictitating membrane
         f) Denticles (toothlike) rather than scales like a fish
         g) Inflexible fins–tail fin is the driving force.
         h) Teeth grow continuously.
         i) Reproduction is internal.

III. Dangerous versus Harmless Sharks
  A. Dangerous sharks (piscivorous feeders)
    1. Tiger
    2. Great White
    3. Hammerhead
  B. Harmless sharks (plankton feeders)
    1. Basking
    2. Megamouth
    3. Whale shark
IV. Preventing Shark Attacks
  A. Sharks hunt using recognized signals of prey:
    1. Thrashing of a wounded fish
    2. Smell of blood or other body fluids
    3. Flailing of appendages of weakened prey
  B. Swimmers should
    1. Avoid swimming alone
    2. Wear low-contrast clothing
    3. Avoid wearing shiny jewelry
    4. Avoid wild splashing and erratic swimming
    5. Stay close to shore
    6. Avoid murky rivermouth areas
    7. Avoid deep channels
    8. Avoid swimming at night
    9. Surfers should be alert to sharks: paddle calmly toward shore if one is spotted.
    10. Divers spearing fish should tow their kill on a long line away from their bodies.

Ms. Avila introduces her students to a smartphone application called "Sharkbytes" that features facts about sharks, as well as shark encounters around the globe.

Learning Activities

Ms. Avila has taken a class in content area literacy, and she is able to capitalize on a number of teaching strategies. For the opening lesson of this unit, she decided to use a comprehension strategy called *Talking Drawings* (Bean, 2010) to introduce the unit. Talking drawings asks students to draw stick figure drawings or doodles that represent what they know about a topic to be studied. These rough sketches become visual prompts for a prereading discussion of the topic in pairs or small groups. Following the text reading, students can revise their talking drawings to include the information they learned, and erroneous information can be removed.

The opening lesson focuses on how sharks hunt for food. Ms. Avila's lesson plan follows. It contains all the elements of a good *lesson plan*: (a) objective(s); (b) set induction; (c) content outline; (d) activities; (e) closure; (f) resources and materials; (g) evaluation; and (h) assignment.

Her objective for this lesson contains the four key elements of any good *objective*: (a) a clear statement of the performance expected of students; (b) the product that should result from this performance; (c) the conditions for demonstrating the expected performance and product; and (d) the criteria for successful demonstration of the expected performance and product. Thus, for the lesson on how sharks hunt for food, Ms. Avila wrote the following lesson plan and related objective.

Ms. Avila's Lesson

Topic: How Sharks Hunt for Food

Objective: Students will verbally discuss their revised shark drawings in groups of four. Their revised drawings should have two anatomic features that assist hunting for food.

In this objective, the expected performance is a shark drawing. The expected product is a revised version of the original shark drawing. The condition for demonstrating success at this task is a small group discussion of students' revised shark drawings. The criterion for success is the inclusion of two anatomic features that assist sharks in hunting for food.

Set Induction

1. Using the talking drawings format, Ms. Avila has students draw their impressions of a tiger shark's features. The following drawing was produced by one of her students prior to any reading and study about tiger sharks:

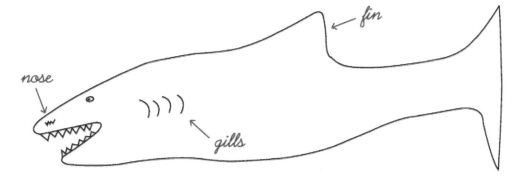

Lesson Content Steps, Outline, and Activities

2. Students then shared and discussed their initial drawings in groups of four. A recorder kept track of the information they provided about the shark's

features. For example, the group that labeled the previous drawing here understood a few anatomic features of tiger sharks that might be important for hunting. They included the nose and sense of smell, the gills for breathing, and the dorsal fin for swimming. However, they also felt that sharks might navigate to their prey using sonar.

3. A whole-group teacher-guided discussion led to the development of a shark features drawing on the board with labels for those features mentioned by students at this initial stage of the lesson. The second drawing, which resembled a tiger shark more closely than the drawing produced by the group in step 1, had a few additional features useful in hunting, including the pectoral fin.

4. Students were then assigned a text passage to read, and internet material to search.

5. Following text reading, they revised their initial shark drawings:

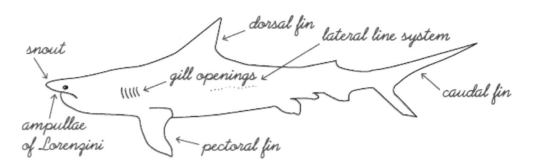

The final phases of a lesson plan structure consist of (a) lesson closure; (b) evaluation; and (c) assignment. In the case of the shark lesson, students completed the following steps:

6. Small-group sharing of the revised drawings, with a recorder keeping track of changes and additions to the original drawings. This small-group discussion provided the material for the final lesson activity.

Lesson Closure, Evaluation, and Assignment

7. A whole-class discussion resulted in a final composite drawing on the board of the tiger shark and its various anatomic parts that assist hunting. These included the tiger shark's sense of smell and its ability to use its lateral line system or pores along the body to detect vibrations in the water. In addition, highly sensitive pores beneath the shark's snout, termed "ampullae of Lorenzini," assist the shark in the final phases of attack by detecting very weak

electrical fields emitted by its prey. In short, the tiger shark is a well-equipped hunter, even without sonar.

To close the lesson, Ms. Avila advised students to read the section in their book on Great White sharks, as that topic would be taken up in the next class.

Lesson Resources and Materials

Ms. Avila listed drawing paper, felt-tip pens, overhead transparencies, overhead pens, a book on sharks in Hawaii, and Internet search tasks on sharks of Hawaii. Additional learning activities in the overall unit on sharks included shark videos from the local library, a fisheries biologist well known as a shark researcher as a guest speaker, and a field trip back to the local museum, where a shark exhibit further countered students' misconceptions about shark vision, teeth regeneration, and reproduction. Students also read and critiqued popular novels that involved sharks based on the accuracy of the scientific information used by the author in describing shark behavior. In addition, the field trip exposed students to some of the large yet harmless species of sharks, including the whale shark and megamouth. Finally, students were asked to develop shark attack prevention brochures for use by the Department of Fisheries in its community education program.

Unit Resources and Materials

Ms. Avila selected videos, a list of potential guest speakers, felt-tip pens, overhead transparencies, media supplies for brochure drafts, and trade books.

Evaluation

This included text-based quizzes and tests, as well as a panel review of students' brochures using specific criteria in a checklist of features. Thus, both ongoing and final project evaluation can be used to judge students' performance within individual lessons and across the overall unit.

Table 6.1 presents the components needed to design lesson plans for a conventional unit as well as designing lessons within the unit structure.

TABLE 6.1

Designing Lesson Plans

CONVENTIONAL UNIT	LESSON WITHIN THE UNIT STRUCTURE
1. Topic	1. Topic
2. Goals and Objectives	2. Objectives
3. Content Outline	3. Set Induction
4. Learning Activities	4. Content Outline
5. Resources and Materials	5. Activities
6. Evaluation Plan	6. Closure
	7. Resources and Materials
	8. Evaluation
	9. Assignment

The vocabulary, comprehension, writing, and studying strategies introduced later in the book fit within unit section number 4, Learning Activities. Ms. Avila's use of talking drawings demonstrates how content area literacy strategies fit within the larger framework of a lesson and unit.

All of these planning elements are important, but your delivery of a lesson needs to be flexible enough to allow for students' varying prior knowledge, interest, and achievement. In order to experiment with the process of developing and delivering a lesson, try the activity in Application 6.1.

Five-minute lessons can cover topics like how to polish shoes correctly, how to slice an onion properly, using a kitchen fire extinguisher, making a child's paper helicopter, tuning a guitar, and any number of other possible topics that lend themselves to a single objective. The process of developing and delivering a five-minute lesson will strengthen your skills in lesson planning and delivery that adheres to clear objectives. Remember, a good objective includes four important elements:

a. A clear statement of the performance expected of students;

b. The product that should result from this performance;

c. The conditions for demonstrating the expected performance and product;

d. The criteria for successful demonstration of the expected performance and product.

The Five-Minute Lesson

One of the best ways to get accustomed to lesson planning and delivery is to microteach a brief, five-minute lesson focusing on a single, attainable objective. Using the following example as a model, develop and deliver a five-minute lesson based on your favorite hobby. For instance, a teacher interested in horses devised the following five-minute lesson.

Topic: How to Tie a Quick Release Knot

Objective: Students will be able to verbally state the purpose of the quick release knot in horsemanship with 100% accuracy.

Set induction: "You finish a trail ride with your horse, and it's time to remove the saddle to give your horse a bath. You need to tie your horse while you remove the saddle. How would you do this so you can easily untie your horse if he gets spooked?"

Content outline and activity: Demonstrate how to tie the quick release knot using a short piece of halter rope and an overhead transparency showing the steps necessary to tie the knot correctly.

Closure and assessment: Students in small groups of four will have the group leader verbally state the purpose of the quick release knot with 100% accuracy.

Resources and materials: Transparencies of the quick release knot steps, short halter rope to demonstrate tying the knot around a chair leg, and book on working with horses.

The first transparency shows a horse tied correctly with the quick release knot. In an emergency, a sharp tug on the free end will release the horse.

The second transparency shows the four steps needed to tie a quick release knot: (1) Loop the rope through the breakaway string on the tie down; (2) with the end of the loop, make a bow; (3) tighten the bow to secure the horse; and (4) lock the knot by running the loose end through the bow so it will stay secure.

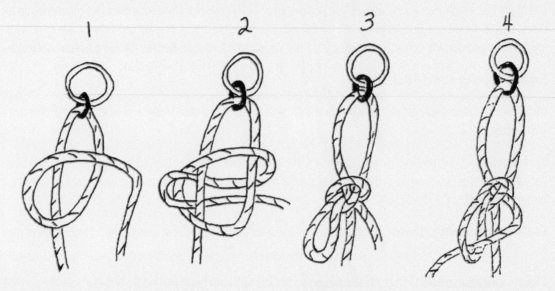

Assignment: Based on this lesson, students would be given short lengths of halter rope to go home and practice the quick release knot for a short performance test at the next class meeting.

The unit and lesson planning framework we have explored so far provides a good beginning point in your planning and use of content area literacy strategies. However, other planning models have been emerging in the last few years that capitalize on core area teacher teams from English, mathematics, science, and social studies engaged in regular lesson and unit planning meetings to develop thematic units that integrate content from diverse subject areas.

PLANNING THEMATIC UNITS AND LESSONS

The development and delivery of a *thematic unit* require a school structure that provides regular planning time for teams of teachers to meet and create curriculum. In addition, a team of core subject area teachers from English, mathematics, science, and social studies typically share the same students. In a secondary school, about 130 students are usually served by a core team of teachers. Additionally, teachers from the elective areas of art, music, industrial arts, and physical education may also be involved in planning *integrated thematic units*. It is only at the point of actually carrying out the unit for the first time that all the "bugs" can be worked out. This is equally true for lessons and conventional, single-subject units.

Before considering additional examples of unit planning, we want to share recent ideas about educating for creativity and using technology-based blended learning (Gaut, 2014; Kist, 2015). Because creativity is a kind of disposition combined with motivation to act on an idea, it is possible to create classroom conditions likely to foster student creativity and problem solving. For example, in eighth-grade physics, a popular project engages students in the design and construction of an amusement park roller coaster (Walker, Bean, & Dillard, 2010). Students locate information on the Internet about constructing roller coasters and use simple, inexpensive pipe insulation tubing and duct tape to construct their prototypes, using a marble to represent a roller coaster car. They learn about momentum, gravity, various forms of energy, and take photos and notes related to physics concepts. Ultimately, they are able to apply these concepts to test runs of their roller coasters, calculating speed and velocity, as well as creating Quicktime movies of their roller coasters.

Teaching for creativity will vary across disciplines because each content area has its own domain knowledge and structure. For example, in history, students can begin to critically evaluate sources of information in texts and even create counterpoint interpretations. In a British literature class, students can take one of Shakespeare's sonnets and rewrite it as a rap or dialect poem. Based on a rich understanding of the original text, they can create novel versions in a new form. As Gaut (2014) notes, "The student, in short, is being equipped to become a thinker who can make new and valuable discoveries, building on her preexisting capacities, by imitation of good models and practice under the guidance of a teacher." (p. 178)

Steps for Creating a Powerful Thematic Unit

A well-designed thematic unit contains the following steps:

1. **Create a binding theme.**
   For example, one middle school decided to concentrate on eradicating litter on its campus. The core team and elective teachers developed a quarter term thematic unit on environmental beautification using their campus as a test case. All 130 seventh- and eighth-grade students would be involved in the unit across their various core and elective classes.

2. **Use concept mapping or outlining to brainstorm and design a preliminary plan for the unit.** (See Figure 6.1)

3. **Decide what concepts will be developed within each content area.**
   For example, the mathematics, science, and social studies teachers decided to have their students use a campus map and tour the campus to collect specific data on amounts of litter at various key areas of the school. This information was then entered in a computer database, and descriptive bar graphs showing areas of substantial litter were plotted. The English teachers assisted students in writing research reports chronicling the location of litter and potential solutions to the problem. Elective art teachers had students videotape the data collection process, and ultimately students developed antilitter posters. In music, they created songs related to litter eradication, and the English classes developed skits for a whole school assembly to recognize the custodial staff and introduce a campus beautification incentive program. New trash cans were placed at key litter sites mapped by students and a weekly drawing awarded prizes for litter control.

FIGURE 6.1   *Concept Map for Environmental Beautification*

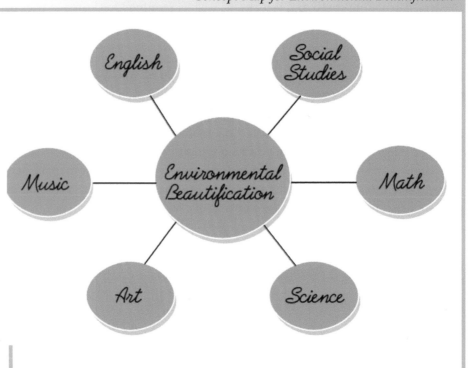

Courtesy Thomas Bean

This third step of listing key concepts parallels the lesson and unit planning steps explored earlier in the chapter, but it relies on all team members coordinating their content around the central theme. Many middle and secondary schools are moving toward this model because it results in students seeing connections across diverse content areas and it allows teachers to track student progress and engage in cooperative problem solving when they notice a student falling behind. Elementary teachers can create thematic, integrated units of instruction within their own classrooms.

4. **Decide how the concepts in step 3 are connected across content areas.**
   Each content area contributes the special skills it has to offer. Thus, the art department capitalized on poster-making talents, the mathematics area on data analysis, the social studies area on mapping skills, science on data collection, and English on report writing. The music teacher gave students a chance to put their ideas to song and rap.

5. **Develop cooperative activities.**
   The central, cooperative activity that started this unit was the campus mapping and data collection about litter. This activity necessitated reading materials on environmental beautification, and learning a great deal about working in groups with specific assignments for each group member. Some students had to count litter in various locations, others recorded the data, and each team had to share its findings with the other teams mapping campus litter.

6. **Locate resources.**
   A number of websites provide resource materials for lesson planning. These sites change frequently, but they can be found with most popular search engines.

Apart from the library, computer, video, presentation software and hardware, Internet, and other resources needed for this thematic unit, students and teachers received a small grant from the local Rotary Club to assist in purchasing trash cans and developing posters, brochures, and incentive awards.

When you are designing integrated, thematic units, try to pick topics that are likely to generate excitement and interest. Students should be involved in the planning stages as well as helping to design projects and grouping structures. If possible, seek whole-school involvement since it makes clear to students just how crucial this activity is to the whole school. In the case of the litter eradication example, litter was a problem that had gotten steadily worse with everyone assuming someone else—the custodians, teachers, and others—responsible. This was a unit that had an obvious impact on the whole school. Unfortunately, it is rare that our day-to-day curriculum has this kind of obvious impact on students' lives. Carefully planned thematic units can have a tremendous impact, but they do take time to create and implement.

One potential problem in unit planning that we have not yet addressed is the wide range of individual differences that students bring to classes. You may need to vary lesson assignments in your classes based on students' prior knowledge, interest, reading achievement, language variation, and learning difficulties. In

Chapter 3 we reviewed some of the current legislation in the area of inclusion, and we discussed second language learners and various approaches. In the section that follows, we explore the nature of individual differences and consequences for planning instruction.

ACCOMMODATING INDIVIDUAL DIFFERENCES IN PLANNING

Teaching requires helping individuals to change. Learning occurs by making whatever adjustments are necessary in the learning situation, accommodating instructional methods to match student abilities, and guiding students as they try to cope with new learning situations. In Chapter 3 you learned about two factors (among many) that affect students' ability to learn from text—prior knowledge and language knowledge. The quantity and quality of the prior experiences of individuals and their language sophistication vary greatly. Other individual factors that may affect reading achievement as they interact with each other are the following:

1. Physical development

2. Emotional development

3. Rate of learning

4. Mode of learning

5. Motivation

6. Practice needed.

Because of their interactive nature, it might be difficult to speak of each factor singularly. For instance, physical development may influence one's emotional well-being. The same might be said for rate and mode of learning.

The notion of *passive failure,* or learned helplessness, is another learning difference to be recognized. Students who exhibit passive failure may be defined as those students who are resigned to fail and believe they do not have the ability to succeed in their learning. When faced with failure, they do not persist; they give up. On the other hand, when these students do succeed, they usually attribute it to factors other than themselves, such as luck, good teaching, or the ease of the task. The important point to be made about these students is that they do not fail because of lack of ability; rather, they do not, and will not, employ the appropriate strategies necessary for effective learning.

One last principle regarding individual differences is that sometimes a factor may vary almost as greatly within an individual as it does among individuals. For instance, a student's interest in school may fluctuate dramatically according to subject area. Changing interests, motivations, and life goals are differences that may differ greatly within an individual, especially over time.

A Definition

Accommodating individual differences means many different things to many different people. It does not mean largely undifferentiated, whole-group instruction in which the subject, rather than the student, is the focus of instruction. The problems inherent in such instruction have been recognized for some time. For instance, as far back as 1950, Hunt and Sheldon offered that "High school teachers must also realize that much of their frustration is derived from attempting to teach forty pupils as if all the children were able to perform on the same level." (pp. 352–353) Nonetheless, the lecture method is still predominant in content area teaching.

At the other extreme is complete individualization, in which instruction takes place totally on a one-to-one basis. This may be an ideal to which some educators aspire; however, given the rigors of day-to-day classroom experiences with large numbers of students, complete individualization is an unrealistic and counterproductive goal.

We recommend a compromise between the two extremes cited earlier. It does not embrace complete individualization, which requires individual preparation or text material for each student, nor does it call for the abandonment of grouping strategies. Rather, it incorporates the gamut of grouping procedures—whole group, small group, and individual—and utilizes these grouping procedures within the structure of unit and lesson planning.

We recommend grouping, and collaborative discussion within grouping procedures, because we feel that active student involvement in a group situation facilitates productivity in learning, for example, through plays, science experiments, or unit reviews (Walker, Bean, & Dillard, 2010). Students can learn from one another and provide new insight into learning by modeling their thinking for others. Feelings of belonging cannot be disregarded in grouping situations either. Additionally, teachers can move into their most appropriate role, as facilitators of learning, through the use of different group structures.

For example, the following are some of the numerous different types of small groups that teachers might employ:

1. Instruction groups—allow teachers to teach a specific process or issue with more individual contact than is possible in a large group;

2. Research groups—gather information on a problem and report the results to the large group;

3. Debate groups—present a contest of ideas to the large group;

4. Digressive groups—brainstorm to generate creative solutions to a problem.

Teachers need to be aware that making an overnight transformation from total whole-group instruction to the practices for accommodating individual differences is unrealistic. Slow, careful adaptation is crucial to the eventual successful implementation of these practices.

Some Suggestions

In order to realistically consider accommodating students' individual differences, teachers must modify the way they present the textbook within the context of the instructional paradigm. Consequently, you must be willing to make these necessary alterations in order to insure that each student has optimal opportunity for success in your classroom.

> **Types of Small Groups**
> o Instruction
> o Research
> o Debate
> o Digressive

The following are suggested modifications for teachers to consider as they employ the instructional paradigm of prereading, reading, and postreading phases:

1. Modifying students' prior knowledge

2. Modifying the way in which the material is presented

3. Considering alternatives to the text material

4. Modifying assignments.

These suggestions are our attempt to offer you practical instructional techniques to help you answer the commonly asked question, "What do I do on Monday?"

MODIFICATIONS IN THE PREREADING PHASE. The degree to which readers utilize their prior experiences in reading and learning with a text greatly influences their understanding of that material. Students' failure to associate new information with previously known information as they attempt to assimilate text material increases the difficulty of their comprehension task. Additionally, some students simply do not have the necessary prior knowledge about all the topics they encounter in text material.

Fortunately, while students prepare to read their texts, you can intervene to modify their knowledge of a topic as well as their interest in it. You can provide guided instruction to activate, or modify, students' schemata through the use of prereading strategies, which serve to activate appropriate schemata and modify them as new information is entered, thus allowing comprehension.

Another way to activate prior knowledge at the prereading stage of an integrated unit is to create a central question that puts students in the role of the problem solvers. Central questions should do the following:

1. Tap meaningful issues;

2. Be provocative and emotionally engaging;

3. Connect with students' worlds;

4. Give students active, investigative roles versus passive processing of content;

5. Allow for multiple responses.

For example, in the shark unit, a central question might be, "Why do tiger sharks attack people?" Central questions lend themselves to culminating activities that are based on performance standards. Thus, students may do a performance such as a one-act play, a presentation, a video, or guide a field trip. The possibilities are endless. A well-crafted central question will frame a unit and provide an overarching focus for inquiry.

MODIFICATIONS IN THE READING PHASE. Certainly there is cause to wonder about instruction that presents the same material in the same way to all students. Obviously, this type of instruction does not heed the differences in the way students learn or how well individual students deal with the difficulty of the concepts and vocabulary inherent in text. Because of these differences, methods for reducing the difficulty level of the learning material need to be considered. With some students it may be necessary to modify the way the material is presented, or even the material itself.

Some students may find the text too difficult to read; others may prefer an alternate means of text presentation. In these situations it is advantageous to capitalize on students' ability to listen and comprehend the material. Listening can be an effective means for student readers to communicate with text authors. We feel that active listening strategies are utilized too infrequently and that students could benefit extensively from these strategies.

The teacher may read aloud the selected passage from the text after instructing students to listen for particular concepts or other purposes. Students who are able to read the text with ease may be asked to read it to other students who are having difficulty with the reading. Another alternative is to use a tape recorder. Either the teacher or selected students may tape a portion of the text for those experiencing difficulty. These students may follow along as the text is being read, again with specific instructions about what they should be listening for. If a more structured approach is desired while students are listening to a selected passage, *listening guides* are suggested. A listening guide is a skeletal outline of the important concepts in the passage presented in the order and relationship in which they are set out in the passage. Students are asked to write in the desired information as they listen to the selection. The task of filling in the listening guides gives students additional guidance through the outline structure provided. Activities for reinforcement and extension may follow as planned.

Figure 6.2 is an example of a listening guide. If a listening guide was employed with the section of Chapter 8 entitled "Principles of Effective Vocabulary Instruction," it might look like this:

FIGURE 6.2 — *Sample Listening Guide*

Principle	Notes
1._____	_____
	_____
2._____	_____
	_____
3._____	_____
	_____
4._____	_____
	_____

MODIFICATIONS IN THE POSTREADING PHASE. In addition to modifying students' prior knowledge, the method, or the presentation of the material, and assignments required of students may also be modified. Usually the students' comprehension of text material is checked by having them answer a series of questions either found at the end of the chapter or in a study guide constructed by the teacher. However, having the whole group of students deal with exactly the same questions is the antithesis of accommodating divergent student abilities.

The use of a technique called *slicing* in assigning tasks to students is suggested as a means to modify assignments. Specifically, slicing refers to simplifying the complexity of these tasks by reexamining those that are required and recasting them to ease the demands placed on students.

Text assignments may be sliced in a variety of ways. Slicing enables teachers to accommodate individual differences by graduating the learning steps involved in completing assignments and by providing structured guidance in doing so. Slicing may be utilized in the following aspects of text assignments: (1) length of passage; (2) scope of information search; and (3) information index.

1. **Length of passage.** Though obviously more of a reading task than a post-reading one, length of passage is discussed here under the umbrella strategy of slicing. Sometimes assigning a whole chapter at a time for reading represents too sizeable a chunk of text for some students, yet this size assignment is very prevalent. In some cases, poor readers might be overwhelmed by as little as five pages; therefore, it seems appropriate to consider slicing the length of reading task for certain students to accommodate their divergent abilities. Reading assignments should be varied according to the number of concepts assigned to each student. Slicing the length of the passage to even a section or paragraph might be appropriate for certain students to insure their comprehension. Caution should be exercised regarding pictorial aids in text. Authors sometimes use such aids to express what could take a large numbers of words. Such aids might be considered a unit of instruction for some students, whereas other students may focus on the running text elaborating upon a particular aid.

2. **Scope of information search.** Content textbooks and websites are bursting with information. It is unrealistic to consider teaching all concepts presented; therefore, the teacher must conduct some form of content analysis in order to make decisions regarding the relative importance of the concepts. The *scope of information search* is determined by the number of concepts for which students are then held responsible. As concepts increase in number, the more exhaustive the scope of the search becomes. On the other hand, the fewer the concepts to be mastered, the more limited the search. The less proficient the student's reading ability, the more difficult an exhaustive search will be, and the greater the chance of negative effects on motivation and retention of new learning. Therefore, slicing the scope of information search according to students' individual differences is appropriate.

   The number of concepts for which students are responsible should depend on their differential abilities and the importance of the concepts in the chapter. The number of concepts can be varied by adding or subtracting from the number of assigned tasks on students' end-of-chapter or study guide questions. For example, more proficient readers may be responsible for 12 concepts whereas others need to deal with only three or four. No matter how many concepts are assigned to individual students in the class, whole-group discussion should follow the completion of work so that all students are exposed to the selected information.

Two points should be remembered concerning the scope of information search. First, limiting the search does not necessitate that only literal thinking be involved. It is not the level of thinking that is limited, only the number of concepts. Since all students can think and all students should be involved in higher-level comprehension processes, it is misguided to limit such thinking in an endeavor to reduce the scope of the information search. Second, there is a difference between varying the scope of the search and varying the length of the passage to be read. The number of concepts assigned may be varied while the length of the passage is held constant. For example, in a three-page selection certain students may be responsible for one concept per page whereas others may be held responsible for numerous concepts.

3. **Information index.** Keying students into the location of important concepts or in some way structuring their search for that information is the intent of using an *information index.* The extent to which the index is used depends on students' differential abilities, the importance of the information, and the depth of understanding required.

Two ways are suggested for teachers to slice the demands of the learning task using the information index. The first method is to intersperse questions throughout the text. Students can be directed to lightly mark question numbers at the appropriate places in the text chapter. In this way questions can be dealt with at the time they are encountered during the reading, thus slicing the search for the information. For some teachers this marking of questions may also serve as a preliminary step to their eventual development and use of study guides (Chapter 10).

A second method of providing the information index is to provide an actual informational key to the questions. Questions may be keyed to the page, section, paragraph, and/or sentence where students may find the appropriate answer or the information on which the answer is based. This type of information is frequently provided by content teachers when they use study guides with their students. This is an example of the type of information index provided:

What were the causes of the Revolutionary War? (122:2)

In this case the students are keyed to the page and paragraph numbers.

Similarly, structured internet search assignments provide scaffolding for students to explore questions and topics.

You can find a vast array of useful lesson plans in language arts and English at the ReadWriteThink site supported by the International Reading Association and National Council of Teachers of English (http://www.readwritethink. org/lessons/lesson_view.asp?id=1042). Resources supporting science lesson planning keyed to science standards can be found at Science Net Links: http:// www.sciencenetlinks.com. For social studies, the Smithsonian site includes video clips, cultural histories, and other resources for unit and lesson planning: http://www.smithsonianeducation.org.

MINI PROJECTS

1. Use the "Matter and Energy in the Web of Life" text passage on the website and the lesson planning guidelines in this chapter to design a lesson.
   A. Write two learning objectives for a group of secondary students in a wellness class.
   B. Create a possible set induction activity.
   C. Design a learning activity for the lesson.
   D. Brainstorm additional resources and materials for the lesson.
   E. Brainstorm how you would evaluate students' learning with respect to this material.

2. Meet with colleagues from core and elective content areas to design an integrated, thematic unit.

3. Use planning modifications, such as slicing the task, to accommodate student differences for a lesson in your content area.

4. Develop a list of supplementary materials (including internet material) that you might be able to use to augment or replace a chapter from a textbook in your content area.

5. Use the Internet to explore state performance and curriculum standards in your content area.

RECOMMENDED WEBSITES

- o Blendspace.com—An excellent platform for lesson construction
- o The Teaching Channel—A resource with multiple lesson and unit classroom examples
- o ReadWriteThink—A rich collection of lesson and unit plans across content areas
- o WordPress.com—A great blog and video sharing site

WEBSITE ACTIVITY

Go to the website for Chapter 5 activities.

Literature

VIGNETTE

Setting

Tenth-grade students, Jacob Williams, Daniella Banks and Ashea Baker, along with the rest of their literature circle have just finished reading the novel, *Moon at Nine* by author Deborah Ellis. Despite the somewhat controversial topic, Ms. Moffitt, their English teacher knows it is an important book for them to experience. Set in Iran, this semi-biographical novel tells the story of teenage girls Sadira and Farrin who are persecuted and imprisoned for being in love with each other. At the end of the novel, Farrin learns of Sadira's tragic fate while

© Lolostock/Shutterstock.com

she copes with the realization that she has been sold into marriage. The literature circle has been blogging about their reading on a site Ms. Moffitt has created for them. She reads their posts as they react to the ending of the book:

Jacob: I just… what?… I cant…I can't even form coherent sentences, honestly. I am so glad I finished this book. It was absolutely astounding. The ending is just… One side of me screams unfair, but another side screams fair. I love that they gave Farrin and Sadira a final moment I suppose… I truly hoped they had that moment in real life… I would hope she did… Some people don't.

Daniella: I agree with Jacob. I'm mind blown at the ending of this book. I'm still trying to wrap my head around it. This was such a good read. I can't remember the last time I actually picked up a book and enjoyed reading it. Farrin really progressed as a character, and I just wish we could have answers to all of the unanswered questions!

Ashea: I really liked how they put in the part about them "meeting" at the moon at 9 every night, and I loved how that was the title. And Farrin and Sadira being able to admit their love for one another was as good as it could possibly get, but I wish there was more for them. I just could not believe that being in love with someone of the same gender as you can get you killed or indefinitely damned. But the ways these people were punished not only disgusted and disturbed me, but made me feel so ashamed that no one has stood up and corrected this matter.

The Lesson

After reading their posts, Ms. Moffitt decides that the students need to have the opportunity in class to work through some of their responses to this very moving book. She decides to have the students create a Body Biography for a character of their choice. Ms. Moffitt knows that this response strategy will provide her with another way to gauge the students' comprehension of the text, but more importantly, it gives the group the opportunity to collaborate in a creative and meaningful way. The students select the character of Farrin. As Ms. Moffitt suspects will happen, the students use rich imagery, meaningful quotes and symbols to represent Farrin's life and struggles throughout the novel. As the students' explain their work, Ms. Moffitt reflects on how effective the combination of a thought-provoking novel, the blog and the chance to creatively reflect on their reading has engaged her students – even Jacob, who although an excellent student had admitted he hates to read.

Now that you have had a chance to consider this lesson, write down your thoughts on the following questions:

1. What are the good points about the lesson?
2. What are the weak points about the lesson?
3. What, if anything, would you change about the lesson?

RATIONALE FOR USING LITERATURE IN THE CONTENT AREAS

Author Jamaica Kincaid grew up on the tiny island of Antigua, governed by British rule. Her memories of the library where she spent so much time recalled the quiet, reflective power of reading a good book.

> If you saw the old library, situated as it was, in a big, old wooden building painted a shade of yellow that is beautiful to people like me, with its wide veranda, its big, always open windows, its rows and rows of shelves filled with books, its beautiful wooden tables and chairs for sitting and reading, if you could hear the sound of its quietness (for the quiet in this library was a sound in itself), the smell of the sea (which was a stone's throw away), the heat of the sun (no building could protect us from that), the beauty of us sitting there like communicants at an altar, taking in, again and again, the fairy tale of how we met you, your right to do the things you did, how beautiful you were, are, and always will be; if you could see all of that in just one glimpse, you would see why my heart would break at the dung heap that now passes for a library in Antigua. (Kincaid, 1988, pp. 42–43)

By 1974, the library was damaged in an earthquake and left unrepaired for over a decade with the mocking sign "repairs are pending" (Kincaid, 1988, p. 42). In her book, A Small Place, Jamaica Kincaid vividly charts the tensions between native Antiguans, the colonial British, and the more recent Antiguan independence. In truth, Kincaid's book is a multicultural treatise on the complexities of the aftermath of imperial rule, racism, and pride. But the library provided the chance to explore a vast array of books, although they recounted the lives of whites rather than Antigua natives. Nevertheless, as a little girl, Kincaid gravitated toward the lyrical, captivating world of a good book. She said, "I stole many books from this library. I didn't mean to steal the books, really; it's just that once I had read a book I couldn't bear to part with it." (Kincaid, 1988, p. 45)

Unfortunately, many content area teachers assume that librarians, media specialists, and English teachers should be the ones to acquaint students with powerful fiction books beyond the required texts in social studies, science, mathematics, and elective areas. Yet the field of young adult literature is a rich treasure trove of books that can illuminate concepts about endangered species like Mr. Cousteau's turtles or the flight of a Nigerian family under a military coup (Bean & Harper, 2011; Naidoo, 2000).

152

In any content area it is possible to find young adult literature that enriches textbook readings and course concepts. Your task as a content teacher is to become familiar with this rich treasure trove of literature, understand how to survey students' attitudes and interests, and learn about various strategies you can use to link literature and textbook reading. This may sound like a daunting task, but it is really a matter of starting modestly by reading at least one young adult novel keyed to your particular field. Since most of these novels are relatively short, in the range of 125 pages, you may find this process to be every bit as enjoyable as reading the latest adult fiction bestseller.

Indeed, in the last few years, contemporary young adult realistic fiction has blossomed with a more inclusive collection of titles portraying LGBTQQ (lesbian, gay, bisexual, transgender, queer, questioning)(Blackburn, Clark & Nemeth, 2015). Titles that represent teens with disabilities also expanded in number and encompassed physical and mental disabilities (Koss & Teale, 2009). Yet, as scholar Alfred Tatum (2015) writes, "Social issues in the United States still lead to fears and awkward silencing in a nation still trying to come to discover and rediscover itself. These fears also lead to an endorsed silencing by adults who limit opportunities for students to discover themselves as they negotiate their identities within the milieu of social issues" (p. 539).

In addition to reading young adult literature keyed to your field of study, it is imperative that you provide students with the opportunities to explore both their own identities and social issues as advocated by Tatum. One of the ways that makes it possible to do this is by becoming familiar with the increasingly rich array of multicultural and global literature. The literary canon of assigned readings in English has been very resistant to change. In this chapter we will introduce some of the growing collection of multicultural young adult literature that can be used in content area teaching.

LEARNING OBJECTIVES

o   Use attitude and interest inventories to survey students' reading attitudes and interests in your content area.
o   Select and use tradebooks linked to units of instruction in your content area.
o   Implement a sustained silent-reading program.
o   Use sources of the tradebooks to locate and review books you plan to use in your content area.
o   Create a plan for further development of your knowledge about tradebooks you can use in your discipline.

GRAPHIC ORGANIZER

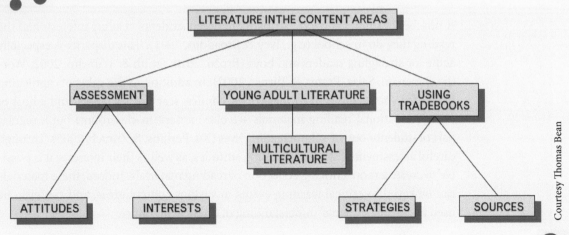

Courtesy Thomas Bean

ASSESSMENT OF READING ATTITUDES AND INTERESTS

Attitudes

Attitudes may be defined as those feelings that cause a reader to approach or avoid a reading situation. Attitudes toward reading are shaped by a variety of factors. For example, reading attitudes are undoubtedly the result of beliefs finely tuned by culture. The motivation to read is multi-faceted and highly individualistic.

In a large-scale survey of 18,185 grade 1 through 6 students' attitudes toward academic and recreational reading, McKenna, Kear, and Ellsworth (1995) noted that reading attitudes declined steadily. By the time students were in sixth grade, they cared little for academic or recreational reading. Unfortunately, the trends described in the 1990's still hold trues today. McKenna and colleagues recently reviewed trends in adolescent reading motivation. They found that according to the most recent recent National Assessment of Educational Progress (NAEP) survey, 32% of eighth graders reported "never or hardly ever" reading for fun. These measures among others indicate that declines in voluntary pleasure-reading parallel declines in national assessment performance on a variety of reading tasks Thus, fostering students' engagement in both academic and recreational reading is extremely important for their future success.

Guthrie and Wigfield (2000) pointed to research indicating that students learn more content from interesting texts. Providing interesting texts in a lesson or unit helps bridge the gap between students' pre-existing interests and new content. In addition to being aware of students' attitudes toward interesting texts, it is important to include in the classroom books that relate to their various cultures. Contemporary multicultural young adult literature has the power to change students' attitudes toward reading for pleasure, but the visibility of this literature in classrooms is all too rare (Bean, 2000).

A number of studies show the disparity between students' reading interests and the reading they do in school (e.g., Ivey & Broaddus, 2001). This disparity is especially acute for struggling readers and boys (Brozo, 2010; Smith & Wilhelm, 2002; Worthy, Patterson, Salas, Prater, & Turner, 2002). In addition to the value of captivating novels for young adults, teen magazines, comics, scary series books, and a host of other recreational reading materials are often absent in classrooms but a regular part of students' out-of-school reading lives (Xu, Perkins, & Zunich, 2005). Through careful assessment of students' reading attitudes, as well as their interests, it is possible to create a more enticing collection of reading materials. Indeed, these materials can be keyed to critical learning events in various content areas, and can even be used to expand students' understanding of classical literature.

ASSESSMENT. Since attitudes are a critical factor in using trade books in content classrooms to develop a lifelong love of reading, you need to know how to assess students' attitudes toward reading. There are a number of methods for assessing reading attitudes, including personal interviews, autobiographies, and behavior checklists. The most common method is the self-report questionnaire. The reading attitude survey in Figure 7.1 was developed for use with middle and secondary school students.

This attitude survey may be used as a pre/posttest for determining the affective impact of programs. It is also possible to look at specific areas of reading attitude. For example, in the Baldwin, Johnson and Peer (BJP) Survey in Figure 7.1:

> Items 1, 7, 12 = Attitude toward libraries
> Items 4, 6, 16, 19 = Reading self-concept
> Other items = General attitude toward reading

It is standard procedure for individual scores to be recorded for purposes of counseling students with bad attitudes. We recommend that this not be done. Students with negative attitudes toward reading are not necessarily unintelligent. As a consequence, if they have any reason to think that they will be singled out and/or questioned because of their negative attitudes, they will take the only intelligent option and lie on the survey. The technical name for this is ***response bias***, writing down what one believes the examiner wants rather than what the test taker really believes. A second reason for not generating individual scores is that students whose attitudes toward books and reading are so bad that they need counseling are painfully conspicuous most of the time, and no test is needed to identify them. On the other hand, trying to determine whether or not a program has created a positive change in group attitudes requires some objective measure. Therefore, we recommend that attitude surveys be anonymous and that class, grade, and school averages be used to assess groups rather than individuals. Additionally, once data have been gathered concerning the attitudes of students, attention should be given to promoting reading related to content areas.

FIGURE 7.1

BJP MIDDLE/SECONDARY READING ATTITUDE SURVEY* **Directions:** This survey tells how you feel about reading and books. The survey is not a test, and it is anonymous. It will not affect your grades or progress in school, but it will help your school to create better programs. Answer as honestly as you can by checking the term or terms that tell how you feel about each statement.	Strongly Agree	Agree	Strongly Disagree	Disagree
1. Library books are dull.				
2. Reading is a waste of time.				
3. Reading is one of my hobbies.				
4. I believe I am a better reader than most other students in my grade.				
5. Reading is almost always boring.				
6. Sometimes I think kids younger than I am read better than I do.				
7. I enjoy going to the library for books.				
8. I can read as well as most students who are a year older than I am.				
9. I don't have enough time to read books.				
10. I believe that I am a poor reader.				
11. I would like to belong to a book club.				
12. I like to take library books home.				
13. Teachers want me to read too much.				
14. You can't learn much from reading.				
15. Books can help us to understand other people.				
16. I almost always get As and Bs in reading and English.				
17. I like to have time to read in class.				
18. Reading gets boring after about ten minutes.				
19. Sometimes I get bad grades in reading and English.				
20. I like to read before I go to bed.				

Scoring: The positive items are 3, 4, 7, 8, 11, 12, 15, 16, 17, 20. Give four points for an *SA*, three points for an *A*, two points for a *D*, and one point for an *SD*. For the negative items, 1, 2, 5, 6, 9, 10, 13, 14, 18, 19, score four points for an *SD*, three for a *D*, two for an *A*, and one for *SA*. Scores can range from 20 to 80.

60–80 = Good
40–59 = Fair
20–39 = Poor

*The survey may be reproduced by individual teachers for noncommercial purposes. From Educational Development Corporation by R. Scott Baldwin, Dale Johnson, & Gary G. Peer. Copyright © 1980 by Educational Development Corporation. Reprinted by permission.

Interests

Reading **interests** are generally defined as the material students actually select to read, while **reading preferences** indicate what they might like to read (Galda, Ash, & Cullinan, 2000). Reading interests are complicated as they are both individualistic and strongly influenced by sociocultural norms and expectations. Knowing something about your students' interests can help you select reading material that will build on this important aspect of their developing identities.

Students naturally prefer to engage in activities that are likely to boost feelings of competence, autonomy, and relatedness to others. In addition, reading interests that develop and endure come from feelings of enjoyment and involvement. Recent studies of adolescent males and females reveal their awareness of the complexity of their lives and the degree to which media and some novels oversimplify teen identity (Bean & Harper, 2007; Brozo, Walter, & Placker, 2002; Harper, 2000; Moje 2000). These studies show a level of self-awareness that allows for diverse in- and out-of-school interests, as well as the need to critique simplistic portrayals of gender and teen life. Thus, rather than expecting a homogenization of teen interests, we can expect a good deal of individual diversity within any content area classroom.

ASSESSMENT. The most useful type of interest assessment is one that permits the teacher to match specific interests with specific materials. However, the general-interest inventory is the most common type of interest assessment (see Figure 7.2).

It is possible to create interest inventories with varying degrees of specificity; for instance, sports can be subclassified into baseball, basketball, football, tennis, curling, and so on. Baseball could be subdivided into fiction stories, nonfiction books about pitching or hitting, and so on. In much the same manner it is possible to create an interest inventory for a specific content area. This type of inventory can provide information about group interests as well as guide outside reading for individuals. The U.S. history interest inventory shown in Figure 7.3 is merely one example in an endless chain of possibilities.

FIGURE 7.2
General Interest Inventory

Directions: The purpose of this inventory is to find out what kinds of things you and your classmates are interested in reading. After every topic there is a blank space. On each space give a grade of A, B, C, D, or F based on how much you would like to read about the topic.

An A means: It's wonderful; I love it! An F means: It's terrible; take the topic away and bury it, quick!

Sports _____	Animals _____	History _____
Science Fiction _____	Fantasy _____	Poetry _____
Folklore _____	Romance _____	Family Life _____
Cars _____	Adventure _____	Plays _____
Humor _____	Mystery _____	Human Drama _____
War _____	The Arts _____	Mathematics _____
Supernatural _____	Foreign Lands _____	Health Sciences _____
Science _____		

Teachers can modify the interest inventory in Figure 7.3 to fit the needs of their teaching objectives. For instance, students might rank each general topic area (e.g., The Colonial Period) 1, 2, 3, 4 instead of ranking all topics at once. This may enable teachers to find appropriate material for each general topic area as it is encountered.

YOUNG ADULT LITERATURE

A cartoon by artist Randy Glasbergen depicts two teachers standing in front of a bank of computers. One, with his arms full of texts says to the other, "*I'm taking an innovative approach to teaching this semester. I'm using books!* While we advocate for the importance of technology in education, so too do we advocate for encouraging students to become voracious readers.

Developing a lifelong love of reading is the result of many influences. Family, friends, and teachers all play a role in making reading pleasurable or something to be avoided at all costs. The more you become familiar with contemporary young adult literature the more you can create units that integrate this captivating medium.

Directions: Everyone in your class is going to be doing some outside reading related to American history. The purpose of this inventory is to help you find books that are actually interesting to *you*. After every topic there is a blank space. On the space next to the topic you would *most* like to read about, put a 1. Place a 2 on the space for your next choice. Place a 3 on the third best choice, and so on until you have evaluated every topic. Do *NOT* use any number more than once.

The Colonial Period (1600–1760)
        Biography _____
        Human Drama _____
        Family Life _____
        Freedom and Justice _____
The Revolutionary War Era (1760–1785)
        Biography _____
        Politics _____
        War _____
The Civil War Era (1850–1876)
        Slavery _____
        Famous Battles _____
        Politics _____
        Biography _____
        Human Drama _____
Western and Frontier Life
        Pioneers _____
        Native Americans _____
        Tales of the Wild West _____
World War II (1939–1945)
        Battles in the Pacific _____
        Military Planes _____
        The War in Europe _____
        Atomic Weapons _____
        Freedom and Justice _____
Post World War II America
        Civil Rights _____
        Women's Liberation _____
        Vietnam War _____
        The Presidency _____
        Biographies of African Americans _____

Case studies of adolescents' reading habits, especially boys, suggest they spend little of their leisure time reading literature (Smith & Wilhelm, 2002; 2006). However, other studies such as Elizabeth Moje and colleagues work (2010) suggest that adolescents do read outside of school, but they may not see the connection, and thus the value, of in-school literacies. As a content area teacher, you can change this apathy or avoidance of young adult literature by becoming personally familiar with at least a small portion of the vast array of books that can be linked to your units and lessons. If you think of adolescents through the lens of your own adolescent experience and the filter of young adult literature from your teen and preteen years, this will limit your horizons. Although we are not saying you should ignore this older literature, we do strongly advocate getting to know the newer young adult authors who portray multicultural characters, actions, and events that more closely mirror those of our students.

The shift toward greater realism in young adult literature began with S. E. Hinton's (1967) *The Outsiders,* written when she was 16. This novel realistically portrayed the passages and transitions adolescents go through as they struggle to find their own identity amidst conflicting peer and family pressures. Young adult literature helps adolescents cope with the dissonance between the ideal and real in daily life by its power to vicariously transport the reader into the lives and times of fictional characters struggling with familiar problems. In more recent times increasingly complex female and multicultural characters emerged. Hispanic authors like Gary Soto offered a positive, insider's view of life in the barrio. Asian American literature explored racial discrimination and oppression. The Vietnam war has been widely chronicled in powerful young adult novels like Walter Dean Myers' (1988) *Fallen Angels.* Myers' novel is a poignant account of two young African American soldiers immersed in the rice paddy skirmishes that robbed their adolescence and forever changed their lives.

More recently, authors have addressed such issues as LGBTQQ (lesbian, gay, bisexual, transgender, queer, questioning) rights, discrimination and persecution such as in the compelling book, *Moon at Nine* (2014) featured in our opening vignette.

Unlike textbooks that present facts to be considered and used in solving problems in science or math, discussing policies in history, or reading the notes of a scale in music, fiction by its nature propels students into high level interpretive thinking. Indeed, critical literacy, by definition, asks readers to carefully examine how characters cope with power relations and, in particular, the way social and cultural forces shape their lives (Janks, 2013). Critical literacy moves the reader beyond response (Rosenblatt, 1978) to examine novels as social constructions that position characters in various ways in terms of gender, ethnicity, class, and race (Bean & Moni, 2003; Stevens & Bean, 2007; Vasquez, Tate & Harste, 2013). Students are encouraged to examine gaps and silences wherein some characters have strong voices and power and others are left by the wayside. Later in this chapter we explore some of the questions you may want to have students explore as you link young adult literature and content area teaching.

What exactly is *young adult literature*? Young adult literature can be defined as literary works (usually fiction but not always) intended for readers between the ages of 12 and 18 (Bean & Harper, 2011). Young adult literature encompasses a wide range of genres including mystery, adventure, science fiction, romance, supernatural, fantasy, sports, humor, and historical fiction. Typical themes revolve around family relationships, rites of passage, alienation, friends and society, death, disabilities, drugs and alcohol, and sexual relationships. A number of powerful novels explore how to define oneself outside the family, coping with the reality that parents are less than perfect, carving out one's own set of moral, ethical, religious, and political principles, developing positive healthy relationships, and projecting possible futures and career choices (Stover & Tway, 1992). For example, Woodson's (2002) powerful novel, *Hush*, explores the life of an African American teenage girl uprooted from her familiar home when her Dad is placed in a witness protection program.

In Carl Deuker's (2007) *Gym Candy*, high school football star Mick Johnson plunges into the world of anabolic steroids to boost his performance on the field. This novel, along with many of Mike Lupica's works, can be used in the health sciences to raise awareness of the effects of performance-enhancing drugs. A wide array of young adult novels span core content areas like mathematics, science, and social studies.

Unfortunately, very few content teachers seem to use or know much about young adult literature. Rather, they often see all literature as the English teacher's exclusive domain and responsibility. Worse still, many teachers have never read a young adult novel, let alone a contemporary young adult novel.

The purpose of using young adult literature in your content area is to enhance students' content learning while also providing the opportunity to engage with texts relevant to their lives. This is a different focus from the English teacher's interest in appreciation and analysis of literature. You can focus on locating those books best keyed to concepts and issues in your course. For example, a history teacher could enrich a unit on slavery with Warner's (1976) diary account, *From Slave to Abolitionist: The Life of William Wells Brown*. This poignant book propels the reader into the day-to-day trials of William Wells Brown, a young slave who eventually escapes his tormentors to become a significant abolitionist writer in the 1850s. His writing far surpasses that of any textbook in its ability to grab the attention of young readers.

Similarly, young adult novels like *1/2986: The Climate Fiction Saga* (Wendeberg, 2014) confronts science-related issues like global climate change. Novels like *Pandemic* (Ventresca, 2014) take up viruses and epidemics, while *A Girl Named Digit* (Monaghan, 2013) tells the story of a self-described math geek and daughter of a math professor who unknowingly cracks a terrorist group's number sequence. These titles offer just a glimpse into a rich array of choices to expand students' understanding of content area concepts, particularly in the core subject areas of English, history, mathematics, and science. Locating useful booklists by topic and theme is relatively easy with online support, and we offer a selected list of trade-books by content area at the close of this chapter, to help you get started.

Developing a Youth Lens

In discussing and encouraging your students to read young adult literature, it is important to realize that adolescents are not a fixed or easily defined group. Thus, ideas of what "stereotypical" adolescents might read are not helpful in selecting YA literature. Nor are stereotypical interpretations of youth portrayed in YA literature. Scholar Robert Petrone and colleagues have recently introduced the notion of the youth lens (YL) when reading and discussing literature with adolescent protagonists. A youth lens is similar to other critical lens or frameworks used in the analysis of text, such as a feminist lens exploring the ways gender is represented, a Marxist lens studying depictions of class, or a postcolonial lens examining nationhood and race (Petrone, Sarigianides, & Lewis, 2015). These scholars build on research that rejects the idea of adolescence as a monolithic, universal experience. Instead, adolescents are seen as being individuals and the experiences of adolescence to be " contingent on and constituted through social arrangements and systems of reasoning available within particular moments and contexts" (p. 509). When viewed as a construct, essentializing the experiences of adolescents is avoided. Thus, when using a YL lens in reading and discussing YA literature, the teacher and students can resist stereotypical interpretations of adolescents. Instead they can ask questions such as:

o How does this text represent adolescent/ce?

o What role does the text play in reinforcing or subverting dominant ideas about adolescence (p. 511)

Petrone and colleagues (2015) use Suzanne Collins' wildly popular *Hunger Games* series to explore how Katniss and other youth characters are portrayed and positioned in relation to the adults in the novels. In their analysis using a youth lens, they posit that Katniss and the other teens in the story have shifting identities based on their context. For example, in her home and in District 12, Katniss is autonomous and assumes adult responsibilities. However, when in the Capitol (including in the actual Games) Katniss and the others are very much dependent on adults, and thus they assume roles and behaviors more typical of adolescents. The researchers go on to explain how *The Hunger Games* " portray conventional adolescence as a strategically performed identity necessary for youth survival in public and political contexts where youth must rely on adults in positions of power" (p. 519).

As you begin to create your own collection of YA texts, we encourage you to explore using a youth lens to read within and beyond texts with your students.

Creating a Classroom Library

Tradebooks must survive on the open market. These are the books you find at popular bookstores, where there is usually a section on young adult literature. Since there is no perfect list of tradebooks to be used with every content area, as a teacher you need to explore books keyed to your area, and develop a classroom library (Donelson & Nilsen, 2008). Given the labor-intensive requirements of creating a classroom library, we suggest you start small by getting to know one or two contemporary young adult novels that relate to one or two topics in your content teaching. In addition, online resources like the American Library Association, journals like *The ALAN Review* (National Council of Teacher of English) and the *Journal of Adolescent & Adult Literacy* (International Literacy Association), as well as Amazon. com and other online print and eBook sources, make finding contemporary young adult lists manageable. We include an annotated bibliography of tradebooks keyed to various content areas at the end of the chapter, but it is important to realize that the list is one we created. You need to develop your own unique collection of novels, magazines, and enjoyable reading material that expands on textbook and class concepts. For example, some authorities on using literature in classrooms recommend creating book clusters (Savage, 1994). A book cluster is a graphic organizer with the title of a unit like sharks and a listing of tradebooks that relate to the unit. Often, the school librarian and/or media specialist can be helpful in suggesting books to use with your proposed unit. In addition, websites like the one offered by the American Library Association, as well as international sites, can be helpful.

Multicultural and Global Literature

One of the most exciting dimensions of young adult literature is the growing number of multicultural and global literature portraying characters' experiences from a bicultural perspective (Hadaway & McKenna, 2007). Books about African Americans, Asian Americans, Native Americans, Hispanics, Pacific Islanders, and the disabled fit within this category. The best of this body of literature affords an opportunity for students to see themselves in the books they read, provided the multicultural literature selected portrays characters in a culturally authentic fashion.

For example, one of Soto's now classic novels, *Buried Onions* (Soto, 1997), charts the struggles of Eddie at 19, trying to find a way out of his Fresno barrio. Throughout the novel, Eddie faces ethical dilemmas that form the basis for powerful classroom discussion and writing (Bean & Rigoni, 2000). We have used this novel in high school Social Studies to engage students in journaling with university graduate students about how they would handle Eddie's problems with his relatives and the police. The novel lends itself to social studies classrooms and issues of citizenship and social justice. In addition, guidance classes might center discussion on the gang issues dealt with in the novel. The writing is lyrical, and peppered with Spanish phrases. Consistent with many other Soto novels, this one includes a glossary of Spanish terms.

In a sequel to *Buried Onions,* entitled *The Afterlife* (Soto, 2003), Chuy, Eddie's cousin in *Buried Onions,* is murdered early in the novel at a high school dance, leaving him to wander Fresno as a ghost. This novel and others offer sites for exploring the social construction of adolescents, often treated as invisible in larger society (Bean & Harper, 2004). Multicultural literature is typically outside the accepted canon of traditional required reading that includes books such as *The Scarlet Letter* and Shakespeare's writing. Yet, all students "have the right to see themselves in what and how we teach" (Gray, 2003, p. 82). Heriberto Godina (1996) recounted his struggles as a teacher to establish a multicultural literature strand at his middle school. He was able, through the use of his own funds and a desire to move beyond one-shot multicultural food days, to engage students in his English classes in the reading and discussion of Rudolfo Anaya's (1972) *Bless Me Ultima.* "Students began to see reflections of themselves in text, and this provided them with a familiar path for thinking critically and scaffolded their writing." (p. 546) Godina makes a persuasive argument for integrating classical, widely accepted canonical literature, and multicultural literature.

More recently, author Elizabeth Wein (2015) explores issues of racial disparity in her book, *White Dove, Black Raven.* Emilia and Teo's lives changed in a fiery, terrifying instant when a bird strike brought down the plane their stunt pilot mothers were flying. Teo's mother died immediately, but Em's survived, determined to raise Teo according to his late mother's wishes -- in a place where he won't be discriminated against because of the color of his skin. However, in 1930s America, they are not sure such a place exists.

In a very powerful classroom project in Corpus Christi, Texas, aimed at integrating multicultural literature and community talents, Brozo, Valerio, and Salazar (1996) also used *Bless Me Ultima* as a basis for exploring cross-cultural approaches to healing. By using take-home learning packets that involved making herbal tea, they were able to bring parents into the reading and discussion of the novel. This community connection made the novel's setting in south Texas come alive for students and families.

As Godina (1996) and Brozo et al. (1996) found, when students see themselves reflected in their reading, they view the content classroom as a place of direct relevance to their lives. Reading at the secondary level, as it has so often been described in literacy autobiographies, is no longer work or a task to complete. Rather, reading has powerful, personal meaning for adolescents' identity development.

Nieto (2003) argues that, to effectively use multicultural literature in the classroom, teachers must become multicultural themselves. The best of multicultural literature confronts racism, bias, and oppression head on. Thus, social issues are a good starting point for selecting multicultural literature. Students from diverse cultures gain pride in their ethnic origins when they see a character overcome obstacles to succeed. They gain a complex view of American and world societies and of issues of social justice.

For example, Native American author Sherman Alexie's (2007) *The Absolutely True Diary of a Part-Time Indian* confronts racism head on. Junior, the main character, comments candidly on the harsh realities of his Washington state reservation life and his decision to attend a white school some distance from his reservation home. Basketball provides a way into the social network of Junior's new school and, despite serious health problems as a child, he is a skilled player. Part autobiography, part fiction, this multimodal novel includes Junior's doodles and the shocking reality in his reservation school that one of his textbooks, now badly out of date, was the same text his mother had with her name still in it. The novel would be a useful addition to social studies content, along with the Joseph Bruchac's (2006) *Geronimo*.

What constitutes good multicultural literature? A number of writers have wrestled with this issue. You should try to select books that sensitively and accurately depict characters. For example, in Asian-Pacific young adult literature, authors should go beyond stereotypes, avoid historical distortions or omissions, avoid the "super minority" view, and reflect the changing status of women (Aoki, 1993, p. 122). Additionally, young adult literature should shun tokenism where characters from divergent cultures are mere window dressing in a story (Stover & Tway, 1992). Essentially, the novels you select should avoid the danger of the single story. That is, that one story or experience speaks to the experiences of everyone in the group. We also need to acknowledge that education, including content area reading is never neutral, and that care must be taken to not perpetuate social structures such as institutionalized racism or heteronormativity. Novels should give the reader an honest, accurate portrayal of the human condition experienced by students from various cultures. For example, Ashley Hope Perez' (2015) *Out of Darkness* is loosely based on a school explosion that took place in New London, Texas in 1937. This is the story of two teenagers: Naomi, who is Mexican, and Wash, who is black, and their dealings with race, segregation, love, and forces beyond their control that hold the power to destroy. This type of historical fiction helps personalize history for students, and it helps them see the cause-and-effect structure of history. In contrast, textbooks present a profusion of objectively documented facts that lose the flavor of the human experience. The best young adult literature is historically accurate, but human drama is at the forefront rather than places and dates.

For example, Donald Gallo's (2007) *First Crossing: Stories About Teen Immigrants* features short stories about Mexican, Chinese, and other displaced groups. These compelling stories can illuminate nonfiction accounts of diasporas in history.

Global literature acknowledges the increasingly permeable boundaries that define teens' social networks and affiliations, often spanning wide-ranging geographic areas (McLean, 2010). For example, Baer and Glasgow (2010) offer an excellent bibliography of young adult literature, depicting Muslim cultures along with Socratic and process drama teaching approaches. Paired with nonfiction history texts, this collection of compelling young adult literature balances the simplistic and often stereotypical media accounts of this diverse group. For example, Randa Abdell-Fatah addresses the often misunderstood practice of Muslim women wearing a hijab or headscarf in *Does My Head Look Big in This?* (2007). Sixteen-year-old Amal makes the decision to start wearing the hijab full- time and everyone has a reaction. Her parents, her teachers, her friends, people on the street. But she stands by her decision to embrace her faith and all that it is, even if it does make her a little different from everyone else. She handles the taunts of "towel head," the prejudice of her classmates while still being true to her beliefs. Brilliantly funny and poignant, Randa Abdel-Fattah's debut novel will resonate with many teenage readers, no matter what their personal beliefs may be. In addition to some of the titles discussed here The International Literacy Association website featuring Notable Books for a Global Society offers a list of K–12 selections (www.clrsig.org)

Once you have browsed sources of young adult and multicultural young adult literature, have found some that relate to topics in your discipline, and have taken the time to read a few books, how can you make these books an integral part of your classroom teaching? In the section that follows we offer a few ideas for using literature across the various content fields.

USING TRADEBOOKS

Tradebooks offer one of the best ways to delve into other cultures or to see how other people cope with the problems inherent in being a young adult. A good novel can illuminate otherwise rote facts in history, science, mathematics, and the elective fields of art, music, physical education, health, agriculture, industrial arts, and a variety of other curricular areas. You really can't afford to not tap this rich resource in your content teaching. The chance to influence students' lifelong love of reading, as well as the potential to improve their concept understanding and critical reading in your subject, is too important a task to leave exclusively to the adopted textbook.

Nonfiction tradebooks can be used to explore text-based topics and as a means to engage students in synthesizing ideas from diverse sources. The librarian is key to locating a good collection of nonfiction tradebooks to support any unit you are working on. In addition, local district resources and the Internet offer resources students can learn to explore independently. For example, in a literature response project, 9th-grade students in English visited the Las Vegas Indian Center and consulted the Internet to learn more about Navajo burial practices. They then used this information to critique and write about the authenticity of Navajo burial traditions described in a novel they were reading and discussing (Bean, Valerio, Money Senior, & White, 1999). Additionally, contemporary young adult literature like Joseph Bruchac's (2006) *Geronimo* treats the capture and imprisonment of the Apache from an insider's point of view that counters earlier accounts viewing Native Americans as savages. Powerful young adult novels like this one can be integrated with content area classes in social studies to give your students a more in-depth understanding of history.

Nonfiction tradebooks and Internet resources are often informative, visually attractive, lively, and up-to-date. Although students may be unaccustomed to reading across multiple sources, taking notes, and synthesizing information, they are unlikely to learn these crucial skills without practice. Indeed, as they move into college and work, these will prove to be essential skills for success. Palmer and Stewart (1997) emphasize the need for teacher guidance in how to read, retrieve, and restructure information in nonfiction tradebooks and other sources.

Reading Aloud to Students

Most contemporary young adult novels lend themselves to reading aloud (Serafini, 2015). For example, Marie Lee's (1997) novel, *Necessary Roughness,* follows main character, Chan Kim, from a cohesive, Korean American community in Los Angeles to a new school in rural Minnesota. Chan plays football and endures overt and sometimes violent discrimination from his teammates and others. The novel should be preceded by a cultural history of Korean immigration patterns to the United States because Chan's father in the novel represents the old world and its norms. Chan tries hard to assimilate, caught between his father's old ways and his teammates' rancor. Marie Lee's writing flows, and the novel's vivid scenes and surprise ending generate vibrant classroom discussion.

Similarly, Genaro Gonzalez's (2009) young adult novel, *A So-Called Vacation,* follows brothers Gabriel and Gustavo on a powerful journey from their comfortable Rio Grande Valley home in Texas to go with their father to spend the summer in a California migrant camp. Their father believes this contemporary rite of passage will make them more attuned to his family's history and culture. This is another novel that works well with social studies nonfiction content on the San Joaquin Valley and migrant workers.

Short-story collections also offer excellent narratives for reading aloud. For example, Donald Gallo's (2004) *First Crossings: Stories about Teen Immigrants* can be read aloud and serve as a springboard to students' recounting, in writing or multimedia, their own experiences with immigration or a move to a new home and school. In addition, nonfiction accounts of adolescents living in war zones like *Thura's Diary* (Al-Windawi, 2004) provide an adolescent insider's look at life in the Middle East. These shorter collections are ideal for reading aloud, but novels can also be subdivided into read-aloud sections.

We recommend starting modestly by identifying a unit where you can include a young adult tradebook novel of about 125 pages. In selecting a novel to read aloud, look for books that have rich, lyrical language. For example, in a unit on slavery Mary Lyons' (1992) *Letters from a Slave Girl: The Story of Harriet Jacobs* takes place in 1861 and vividly recounts Harriet's seven years of confinement in a relative's storeroom before gaining her freedom. The autobiographical letters that formed the basis for this story accurately portray the dialect of the time. At 158 pages *Letters from a Slave Girl: The Story of Harriet Jacobs* is an ideal read-aloud book.

Read the novel once and then skim through it to identify prediction points and places where you can stop reading at the end of a class period. Allow about 10 minutes at the end of a period to read from the novel and build on concepts introduced in the text and other class activities. With some young adult literature, videos can be located to further illuminate events of the time in compelling human terms. We recommend practicing your read aloud with a cassette recorder to ensure you are likely to capture students' attention. In addition, using prediction questions like "What do you predict will happen to Harriet? Will she gain her freedom?" Or, experience-based questions like "What would you do if you were Harriet?" involve students in the story plot and upcoming events. With some novels you can omit passages that you feel do not move the story forward.

Sustained Silent Reading (SSR)

Bard College literature professor and writer, Chinua Achebe, is a Nigerian Ibo villager and is now one of the most influential African intellectuals of our time (Winkler, 1994). The headmaster of his secondary school in Nigeria had a rule that after class, three days-per-week, students closed their textbooks and read novels, poetry, or anything for pleasure. Achebe attributed his love for literature to this period of his life. However, he did not see himself or other Africans portrayed in the stories he read, so he set out to become a writer. His first novel, *Things Fall Apart* (1958), has been translated into over fifty languages.

Sustained Silent Reading is a systematic program that establishes regular reading times for students. Its fundamental objective is to provide students with an opportunity to practice their reading skills using pleasurable content related materials. Sustained Silent Reading has the potential to immerse students in pleasurable reading where they achieve what psychologist Csikszentmihalyi (2002) calls flow. In a state of flow, reading is spontaneous and effortless, with the reader unaware of time passing. SSR has a positive impact on students' attitudes toward reading and their long-term interest in reading for pleasure.

There are two separate phases in SSR: (a) instructional readiness, and (b) the reading activity itself. The books can be selected to match a content unit like the slavery example in the read-aloud section discussed previously, or books may be self-selected by students if you have a well-stocked classroom library or helpful librarian.

INSTRUCTIONAL READINESS. Discuss SSR with students. Let them know how the activity will be carried out and why they are doing it. Emphasize that SSR is supposed to be a pleasurable activity. Tell them that they will not be graded or asked comprehension questions over what they read. It is important to ensure that students are actually reading during SSR and not simply napping with their eyes open. In an action research study at one urban high school, Fisher (2004) observed and charted the fact that fewer than 33 percent of the students participating in the SSR period were actually reading. As a solution to this problem, students in video classes developed a powerful commercial showing how SSR should look in practice. In addition, teachers engaged in professional development sessions to improve the success rate of SSR in their school, and a funded grant helped with purchasing contemporary young adult books like *Monster* (Myers, 1999). Following these changes to the program, follow-up data revealed that 88 percent of the students were actually reading during SSR.

Textbooks are seldom selected for pleasure reading, and comics, magazines, and newspapers lend themselves to picture-looking rather than reading. If you plan to use SSR to further expand students' understanding of events in history, science, or mathematics units, then you will need a well-stocked collection of young adult novels from which students can select. Your guidance in this area will be crucial, as students often have no idea what books match their interests within a content area like science or history. An interest inventory and your own familiarity with literature related to your field will be important preparatory steps before launching into SSR.

Literature Response Journals, Blogging, Podcasts, and Other Response Strategies

Both reading aloud to students and SSR lend themselves to some follow-up dialogue about the book or books being read. Indeed, students generally want to discuss powerful literature, and this is a good opportunity to build on content learning. **Literature Response Journals** ask students to reflect on their reading and share these reflections with the teacher, peers, or parents for further written dialogue (Bean, 2002). Literature Response Journals can be in print or online form. You can give students a few minutes after SSR or reading aloud to write in their journals about how they might handle the situation the main character is in or what they predict will happen next. We recommend collecting journals and responding to them for extra student points. You can collect a few journals each time or collect all of them depending on the schedule you establish with students.

Blogging

Alternatively, you can have students blog about the novel or selection they have been reading. *Blogging* (weblogs) consists of a closed site where students can write to each other about their reading (Johnson, 2010). Numerous programs exist to support literature response blogs across content areas. For example, *Classpress* (www.classpress.com) and other sites like *Edu-blogs* (http://edublogs.org) can be used for literature blogging. We have used Wordpress (www.wordpress.com) with a great deal of success and its selection of templates can be modified for your particular approach and needs.Students can include uploaded pictures, podcasts, videos, and other multimedia to support their assertions about a young adult novel, short story, or other genre.

In addition to student-generated literature response blogs, most young adult authors have their own blog sites where they discuss their latest works. Simply have students use a search engine with the author's name, and a wealth of information will be available.

Podcasts

Podcasts about young adult literature selections involve creating an audio response that can be uploaded to iTunes (Rozema, 2007). Essentially, this is a book talk in recorded and archived audio form. Various software programs provide support for recording a podcast, including Garageband available on Apple Mac computers. Students create scripts to guide their podcasts and, since they can broadcast via iTunes, students are creating content for a real audience. A good example of this form of podcast and a related lesson can be found at the ReadWriteThink website: (http://www.readwritethink.org/lessons/lesson_view.asp?id=901).

In addition to journal writing, blogging, or creating podcasts about tradebook selections, you can organize a panel discussion or debate that asks students to take a position the main character in a novel might advocate or oppose. Using overlapping Venn diagrams, you can compare and contrast cultural mores in multicultural literature. For example, in Crew's (1989) *Children of the River*, Sundara, a Cambodian teenager, struggles with the old ways of her relatives and the contrasting brashness of her Oregon classmates. A Venn diagram (Figure 7.4) consisting of two overlapping circles can be used to discuss those cultural norms that are distinct to Cambodian and European American cultures, and those norms that seem to overlap.

Venn Diagram for Children of the River

FIGURE 7.4

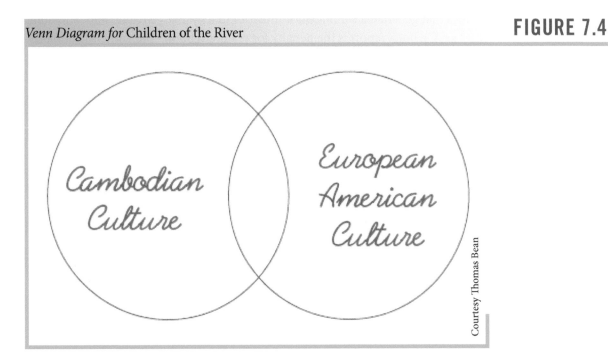

Courtesy Thomas Bean

Art, role-playing, music, and drama offer additional ways of responding to literature. For example in the novel, *Farewell to Manzanar* (Houston, 2012) Jeanne Wakatsuki and her family were sent to a Japanese internment camp at the beginning of WWII. Along with searchlight towers and armed guards, Manzanar ludicrously featured cheerleaders, Boy Scouts, sock hops, baton twirling lessons and a dance band called the Jive Bombers who would play any popular song except the nation's #1 hit: "Don't Fence Me In." Students could take up the roles in the novel and role-play characters in this painful part of American history. In so doing, they can critique the societal fears, predjudices and discrimination that led to the imprisonment of thousands of innocent Americans.

Students engaged in reading international multicultural literature like Gwynne's (2000) Australian-based aboriginal novel, *Nukkin ya*, can e-mail students in an Australian site to gain an insider's understanding of the sociocultural issues explored in international multicultural novels (Bean & Moni, 2003). Discussions of novels via e-mail offer a venue for production exploration of key events in a novel (Love, 2002). Or, as a contemporary alternative to writing, they can make a video with one student interviewing another or a panel of students about the book just read.

Finally, students can write authentic book reviews for online sites like Amazon. com that can be shared with other adolescent readers via discussion forum sites like Ning (www.ning.com), Google Groups (http://groups.google.com), and others. These sites offer real audiences for student writing, and they see their work in venues that generate a significant number of hits by a large readership. Someone once said "a book report is the penalty for reading a book." But authentic book reviews serve a real purpose and provide an audience that goes beyond the teacher as sole audience and judge. In addition to the response modes mentioned, a host of other responses to literature can enliven content area classrooms.

Book Clubs

Book clubs in the content classrooms offer another way to engage students in reading and sharing their interpretations of fiction and nonfiction tradebooks. Book clubs involve small groups of 3–5 students gathering to discuss a common reading (Gray, 2003; McMahon & Raphael, 1997). This sharing helps clarify areas of confusion in reading a novel or other selection, and it offers a good forum for collectively creating interpretations, critiques, and ownership of ideas.

Book clubs can be used in content fields like social studies to expand students' learning. For example, studying World War II through novels that view events from a Japanese perspective helps students evaluate textbook accounts critically. In addition, guided reading across multiple sources helps students learn how to synthesize information.

In a book club discussion in one of our classes, students enrolled in a content area literacy course read David Klass's award winning novel, *California Blue* (Klass, 1994). John, a high school student and the main character, finds a special butterfly while jogging in the woods in a logging area of Northern California. It turns out the butterfly is endangered and the livelihood of the town is about to be threatened because of John's discovery. About halfway through the novel, John longs to tell his Dad about his discovery but realizes there is great risk involved as his family also earns their living through logging. He feels very alone and decides to keep his discovery to himself, ultimately sharing it with his biology teacher and others he decides to trust. In order to prepare for book club discussion of this and other key episodes in the novel, students kept reading logs. Open-ended prompt questions helped students jog their thinking and writing about these episodes. For example, in this episode, students were asked to write and talk about how they would handle the situation where John wants to tell his father about his discovery the next day at breakfast. This prompt question generated a wide array of responses and personal stories about family styles. Some students said they would be secretive because of severe consequences in their families, and others indicated they would take the risk of being grounded or worse to stand for their beliefs. This particular novel is ideal for exploring a range of science and social science issues, particularly issues of citizenship and decision-making.

A host of new novels emerge each year that you can use to expand students' grasp of content area topics. For example, in a biology class considering the topic of infectious diseases, the young adult novel, *Code Orange* (Cooney, 2005) offers a suspenseful look at a potentially fatal virus that could wipe out the entire population of New York City. Roland Smith's (2005) novel, *Cryptid Hunters,* takes the reader on a fast-paced journey to the Congo. The novel is based on cryptozoology involving the search for and study of mysterious and sometimes mythical animals such as Sasquatch and the Loch Ness monster. Similarly, Nancy Werlin's (2004) award winning mystery, *Double Helix,* capitalizes on students' interest in CSI and other crime-detection television series. Your media specialist and librarian can help you create a print-rich environment in your particular content area that is likely to increase students' interest and engagement in both fiction and nonfiction selections.

When you decide to implement book clubs in your classroom, take some time to learn more about other teachers' experiences with this exciting addition to a content classroom. In the recommended reading section for this chapter, we offer selections to help you get started.

Readers Theater

Readers Theater involves a presentation of material that is read aloud in an expressive and dramatic fashion by two or more readers (Young & Vardell, 1993). Readers Theater offers students oral reading and group presentation practice and a chance to review concepts so they can effectively deliver a performance. To engage students in Readers Theater you need to:

a.   select passages from a novel that move the story forward;

b.   reproduce these sections;

c.   delete non-critical lines;

d.   divide the parts for each student to deliver;

e.   label reader parts with students' names; and,

f.   model the process of reading aloud in a dramatic fashion.

Dinner Party

Dinner Party is based on the idea that you could invite characters from a young adult novel (or other forms of text, including nonfiction) to your home for dinner and conversation (Vogt, 2002). The purpose of Dinner Party is for students to take on the role of specific characters in response to prompt questions you develop. Dinner Party is a postreading strategy, and assumes students have read the novel or at least the section being discussed. In addition, Dinner Party, consistent with contemporary theories of critical literacy, offers an opportunity for silenced characters in a novel to have a voice. The following steps will be helpful in guiding a Dinner Party discussion in your classroom:

a.   Decide which characters from the novel will be part of a panel discussion. About 5 to 6 characters, including some whose voices were silenced in the novel, will be about right. You may want to have multiple small groups engaged in Dinner Party discussion.

b.   Assign one of the group members the role of moderator.

c.   Provide an initial prompt question to get the discussion rolling.

d.   Use an excerpt from the novel or an especially conflict-ridden scene to entice students into the discussion.

e.   Debrief at the end of the role-playing to illuminate important issues that were revealed in the discussion, and any content concepts that were considered.

In the example that follows, an excerpt from Klass's (1996) young adult novel, *Danger Zone*, takes up the issue of racism within a U.S. all-star basketball team slated to play in Italy.

DINNER PARTY

Danger Zone

Plot Summary:

Jimmy Doyle, a high school basketball player from a small town in Minnesota, has been selected to play on an American Dream Team slated to compete in Italy. In this scene, he has just completed his first scrimmage with the team. This illustration of Dinner Party involves three major players. Two students volunteer to play Jimmy and Augustus LeMay, an African American player from South Central Los Angeles. Both players are interviewed by a third volunteer playing the role of the team coach.

The key to the conflict in the novel is the fact that both Jimmy and Augustus carry misconceptions about each other. Jimmy thinks Augustus is lucky to live in Los Angeles with its warm climate and beaches. In actuality, Augustus grew up in a tough neighborhood where his father was killed. Moreover, Jimmy replaced Augustus's cousin Devonne after a team infraction, further aggravating the tension between them. Augustus views Jimmy as a rich white kid, but Jimmy is from a poor family, and his father died of a heart attack shortly before the team selection, leaving his mother in difficult financial shape. These layers of truth emerge as the novel unfolds.

Excerpt from the novel (Klass, 1996, p. 67):

Augustus (referring to his cousin, Devonne):
> They dropped him to put some whitebread on our team. That's you, Mr. Minnesota.

Jimmy:
> I am white and I'm from Minnesota. So what? I still don't get it.

Augustus:
> It's just that I don't have much patience with the . . . jive that says a team representing America has to have some rich, blond-haired stiff who wouldn't last five minutes on any playground in this city.

Jimmy:
> I lost all control and swung at him. Then he stepped forward and hit me twice, bam, bam, first on the side of the head and then in the stomach. I found myself lying on my back on the gym floor.

Prompt Question:

In the role of the team coach, what would you want to find out about this fight from Jimmy and Augustus? What advice would you give them once they each tell their respective sides of the story?

Dinner Party is a highly engaging discussion strategy that often leads students to surprisingly creative dramatic performances. Most importantly, it allows for vibrant follow-up discussion aimed at considering both main character voices as well as those characters who may have had little voice in the novel. For example,

Jimmy's mother supported his joining the all-star team, but her strength and voice were largely silent in the novel. During Dinner Party, you can include characters to transform these gaps and silences.

In the area of social studies, a vibrant collection of novels can serve to illuminate and enliven discussions of often abstract or taken-for-granted concepts like freedom and democracy (Bean & Harper, 2006; Harper & Bean, 2006). For example, award-winning novels like *The Breadwinner* by Deborah Ellis (2000), set in Afghanistan, chronicle Afghan women's rights amidst Taliban rule. In a United States urban context, Sharon Flake's (2001) *Money Hungry* takes the reader inside a single parent African American home where the main character, 13-year-old Raspberry, struggles to make ends meet and avoid becoming homeless. Both these novels have sequels and their authors continue to produce additional titles listed in the recommended reading section of the chapter. In addition to creative response strategies like Dinner Party, you can infuse any literature and text discussion with elements of critical literacy examining an array of social justice issues including racism, gay and lesbian issues (Blackburn & Buckley, 2005), and violence (Franzak & Noll, 2006). Critical literacy questions move the reader into a wide-angle lens view of characters, social practices, and the non-neutrality of any text (Stevens & Bean, 2007).

Critical Literacy Discussion

Critical literacy discussions takes a close look at power relationships among characters in a discussion of a novel. Students are asked to carefully consider who has a voice in the novel and how various characters are positioned and treated by others. Novels are viewed as social constructions subject to multiple interpretations. Thus, the narrative world of a novel can be deconstructed through critical questions about gender, race, and class stereotyping (Bean & Moni, 2003; Stevens & Bean, 2007). In the illustration that follows, we pose some generic critical questions along with an excerpt from an Australian novel, *Deadly Unna?* (Gwynne, 1998), centered on two adjacent but ethnically divided communities, one Aboriginal, the other white. Set in a remote fishing community, Aboriginal students walk from their neighborhood to the local high school in the white fishing community. They excel at the fast-paced Aussie football but, outside of this arena, little cross-cultural interchange occurs. During the course of the novel, an Aboriginal player, Dumby Red, is killed in a pub robbery in the white community. Racial tensions underpin this novel and its sequel, *Nunkin Ya* (Gwynne, 2000), when Gary Black, one of the white Aussie players, falls in love with Dumby Red's sister, Clarence. Their affection for each other begins in Gwynne's first novel, *Deadly Unna?*, and the scene that follows foreshadows some of the tensions that escalate between the two communities as the novel unfolds. The derogatory term for Aboriginal people in the white fishing community where Gary Black lives is "Boongs," and this term marks the beginning of the conflict that escalates in the story.

Excerpt from the novel (Gwynne, 1998, p. 121):

In this scene, Gary Black has left their winning high school team celebration dinner with Clarence, an Aboriginal girl whose brother is Dumby Red, a star player but destined for a violent death later in the novel. They go down to an old shed by the fishing harbor to smoke cigarettes. They sit on opposite seats in the shed, which smells of fish guts, cigarette smoke, and stale beer.

Gary:

> The smell didn't really bother me, but something else did. Right above where Clarence was sitting was some graffiti. BOONGS PISS OFF it said . . . BOONGS PISS OFF had been there for ages. I wasn't sure if Clarence had seen it; she didn't say anything. Still, I didn't feel comfortable. I hadn't written it, but I hadn't scratched it out either.

Critical Questions:

1. Who has a voice in this discourse? Who does not have a voice?
2. What are the power relationships involved?
3. What race, class, and gender issues are highlighted?
4. What ideologies are operating to shape this discourse?
5. How could this discourse be shaped differently? For example, if you were to rewrite this passage, how would you change it?

Additional questions can be created to further deconstruct critical elements of key sections of a young adult novel, in this case aimed at illuminating social justice issues. Critical literacy moves beyond reader response and the individual to consider larger, societal problems and issues often raised in contemporary young adult fiction.

Body Biographies

Body biographies involve creating a multimedia interpretation of a character in a novel, short story, or major figure in any content area (Boyd, 2003; Smagorinsky & O'Donnell-Allen, 1998). They can be displayed around the classroom and discussed in a gallery walk where small groups of students explain their illustrations. Following are the steps:

1. Students in small groups place a 7-foot long sheet of butcher paper on the floor and have one student lie down on it. Another student needs to draw an outline of the student's body on the butcher paper.

2. Students in small groups then fill in the body outline with artistic representations of the character's traits, relationships, motivations, and experiences. These can be drawings, clip art, or other multimedia. The body biography should also include relevant quotations and original text about the character. The following details are important to consider in the development of a well-designed body biography, and could be included on a rubric for evaluating this small group work:

   o Placement of the art is important (e.g., the character's heart could feature important relationships).

   o The body biography should help an audience visualize the character's virtues and vices.

   o The effective use of color should help symbolize elements of the character's personality.

   o The effective use of symbols and objects helps capture the character's various dimensions.

   o Poetry can also be used to portray various dimensions of the character.

   o Try to portray contrasting views of the character (e.g., self-view versus how others perceive the character).

   o If the character changes over the course of the story, use text and artwork to show this transformation.

Body biographies offer yet another, creative means for students to explore the complex and often contradictory elements of characters in contemporary young adult fiction. In our experience, this postreading strategy engenders a high degree of engagement and creativity. Figure 7.5 provides an example of a body biography for Farrin, a character in Deborah Ellis' powerful novel, *Moon at Nine*.

Library Power

Good school libraries contain thousands of fascinating novels, biographies, periodicals, and reference works, all waiting to be discovered. The unfortunate thing is that many students never discover the pleasures and satisfactions of the library. You as a content teacher can introduce students to the wealth of the school library via **Library Power**. The following guidelines suggest some of the ways you can do this.

   o **Meet the librarian and media specialist.** It makes sense that before you can guide students in the uses of the library, you need to familiarize your-

Courtesy of Jacob Watson

self with its organization and resources. Find out what periodicals, reference works, videos, and other media are available for your subject area. Most librarians are anxious to help faculty members identify, catalogue, and order materials.

o   **Library orientation.** The school librarian or media specialist is an expert in location skills necessary for finding information. Take advantage of those skills by setting up library orientations for groups of students. Even in senior high school, many students will not know how to use the computerized databases to locate books and materials. Some students will not be able to find a work of fiction. The librarian can provide this basic information as well as answer questions about library hours and special rules.

Glimpse into the Classroom

Imagine that you are a high school history teacher. You want your students to read beyond the class textbook, and you want them to enjoy outside reading as much as possible. In order to meet this objective you do the following things:

1.   You create a list of broad topics from American history, for example, Freedom and Justice.
2.   With the help of the librarian, you catalogue the titles in the school library that fit each topic. (Obviously, the difficulty of the task is determined by the size of the library, the number of topics, and the number of books you require for each topic.)
3.   Create an interest inventory that reflects the original topics, in this case the U.S. History Interest Inventory cited previously.
4.   Administer the inventory to students and then recommend specific titles to individual students on the basis of expressed interest.

The following selected titles reflect the freedom and justice topic on the U.S. History Interest Inventory.

Bruchac, J. (2005). *Pochahontas*. Orlando, FL: Harcourt.
Bruchac, J. (2006). *Geronimo*. New York: Scholastic.
Carlson, L. M. (Ed.). (2005). *Mocassin thunder: American Indian stories for today*. New York: HarperCollins.
Fleischman, P. (1990). *Saturnalia*. New York: HarperCollins.
Gallo, D. R. (2007). *First crossing: Stories about teen immigrants*. New York: Candlewick Press.
Gonzalez, G. (2009). *A so-called vacation*. Houston, TX: Pinata Books.
Myers, W. D. (1988). *Fallen angels*. New York: Scholastic.
Myers, W. D. (2008). *Sunrise over Fallujah*. New York: Scholastic.
Ryan, P. M. (2000). *Esperanza rising*. New York: Scholastic.
Salisbury, G. (2005). *Eyes of the emperor*. New York: Wendy Lamb.
Sandler, M. (2013). Imprisoned: the betrayal of Japanese Americans during WWII.
Stone, T.L. (2013). *Courage has no color*. New York: Candlewick
Taylor, M. D. (1976). *Roll of thunder, hear my cry*. New York: Trumpet Club.
Warner, L. S. (1976). *From slave to abolitionist: The life of William Wells Brown*. New York: Dial.

PART 2: Teaching and Learning Strategies

As recommended earlier in this chapter, perhaps the best way to begin using tradebook novels in your content area is to read one or two young adult novels a year, starting small and building your collection slowly. That way, you will truly have ownership of the books you read aloud to students and recommend they read. Your book discussions will be more informed, and you will be modeling your own interest in young adult literature. Where can you locate tradebooks to use in your content area? And what are some good books in the divergent content areas of science, mathematics, music, social studies, and other content areas? In the section that follows we provide a listing of useful sources as you search for books in your own unit and lesson planning. We also indicate a few books that we have found to be useful in expanding students' knowledge in science, history, mathematics, social studies, and other areas.

Sources of Tradebooks

As a content area teacher in science, social studies, mathematics, English, music, physical education, agriculture, art, and other areas, you may be interested in locating contemporary young adult literature and other tradebooks. The librarian, the Internet, book reviews in journals, teacher conventions, mall bookstores, specialty children's bookstores, and publishers' catalogs are some of the possible sources. Keep in mind that there is no substitute for browsing your local bookstore, reading the first few pages of a young adult novel you think might key into your content area, and spending some time reading it. The process of finding just the right book to read aloud, including it in SSR, and integrating it with a unit in your field is labor-intensive. Viewing the development of your own bibliography of trade-books for your content area over the span of 3–5 years is a reasonable goal. Any of the following sources can help you get started.

Sources of Tradebooks

- o   Librarians

- o   Journals

- o   Book Reviews

- o   Teacher Conventions

- o   Mall Bookstores

- o   Online Resources

- o   Author Websites and Blogs

- o   Specialty Children's Bookstores

- o   Publishers Catalogs

- o   Local Bookstores

JOURNALS.

Young Adult Choices. Each year, the November issue of the *Journal of Adolescent & Adult Literacy* (International Reading Association) publishes an annotated list of recommended books that a team of young adults selected. In addition, regular reviews of young adult literature are featured in each issue.

The *English Journal,* published by the National Council of Teachers of English, also features young adult literature reviews. It is published eight times per year. The middle school publication, *Voices from the Middle* also highlights young adult literature.

ANNOTATED BIBLIOGRAPHIES AND BOOK REVIEWS. Most annotated bibliographies are organized by content area or theme, making it easy to locate books within the topic area you need. These bibliographies are a good starting point, but ultimately, you need to create your own unique bibliography.

The ALAN Review. Assembly on Literature for Adolescents, National Council of Teachers of English. Published three times each year.

The American Library Association lists the annual Top 10 Best Books for Young Adults on their website at: http://www.ala.org/yalsa/booklists/bbya/.

Internet sources (e.g., Amazon.com) also include reviews of novels.

CONVENTIONS AND CATALOGS. Most professional association annual and regional conventions feature a large exhibit hall filled with publishers' displays of books and materials. This is a great place to browse, collect catalogs, and put your name on publishers' mailing lists so you can stay in touch with new books. For example, the annual California Reading Association convention each November features an extensive array of publishers' exhibits with a focus on California's literature initiative. Specialty bookstores display their books and feature a quarterly newsletter with annotations and book ordering information. Other book suppliers have a special emphasis on multicultural books, particularly Asian novels and nonfiction. Publishers like Scholastic in New York have extensive, annotated catalogs and classroom book club order forms.

LOCAL SOURCES. Your local teacher materials and supplies store and the school and public libraries are good places to browse. Local business and philanthropic clubs are usually interested in raising funds to support literacy activities in classrooms. This is an often overlooked source of support. Purchasing a classroom set of books for a unit on endangered species in science may seem prohibitive. But with the help of a small grant from a local philanthropic organization, you can at least get started.

CREATING YOUR OWN BIBLIOGRAPHY. Book lists, catalogs, and journal recommendations of books are convenient, but no substitute for browsing, locating a book you think might key into a unit you teach, and reading it. Table 7.1 includes some of the content areas in which tradebooks can be used to illuminate textbook concepts. Many books are also appropriate for art, music, mathematics, agriculture, industrial arts, foreign language, drama, health, guidance, and physical education. This bibliography is merely a brief listing to get you started on developing your own collection of books and materials.

As a content teacher, with a well developed knowledge of students' reading attitudes and interests, as well as a working knowledge of young adult literature you can tie to your units, you will make learning in your classroom a rich experience.

Annotated List of Tradebooks for Content Areas	**TABLE 7.1**

ENGLISH

Anderson, L. H. (2009). *Wintergirls*. New York: Viking. The author of *Speak* continues to tackle difficult topics, in this case anorexia.

Cast, P. C. (2008). *Immortal: Love stories with bite*. Nashville, TN: Borders Books. This edited collection of short stories features seven authors with a presence in the hugely popular vampire literature for teens.

Flake, S. G. (2005). *Who am I without him? Short stories about girls and the boys in their lives*. New York: Jump at the Sun. Award winning author Sharon Flake's collection of a dozen short stories traces the challenges teens face in relationships.

Loughery, J. (1993). *First sightings: Contemporary stories of American youth*. New York: Persea. (ISBN 0-89255-187-9). This anthology contains 20 stories selected from a variety of award winning authors.

Mazer, A. (1993). *American street: A multicultural anthology of stories*. New York: Persea. (ISBN 0-89255-191-7). Includes short stories from Native American author Duane Big Eagle and "The No Guitar Blues" by Gary Soto. A wide range of cultures and times are represented in this anthology.

Tannenbaum, J. (2006). *Solid ground*. San Francisco: WritersCorp. Written by adolescent writers based in San Francisco, this edited collection of poetry by urban youth captures life in a vibrant city, 100 years after the great earthquake of 1906.

HISTORY AND GEOGRAPHY

Bruchac, J. (2006). *Geronimo*. New York: Scholastic. The account by Native American author Joseph Bruchac follows Geronimo on his cross-country journey to prison in Florida. Told through the eyes of his grandson, we see a powerful leader displaced from his Rocky Mountain home.

Choi, S. N. (1991). *Year of impossible goodbyes.* New York: Dell. (ISBN 0-440-40759-1). Chronicles the occupation of Korea in 1945 and its impact on one family.

Ellis, D. (2000). *The breadwinner.* Toronto, Canada: Groundwood Books. This novel explores life in Afghanistan through the eyes of a young girl living under Taliban rule.

Fleischman, P. (1990). *Saturnalia.* New York: HarperCollins. (ISBN 006-447089-X). William is a Narraganset Indian in colonial Boston, where he must serve as an indentured servant to a printer. It is 1681 and the servants await Saturnalia, a 24-hour respite when servants and masters trade places.

Gallo, D. R. (2007). *First crossings: Stories about teen immigrants.* New York: Candlewick Press. This collection encompasses accounts of Mexican, Chinese, and other immigrant groups.

Myers, W. D. (1988). *Fallen angels.* New York: Scholastic. (ISBN 0-59040943-3). The Vietnam War in 1968 through the eyes of a 17-year-old African American soldier from New York.

Myers, W. D. (2008). *Sunrise over Fallujah.* New York: Scholastic. The war in Iraq seen through a young African American soldier's eyes is a compelling account of the dissonance between intention and action in war.

Naidoo, B. (2000). *The other side of truth.* New York: HarperCollins. Follows a 12-year-old Sade into a forced exile from Nigeria to London following the murder of her mother, caught in the crossfire of an assassination plot aimed at her journalist father for protesting the military government in Lagos, Nigeria.

Ryan, P. (2000). *Esperanza rising.* New York: Scholastic. A young girl's life in a Mexican farm labor camp during the Great Depression is the setting for this novel.

Slade, A. (2001). *Dust.* Toronto, Canada: HarperCollins. Canadian prairie life during the Dustbowl forms the backdrop for this young adult fantasy.

Taylor, M. D. (1976). *Roll of thunder, hear my cry.* New York: Trumpet Club. (ISBN 0-440-84387-1). The Logan family in Mississippi in the 1930s struggles with discrimination, racism, and oppression.

Uchida, Y. (1983). *The best bad thing.* New York: Macmillan. (ISBN 0689-71069-0). Rinko, a Japanese American living in California in the 1930s, experiences prejudice.

Yep, L. (1993). *Dragons's gate.* New York: HarperCollins. This novel chronicles the Chinese workers' experiences while building the transcontinental railroad in brutal physical and psychological conditions.

ART AND MUSIC

Balliett, B. (2005). *Chasing Vermeer.* New York: Scholastic. This young adult novel revolves around an international art scandal and incorporates elements of problem-solving overlapping with geometry and the linear quality of Dutch painter Vermeer's art.

Landis, J. D. (1989). *The band never dances.* New York: HarperCollins. The main character is a female drummer who rides the wave of success into the world of rock arenas while simultaneously struggling with her brother's suicide.

PHYSICAL EDUCATION

Cannon, A. E. (1990). *The shadow brothers.* New York: Bantam. Recounts the problems Marcus and his Navajo foster brother Henry experience in high school track and through Henry's growing interest in his Navajo culture, which propels him away from his foster family.

Deuker, C. (2007). *Gym candy.* Boston: Houghton, Mifflin Harcourt. This author of realistic young adult fiction takes the reader into a high school quarterback's use of anabolic steroids.

Klass, D. (1996). *Danger zone*. New York: Scholastic. Racial tensions swirl around a star basketball team getting ready to play in Italy. African American player Augustus LeMay and a new player, Jimmy Doyle, clash on and off the court.

Klass, D. (2002). *Home of the braves*. New York: Farrar, Straus, and Giroux. Chronicles the experiences of a senior high soccer captain, Joe Brickman, and a Brazilian soccer star who transforms the team, resulting in tensions with Lawndale High's football players.

Lipsyte, R. (1993). *The chief*. New York: HarperCollins. In this ongoing series, Lipsyte presents an insider's view of the gritty world of boxing.

Lupica, M. (2006). *Heat*. New York: Puffin Books. Main character Michael Arroyo is underage and living with his older Cuban brother. His baseball skills are beyond reproach, but Social Services is on a path to separate Michael from his caretaker brother.

Myers, W. D. (1996). *Slam!* New York: Scholastic. "Slam" Harris's superb basketball playing offers a way out of New York's inner city, but his grades haunt his dreams.

Zusak, M. (2000). *Fighting Ruben Wolfe*. New York: Scholastic. A strong novel set in the rough world of illegal boxing and betting.

SCIENCE, MATHEMATICS, AND TECHNOLOGY

Anderson, L. H. (2002). *Catalyst*. New York: Penguin. This novel features a main character with a strong interest in math and science and a related desire to organize her world based on logic. Needless to say, life intervenes, disrupting her orderly world.

Cooney, C. B. (2005). *Code orange*. New York: Delacorte. The main character in this thriller finds a virus that has the potential to wipe out New York City. Combining suspense, mystery, and allusions to the powerful pull of technology in adolescents' lives, this novel links nicely to problem solving in biology around the topic of infectious diseases.

George, J. C. (1989). *Shark beneath the reef*. New York: HarperCollins. (ISBN 0-06-440308-4). Fourteen-year-old Tomas Torres wants to become a marine biologist and struggles with staying in or dropping out of school.

Hobbs, W. (1988). *Changes in latitudes*. New York: Avon. (ISBN 0-38071-619-4). A family vacation in Mexico leads to Teddy's interest in turtles and efforts to protect their welfare as endangered species.

Johansen, K. V. (2006). *The Cassandra virus*. Victoria, Canada: Orca. This short novel deals with computer viruses from the point of view of a bored student over summer vacation. Orca publishes a number of short titles on topics in science (e.g., tornadoes), generally running about 100 to 150 pages.

Klass, D. (1994). *California blue*. New York: Scholastic. John, the main character, discovers the double-edged sword of trying to protect an endangered butterfly in a small logging community.

SOCIAL STUDIES: CULTURAL AND ETHNIC IDENTITY

Alexie, S. (2007). *The absolutely true diary of a part-time Indian*. New York: Little, Brown. Sherman Alexie, in a semi-autobiographical account, follows main character Junior from the comfort zone of his reservation surroundings to commute to a predominantly white, upscale school where basketball and a bright mind becomes his saving grace against racism.

Al-Windawi, T. (2004). *Thura's diary*. London: Penguin. This account chronicles the war in Baghdad from the point-of-view of an Iraqi teenager. Along with young adult novels and other non-fiction accounts of adolescents in war zones, these selections offer powerful insights into the human impact of global conflicts.

Chock, E., Harstad, J. R., Lum, D. H. Y., & Teter, B. (1998). *Growing up local: An anthology of poetry and prose from Hawai'i.* Honolulu, HI: Bamboo Ridge. This collection of short stories and poetry includes the major authors from Hawai'i (e.g., Lois Ann Yamanaka) as well as new teen voices. The writing is true to Hawai'i's local scene with pidgin dialect an integral part of many of the author's voices.

Ellis, D. (2002). *Parvana's journey.* Toronto, Canada: Groundwood.

Ellis, D. (2003). *Mud city.* Toronto, Canada: Groundwood. Each of these sequels to Ellis's (2000) award winning book, *The Breadwinner,* traces a young adolescent girl's flight from war-torn Afghanistan to the streets of Peshawar, Pakistan. These books and others in this list, set in the Middle East, offer a strong collection of writing to support a unit in world history or cultural geography.

Ellis, D. (2004). *Three wishes: Palistinian and Israeli children speak.* Toronto, Canada: Groundwood. Adolescents in the Middle East candidly describe their lives and advance proposals for peace. Much like *Thura's diary* (annotated earlier), this series of young voices provides a compelling, insider's view of war.

Flake, S. G. (2001). *Money hungry.* New York: Hyperion Paperbacks. Thirteen-year-old African American character Raspberry Hill has lived in a car and project housing. Her fear of becoming homeless drives her entrepreneurial efforts, but she is constantly in trouble with endless schemes to make and keep cash on hand.

Flake, S. G. (2004). *Begging for change.* New York: Hyperion. This sequel to Flake's (2001) *Money Hungry* continues Raspberry's quest for a permanent home for herself and her mom, as well as Raspberry's pursuit of financial security.

Flake, S. G. (2005). *Who am I without him? Short stories about girls and the boys in their lives.* New York: Jump at the Sun. This collection centers on the challenges of relationships in teens' lives.

Gallo, D. R. (2004). *First crossings: Stories about teen immigrants.* New York: Candlewick Press. Donald Gallo's short story collections always feature engaging accounts to which adolescents can relate.

Gonzalez, G. (2009). *A so-called vacation.* Houston, TX: Pinata Books. The father in this family feels his two boys will benefit from a trip away from their suburban Texas home to work for a summer in the field in a California migrant camp.

Hamilton, V. (1993). *Plain city.* New York: Scholastic. Buhlaire Sims slowly forms a positive sense of the good dimensions of her life imparted by her African American mother and long-departed half-Caucasian dad.

Hernandez, I. B. (1992). *Heartbeat drumbeat.* Houston, TX: Arte Publico Press. This novel chronicles Morgana Cruz's search for her identity based on her mother's Navajo traditions and her father's Mexican culture.

Lee, M. (1992). *Finding my voice.* Boston: Houghton Mifflin. A Korean American high school student, Ellen Sung, struggles with violent racism and its impact on her identity in a small Minnesota town.

Lee, M. (1997). *Necessary roughness.* New York: HarperCollins. Chan Kim's family moves in his senior year from a close-knit Los Angeles Korean community to a rural Minnesota town. Chan begins to play football there amidst prejudice and his father's old world expectations.

McMillen, G. K. (2005). *School for Hawaiian girls.* Sag Harbor, NY: Permanent Press. Spanning the 1920s to the 1980s, this young adult novel recounts the murder and rape of 16-year-old Lydia Kaluhi. A novel of struggle and cultural survival, much like Salisbury's (2005) *Eyes of the Emperor*, it could fit within a United States history course by offering an insider's postcolonial lens of past events.

Myers, W. D. (2000). *Monster.* New York: Scholastic. Sixteen-year-old Steve Harmon's trial in the murder of a convenience store owner during a robbery forms the backdrop for his simultaneously writing a screenplay about the trial and wrestling with the moral dilemmas in his life. This avante-garde novel, written by Walter Dean Myers and illustrated by his son, Chris Myers, moves the young adult novel into a multi-task framework familiar to contemporary teens.

Myers, W. D. (2003). *The beast.* New York: Scholastic. The main characters in this powerful novel represent the varying opportunities available to urban youth, often beset by street pressures to embrace drug addiction. The double-edged sword of community and family loyalty and the need to form an independent life play out in this story.

Rifa'l, A., & Ainbinder, O. (2003). *We just want to live here.* New York: St. Martin's Griffen. Two 18-year-old girls, one Palestinian and the other Israeli, attend a student exchange program in Switzerland. Following their return to their respective homes, they continued corresponding. The resulting letters, compiled by Middle East correspondent Sylke Temple, provide a strongly human picture of their lives amidst suicide bombings and constant restrictions on their mobility. Along with Thura's diary and Deborah Ellis's trilogy, this book could support a unit in world history or geography.

Soto, G. (1997). *Buried onions.* New York: Scholastic. Nineteen-year-old Eddie drops out of school to work at menial jobs, avoid gang confrontations, and find a way to cope with constant problems in a Fresno barrio.

Soto, G. (2003). *The afterlife.* Orlando, FL: Harcourt. This sequel to Gary Soto's (1997) *Buried Onions* follows Chuy, Eddie's cousin, who was murdered in that novel and returns as a ghost with powers that allow him to take a wide-angle look at his neighborhood, family, and barrio life in Fresno, CA.

Now go back to the literature vignette at the beginning of the chapter. React again to the lesson as you did before. Compare your answers with those you made before you read the chapter.

MINI PROJECTS

1. Interview two adolescent students, one male and one female, to determine: (a) what their reading interests are, and, (b) to what extent their interests are represented in the classroom by the content area reading they do in school.

2. Administer the BJP attitude survey presented in this chapter to a group of middle or secondary students. Summarize the results.

3. Create a reading interest inventory for your content area.

4. Read one young adult novel related to your content area and share it with another person in your field. Use the novel in a read aloud or independent reading fashion within a unit of instruction in your content area.

5. Develop a bibliography of young adult literature for use in your content area. Use Internet resources to research contemporary young adult books.

WEB RESOURCES

Go to the website for Chapter 5 activities.

American Library Association YA Forum
http://www.ala.org/yaforum/

Educating Zombies
http://educatingzombies.com/Welcome.html

Book Country
http://www.bookcountry.com/readandreview/books/genremap/youngadult.aspx

Good Reads
https://www.goodreads.com/list/tag/young-adult

Diversity in YA
http://www.diversityinya.com/category/book-lists/

CHAPTER 8

Vocabulary

VIGNETTE

Setting

Matha Matix's seventh-grade math class, a diverse group of students in a multicultural setting. In her unit on Geometry, Ms. Matix is teaching a lesson on angles.

The Lesson

Ms. Matix begins class by displaying the following words on the smart board: straight, right, obtuse, acute, vertical, corresponding, adjacent, complementary, and supplementary. She then goes back to each word, pronounces it, provides a definition, and gives a pictorial example. Some students are seen writing in their notes. She emphasizes to the class that they will be using the words throughout the lesson on angles. Later, as the bell rings, Ms. Matix gives a homework assignment for students to find other examples of these angles by searching the Internet for photos of buildings and other objects that use each of the angles. She tells students they will review the vocabulary words the next day by sharing their visual examples on their laptops and tablets.

Bearing in mind that much of this lesson concerns vocabulary, jot down your thoughts on the following questions:

1. What are the good points about the lesson?

2. What are the weak points about the lesson?

3. What, if anything, would you change about the lesson?

RATIONALE

Sometimes a mob might "grift" all day without "turning them over," but this is unlikely except in the case of a "jug mob" which takes a limited number of "pokes." Any pick-pocket who has on his person more than one wallet is something of a hazard both to himself and to the mob, for each wallet can count as a separate offense if he should be caught. Therefore, it is safer to have cash only. "Class mobs" usually count the money each time they "skin the pokes," one stall commonly is responsible for all of it, and an accounting in full is made at the end of the day. (Maurer, 1955, p. 194)

All groups of people, whether they be pickpockets, bridge players, or educators, share special idioms and technical terminology which characterize the group. "Insiders" use this vocabulary freely and through it gain access to the collective knowledge of the group. Likewise, "outsiders" are identified as such and are restricted in their social and intellectual intercourse with the group due, in part, to their ignorance of its specialized vocabulary.

The task of the content teacher is to help students become insiders whose minds move easily in the fields of science, English, social studies, mathematics, music, the arts, or physical education and health. To a large extent, this is accomplished by teaching them the technical terminology of each discipline. The following example, in which one student is explaining a mathematical problem to another student, suggests the gravity of vocabulary acquisition in content areas:

"I don't remember what you call it, but it's like if you have three numbers—5, 9, and 6—and you want to multiply them. It doesn't matter what order you do it in. You always get the same answer, 270."

This student apparently understands the concept of the commutative principle, the process of combining elements in such a manner that the order of multiplication is unimportant. Unfortunately, not knowing the word for this concept limits the student's capacity to utilize it. For instance, one might expect the student's reading or listening comprehension to be seriously impaired, given the following textbook statement, ". . . The commutative principle applies to the preceding series of algebraic equations."

In all content areas, new concepts are sequentially introduced and defined in terms of concepts presented earlier. As students progress through texts, reading comprehension can diminish to the point of extinction if students have failed to master the words that symbolize important concepts, even when they have mastered the concepts themselves! In addition, teaching vocabulary can have a powerful and positive impact on reading comprehension. For this reason, considerable attention to vocabulary is fundamental to the purposes of every classroom teacher.

LEARNING OBJECTIVES

o   Discuss the pros and cons of various decoding strategies.

o   Understand the general principles of vocabulary instruction.

o   Justify direct vocabulary instruction as an essential component in your own content area.

o   Implement a variety of instructional strategies for introducing and reinforcing new vocabulary.

GRAPHIC ORGANIZER

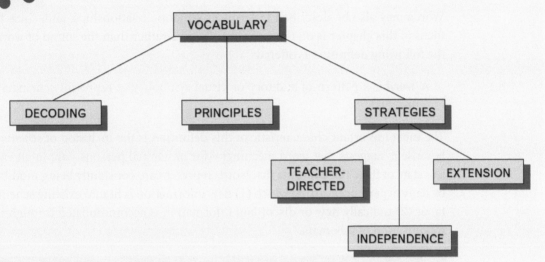

Courtesy Thomas Bean

WORDS

For a variety of technical reasons, the concept of "word" is extremely difficult to define as a unit of language. Curiously, adult language users have little difficulty agreeing whether or not a particular sequence of sounds or symbols is a word. This common sensitivity to the concept of "word" is a result of defining words as prefabricated units that speakers know are not to be interrupted with linguistic fillers such as "um" or "uh" during speech. For instance, it would be quite natural for a speaker to say "The-workman-um-will-finish-um-Saturday," but not "The-work-um-man-will-fin-um-ish-Saturday."

Words may also be described in terms of semantic relationships; and, since the focus of this chapter is on the meaning of words rather than the sound of words, the following definition is offered:

> A *word* is a pattern of auditory or visual symbols that represent schemata (concepts).

The most important characteristic of this definition is the inclusion of *schemata*, because it suggests that word meanings—for individual persons—are in an endless state of flux. The concepts that words represent are constantly being modified by daily experiences during which (1) new information is fit into existing schemata, or (2) radically new or discordant information is accommodated through the modification of schemata.

CONSIDER THIS!

For instance, most people have internalized the concept of "cat," but do they know all breeds by name? Could they correctly identify the habitats and mating customs of each? Could they name a type of cat that does not have retractable claws? If not, then there is a clear potential for the modification of their cat schema.

The point is that the question of knowing the meaning of a word is not subject to a simple yes or no. There is always a need for qualification because a word is known or unknown, strange or familiar, to some degree, which is determined by the richness of its known associations.

Learning a new word (concept) requires more than a simple explanation, because individual words are not simple isolated bits of information. Words are defined by the ways and the extent to which they are related to all other words. For instance, it would be possible to define the concept "anchor" as a device used on a boat or ship to keep the vessel stationary. However, such a definition does little to build an anchor schema that will allow a student to comprehend and use the word at will. A more effective strategy, one that builds a richer schema, might entail the following:

1. Demonstrating the variation in sizes and shapes of anchors;

2. Letting students touch or try to lift an anchor;

3. Explaining how sailors get an anchor in and out of the water;

4. Describing how an anchor keeps a ship from drifting;

5. Explaining why it is a good idea to keep boats from drifting.

On a more abstract level, knowing a word requires understanding its connotations as well as its denotations—sometimes referred to as contextual versus definitional knowledge.

o The *denotation* of a word is its broad meaning; in this sense, old/aged, end/finale, and surface/superficial are synonymous pairs of words.

o A word's *connotations* are its subtle shades of meaning and the specific contextual conditions in which it can occur.

Connotations are meanings that differentiate among words that would otherwise be considered synonyms. Connotatively, old and aged are not synonyms because they cannot be used in the same context. For example, you can talk about "an old rock" but not "an aged rock" because aged connotes "living" as in "an aged woman." In this sense, there are probably few, if any, exact synonyms in English.

CONSIDER THIS!

The following four sentences were written by students in a ninth-grade English class. The sentences were constructed as part of an assignment in which the students wrote sentences and then made word substitutions based on an inspection of the classroom thesaurus. The italicized words are those selected from the thesaurus.

1. The dirty old man went to church to ask God for *immunity*.
2. The car had a *putrefaction*.
3. It was clear from her actions that Susan was a fine *madam*.
4. It pays to be a *chivalrous* driver.

Aside from the amusing pictures which some of these sentences paint, what precisely is wrong with them? Denotatively, the words selected from the thesaurus are quite reasonable since pairs like immunity/forgiveness and breakdown/putrefaction are synonymous, or at least closely related in meaning. However, the members of each pair have different connotations that make them unacceptable substitutes in most contexts. For instance, putrefaction connotes a breakdown of a biological nature, and it is anomalous to use the word in reference to something made of steel and rubber.

What we are suggesting is that the acquisition of new word meanings is sufficiently complex that vocabulary instruction should not be consigned to a mindless list of strange words followed by one-line definitions. If it is, the lack of examples and supporting contexts will doom students' understanding of new words to be both superficial and tentative.

VOCABULARIES

A *vocabulary* is a corpus of many thousands of words and their associated meanings. An individual's vocabulary may be analyzed in several ways. For instance, every person has a *receptive* vocabulary and an *expressive* vocabulary. Receptive refers to words that can be read and comprehended in print or heard and understood in spoken context. Expressive refers to lexical items that a person can use properly when speaking or writing. In a sense, people have four vocabularies: listening, reading, speaking, and writing, and these categories are not mutually inclusive. Children usually begin school with respectable listening and speaking vocabularies but considerably less reading and writing vocabularies. On the other hand, the listening and reading vocabularies of literate adults—and secondary students—far outstrip their speaking and writing vocabularies. This is true because the schemata necessary to place words in proper contexts must be more fully developed than those required for recognizing word meanings when context has already been provided.

Finally, vocabularies may be classified as *technical* or *general*. Technical vocabulary refers to words such as denouement, secant, Bull Market, secede, and so on, which are uniquely or usually related to individual academic disciplines. General vocabulary refers to words that are not specifically associated with any one teaching area; for example, germane, astute, and ubiquitous.

By the time students are intellectually prepared to learn words such as "germane" or "astute," they already possess the concepts that those words symbolize; that is, significant/relevant and alert/perceptive. Consequently, "germane" and "astute" are new, perhaps more efficient, labels for previously acquired concepts. Learning them does not demand a radical modification of existing concepts. In contrast, technical vocabulary presents labels for unfamiliar concepts.

Vocabulary and reading comprehension are intertwined (Ford-Connor's & Paratore, 2015). These researchers set out to determine what features of instruction best support students' vocabulary learning in the content areas. They found, not surprisingly, that single encounters with words and their dictionary definitions fail to develop deep knowledge of content area words and concepts. Indeed, from grades 5 through 12, they defined knowing a word as being able to do things

194

with it through discussion, writing, or performing some activity (e.g. solving a mathematics problem). The factors that were associated with deep word learning included the following:

o Wide reading in complex texts

o Using a combination of context clues and morphemic features of words (e.g. prefixes, affixes, and suffixes) to help students learn word meanings

o Direct instruction in unfamiliar vocabulary

o Repeated opportunities to hear and use words in authentic learning (e.g. solving a problem, conducting an experiment on water quality, and problem solving)

o Rich classroom discussion using target vocabulary

Academic Vocabulary

Another way of thinking about both general and technical terminology that students encounter in the content areas is *academic vocabulary* (Townsend, 2009) or academic language (Templeton, et al., 2015; Kieffer & Lesaux, 2010). These words cause difficulty for many students including English language learners. Some of these words are technical and specific to particular content areas (e.g., "percent"), whereas others are more general (e.g., "assume"). The *Academic Word List* (Coxhead, 2000) is a very useful resource for evaluating the frequency of occurrence of these general academic words. This list focuses exclusively on general vocabulary that occurs in various content areas, posing problems for students. For example, general terms like "principle" take on specific meanings in biology or economics. Townsend (2009) recommends using a language workshop approach to help students become insiders with these slippery words. We look at some of the engaging game approaches recommended by Townsend later in this chapter.

Content area teachers are primarily concerned with transmitting novel information and helping students develop new concepts; for example, Bull Market or secant. For this reason, the focus of the present chapter is on the teaching of technical vocabulary and a general strategy for independently decoding unfamiliar words.

DECODING UNFAMILIAR VOCABULARY

Decoding is a process whereby a coded message is converted back into thought. For example, a chef reads a waiter's written message about your order and decodes it, that is, comprehends how you want your steak prepared.

The process is similar in content area textbook communication. Authors put down their thoughts in a written form that their readers then decode. When the decoding process breaks down, comprehension suffers. In our opinion the major stumbling block to efficient decoding of text is the students' inability to cope with unfamiliar words and concepts. There are three basic strategies for unlocking the meanings of unfamiliar words in text: *morphemic analysis, context clues,* and *external references.*

Morphemic Analysis

When students encounter long words in print, it is valuable to break such words into more manageable parts. It is well known that a word part may have a meaning of its own. Such a word part is called a morpheme. A *morpheme* is the smallest unit of language with an associated meaning, that is, it possesses a definite meaning and cannot be subdivided into smaller units that have meaning. There are two types of morphemes: free and bound.

o A *free morpheme* can function alone as a word, e.g., "some" or "thing."

o *Bound morphemes* are those meaningful language units that occur only as attachments to words or other morphemes, e.g., "tele-," "-er," or "-cide." In essence, they are prefixes, suffixes, or roots.

Just as a word may be a symbol that represents a schema in our knowledge structure, so may a word part or morpheme. Additionally, two or more morphemes may combine to give a combination of ideas, thus modifying a schema. For instance, "blue" and "berry," two separate morphemes, may be combined to form a new or modified schema conveying a combination of meanings. Thus, *morphemic analysis* is a process by which readers can determine the meaning of an unfamiliar word by analyzing its component parts (Mountain, 2015). For example, the root word "migr" means to move and it provides clues to the meaning of related words like "migrate" and "immigrant." (Mountain, 2015) Morphemic analysis gives students a bridge to figure out word meanings across content areas.

Attention to word parts to reveal the meanings of unfamiliar words is a process that goes on all the time. For instance, if a reader encounters a word such as "patricide" in a contextual setting, he or she is likely to focus on the morphemes of the word, "patri-" and "-cide" to determine its meaning, particularly if the context is anomalous, or provides no clear interpretation. Such an anomalous context would be

Robert has committed patricide.

Of course, the reader cannot perform such an analysis without prior knowledge of the two morphemes in "patricide." Yet, because morphemic analysis focuses on meaning, it provides a more sensible approach to analyzing unfamiliar words than does phonics. Additionally, approximately 80% of the words listed in an English dictionary contain words composed of Latin or Greek morphemes. Consequently, a knowledge of these roots and affixes can be valuable in analyzing and remembering the meanings of unfamiliar polysyllabic words.

We are certainly not arguing that content teachers should have their students master lists of affixes and roots. This procedure is restrictive in that students memorize without meaningful context. Inserting information into long-term memory is best accomplished by making the information interesting and relevant—descriptors that hardly apply to lengthy lists of strange-looking morphemes.

APPLICATION 8.1

Use your knowledge of morphemes to analyze the following unfamiliar polysyllabic word. Try to derive the meaning of it.

PNEUMONOULTRAMICROSCOPICSILICOVOLCANOCONIOSIS

Were you able to arrive at a definition without consulting a dictionary, or did you panic because the word appears ominous? What you have encountered is one of the longest words in the English language, yet one that readily lends itself to morphemic analysis. Perhaps the following context will help you come up with the definition:

Because of his proximity to Mount St. Helens, he contracted pneumonoultramicroscopicsilicovolcanoconiosis.

Using the context clues present in the sentence, in combination with your knowledge of morphemes, probably gave you the definition. The following morphemes are present in the word:

Pneumono—related to the lungs
Ultra—transcending; super
Micro—small
Scopic—related to a viewing instrument
Silico—the mineral, silicon
Volcano—eruption in the earth from which molten rock, steam, and dust issue
Coni (konis)—dust
Osis—referring to a disease condition

Thus, pneumonoultramicroscopicsilicovolcanoconiosis is a disease of the lungs caused by habitual inhalation of very fine silicon dust particles.

Direct teaching of morphemes has been shown to improve both middle school students' vocabulary growth and comprehension over an 18-week span (Kieffer & Lesaux, 2010). A number of principles underpin high-quality morphemic analysis teaching (Kieffer & Lesaux, 2010):

o Integrate morphemic analysis instruction with rich print contexts (e.g., if you are teaching the word "strategy," expand this instruction to include "strategic," "strategize," and so on).

o Teach morphemic analysis as a valuable cognitive strategy (e.g., upon encountering a word like "unilateral," analyze the word for known morphemes; "uni" means "one"). Use a four-step approach that includes the following: (1) Acknowledge that you do not know the word; (2) Analyze the word for parts you do know (i.e., roots, prefixes, suffixes); (3) Generate a possible meaning for the word based on words parts; and, (4) Check this estimate against the context where the word appears (e.g., "The chair of the committee made a unilateral decision to purchase the new software for the school—a one-sided decision.").

o Introduce word parts carefully with practice and review opportunities (e.g., a classroom) and a Word Form Chart that displays action verbs (e.g., "prepare"), nouns (e.g., "preparation"), adjectives, and adverbs helps solidify these words in students' academic vocabularies.

In summary, we suggest that knowledge of morphemes has the potential for transfer to unfamiliar words that possess the same morphemes. Students should be taught to apply their knowledge of word parts to unfamiliar words they encounter. In this way they are encouraged to discover their own generalizations by intelligent inference or informed guessing. For instance, in the word you were asked to analyze in Application 8.1, you may not have extracted the morpheme "pneumon" and attached meaning to it directly. Rather, you may have associated the morpheme with the word "pneumonia" to arrive at a meaning for it. It is this type of learning process that the authors advocate.

Context Clues

All human experience is context dependent. Indeed, human behavior can hardly be interpreted without context. As an example, consider the question, "Is it okay for me to take my clothes off?" The answer obviously depends upon the context—at a nudist colony, yes; in church, no! Context is, therefore, a necessary and natural part of human functioning. Such is also the case in reading. For instance, if given the sentence, "Bella loves her new red _____," you would be able to supply a word in the blank even though no graphophonic information is present. Additionally, many investigators in reading education have stressed the importance of readers' use of context in interpreting and verifying the meaning of words and sentences to be comprehended. The appropriate use of context leads to more effective processing and overall accuracy in deriving the meaning of unfamiliar words. It is in combination with readers' experiential background that the analysis of context provides meaning to the semantic subtleties of print.

To assess the value of context clues in decoding new vocabulary, we need to examine how context can supply meaning. There are three main types of *context clues*:

> **Context Clues**
> o Definition
> o Description
> o Contrast

A. Definition: The word is defined, usually in the same sentence. For example,

1. *Uxoricide,* which means to murder one's wife, is the ultimate form of marital abuse.

B. Description: The word is described by the context in such a way that the reader can take a good guess at its meaning. For example,

2. Their *vociferous* chatter made me wish I had ear plugs.

C. Contrast: The word is compared with some other word or concept, often an opposite. For example,

3. Mike was *loquacious* whereas Susan said very little.

Most textbooks rely on context clues when introducing new concepts. Generally, these new words are *italicized*, underlined, or written in **bold print** to call attention to the fact that a new word is being introduced. Typically, the context clue is some form of definition.

It is fairly obvious that context clues work in the sentences above, and students are capable of using such clues when they are presented. The real issue is whether sentences such as those in (B) and (C) above occur with sufficient frequency to make context clues a valid strategy for decoding unfamiliar words. Research based on the naturally occurring prose of novels, magazines, and textbooks strongly suggests that context clues are not nearly as useful for decoding unfamiliar words as has traditionally been assumed. Rather, both definitional and contextual information are crucial for learning new vocabulary, along with multiple encounters with new words.

Moreover, context clues only seem to work well in the decoding process when the word in question is redundant in the passage and, therefore, unimportant to the overall meaning of the passage. Since the major purpose of a decoding strategy is to promote comprehension during reading, context clues are less valuable than external references as an independent decoding strategy.

External References

An *external reference* is a source of information that falls outside the passage in which the unfamiliar word occurs. In this sense phonics, context clues, and morphemic analysis are internal sources of information, whereas textbook aids, dictionaries, encyclopedias, and online resources are external.

Textbook Aids

Textbook aids are elements included in the text to help students with new vocabulary. When students encounter an unfamiliar word, context clues and morphemic analysis usually will not be enough to decode its meaning. In most cases, references outside the passage must be used to find the meaning of the unknown words. The three most important references are the glossary, index, and dictionary. Online texts often include additional support in the form of searchable glossary elements by simply clicking on an unknown word. If a text fails to offer a glossary, most smart phones can support a quick online search to locate a word's definition, pronunciation, and so on. These are useful for all learners but especially English language learners. Encountering a word like "paradigm" along with its definition does not guarantee a student has any idea how it is pronounced.

GLOSSARY. A *glossary* is an alphabetized list of the technical words used in a textbook. With each word is the definition of the word as it is used in the book. Not all textbooks have glossaries, but those that do usually place the glossary at the back of the book (like this one). Sometimes authors put the glossary at the beginning or end of each chapter in the text.

INDEX. When a textbook does not contain a glossary, the index is another good reference for finding word meanings. An *index* is an alphabetized list of important terms and topics included in the text. It is always located at the back of the text. Locate the index for this textbook. The index lists the page numbers in the text where information can be found on each topic. Frequently, the word for which a student is hunting will be defined in context on one of those pages. This is particularly true of technical vocabulary.

DICTIONARY. When students need to find the meaning of a nontechnical word, they should use a dictionary. The standard word dictionary is undoubtedly the most common reference tool. Unfortunately, it is also probably one of the most misunderstood and misused. Because the dictionary is used so widely, teachers have a tendency to assume that students know how to use a dictionary. This is a dangerous assumption.

For example, one of us once asked a ninth grader in his English class to look up the word "embroil." After a few minutes he returned to the student's desk only to find her moving her finger laboriously from entry to entry on page four of the As. The student did not know that words in a dictionary are arranged alphabetically! This remarkable incident led the author to discover that half the class did not know what guide words were, and that over half did not know how to use the pronunciation key or how to choose from among the multiple definitions of a word.

If you want your students to use the dictionary, particularly for verifying the meanings of unfamiliar words in print, it is worth your time to diagnose their familiarity with this important book. The guide words and entry in Figure 8.1 indicate the most common and important features of dictionaries.

Dictionary skills can be assessed informally by asking students to seek out and explain the various features of specific entries in the dictionary, either in print or online form. This can easily be conducted as a group activity in which students must find an answer and then explain how they arrived at it. For example,

"Turn to page 253 of your dictionary and figure out how to pronounce the word "___" (e.g., "daguerreotype" is written on the board). Raise your hand when you have the answer, but be prepared to explain to the rest of the class how you got it."

Features of the Dictionary

FIGURE 8.1

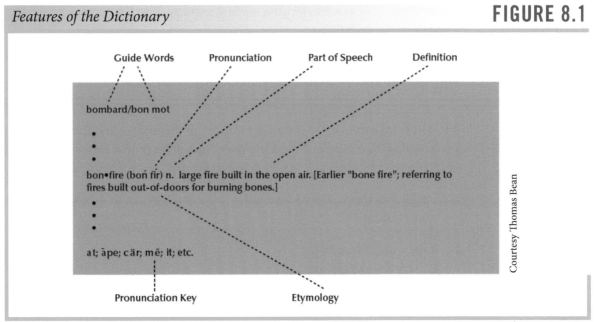

Courtesy Thomas Bean

Once you have ascertained which dictionary features students need to practice, discuss them and then provide practice in identifying and interpreting those features. It is, of course, possible to create exercises for students. However, a simpler and more enjoyable activity is for students to compete with each other or with the clock to see how fast they can identify parts of speech, specific guide words, etymologies, and so on.

For those students interested in pursuing the dictionary through the Internet, they are directed to One Look Dictionaries (Available: www.onelook.com). This is a website which can search the dictionary world to provide comprehensive definitions of words.

In addition, dictionary.com and other dictionary sites offer students a self-monitoring vehicle for learning new words (Ebner & Ehri, 2013). The recommended steps applied, for example, to learning about "exercise persistence" in Physical Education might include the following:

o Read the online dictionary entry for the words (i.e., exercise persistence).

o Avoid distractions (e.g., pop up ads) and stay focused on the goal.

o Write down the definition of the term and related examples (e.g., keeping an exercise journal).

APPLICATION 8.2

Directions: Create an activity for giving middle or secondary students practice in using one or more features of the dictionary.

A GENERAL DECODING STRATEGY FOR TEXTBOOKS

When students encounter an unfamiliar word while they are reading, they should first finish reading the sentence. If they determine the word is crucial for comprehension, we recommend that they rely heavily on external references, following these steps:

1. Decide whether the word is technical or general. When in doubt, assume the word is technical.

2. If the word is technical,
   a. Try the glossary first.
   b. Then try the index.
   c. Then try the dictionary.

3. If the word is general,
    a. Try the dictionary first.
    b. Then try the glossary.
    c. Then try the index.

4. After finding a meaning for the word, check the meaning in the context of the sentence to make sure that the definition fits. This is particularly important when using a dictionary. Context is critical as a verification procedure.

This strategy is recommended as a way for students to deal systematically and independently with unfamiliar words in print. The strategy concentrates on meaning since that is the task of students when they are reading textbook assignments. The strategy also avoids the pitfalls of haphazard or misleading guessing associated with context clues and morphemic analysis. Those who are knowledgeable in a subject area do not need to guess at the meanings of important words: those who are less knowledgeable should not.

PRINCIPLES FOR EFFECTIVE VOCABULARY INSTRUCTION

If there is one thing that contributes most heavily to the burden of learning technical vocabulary, it is the simple lack of direct instruction. Teachers frequently assume that students will automatically assimilate new words just because they are introduced in textbook assignments. This is a mistake. While incidental learning of word meanings may occur with narrative, story-type material, even across cultures, this will, more than likely, not occur with textbook material. Consequently, almost any kind of direct instruction you provide is better than none at all. The following principles should be considered in conjunction with the specific teaching strategies presented later in the chapter, as well as the information presented about lesson and unit planning in Chapter 6.

Be an Enthusiastic Model of Vocabulary Use

Reach out to your students and make them see that you believe vocabulary development is something more than a dead paragraph from your teacher's syllabus. Let them see you using a dictionary once in a while, and make an effort to use words you expect the students to learn. In addition to exemplifying new terms in appropriate verbal contexts, you will be demonstrating that they have some practical value. Nothing will facilitate the acquisition of vocabulary more than the enthusiasm that you convey to students.

Make Vocabulary Meaningful

Vocabulary instruction should have a long-term impact upon individual powers of communication and concept development. A vocabulary program that encourages students to squeeze the definitions for 20 words into a temporary memory store so that they can pass Friday's quiz is a waste of time. New words and their meanings must be stored in long-term memory if they are to add to the students' powers of perception and articulation. As we pointed out in Chapter 3, placing information in long-term memory is difficult unless the information is meaningful in terms of prior knowledge. Consequently, new words should be (1) defined in multiple contexts; (2) drawn from reading or other experiences immediately pertinent to the student; and (3) defined in terms and with examples that clearly fall within the boundaries of the students' prior knowledge.

In general, the greater the quantity of meaningful associations that teachers can tie to new words, the greater the likelihood that the students will remember and use them (Cunningham, 1992).

Reinforce Vocabulary

Give students an opportunity to use their new words as they read, write, speak, and listen. There is no substitute for meaningful practice. Drill, practice, and multiple exposures to a new word in various contexts will improve word knowledge and comprehension.

Be Eclectic

There are as many good ways to teach vocabulary as there are creative teachers, and probably no single one is the best. However, any method can become boring if it is overused. A successful vocabulary program will employ a variety of methods. Moreover, a balanced program emphasizing both contextual and definitional strategies is likely to work best. In the recommended reading section of this chapter we highlight some of the many approaches available that are supported by research (e.g., Baumann & Graves, 2010). For example, these authorities recommend thinking about academic vocabulary in terms of a classification scheme that includes five elements:

o Domain-specific vocabulary (relevant to your discipline, e.g., "ratio")

o General academic vocabulary (e.g., "inquire")

o Literary vocabulary (e.g., "exegesis")

o Symbols (e.g., ">")

o Metalanguage (e.g., "summarize")

Teaching new vocabulary prior to reading assignments is a direct application of the *readiness principle.* Readiness refers to the mental state in which an individual is prepared to derive maximum meaning from a learning situation, with a minimum of frustration. Preteaching content area vocabulary is a readiness aid that gives students direction and purpose for reading.

Introducing vocabulary facilitates reading comprehension by reducing the number of unfamiliar words in textbook and online reading assignments. If new terms are introduced in a meaningful and interesting manner, this will reinforce vocabulary, generate enthusiasm for the reading task, and provide background information that will help students relate what they know to the content of the text. The strategies for introducing vocabulary that follow are adaptable to reading assignments in most content areas.

Troubleshoot reading assignments for the students by identifying important words that are likely to confuse them as they read. Then introduce those words before they begin their reading assignments. By introducing difficult terminology, the teacher facilitates the retention of pivotal vocabulary, provides students with critical prior knowledge of the content they are being asked to assimilate, and improves reading comprehension by reducing the number of alien words in the text. In most subject areas, reading assignments introduce so many unfamiliar words that it is impossible to teach all of them.

Tips for Selecting Words to Teach

1. Restrict your selections to words that are critical to comprehending the selection.

2. Choose words that define key concepts.

3. Choose terms that you might include in a test.

4. Choose words that have a new technical meaning in addition to a general, familiar meaning, e.g., "complementary" angles as opposed to "complimentary" actions in social situations.

5. Ignore terms that will be of little or no use once a student has passed the test.

6. Do not spend time reinforcing the meanings of words just because they appear in italics.

Teacher-Directed Vocabulary Strategies

o Contextual redefinition
o Personal glossary
o Graphic organizers
o Word origins
o Semantic mapping
o Clues and questions

In addition to preteaching strategies, it is also good teaching to reinforce new vocabulary after reading. Reinforcing new vocabulary allows students to review the words that you introduced before reading and words they encountered during reading. In essence, reinforcement makes the words more meaningful to students. The following teacher-directed strategies for introducing and reinforcing vocabulary are adaptable to reading assignments in most content areas and should be modified as necessary to fit the idiosyncratic nature of individual classrooms.

Contextual Redefinition

We recommend a strategy described by Tierney and Readence (2005) for its simplicity and ease for content teachers. To illustrate contextual redefinition, define each of the following words using only your own prior knowledge.

1. Carapace _____

2. Nonsectarian _____

3. Insipid _____

Were you able to write a definition without going to a dictionary? If not, read the following sentences and see if they help you with the definition of the words. After you write a definition, check the dictionary for your definition.

1. Without its *carapace,* the turtle would be subject to certain death from its enemies or the elements.

2. Although he was a believer in God, he had a *nonsectarian* attitude toward religion.

3. His teaching lacked spirit. He had presented his lesson in a dull manner, failing to challenge or stimulate the students. The teacher knew he had made an *insipid* presentation.

Did the sentences help you with the meaning of the unknown words? If they did, you were utilizing the surrounding context as clues to the meaning of the words. *Contextual redefinition* is a strategy that introduces new vocabulary in rich contexts that help define words and facilitate memory by giving the words meaningful associations.

206

Steps for Contextual Redefinition

1. **Select unfamiliar words.** Identify those words that may present trouble to your students and that may be central to understanding the important concepts they will encounter in their reading. Select only a few words to be presented at one time to prevent the lesson from becoming tedious.

2. **Write a sentence.** An appropriate context for each word should be written with clues to its meaning. The categories of clues discussed earlier should be utilized in writing these sentences. In the sample sentences provided, "carapace" could be identified by previous experience, "nonsectarian" by comparison and contrast, and "insipid" by description or mood. If such a context already exists in the text material the students are about to read, it is appropriate to use that, in lieu of creating a new context for it.

3. **Present the words in isolation.** Using the whiteboard, smart board, or other display, ask students to provide you with a meaning for the unfamiliar word. Some guesses may be off base or even humorous, but students should be asked to come to a consensus about the best meaning.

4. **Present the words in a sentence.** Using the sentence you developed previously, now present the word in context. Again, ask the students to provide a meaning for the unfamiliar word. It is important that students who volunteer definitions defend their guess by providing the rationale for it. In this way poor readers will be able to experience the thinking processes of other students and how they arrive at meaning. In essence, students can act as models for each other.

5. **Dictionary verification.** A volunteer or volunteers can look up the word in the online or print-based dictionary to verify the guesses offered by the class. This step also provides students and the teacher an opportunity to examine any morphemes present in the word and how they might help in its verification.

Students gain several benefits from this strategy. First, they realize that trying to identify an unfamiliar word by simply focusing on the word as an isolated element is frustrating, it makes for haphazard guessing, and it probably is not very accurate. They are prompted to develop more reliable methods for determining meaning. Second, students become actively involved in a more profitable process of discovering new words rather than in their rote memorization. Finally, the dictionary is cast in its most appropriate role—that of a tool used to verify the meanings of unfamiliar words by selecting the definition that is syntactically and semantically acceptable in a particular context.

Personal Glossary

Having students keep a *personal glossary* is a valuable addition to the context re-definition strategy (Bean, Readence, & Baldwin, 2012). A personal glossary will aid students' long-term retention of word definitions. The following steps demonstrate how to guide students' development of their own personal glossaries:

Steps for Personal Glossary Development

1. **Introduce the glossary format.** Although the format for entries in a standard dictionary is comprehensive, it may present more features than are necessary for students' personal glossaries. We recommend the following components for a personal glossary: (a) the word; (b) its definition; and (c) a sentence using the word in context. You may find that the pronunciation of the word, its part of speech, and/or its etymology useful for your students. Introduce the format you want your students to use and show students how their personal glossary should look. For instance, using our previous example, *bonfire*, a personal glossary entry might look like the following:

   bonfire

   Definition: large fire built in the open air.

   Sentence: The football team built a bonfire at its party to celebrate its victory over their main rival.

2. **Direct students in its usage.** The personal glossary is used individually by students to help them retain word meanings, so tell students to enter difficult words introduced by you as well as problematic words they encounter in their own class reading. Explain that their glossaries are their responsibility to maintain and that they are important to help them learn and retain key vocabulary words and their meanings, particularly if you use them in a test. Demonstrate that they can use the words to quiz themselves about the definition of the word and how it might be used in a sentence. Emphasize that they can make the words part of their permanent vocabulary through periodic rehearsal of the words' definitions and their use in context.

Graphic Organizers

A *graphic organizer* is a visual aid that defines hierarchical relationships among concepts. It lends itself particularly well to the teaching of technical vocabulary. The graphic organizer may be used in a variety of ways. It may be used as an introductory strategy, as exemplified by the organizers at the beginning of each chapter

208

in this text. Such usage is designed to provide relational guides to the prose that follows them. A graphic organizer may also be used as a postreading technique to reinforce and summarize. Additionally, the graphic organizer is one strategy that can be used in the same lesson to enhance both readiness and recall of material. In all cases, the graphic organizer can be an excellent mechanism for defining related concepts. Certainly, modeling the use of graphic organizers for students will help them see their usefulness.

Steps for Generating Graphic Organizers

1. **Concept Identification.** An analysis of the content is undertaken to identify all new terms and concepts that will be introduced in the reading assignment. Since there will often be a large number of these terms and concepts, it will save time simply to mark them in your own text. The following list was derived from one chapter in a science text dealing with matter and how it is structured.

Structure of matter	Natural elements
Elements	Compounds
Metals	Nonmetals
Nucleus	Atoms
Mixtures	Physical combination
Natural elements	Orbits
Particles	Electrons
Protons	Neutrons
Electron shell	Energy levels
Molecule	Electrolysis
Inert gases	Positive electrical charge
Negative electrical charge	
Atomic theory of matter	
Law of definite or constant proportions	
Chemical combinations	

2. **Concept Selection.** In order to prevent the organizer from being overly complex, it is critical to prune the initial list until it consists only of superordinate concepts, that is, those that are most important or most essential to the integrity of the reading selection. The organizer is supposed to supplement the reading assignment, not replace it. Once the list has been reduced, subclassify the remaining terms in an informal outline.

Structure of matter
    Chemical combinations
        Compounds
        Molecules
        Elements
    Natural elements
        Metals
        Nonmetals
    Physical combinations
        Mixtures
            Compounds
            Elements

3. **Diagram Construction.** Arrange the terms in a tree diagram that reflects the structure established in Step 2. (See Fig. 8.2.)

4. **Initial Evaluation.** Once you have created the organizer, step back and evaluate it. Does the organizer accurately convey the concepts you wish to teach? If not, rearrange the diagram until you are satisfied. One of the advantages of the graphic organizer is that it helps teachers to organize and clarify their own purposes. In addition to accuracy, consider the complexity of the diagram. Students can be overwhelmed if the visual display is too complicated. Under such conditions it may be desirable to present the organizer piece by piece.

FIGURE 8.2 *Graphic Organizer on the Structure of Matter*

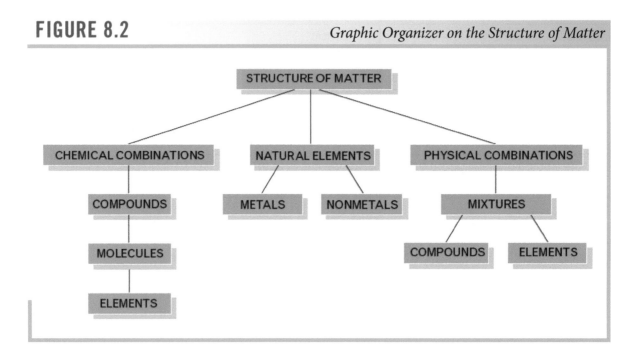

5. **Organizer Presentation.** The physical presentation of the organizer is unimportant. Handouts, a permanent poster, overhead transparency, or chalkboard may be used as the teacher's resources dictate. The time required for the presentation will vary depending on the complexity of the organizer and the extent to which the concepts in question are unfamiliar to students. Begin the presentation with a general explanation of the purpose of the organizer and an explanation of how a tree diagram works. Talk students through the organizer, explaining each term, encouraging student questions and discussion, and indicating the ways in which terms are related to each other. In so doing you will be developing vocabulary, improving reading comprehension, and enriching schemata in ways that will make subject matter more meaningful to students.

APPLICATION 8.3

Directions: Using the following words, create a graphic organizer. Be prepared to justify your arrangement.

Vertebrate	Mammal	Invertebrate
Snake	Grasshopper	Reptile
Cockroach	Crustacean	Aardvark
Animal	Whale	Insect
Lobster	Shrimp	Crocodile

Word Origins (Etymologies)

Introductory strategies for vocabulary are successful to the extent that they are interesting and build meaningful schemata. Etymologies offer a colorful means of helping students remember word meanings. This is especially true for social studies and English, where many relevant words have interesting etymologies.

The *etymology* of a word is its history, where it originated, and how it came to be a part of the language. Language is not a static feature of human behavior; all languages are in a constant state of change. Grammar mutates from one form to another; lexical items become popular and then fall into disuse, for example, groovy. The meanings of words change, too. Every word that is now a part of the English language has a past, a present, and a future. Many word histories are quite interesting and can add flavor to an otherwise banal vocabulary lesson.

The etymological portion of a dictionary entry follows the pronunciation guide and part of speech and is enclosed in bold face brackets, although some dictionaries do not include any etymological information at all.

CONSIDER THIS!

This is the more colorful portion of the etymology for the word "chauvinism" taken from *Webster's New Collegiate Dictionary*.

> [F "chauvinisme," fr. Nicolas "Chauvin" fl 1815 F soldier of excessive patriotism and devotion to Napoleon]

The F is an abbreviation for "French," *fr.* stands for "from," and *fl* is an abbreviation of a Latin word that means "flourished about." In addition to its interesting origin, "chauvinism" provides an example of how word meanings change over time. Originally, "chauvinism" referred to excessive patriotism or loyalty to a cause or creed. However, now the meaning of the word has narrowed so that it refers primarily to men who are so loyal to their sex that they have condescending or disparaging attitudes toward women, that is, "male chauvinist pigs."

Other sources of word histories are books that provide more complete story lines.

CONSIDER THIS!

The following etymology of the word "berserk" is quoted from *Thereby Hangs a Tale: Stories of Curious Word Origins* (Funk, 1950):

> In Norse mythology there was a famous furious fighter who scorned the use of heavy mail, entering battle without armor. His only protection was the skin of a bear fastened over one shoulder. From this he became known as "berserk," or "bear shirt." It was said of him that he could assume the form of a wild beast, and that neither iron nor fire could harm him, for he fought with the fury of a beast of the forest and his foes were unable to touch him. Each of his twelve sons, in turn, also carried the name "berserk," and each was as furious a fighter as the father. From these Norse heroes, it came to be that any person so inflamed with the fury of fighting as to be equally dangerous to friend and foe as was that legendary family when engaged in battle, was called "berserk" or "berserker." (p. 48)

We submit that few students could forget the word "berserk" if it were introduced in conjunction with the story of bear shirt! This is a clear example of how rich and meaningful associations can facilitate the learning of new words.

It may be useful for advanced students to check the etymologies of words in a dictionary. However, the numerous abbreviations, references to classical languages, and clipped versions of the histories may rob interest from otherwise interesting stories. For this reason, dictionary etymologies may be more useful as sources of information that teachers may incidentally insert into vocabulary presentations.

Not all words have flashy histories, and we are not recommending that the etymology of every new word be explored with students. Nevertheless, tossing one or two into a lesson is an excellent means of building interest and promoting recall. Collections of word histories are standard volumes in most secondary school libraries and can be found under the headings *English Language* or *Etymologies*. See Application 8.4 for more interesting etymologies.

Semantic Mapping

A *semantic map* is a diagram that groups related concepts; it combines this grouping activity with the structure the graphic organizer provides. Semantic maps may be used as prereading or postreading exercises that reinforce new vocabulary and help students relate their prior knowledge to new experiences and concepts. You and your students can construct a semantic map using the steps given in the example that follows:

1. Select an important word or topic from the lecture or reading assignment. This example is based on disastrous volcanoes. The topic in this case will be "volcano."

2. Write the topic (volcano) on the board or overhead projector.

3. Ask students to write down as many related words as they can think of from their own experiences or from their reading of the text. In this case we assume that students have read the text.

Vesuvius	Vulcanian	Pompeii
Mount St. Helens	Cataclysm	Lava
Ash	Earthquake	Ring of Fire
Vent	Conduit	Volcanic bombs
Gas	Blocks	Tsunami
Explosions	Plug	Krakatoa
Pressure	Hell	Terrifying plate
Tectonics	Magma	Shield volcano

4. Organize the words into a diagram as in Figure 8.3.

APPLICATION 8.4

Directions: The following words, listed by content area, have interesting word origins. Select one of the lists and use an unabridged dictionary, an etymological dictionary, or a book on interesting word origins to determine their histories. Describe how you might work one or more of these words into a lesson in your own content area.

Science	Social Studies	English
Alkali	Assassin	Anecdote
Barnacle	Ballot	Dumbbell
Cobalt	Boycott	Enthrall
Crayfish	Filibuster	Fib
Hurricane	Indenture	Gossip
Larva	Lynch	Quixotic
Nicotine	Senate	Sarcasm
Parasite	Sinecure	Tragedy

_____

_____

_____

_____

_____

_____

_____

_____

_____

_____

_____

_____

_____

5. Students share words while you write them on the board. As new categories emerge, give the map new arms or add categories of your own. The diagram itself can be as simple or as complex as you desire.

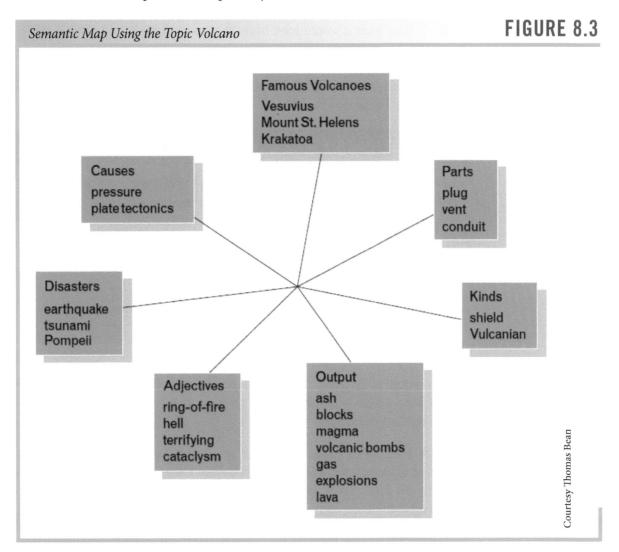

Semantic Map Using the Topic Volcano

FIGURE 8.3

Famous Volcanoes
Vesuvius
Mount St. Helens
Krakatoa

Parts
plug
vent
conduit

Causes
pressure
plate tectonics

Disasters
earthquake
tsunami
Pompeii

Kinds
shield
Vulcanian

Adjectives
ring-of-fire
hell
terrifying
cataclysm

Output
ash
blocks
magma
volcanic bombs
gas
explosions
lava

Courtesy Thomas Bean

6. Have students name the various categories or break categories into subcategories.

Famous volcanoes   Volcanic output
Parts of volcanoes   Related disasters
Adjectives that describe volcanoes Kinds of volcanoes
Causes of volcanoes

7. Perhaps the most important step in this activity is the discussion and questioning activities that accompany the diagram. For example,

   a. Why are volcanoes considered disastrous?

b. Which do you think was the all-time most disastrous volcano?

c. Why is "Ring of Fire" a good name?

d. In what ways are Mauna Loa and Vesuvius different? How are they the same?

e. Tell us what it would have been like to be on the island of Krakatoa in 1883.

f. "Mark, imagine that you are Krakatoa. Susan, imagine that you are Mount St. Helens. Now, each of you try to convince the other that you are the world's greatest volcano."

APPLICATION 8.5

Directions: Imagine that you have just finished teaching a series of units on human physiology, that is, parts of the body. Describe how you would conduct an appropriate semantic mapping lesson with your class. Be sure to include the following:

1. 20–30 terms likely to be elicited from students.

2. Probable groups and labels for those terms.

Clues and Questions

This procedure is designed to help students review technical vocabulary. What makes *Clues and Questions* interesting is the fact that students provide the questions as well as the answers.

The teacher begins by collecting content area vocabulary for students to review. Each word is typed on a notecard and placed in a shoebox or card file. Students randomly select several of these cards. Their task is to write questions whose answers are the words on each card.

The teacher encourages the students to use the textbook index to find where their vocabulary words are introduced and used. In addition, the teacher provides examples of different kinds of questions and clues, for example, definition, analogy, comparison–contrast, context (see the following example on "molecule"). As students finish writing questions, the teacher checks them for clarity and accuracy, and then has the student print them on a vocabulary card or smart phone display directly below the word.

When the vocabulary cards have been completed, the class is subdivided into small groups, with each group having a portion of the vocabulary cards. One student shows a card to the others in the group but does not look at the card. Each of the other students asks a question or supplies a clue until the word is identified.

The activity proceeds in round-robin fashion until the cards have been exhausted, at which point students exchange cards and the clue sessions begin anew.

As a vocabulary builder, the clues and questions procedure has a number of strengths. First, allowing students to create their own questions for a game gives them a novel purpose for using the text. Second, students will benefit from trying to write clear and meaningful questions. And third, participating in the vocabulary review will itself enlarge and reinforce students' technical vocabularies.

Molecule

1. _____ is to compound as atom is to element.

2. What is the smallest unit of a compound that retains all the characteristics of that compound?

3. Two hydrogen atoms and one oxygen atom make one _____ of water.

STRATEGIES FOR VOCABULARY INDEPENDENCE

Students need to have their own repertoire of strategies to help them learn new words independently. In this section we describe four strategies that are relatively easy for students to learn and use across various content areas. However, as with any learning strategy, students need to be shown how to apply them when reading and learning with text.

Verbal and Visual Word Association

Students can use this strategy on their own, to learn and retain both general and technical vocabulary. The *verbal and visual word association strategy* we describe here is especially effective for struggling readers (Bean, Readence, & Baldwin, 2012). In our own work we have found that this strategy can be learned and used effectively, with adaptations, by second language learners in content area classes.

> **Vocabulary Independence Strategies**
> o Verbal and visual word association
> o Vocabulary self-collection
> o Word map
> o TOAST

Suppose you are reading along in a novel and you encounter the following passage:

> *"Joan had recently taken up jogging. She used to live life in the fast lane— staying out all night dancing and partying till dawn. Now that she was middle-aged, Joan strived for a more salubrious lifestyle."*

The word "salubrious" is a general vocabulary term not well known by most people. Let us assume you need to learn and remember this word. The following steps of the verbal and visual word association strategy will help you associate the word "salubrious" with personal experiences:

FIGURE 8.4

Verbal and Visual Word Association for "Salubrious"

Surfing	Salubrious
Promoting health	Smoking

1. Draw a square with four boxes in it. Write the word "salubrious" in the top right square and its definition in the bottom left square (see Figure 8.4). Salubrious, as you may have guessed by now, means healthful. Hence, Joan's jogging suggests she is now leading a salubrious lifestyle.

2. Now in the top left square you need to write a personal association for the word "salubrious"—something you do in your own life that is salubrious. For example, surfing is a healthful activity so you might put that in the upper left square.

3. In the bottom right square you need to include a word that describes something you do or something you experience that is not salubrious. Thus, smoking, an unhealthful habit, might go here. This verbal association for the word "salubrious" can then be used to study and retain a personally meaningful conception of the word. In speaking and writing activities, the word "salubrious" is one you might feel comfortable using.

A student in social studies trying to learn the word "diplomatic" formed the following verbal association in Figure 8.5. His association for someone diplomatic was Franklin D. Roosevelt, a successful American diplomat of World War II. This student's non-example, also from World War II—someone clearly not a diplomatic person—was Adolf Hitler.

FIGURE 8.5

Verbal and Visual Association for "Diplomatic"

Diplomatic	Franklin D. Roosevelt
Skilled in international relations	Adolf Hitler

STRATEGY MODIFICATION. Second language students benefit from a modification of the original verbal association strategy. By including a visual association with the verbal symbol and omitting the non-example, second language students can quickly grasp and learn unfamiliar general and technical vocabulary. For example, the word "nocturnal" can be associated with the drawing of a half moon and stars against a black background (see Figure 8.6). Then, in the lower right corner, this student's personal association, "owl," is written to reinforce the idea of a creature that hunts at night. Thus, concept development was enhanced with this strategy modification by providing additional reinforcement rather than the constructive non-example.

Verbal and Visual Association for "Nocturnal" **FIGURE 8.6**

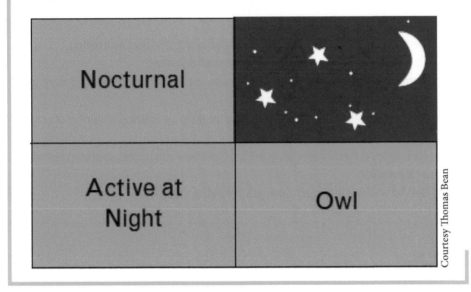

Courtesy Thomas Bean

The visual and verbal association strategy can be introduced to students easily and, given some guided practice, it should quickly become part of their repertoire of independent strategies for learning new vocabulary. It works best for nouns and descriptive adjectives. Highly technical terms such as "photosynthesis" require the more elaborate conceptual networks that may be formed using a graphic organizer, semantic mapping, or the vocabulary self-collection strategy that follows.

View the video clip on the website showing the creative products of the verbal and visual word association strategy with middle school students.

Vocabulary Self-Collection

Given the enormous numbers of new words that students encounter in reading assignments, it is not surprising that most students have a difficult time deciding which unfamiliar words to learn. The *vocabulary self-collection strategy* (VSS) (Ruddell & Shearer, 2002) is a vocabulary acquisition technique that is designed to teach students how to select the most important vocabulary from reading assignments. VSS should first be introduced as a postreading group activity.

GUIDELINES FOR VOCABULARY SELF-COLLECTION

1. Student teams identify a word or term important for learning content information. The teacher identifies one word or term.
2. Teacher writes the words on the chalkboard as teams give definitions from context.
3. Class members add any information they can to each definition.
4. Teacher and students consult external references, e.g., glossary, index, and dictionary, for definitions that are incomplete or unclear.
5. Students and teacher discuss and then narrow the list to a predetermined number of words for a final class list.
6. Students record the class list with agreed-upon definitions in notebooks, vocabulary journals, or on notecards.
7. Class list words are used in extension activities and class tests.

Word Map

Once students are proficient at categorizing technical vocabulary through the semantic mapping strategy, they can learn to use word maps to develop ownership of important terminology. Word maps provide students with a procedure for independently studying content area vocabulary (Tierney & Readence, 2005). A *word map* is a visual representation of a definition, displaying three categories of semantic knowledge: (a) the general class or category to which the concept belongs; (b) the primary properties of the concept and how these properties distinguish it from other members of the class; and (c) examples of the concept.

Figure 8.7 demonstrates a student's effort to develop a word map in science class for the word "reptile." Steps to make students independent users of word maps follow:

1. Discuss the word map with students, emphasizing its value as a word study technique.

2. Walk through the incomplete word map, modeling the process with familiar words like "skateboard," "ice cream," "computer," and "sandwich." Have students brainstorm associations for these words as you would in semantic mapping, and then align the associations with category labels.

3. Give students independent guided practice with technical words in a rich sentence context. Then progress to words in less rich contexts that require students to consult another source of information such as a dictionary, glossary, or encyclopedia.

After students have constructed a word map, you may want to add the requirement that they then create a sentence using the word to see if they have, in fact, internalized its meaning and truly own the word in writing and speaking. For example, the student studying reptiles wrote, "Snakes are reptiles most people fear." This sentence demonstrates that the student knows specific examples of reptiles.

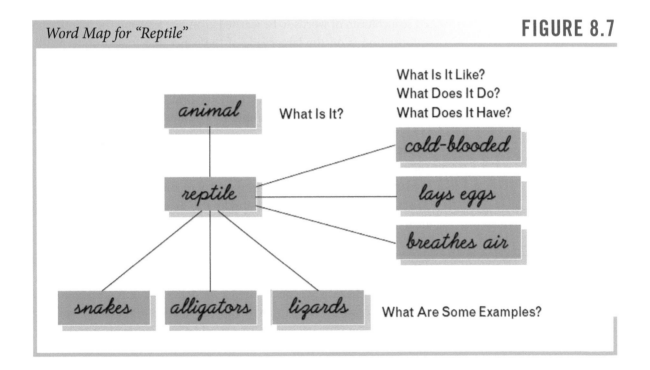

Word Map for "Reptile"   **FIGURE 8.7**

TOAST

A final strategy to help students achieve vocabulary independence is *TOAST,* an acronym which corresponds to the steps in the procedure—*t*est, *o*rganize, *a*nchor, *s*ay, and *t*est. TOAST was developed by Dana and Rodriguez (1992) to provide students with a system for independently studying vocabulary so they can learn at their own rate and focus on the words that seem the most difficult. For many students TOAST represents a viable alternative to the method they themselves use as a means of studying words—which is probably unsystematic at best. Additionally, the strategy is a good rehearsal activity for second language learners. TOAST has the following steps:

Test   Students first pretest themselves on new vocabulary introduced to them in class; by doing so, they determine which words are already known to them, which ones they are somewhat familiar with, and which require additional study time. Students can make vocabulary cards with the word to be learned on one side and the definition and a sentence with that word on the other side. An alternative is to use a piece of paper folded so a column of words to be learned is on one side and the identifying information is on the larger side of the paper and folded underneath. Students examine each word and attempt to guess the definition and provide a sentence; guesses could be verified by checking the other side of the card or paper. The pretest could be oral, silent, or written. It also may be done with a partner if time and circumstances allow.

Organize Students organize their words into some framework that will enhance their ability to learn the new vocabulary. They might arrange them into semantically related groups or place them into categories according to structural similarities. They might also arrange them according to degree of familiarity or unfamiliarity. Some type of organization is important, as it helps students mnemonically and facilitates their learning of the words.

Anchor   Some type of strategy is necessary for students to commit the words to long-term memory. This might entail, but not be limited to (a) working with a partner to teach and test each other, or even compete with one another; (b) using a tape recorder to tape, listen, and recite definitions and sentences; (c) using timed trials to figure out improvement over a series of trials in writing or reciting the words and their definitions; (d) trying to find another word to act as a mnemonic link to the target word; or (e) examining the morphemes present in each word.

Say   This step constitutes the review stage of the procedure. To avoid forgetting newly learned words, these must be periodically rehearsed and reviewed. The first review session should occur 5–10 minutes after learning the words; other review sessions can occur later the same day, a week later, and just before the test. Vocabulary that has been forgotten should be relearned using the anchoring strategies from the previous step.

Test Students need to conduct a posttest after each review to check how well they have learned the words. This test may be conducted in the same way as the pretest.

EXTENSION ACTIVITIES

Extension activities are pencil-and-paper exercises designed to reinforce and expand the schemata of newly acquired content area vocabulary. These activities allow students to explore word relationships and, in general, to manipulate and practice new terminology in a variety of ways. Recall and memorization are certainly a part of extension activities; however, these activities should also force students to think about the terms they are learning. The following extension activities are examples of exercises that teachers can use to enhance the acquisition of vocabulary in their own content area classrooms. Additional extension activities for English language learners are offered in Townsend (2009), one of the recommended readings for this chapter. These include Picture Puzzlers, Music Puzzlers, Action Jeopardy, and others.

Analogies

Word analogies are useful thinking exercises. They require students to draw inferences, and they are an attractive method of exposing subtle word associations. In addition, analogies lend themselves to creative and divergent thinking. A word of caution: analogies can be extremely difficult, especially for students who have never worked with them. Be prepared to provide students with simple analogies that can be used as models for verbalizing relationships. For instance,

> **Pencil-and-Paper Extension Activities**
> o Analogies
> o Hidden-word puzzles
> o Matching definitions to scrambled words
> o Crossword puzzles

Night is to *day* as *big* is to_____

Large, black, little, simple

Verbalization: Night is the opposite of day, so big must be the opposite of something.

What is the opposite of big? Little.

Analogies are easier to complete if answers are provided; however, that leaves only one correct answer for each analogy. If no answers are provided, the analogies are more difficult, but they allow for divergent answers and interesting discussion. (See Figure 8.8.) The decision should be based on the capabilities of the class.

FIGURE 8.8 — *Sample Analogy Activity*

Directions: The following analogies are about science vocabulary that we have just studied. Pick the answer you feel makes the most sense.

1. *Gas* is to *liquid* as *liquid* is to _____.
2. *Proton* is to *positive* as *electron* is to _____.
3. *Atom* is to *element* as _____ is to *compound*.
4. *Physical* is to *mixture* as _____ is to *compound*.
5. *Hg* is to *mercury* as _____ is to *silver*.

Solid	Atomic	Water	Energy	Molecule	Negative
K	S	Chemical	Ag	Salt	

Hidden-Word Puzzles

Hidden-word puzzles are activities that almost all students respond to positively. Consequently, they make good motivational devices for vocabulary review. Hidden-word puzzles are easy to make, using computer software. A word of caution: always give clues that define the hidden words in some way. If the clues are eliminated, the hidden-word puzzle simply becomes an exercise in word recognition rather than an extension activity for vocabulary development. (See companion website Chapter 8 Activities for puzzle software.)

Matching Definitions to Scrambled Words

This exercise provides straightforward reinforcement for meanings of basic vocabulary. Scrambling the spellings adds an extra challenge and makes the activity more interesting. See Figure 8.9 for an example.

Directions: Below are two lists. The numbered list on the left has some basic math terms that we have studied. (Notice that the spellings are mixed up.) The lettered list on the right is composed of definitions for the math terms. Place the letter of each definition on the line next to the appropriate math term.

1. rcleci _____
2. ip _____
3. ets _____
4. toinp _____
5. recpiorclas _____
6. nogatnep _____
7. hcord _____
8. irccumfreence _____
9. daiemtre _____
10. miepr _____

A. A number that has only two whole number factors
B. A line segment with endpoints on a circle
C. A closed curved figure on which every point is an equal distance from a fixed point within the curve
D. 3.14159265
E. Two of these are necessary to determine a line
F. A polygon that has five sides
G. A collection of mathematical elements that have something in common
H. A chord running through the center of a circle
I. Two fractions whose product is 1
J. The perimeter of a circle

Crossword Puzzles

The best way to develop your own puzzles is to use crossword puzzle generator software. Many of these programs offer free demonstration downloads on the web. They allow you to use your own word lists or to tap into their previously set-up dictionaries to develop crossword puzzles. We suggest you consider searching for your own crossword puzzle software on the web. You will find this can be a lot of fun!

NOW go back to the vocabulary vignette at the beginning of the chapter. React again to the lesson as you did before. Compare your answers with those you made before you read the chapter.

MINI PROJECTS

Using the text chapter on the website entitled "The Use and Misuse of Alcohol," do one or all of the following:

1. Choose a teacher-directed vocabulary strategy from Chapter 8 and design an activity appropriate for use in a high school health class.

2. Select a strategy for vocabulary independence and demonstrate how you would use it with students.

3. Develop an extension activity to foster creative and divergent thinking about the key vocabulary related to alcohol.

RECOMMENDED WEBSITES

o Dictionary of affixes: http://www.affixes.org/index.html
o Online dictionary/thesaurus with 1400 affixes: http://memidex.com
o Online dictionary: dictionary.com
o ReadWriteThink lesson planning for vocabulary:
   http://www.readwritethink.org/professional-development/strategy/guides/introducing-ideas-vocabulary/with-30953.html

WEBSITE ACTIVITY

Go to the website for Chapter 5 activities.

Comprehension:
Principles and Integrated Approaches

CHAPTER 9

VIGNETTE

Setting

Jake Spear's ninth-grade literature class. Mr. Spear is in his first teaching job in a diverse urban high school. As the class nears an end, he is about to introduce the next novel the students will read, Les Miserables by Victor Hugo.

The Lesson

Mr. Spear: *"Today we are about to begin reading our next class novel, Les Miserables by Victor Hugo. Does anyone know anything about it?"*

Eunsook: *"I think it's a play that my parents went to see."*

Mr. Spear: *"Yes. Anything else?"*

Students: *Some shuffling of papers and yawning is seen to occur.*

Mr. Spear: *"Okay. This story is set in France in the 18th century. What do you know about that time?"*

Manuel: *"Wasn't France involved in a revolution?"*

Mr. Spear: *"Yes, what else?"*

Students: *Many heads are bowed and some students seem to be occupied with other things.*

Mr. Spear: *"Well, I believe we're in for a treat in reading this novel. It is one of my all-time favorite works of literature, and I'm sure after reading it you'll think the same!"*

Students: *Two students are texting each other. Others are seen staring off into space.*

Mr. Spear: *"I want you to read the first 20 pages of the novel for tomorrow. In reading these pages, I'd like you to think about the answers to some questions I'm going to pass out about your reading. Any questions?" He begins to pass out the questions.*

Billy: *"When did you say we had to read the pages by?" The bell rings.*

Keeping in mind what you already know about the comprehension process, jot down your thoughts on the following questions:

1. What are the good points about the lesson?

2. What are the weak points about the lesson?

3. What, if anything, would you change about the lesson?

RATIONALE

Comprehension of challenging ideas in a content area is rarely easy for students. No collection of textbook aids can be a substitute for the careful guidance you can provide. Academic literacy ultimately requires the ability to monitor one's comprehension independently. By engaging students in participatory, guided instruction in comprehension, they can move successfully toward independent comprehension strategies. In order to accomplish this in your particular content area, you must have a working knowledge of some basic notions about the comprehension process and an array of strategies at your disposal.

In this chapter and the next we explore the comprehension process. Specifically, in Chapter 10 we examine various strategies to facilitate the comprehension process before, during, and after reading. The aim of this chapter is to explore some principles of comprehension and how they are linked to the instructional lesson. Then, we describe various strategies and how they are integrated across the lesson.

LEARNING OBJECTIVES

o Be able to explain the principles of guiding comprehension in a content area.
o Be able to apply specific integrated strategies in your content area that provide guidance before, during, and after reading.

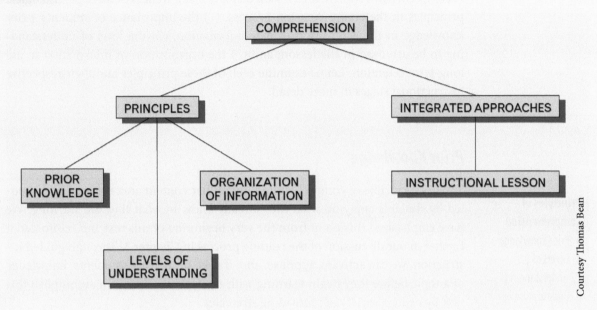

Courtesy Thomas Bean

PRINCIPLES OF COMPREHENSION

A comprehensive content area lesson displays an awareness of three psychological principles in the comprehension process: (1) the importance of students' prior knowledge in the acquisition of new information; (2) the level of understanding to be achieved in the lesson; and (3) the organization of information to aid long-term retention. Let us examine each of these principles and their respective instructional stages in more detail.

Prior Knowledge

Principles of Comprehension
o Prior knowledge
o Levels of understanding
o Organization of information

The first principle of comprehending unfamiliar content area material is embodied by students applying what they already know to what they are learning. We have emphasized this point from the very beginning of this text and reinforced it further in our discussion of the reading process in Chapter 3. Through guided instruction, we can activate, appraise, and, if need be, increase students' knowledge of a topic before they begin learning with the text. Teachers can accomplish this task by using a variety of prereading strategies.

Levels of Understanding

Levels of Understanding
o Text explicit
o Text implicit
o Experience based

The second principle of comprehension emphasizes the fact that content material frequently demands in-depth study beyond the factual, literal level for adequate understanding and application in future lessons. Thus, students must be encouraged to think deeply about what they are learning, as it is a key factor in the retention of information. A content teacher can guide this process during the reading stage by insuring that students adopt an active, self-questioning approach to the text (Bean, Baldwin, & Readence, 2012). In order to construct lessons that guide students in the assimilation of factual text concepts with their own experiences, it is helpful to have a procedure for characterizing different levels of understanding. Those levels are *text explicit*, *text implicit*, and *experience based*. Students should be given every opportunity to reason across this full range of understanding.

These categories, in our opinion, offer the best description of the processes involved in comprehending text at various levels of understanding. This simple framework captures the essence of comprehension—the interaction of prior experience with printed information. In order to gain a more concrete understanding of the three categories, try the following activity:

230

Read the paragraph below and answer the questions that follow.

Failing to remember things is a problem that plagues most of us. We forget to perform routine tasks like stopping at a grocery store on the way home or picking up the dry-cleaning. Worse still, we may forget important information such as a new student's name. Fortunately, there are some reasonable solutions to our forgetfulness.

Q: 1. What is a problem that plagues most of us?

A:

Q: 2. What specific group or audience is the paragraph addressing?

A:

Q: 3. What are your solutions to the problem posed in the paragraph?

A:

In answering question 1 from Application 9.1 (What is a problem that plagues most of us?) your response, forgetfulness, was taken directly from the text. In fact, you were able to point to the answer in the paragraph because it was literally stated by the author. Such comprehension is called *text explicit*.

In question 2 (What specific group or audience is the paragraph addressing?) you had to engage in a different type of comprehension from question one. Your response did not come explicitly from the text; rather, it had to be inferred from a hint in the passage. The phrase *new student's name* implies that teachers are the audience being addressed. When you must infer from the text to derive an answer to a question, you are engaging in *text implicit* comprehension.

Finally, answering question 3 (What are your solutions to the problem posed in the paragraph?) requires yet another form of comprehension. Your response this time was drawn from your previous experience. You had to search your schema for strategies you might use to remember a new student's name. In doing so, you may have responded in a number of different ways, including bizarre associations, where the student sits, and so on. Your inference was not derived from the text, but from your existing schema or knowledge structure. This is called *experience-based* comprehension. This type of thinking is at the heart of curiosity, invention, and problem solving. It is also one of the most neglected forms of questioning in many classrooms.

Explicating Levels of Comprehension

Let us examine each of the three levels of comprehension in depth. We examine question and answer relationships, rather than classifying questions in isolation.

TEXT-EXPLICIT COMPREHENSION. This involves getting the facts of a passage as stated by the author. The question asked is based directly on the text, and the answer is explicitly cued by the language of the text. Raphael, Highfield, and Au (2006), in an effort to use language familiar to students, use the phrase, *right there on the page*, to describe text-explicit comprehension. Answers are literally found on the page and readers can actually point to the answer. In essence, you are reading the lines. Text-explicit comprehension requires you to tell what the author said, and there is usually only one answer. Therefore, answers to such questions have no middle ground—they are either right or wrong.

Text-implicit and experience-based comprehension, on the other hand, require you to think about your answers—they are not explicitly stated by the author, and answers may vary depending on each respondent's experiential background. In fact, the less the text is involved and the more experiential background comes into play, the larger the number of possible answers.

TEXT-IMPLICIT COMPREHENSION. This involves answering a question derived directly from the language of the text, but also requires the reader to derive an answer when there are no obvious clues to it in the passage. You are asked to infer what the author meant. Thus, the relationship between the question and the answer is implicit; it necessarily requires some logic to get from the question to the answer. Raphael, Highfield, and Au (2006) call this *think and search*. As such, questions that require paraphrases of text information result in text-implicit comprehension. In essence, you take the facts presented by the author and add knowledge from your experiential background to derive a reasonable implicit relationship. In other words, you are asked to read between the lines.

EXPERIENCE-BASED COMPREHENSION. This results when a question is asked and the plausible answer is derived almost exclusively from previous knowledge. Thus, the answer cannot be derived directly from the text. In Raphael, Highfield, and Au's (2006) words, you are *on your own*. Students draw inferences from previous knowledge; hence, they are involved in reading between the lines.

Table 9.1 summarizes the distinctions between the three levels of comprehension:

LEVEL	INFORMATION SOURCE			NUMBER OF POSSIBLE ANSWERS	ALTERNATE DEFINITION
	QUESTION	INFERENCE	ANSWER		
Text explicit	Text	No	Text	One	Right on the page
Text implicit	Text	Yes	Text	One plus	Think and search
Experience based	Text	Yes	Reader	Many	On your own

Implications Concerning Questions

Questions are one of the most prominent forms of comprehension instruction used. Questions are used to activate students' memory processes of text, focus their attention on significant aspects of text material, and aid them in synthesizing seemingly different parts of text into a coherent whole. Teachers who are good questioners promote the process of comprehension, as well as modeling and scaffolding student self-questioning. However, there are certain considerations when you attempt to use questions effectively.

1. It takes time and thought to compose good questions. Good questions do not flow like water from a fountain. You need to examine carefully the material you have covered in order to ascertain the best kinds of questions to ask. You possess a wealth of information concerning your subject matter area: students do not. Asking questions that come from your knowledge base, rather than from the text, will do nothing more than confuse and befuddle your students.

2. In asking good questions, be sure not to ask too many text-explicit questions. Answers to such questions, though they form the basis for questions at higher levels of comprehension, require little or no thought, do not challenge the student, and do not enhance your role as a facilitator of learning.

3. Asking questions at higher levels of comprehension requires that you give students the freedom to respond. Without this, you may inhibit divergent responses.

4. Be aware that sometimes you may not get the type of comprehension you expect. For example, consider the following sentences:

   Tom rode through the park at a slow gait, thinking about the day's activities. As Tom daydreamed, he searched the afternoon shadows for a few blades of grass.

Your intended text-implicit question to students might be, "What kind of animal is Tom riding?" Although most students are likely to respond, horse, a few may say, mare. Thus, at times you may be pleasantly surprised at divergent, high-level responses to a seemingly straightforward question. The student has just processed your question differently to draw the above-mentioned inference. The point is that you should be prepared for divergent responses to your expectations.

5. The levels of comprehension model has implications for textbook questions also. Take care to avoid relying entirely on questions provided by text authors. Such questions are written by experts in their field; as good as these authors may be, they cannot possibly understand your students' special needs. Only you, their teacher, can tailor questions that involve your particular students in comprehension at varying levels. Questions so intended by text authors may not accomplish that task.

6. Students can be taught to generate their own questions. If you truly want your students to become active, critical readers of text, you need to become familiar with strategies designed to help them develop a questioning approach to reading (Stevens, 2001; Stevens & Bean, 2007). Helping students adopt this inquisitive stance can boost their interest in pursuing a topic that may otherwise seem distant from their own personal lives.

7. Though *questions* are a major means to teach students, the value of *statements* should not be neglected (Bean, 2000; Tierney & Readence, 2005). It is suggested that using statements at first helps students to recognize information before they are required to produce it through the use of questions. Such statements simulate comprehension at higher levels of thinking and familiarize students with that process. Once familiarity has been achieved, questions again become an appropriate and valuable way to help students comprehend text material. In the next chapter we discuss the Anticipation–Reaction Guide, a strategy that exemplifies the value of statements as a means of enhancing students' comprehension.

Organization of Information

The third principle of understanding, organizing for long-term retention of information, is the most often neglected aspect of comprehension instruction. In the postreading phase, ideas are refined and extended. Additionally, this final instructional stage relates directly to how well new information will be understood in a subsequent lesson. The postreading stage of a lesson must involve activities that encourage students to synthesize and organize information.

Specifically, organization of information relates to the ability to perceive an author's *text structure* or organizational pattern in traditional text. It is important to note that reading comprehension becomes more complex when students search the Internet for information in online texts (Tierney, 2009). We say more on this and the use of multiple texts later in this chapter. For now, our focus is on more traditional text reading comprehension.

When you alert students to the structure of an author's thoughts, you provide them with a powerful strategy for organizing information in a memorable fashion. Moreover, as you develop strategies to guide students' comprehension, your analysis of a text passage should reveal the author's pattern of organization. With adequate guidance, students can eventually become adept at detecting an author's structure independently.

The following activity (Application 9.2) will give you an idea of your well-developed, largely unconscious use of patterns in your own reading:

APPLICATION 9.2

Read the following sentences. Place them in the proper order of occurrence.

He was well thought of by his peers.

John volunteered for extracurricular activities.

His principal gave him an excellent recommendation for the university doctoral program.

He never missed school unless he was very ill.

John was a conscientious teacher.

Recognizing the structure of prose is a great aid for students in comprehending and recalling text material. Students who can perceive the structure that binds the ideas in text will understand and remember ideas much better than if they are viewed only as separate entities. In Application 9.2, your recognition of the *cause–effect* pattern should have enabled you to organize the text in its proper sequence. Because John was such a good teacher and did fine things for his school, his principal was only too happy to fulfill his desire. Additionally, with your knowledge of the apparent organizational pattern, you, more than likely, started the sequence with "John was a conscientious teacher" because the other attributes concerning his abilities logically follow that topic sentence. This same knowledge allowed you to place this sentence last: "His principal gave him an excellent recommendation for the university doctoral program." In essence, your knowledge about the world and the organization of text allowed you to make logical predictions about the arrangement and sequence of the above sentences. It is this same knowledge that students use, or should be taught to use, with their content textbooks.

Helping your students perceive an author's text structure gives them a valuable independent strategy they can use to comprehend text efficiently. Teaching students to think like authors makes them more aware of text structure patterns that provide a framework for remembering important content. For example, history texts often feature a problem–solution text pattern. Placing this pattern in a visual frame assists students in writing a summary of the major ideas and supporting details highlighted in the passage. Thus, a frame guide in history would include three items: (a) a sentence explaining what the problem is; (b) a second sentence telling what action has been taken to solve the problem; and (c) a third sentence explaining what happened as a result of this action. Students can then develop coherent summaries using information in each section of the frame. Your efforts to help students use text structure in comprehension and recall will reap benefits in their reading and writing.

Text structure serves a dual purpose in print: (1) to help writers communicate their thoughts; and (2) to help readers comprehend what authors are attempting to communicate.

Since reading is an interaction between the thoughts and language of both writers and readers, text structure serves as a convenient vehicle to facilitate this communication.

There is an obvious connection in communication between authors and readers. It certainly cannot be denied that authors attempt to communicate their thoughts to readers through structural patterns in text. These patterns are real, and they are visible on the printed page. On the other hand, one also cannot deny that readers attempt to use their logic in thought and reasoning to understand the printed page. The continuous process that readers employ in imposing their own organizational structure to communicate with authors, though not visible, is also very real, as previously discussed in this text. Meaning construction entails active interchange between writers and readers.

Explicating Text Structure

Knowledge of text structure helps to guide students' comprehension of text. These are some of the prominent types of patterns of organization in written materials:

1. **Cause/Effect:** This pattern links reasons with results. It is characterized by an interaction between at least two ideas or events, one taking an action and another resulting from that action.

   Example: Because it snowed so heavily, the city traffic came to a standstill.

2. **Comparison/Contrast:** *Comparison/contrast* patterns of organization demonstrate apparent likenesses and differences between two or more things.

   Example: Whereas a lion and a giraffe are both mammals and bear live young, the lion is a carnivore and the giraffe is an herbivore.

3. **Time order:** *Time order* is exemplified by a sequential relationship between ideas or events considered in presence of the passage of time.

   Example: In December Scott took a job with a new company. Things went so well with the new job that he soon became a supervisor. Now, because of continued successes, he is vice president of the firm.

4. **Problem/Solution:** Similar to the cause/effect pattern, the *problem/solution* pattern is exemplified by an interaction between at least two factors, one citing a problem and another providing a potential answer to that problem.

   Example: Certain plants need an environment with a constant, moderate temperature and high humidity or they will die. Consequently, a greenhouse is ideal for those plants.

To further help students recognize such patterns, key words or phrases that signal, or cue, a particular text type should be pointed out. Such *signal words* provide mind-sets that enhance the perception of text structure and learning from text. See Table 9.2 for examples of signal words. It should be noted that cue words signaling the problem/solution pattern are similar to those signaling the cause/effect pattern.

Teaching students to be on the lookout for signal words helps with awareness of an author's text structure and improves their recall. In addition, helping them discern signal words and their related text structures gives them a strategy for distinguishing important concepts from unimportant, or even misleading, information in a text passage. Many of the texts students read in a contemporary medium like the Internet are laden with extraneous items that actually detract from the main idea. Students are bombarded with information and need a means of separating the essential concepts in a text from the surrounding noise. Signal words and text structure knowledge can be very useful if their application is carefully modeled through teacher think-alouds and guided practice. In the section that follows we outline an instructional procedure for developing your students' ability to use text structure to their advantage.

TABLE 9.2

Signal Words

CAUSE/EFFECT	COMPARISON/CONTRAST	TIME ORDER
because	however	on (date)
since	but	not long after
therefore	as well as	now
consequently	on the other hand	before
as a result	not only . . . but also	after
	either . . . or	

Suggestions for Helping Students Perceive Text Structure

Perhaps the key factor in teaching students to actively use the organizational structure of text is you, the content teacher. It is erroneous to assume students will recognize and utilize organizational patterns. Direct teaching of the recognition of patterns is essential, and all patterns should be pointed out continually to students. The time you spend in stimulating the perception of organizational patterns will take little away from your instructional time and will facilitate comprehension.

Tips for Teaching Students to Perceive Patterns of Text Organization

1. **Modeling.** You should demonstrate the use of text structure first before expecting students to utilize it. Passages drawn from their reading should be used to illustrate your demonstration because they are most relevant to the students. Showing students a particular organizational pattern and pointing out why it is a certain type and how that pattern type is organized is essential. Any signal words that cue the reader to the organization of the material should also be pointed out and discussed.

2. **Recognition.** Next, you should walk students through a particular passage type by asking judicious questions that focus their attention on the text structure. For students experiencing difficulty, you may wish to read the material to them first rather than having them read it. In this way your students can concentrate entirely on perceiving the pattern. You may also wish to start with sentences only and then move to paragraphs and longer passages. Essential to this recognition step is students' verbalization of the how and why of the text structure.

3. **Production.** Producing a communication is a logical extension of receiving one. Writing, therefore, becomes a valuable means to reinforce text structure.

From time to time all content teachers require students to write. Requiring logical organization in students' own writing can become a vital extension of perceiving text organization. As part of a writing assignment, you should ask students to frame a logical response by utilizing a particular pattern of organization and the signal words associated with it. Skeletal outlines or a graphic organizer may also be provided to facilitate production of an organized writing sample. We demonstrate how to teach structure awareness through writing in Chapter 11.

Reading and Comprehending Multiple Digital Texts

Throughout the book we note that the process of reading and navigating digital texts, particularly the Internet, require guidance beyond that associated with the patterns of text organization typical in static, printed texts. Some of these ideas were introduced in Chapter 2 on Technology, and they are reinforced in Chapter 12 on Studying. As a prelude to guiding students' reading and search strategies, it is important to observe and note their current approaches (Bean, 2010; Bean, 2016). You can note sites that students select and their persistence in reading related texts on various sites. This is important as the complexity and skills needed to navigate the maze of idiosyncratic websites include some skills relevant to print and others unique to online context. Tierney (2009) noted the following skills in reading online texts:

o   **Forward inferencing:** As readers visit a particular site, they need to use prediction strategies to think about upcoming sites not yet visited.

o   **Evaluating relevance:** After doing a keyword search, a wide array of sites may be listed and the reader needs to evaluate their likely contribution to the information search they are conducting.

o   **Source evaluation:** Readers need to decide if the information they find on a particular site is biased or related to an ideological position that may limit the truth-value of the information.

o   **Strategic searching:** Reading and searching for information online requires strong metacognitive, self-regulating strategies to avoid getting lost in the Internet or becoming enamored by seductive details, advertisements, pop-ups, and other distractions.

o   **Making intertextual connections between sources:** Reading multiple texts on the Internet requires the creation of an information chain that connects these multiple sources in a coherent argument or line of reasoning.

If a student exhibits difficulty comprehending hypertext, consider slicing the task into a smaller collection of suggested web pages that make a topic search more manageable. Bean (2010) suggests having students do the following:

1. Think aloud by talking about their rationale for selecting particular sites.

2. Keep an annotated hyperlink log to reflect on the pathway they took on a site.

3. Keep an archival record of their searches using the bookmark function on their search engine.

In many ways, reading digital texts is related to learning how to comprehend and construct connections across printed texts. *Intertextuality,* or the process of reading and making conceptual connections across a range of texts (broadly defined to include internet- and media-based texts), requires careful guidance as students are not necessarily skilled at this process. Recent work on teacher's use of *multiple texts* in content area classrooms offers some guidelines.

Teaching in the Content Areas with Multiple Texts and Close Reading

Accomplished teachers in a variety of content areas often guide students' use of multiple print and nonprint texts to enhance their comprehension of key concepts in science, events in history, and the dynamics of economics (Walker, Bean, & Dillard, 2010). Part of the rationale for using multiple texts is a recognition that textbooks alone are best used as one resource among many in a content area. Textbooks, although useful, must be augmented with primary source documents and the Internet, particularly in inquiry and project-based classrooms. For example, Behrman (2003) conducted a study of students in a high school biology classroom where they were asked to determine guilt or innocence based on DNA analysis in a hypothetical murder. In addition to community resource experts (e.g., a director of a county forensic laboratory), students could self-select texts from any source that would help them solve the crime. As might be expected, they gravitated toward information from real-life experts in the community and Internet-based information.

Similarly, in an ongoing series of studies exploring content area teachers' use of multiple texts through classroom observations and teacher interviews, Walker, Bean, and Dillard (2010) found that accomplished teachers saw multiple texts as a way to enrich content area teaching for their students. For example, Maria, an eighth-grade physical science teacher, immersed her students in designing and creating roller coasters to grasp scientific principles including potential and kinetic energy. In an interview, she talked about her rationale for using multiple texts and using the core textbook in physical science as one resource among many:

I try to give them the opportunity to learn the information other than with the textbook. The articles are pretty good, and they did a better job than the textbook. The textbook gets too technical, and I wanted it to be more interesting for them.

Maria's articles that students used to augment the textbook included material from magazines, and internet sites considering theme parks and roller coaster safety and design. Based on redesigning a financially struggling theme park, students adopted various roles including researcher, engineer, public relations director, and architect.

Many of the integrated strategies in this chapter and those in Chapters 10 and 11 are useful in guiding students' reading, discussion, writing, and application of multiple texts in your content area. In addition, these strategies fit nicely with the recent emphasis on close reading of complex multiple texts (Ford-Connors, Dougherty, Robertson, & Paratore, 2015). These educators worked with two teachers on an interdisciplinary unit in English language, arts, and social studies. Set in an urban middle school with a significant number of struggling readers, these teachers collaborated to create multimodal text sets on the Civil Rights Movement in the United States. These text sets spanned various reading levels to facilitate students' independent and teacher-guided reading during this three-week unit. The multimodal material included video clips, texts, newscasts, and nonfiction and fiction trade books. They began the unit with free videos on the Civil Rights Movement available from the Public Broadcasting Service website, www.pbs.org.

The ELA teacher used read-alouds to model how to create graphic organizers, timelines, and conceptual maps encompassing students' developing knowledge about the Civil Rights Movement. In addition, students were able to self-select autobiographies of key figures in the movement, as well as read across picture books, graphic novels, photo essays, and a range of material to accommodate information gathering. Students used reading, writing, technology, and discussion as research tools to expand their understanding of the Civil Rights Movement and the social conditions of the time.

A number of sources provide classroom examples of teachers' use of multiple texts. For example, if you are planning to use multiple texts in history, Stahl and Shanahan (2004) have studied and developed an approach designed to maximize students' success. In particular, a strategy we include in this chapter called "Questioning the Author" (Tierney & Readence, 2005) has been recommended for guiding students' reading and discussion of multiple texts. Information on teaching with multiple texts in science based on Cynthia Shanahan's (2004) work, as well as vignettes of successful biology and English teachers using multiple texts in Sturtevant et al. (2006), offers classroom views of this practice. Finally, recommended readings at the close of the chapter list useful resources as you explore expanding students' use of multiple texts in your content area.

INTEGRATED APPROACHES

Integrated Teaching and Learning Strategies

o K-W-L
o Inquiry charts
o Listen-Read-Discuss
o Scaffolded reading experience
o Questioning the author
o Critical media literacy

In Chapter 1 we introduced the notion that helping students learn content needs to be integrated through all stages of the instructional lesson, i.e., students generally need to be prepared to read a text during prereading, need guidance in searching for selected ideas during reading, and need reinforcement to retain the material learned during postreading. Earlier in this chapter we explored further critical principles of comprehension and related instructional stages. While there are strategies that may only focus on certain aspects of the instructional lesson (see Chapter 10 for a discussion of these strategies), we describe here a series of strategies that should be viewed as more comprehensive in nature. Rather than focusing on one aspect of an instructional lesson, these strategies are integrated across all stages of the lesson—prereading, reading, and postreading—and provide a more holistic view of the comprehension process and integrated lesson planning.

K-W-L

This is a widely used three-step integrated strategy designed to encourage active reading of expository text. The **K-W-L** strategy consists of a prereading stage aimed at activating prior knowledge, a reading stage where students seek answers to predetermined questions, and a postreading stage where they can distill what was learned through the reading. K-W-L relies on three categories of information:

o   K—What we *k*now (before reading)

o   W—What we *w*ant to find out (during reading); and

o   L—What we *l*earned (as a result of text reading).

In addition, you should assist students to anticipate the organizational structure or likely categories of information a text author will introduce. In the example that follows, the topic of killer bees might present their recent invasion of the southern United States as a problem to be solved. Thus, the category section would include the labels "problem" and "solution." To prepare a K-W-L lesson, create a framework like the one in Figure 9.1 on the board or overhead and ensure that each student has a copy of this framework.

FIGURE 9.1

K-W-L Lesson Framework

K—What we know   W—What we want to find out   L—What we learned

Categories of Information

1.

2.

3.

Steps to Utilize the K-W-L Framework

1. Engage students in a brainstorming session on the topic they are about to read in the text. Students can draw their visualization of the topic (e.g., killer bees) to activate prior knowledge. Next, elicit possible categories the author might use to organize this information on killer bees. The lesson framework in Figure 9.2 displays students' comments concerning the killer bees selection they were about to read in the K column.

2. To help students develop a clear purpose for reading a selection, create questions the text might answer. The framework in Figure 9.2 shows some of the questions students generated for the killer bee text in the W column.

3. Finally, students need to record the information they have learned in the framework (see the L column on the next page). In addition, you may wish to have students develop a visual representation such as a graphic organizer or map, or they can write a short summary statement. Students can then share this information in small discussion groups.

FIGURE 9.2

K–W–L Lesson Framework on Killer Bees

K–What we know	W–What we want to find out	L–What we learned
1. They can kill people.	1. Why are they called "killer bees?"	1. They are more aggressive than the common honey bee.
2. They kill other bees.	2. Where are they found?	2. The southern and western United States
3. Their sting is worse than honey bees.	3. Where are they from?	3. Africa originally. They were brought to Brazil by accident in 1956.
	4. How dangerous are they?	4. Very aggressive, but their sting is no more dangerous than other bees. However, they can interfere with the pollination of many fruits and vegetables by the common honey bee, raising the cost of these items.
	5. How can we get rid of them?	5. Scientists claim it is impossible.
Categories of information		
1. Problem of killer bees		
2. Solution to this problem		

Integrated strategies like K-W-L can form a solid foundation for extended research and writing projects. You can have students explore the source and reliability of information gained from reading. Given the vast volume of information on any topic available via the Internet and other media, this is an important, critical reading element. K-W-L also might be extended by having students explore a fourth category of information: What they still need to learn. For example, is it really impossible to rid the United States of killer bees? Perhaps additional reading and research with other texts might provide an alternative viewpoint. Thus, K-W-L can lead into more detailed exploration of a topic or theme spanning a full unit that may take weeks to complete.

In addition, it may be important to modify K-W-L to better represent the particular content area's approach to knowledge. For example, in a mathematics classroom a K-W-S (What do I know? What do I want to know? and What strategies might I use?) might offer a better fit (Draper et al., 2010). Thus, in solving a word problem about a 10K runner's approach to a race, the strategy column might contain a number of possible approaches including making a table, drawing a chart, creating a function, or solving an equation to suggest a particular pace per mile for the runner. The point is not to feel you have to adhere to a particular strategy exactly as it is written. The unique demands of various content areas suggest that strategies like K-W-L can be appropriately applied with some modification to account for how knowledge is constructed across various content areas.

Various modifications have been proposed to improve K-W-L, including a three-column process that questions the sources of information students mention and a more tentative and critical look at a topic (Finders & Balcerzak, 2013). They term this approach, H-Q-Q: H (ask students to indicate what they have heard about a topic); Q (collaboratively generate questions related to the topic); and, Q (after learning about the topic, pose additional questions for further inquiry). For example, if the topic was about solar cars, students might write:

o   H: We have heard that solar cars use energy from the sun.

o   Q: Our questions are these: What does a cloudy day do to a solar car? How far can we go in a solar car? How long can we drive our solar car before it needs more energy? How much can we carry in a solar car? How is energy stored in a solar car? How fast can one go?

o   Q: Why are there so few solar cars in the United States? How much does one cost? What are other electronic options that might increase the use of solar energy–powered cars?

Other modifications might be considered for students in diverse classrooms. Small groups might be used to generate the information in steps one and two rather than a large group forum. Students might first work in a small group to record what they know and then report it to the large group. The same can be done for information they might seek. This should enable more students to participate and make the learning environment more collaborative and less threatening. In step three a small group might be a better conduit to get students to record/summarize what they found out. Teachers might also modify the strategy by incorporating more modeling and direction until students are comfortable with it. For particularly difficult topics or topics where little prior knowledge exists, the use of a shorter text or a video might be considered. These could serve as an advance organizer to give the students some familiarity with the topic before they actually have to read the assigned text. Similarly, a video could serve to augment, or even substitute, the text.

Inquiry Charts

Inquiry charts, or I-Charts (Hoffman, 1992; Tierney & Readence, 2005), nurture critical reading in content classrooms by having students examine multiple sources of information for points of consistency and inconsistency. Based upon the work of Ogle with K-W-L, students use a data chart to record what they know about a topic, what they want to know about it, and what they found from their readings. The chart allows the students to gather the information they get from multiple sources and organize it for summarization, comparison, and evaluation.

Steps for Using the I-Chart Strategy

1. **Planning.** In planning, teachers must decide (a) the topic is to be explored; (b) the questions to drive the inquiry process; and (c) the sources to be used for data collection. For example, let us say the topic is the Civil War, and the teacher decides the questions to be explored are as follows: (a) What were the causes of the Civil War? (b) What were the immediate effects of the war for each side? (c) What were the long-term consequences of the war? (d) What would the United States be like today if the South had won the war? The teacher might decide that besides the class text, the classroom set of encyclopedias and other textbooks and trade books from the school library would serve as resources. Once planning is completed, the I-Chart should be constructed with this information displayed on it (see Figure 9.3).

2. **Interacting.** In this step, students work with the teacher to explore their prior knowledge, share interesting facts and new questions, read, and record. First, students respond to each guiding question along the lines of what they already know. This information is recorded on the I-Chart in the "What We Know" row under the appropriate question. This information is recorded whether it is accurate or contradictory. Next, any interesting facts the students come up with and any new questions they think of, unrelated to the guiding questions, should also be recorded in the appropriate space on the I-Chart. Finally, students are asked to go to the additional source material to answer the guiding questions. The amount of time this will take depends on the number of available sources as well as the number of questions. Following the discussion of each source, the teacher records the appropriate information for each question on the I-Chart.

Guiding Questions

SOURCES	TOPIC Civil War	What were the causes of the Civil War?	What were the immedi-ate effects of the war for each side?	What were the long-term consequences of the war?	What would the United States be like today if the South had won the war?	Interesting facts and figures	New questions
	WHAT WE KNOW						
	1. Class text						
	2. Encyclo-pedias						
	3. Library trade books						
	SUMMARY						

In this case the information should be as accurate as possible; any new questions or interesting information from the reading should be recorded as well. It is important to understand that the eventual size of the I-Chart will be dictated by the scope of the topic and search required.

3. **Interacting and Evaluating.** In this step the I-Chart is completed, and the findings are evaluated and shared. First, the students are asked to generate summary statements for each of the guiding questions and the interesting facts column. Thus, students are asked to synthesize the information previously recorded, taking into account both converging and conflicting information. Summary statements are recorded on the bottom row of the I-Chart. Next, students compare the information gained from their readings with their prior knowledge and reconcile any misconceptions. Now, students are ready to deal with the new, unanswered questions that arose during their data col-

lection. These questions become the basis for additional research, either individually or in small groups. Finally, students report back to the whole class their findings regarding the unanswered questions.

Once students become familiar with the strategy, teachers can fade their responsibility; students may begin to select their own topics, generate their own guiding questions, and decide what to record on the I-Chart. Eventually, the strategy could be used with small groups or even for individual inquiry. Once students become proficient in synthesizing information into summaries, these may become the basis for students to expand them into paragraphs and, later, complete written reports. Finally, the I-Chart seems to be an ideal tool for exploring multicultural issues in the classroom.

Listen-Read-Discuss

The integrated strategy of *Listen-Read-Discuss* was developed to ensure that students genuinely grasp content information (Manzo, Casale, & Thomas, 2004). Because students receive multiple exposures to concepts through listening, reading, and discussion, they are more likely to learn and retain information you feel is worthy of this intensive process.

Steps for a Listen-Read-Discuss Lesson

1. The first part of the lesson entails presenting a well-structured lecture on the material students are about to read in the text. Students need to have a good grasp of the content you are presenting if they are to participate actively in a listen-read-discuss lesson. Therefore, provide a clear lecture guide, perhaps in the form of a graphic organizer that will serve to cue students to the text's structure. For example, the graphic organizer in Figure 9.4 might be used to assist high school students' comprehension of a lecture on Japan's rise to a world power. Reading their text would follow about a 15-minute lecture on the topic. Notice that the graphic organizer displays the cause–effect structure of the text. Items one and three would be provided by the teacher on the graphic organizer lecture guide passed out to students. Those items in script would be filled in by students as the lecture progresses, with clear cues from the teacher signaling each important point.

    Once the lecture is completed and students have filled in their graphic organizer lecture guides, the teacher is ready to progress to step two, the reading portion of a listen-read-discuss lesson.

2. The teacher directs students to read the text pages on which the lecture was based. Their purpose for reading should be to compare their understanding

FIGURE 9.4

Sample Graphic Organizer and Lecture Guide for Listen-Read-Discuss

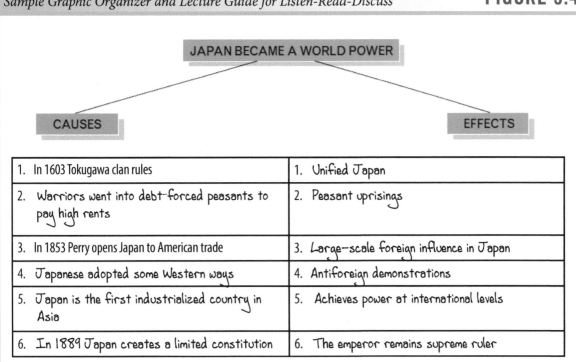

CAUSES	EFFECTS
1. In 1603 Tokugawa clan rules	1. Unified Japan
2. Warriors went into debt-forced peasants to pay high rents	2. Peasant uprisings
3. In 1853 Perry opens Japan to American trade	3. Large-scale foreign influence in Japan
4. Japanese adopted some Western ways	4. Antiforeign demonstrations
5. Japan is the first industrialized country in Asia	5. Achieves power at international levels
6. In 1889 Japan creates a limited constitution	6. The emperor remains supreme ruler

of the lecture with the information presented in the text. In addition, they can identify vocabulary and concepts that need clarification and pinpoint any inconsistencies between the text and the teacher's lecture. They are then ready to discuss the information on Japan's rise to international power.

3. The discussion step can begin with small groups and progress to a summary discussion as a whole class. Three major questions should guide students' discussion of the lecture and text reading: (a) What did you understand best from what you heard and read? (b) What did you understand least from what you heard and read? (c) What questions or thoughts did the topic raise in your mind? This last question is one that is often glossed over in our desire to cover the content. Yet it goes to the heart of students' personal interest in a topic. For example, Japan's influence on our economy has grown considerably over the years. It would be important to raise and consider contemporary issues like this, which have their roots in the mid-1800s.

Scaffolded Reading Experience

The *Scaffolded Reading Experience* (SRE) is a comprehensive lesson framework with a good deal of flexibility in its implementation (Tierney & Readence, 2005). *Scaffold-*

ing refers to the degree of support and guidance a teacher may need to provide to help students engage in text that would be too difficult, left to their own devices. As in all lesson frameworks, you need to first carefully consider what prior knowledge students may bring to the topic. For example, in an art history class, it is unlikely that contemporary students would have much knowledge of the Surrealists, let alone specific artists and their beliefs. A sense of students' prior knowledge about the topic helps suggest the level of prereading, reading, and postreading scaffolding needed. For example, in an art history lesson on the Surrealist Salvador Dali (Martin, 1999), students might consider one of his paintings before doing any text reading about his philosophy and beliefs. The actual lesson steps follow, but keep in mind that this is an overall lesson framework with a great deal of flexibility in implementation.

Steps for Implementing a Scaffolded Reading Experience

1. At the prereading stage, the teacher can ask students to pair up with a class-mate and look at the slide of a famous Salvador Dali painting, *The Persistence of Memory*. The landscape shows three timepieces bent as if melted by a hot fire. There is a sheer stone cliff in the background and the contorted clocks in the foreground. The colors are mainly dark and foreboding, and one clock face hangs from a sparse gray tree limb by the middle of its limp clock face. The teacher uses a prereading question "What does this painting remind you of?" to give students a chance to explore their prior knowledge. They comment on its dreamlike quality and scary looking landscape. The teacher then offers a definition of surrealism with its intense interest in dreams and the unconscious. Because Freudian influences also weighed heavily on Dali during his life (1904–1989), the teacher also offers a brief cultural history based on the text.

2. Based on the foundational information in the prereading stage of the SRE, students are given a broad study guide question to consider as they read the text about Salvador Dali: How was Dali regarded as a Surrealist painter during his lifetime?

The World of Dreams and Salvador Dali's Art

Salvador Dali sought to tap into his dreams and represent the more bizarre dimensions of the unconscious mind. He painted in a realistic style such that familiar objects are easily recognizable, even if juxtaposed in odd ways. Despite the fact that many people now know Dali and perhaps few other famous Surrealists, he was actually tossed out of the Surrealist group by another artist, Andre Breton. Dali tended to reveal his interest in Freud and subconscious dreams in a fashion that many critics thought was too obvious and literal. Indeed, Dali had little use for abstract painting, which may explain some of his appeal and notoriety with the masses. He was, on the one hand, irreverent, and, on the other, meticulous in his planning for a painting. He was criticized for being too academic in his planning and execution compared with the more abstract Surrealists. Nevertheless, his 1931 painting, *The Persistence of Memory*, is widely associated with Surrealism and serves as an introduction to this artistic movement for many people.

3. At the postreading stage, a number of options for critical response to the text are possible. For example, questioning, discussion, writing, drama, art, media, and other response modes might be adopted. In the example of the Dali text, the teacher could ask students to write a short play where Dali attempts to defend his contribution to Surrealism in the face of criticism that he was too realistic in his work. Or, students might research other artists of the period who contrasted with Dali's style and include examples of their works in a gallery set up around the classroom. Other students could then browse these posters containing photos and brief text explaining the philosophy of each artist. Slide shows, videos, and other hypermedia might be used. The possibilities are endless, so it may be helpful, before planning and SRE, to consult additional sources.

The SRE helps students grasp key ideas in a text selection. The next two strategies, *Questioning the Author* (Tierney & Readence, 2005), and *Critical Media Literacy* (Dunkerly-Bean, Bean, & Alnajjar, 2014; Morrell, Duenas, Garcia, & Lopez, 2013; Stevens & Bean, 2007) emphasize critical literacy.

Questioning the Author

This strategy is particularly useful for narrative and expository texts that are unfriendly and likely to challenge students. The strategy unfolds in three separate stages: planning, discussion, and implementation.

PLANNING. Start by doing a careful content analysis of the text you plan to use. The teacher's manual may be helpful for major ideas and questions. Then, read the material imagining yourself as a student who is a less skilled reader and likely to struggle with the text. Identify key ideas and logical segments of text. Based on the key ideas you discern and the segmented text, create some queries that will help guide students as they read. You will be asking students to stop reading at particular points in the text and to respond to these queries. Unlike much of the prereading and postreading guidance we have emphasized thus far, these queries will interrupt the reader *during reading*. Broad questions such as "What is the author trying to say here?" encourage students to reflect on the material just read.

IMPLEMENTATION. In the example that follows, we accompany a student attempting to read a passage in agriculture on horse communication (adapted from Budiansky, 1997).

Horse Communication

The widely popular 1960s television show, *Mr. Ed*, featured a horse that could talk. Indeed, Mr. Ed sometimes seemed to be much more on top of things than his human owners. This desire to attribute human-like traits to wild animals is unfortunate. People are prone to anthropomorphism and sentimentality when it comes to animals, particularly domesticated ones like dogs and horses.

Query: What is the author trying to say about our view of horse communication?

In fact, horses use sounds to communicate but in a fashion quite different from that depicted in *Mr. Ed*. They actually use four basic sounds: (1) the nicker (low pitched like the key of G); (2) the blow (a low nontonal sound); (3) the squeal (louder and like a C two octaves above middle C); and the (4) whinny (very loud).

Query: How does the author help you understand what each horse signal sounds like?

Each signal has particular uses. For example, the whinny is used for long-distance communication when horses are out of visual range of other horses they socialize with.

DISCUSSION. Based on responses to the various text queries, students can then discuss the section of the chapter they read. This is a good place to raise issues of accuracy in what the author presented and help students make connections to their prior experiences and reading. For example, students who have some experiences with horses and their various signals might offer insights during the discussion stage.

This strategy is flexible and lends itself to the creation of higher-order questions for various queries in a text. Questions can range from those that are variously text-based and guide the reader, to those that are open-ended and extend understanding of the text.

Critical Media Literacy

Contemporary adolescents encounter a broad range of texts that include television, films, and music. These popular media help engage students' interest, but are rarely treated as a forum for discussion and critique. Recent efforts to infuse popular culture and critical media literacy in content classrooms show how critical thinking can be developed through the inclusion of contemporary media (Dunkerly-Bean, Bean, & Alnajjar, 2014). The critical media literacy lesson framework that follows will help demystify this process. Recommended readings for this chapter offer additional resources as you begin to work with popular culture material in your content area.

Steps for a Critical Media Literacy Lesson

1. Planning a critical media lesson must involve a clear awareness of district policies regarding appropriate films and music. Movie clips need to acknowledge students' interests, jog their thinking about concepts, and be deemed acceptable within district norms. For example, Stevens (2001) and a middle school physical science teacher collaborated on the development of a popular media lesson involving the three basic laws of motion. At the planning stage, they decided to ask students to critique action sequences in films to judge the degree to which they were consistent with the laws of physics. Movies rated G and PG were selected with a parent consent letter for a 5-minute action sequence from *Jumanji* (1995). They were especially interested in how students reacted and judged those movie sequences where they were expected by the film's producer and director to suspend an understanding of physical laws and what is actually possible.

2. Ask students to watch or listen to the media clip (in this example, a scene from *Jumanji*) and write down their conclusions about the scene's consistency with the laws of physics. They can use their textbook as a reference to cross-check any concepts that may help with their critique. For example, in *Jumanji*, a hunter shoots a bullet, and it stops in the air. Physical laws of motion do not support this scene, and students used both the film clip of this action and their book to critique its veracity.

Our definition of what constitutes a text must be expanded to include the wide array of media material students encounter. More importantly, this material offers an exciting platform for the development of critical thinking and critical discourse. Popular film, music, and television offer a readily available means to challenge students' thinking and assumptions.

Needless to say, the Critical Media Literacy strategy, as well as the K-W-L, I-Chart, Listen-Read-Discuss, Questioning the Author, and SRE strategies, will require a good block of time to complete. They should be reserved for topics you feel are important enough to warrant the extra time. Because of the integrated nature of these strategies, students receive multiple exposures to concepts. This may be especially useful for those students who often need extra time to learn content material.

Now go back to the comprehension vignette at the beginning of the chapter. React again to the lesson as you did before. Compare your responses with those you made before you read the chapter.

MINI PROJECTS

Using the website excerpt, "Ears and Hearing" on the website, do one or both of the following:

1. Develop three questions at each of the three levels of understanding and identify the predominant text structure present.

2. Develop a lesson based on K-W-L, the I-Chart, Listen-Read-Discuss, Questioning the Author, or the Scaffolded Reading Experience. Try out the lesson with a small group of students or your peers. Evaluate the success of the strategy upon completion.

RECOMMENDED WEBSITES

o Public Broadcasting Service: www.pbs.org
o Example of a student-created human rights video from the article (Dunkerly-Bean, Bean, & Alnajjar, 2014 in Recommended Readings: http://www.youtube.com/watch?v=Qgo7P-f5ba4
o Annenberg Media Learner: http://www.annenbergclassroom.org
o Smithsonian Museum: www.smithsonianeducation.org

WEBSITE ACTIVITY

Go to the website for Chapter 5 activities.

CHAPTER 10

Comprehension:
Guiding Content Literacy

VIGNETTE

© Monkey Business Images/Shutterstock.com

Setting

Lydian Flat's high school band class. In the previous class, Mr. Flat began a lesson on scale theory. In this class he plans to expand on this foundational information by exploring the seven modes of the major scale.

The Lesson

Mr. Flat begins class by reviewing concepts about scale theory introduced in the previous class lesson. He does this by asking students to respond to questions he throws out to the whole class at the beginning of the period. In the scene that follows, T = the teacher, Mr. Flat, and S = the students.

T: *"Can anyone tell me what a scale is?"*

S: *Some students attempt to assemble their instruments, honking on saxes and clarinets, while others raise their hands to answer. Mr. Flat calls on Phil, a guitarist, who answers with a textbook definition:*

S: *"A scale is a series of tones organized according to a specific arrangement of intervals. An interval is the distance between any two tones or pitches. The smallest interval is the half step which on my guitar is the difference in pitch between two notes one fret apart on the same string."*

T: *"Okay, Phil, nice answer. Now let's try a tough one. What's a pentatonic scale?"*

S: *Phil snickers. Clearly this is an easy question for him, but the other students become even more intent on fussing with their instruments, resulting in growing cacophony.*

T: *"Alright, alright. Phil, tell us what a pentatonic scale is."*

S: *Phil doesn't answer. Instead he cradles his guitar and plays a slow A minor blues riff built on a minor pentatonic scale.*

T: *"Yes, that's a minor pentatonic scale, but it's a little ahead of where we are in this unit on scales. We need to consider and play the major scales and learn their key signatures first. And today we'll also be looking at the seven modes of the major scale: the Dorian mode in jazz and rock, the Phrygian mode, which you may recognize from flamenco music, the Lydian mode from jazz, the Mixolydian mode used in a lot of folk music, and the Aeolian mode and the Locrian mode used in jazz. But before we go any farther, let's start by playing a C major scale together."*

S: *Students launch into scale practice under Mr. Flat's guidance.*

T: *Near the end of the class, Mr. Flat hands out a worksheet that lists the major keys and their relative minor keys (e.g., C major and A minor). He informs students that there will be a quiz over this material next week on Wednesday.*

S: *Before the bell rings, students take apart and clean their instruments, frantically tossing the worksheet into folders and backpacks.*

Keeping in mind that this lesson is concerned with understanding scale theory and applying this theory in playing band instruments, jot down your thoughts on the following questions:

1. What are the good points about the lesson?

2. What are the weak points about the lesson?

3. What, if anything, would you change about the lesson?

RATIONALE

All the integrated approaches to comprehension introduced in Chapter 9 have advocated guiding students before, during, and after reading. To reinforce the integrated notion that this text recommends, these strategies also advocate the use of all language processes and small groups whenever possible.

To continue in that vein this chapter describes various strategies that can be predominantly classified as prereading, reading, or postreading in scope. Although we realize that a holistic view of the comprehension process encompasses all stages of the instructional lesson and that each stage is not necessarily a separate entity, for example, the postreading stage of one lesson may serve as the prereading stage of the next lesson, the strategies are divided to facilitate our discussion of each of them. The intent of all of these strategies, however, is similar: to increase students' interaction with the ideas presented in print and online texts so they will acquire and be able to act on important content information. Therefore, the aim of this chapter is to introduce and demonstrate an array of comprehension strategies, with the caveat that your particular discipline will guide the selection, use, and modification of any particular strategy (Dunkerly-Bean, & Bean, 2016).

Many of the strategies introduced in this chapter engage students in scaffolded discussion of key content area concepts. An extensive body of research into classroom discussion shows that discussion that moves beyond a simplistic teacher–student ping-pong discussion toward more open-ended dialogue produces significant growth in comprehension (Almasi & Garas-York, 2009). Thus, we tend to high-light comprehension strategies that move students beyond text-explicit understanding of content area concepts.

 ## LEARNING OBJECTIVES

o   Be familiar with a wide array of prereading, reading, and postreading strategies for guiding students' comprehension of content area concepts.
o   Be able to apply specific teaching strategies in your content area in order to guide students' understanding of your course content.

 ## GRAPHIC ORGANIZER

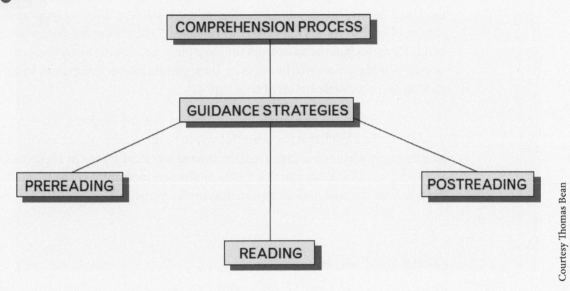

Courtesy Thomas Bean

PREREADING STRATEGIES

Throughout this chapter we emphasize careful, thoughtful, critical close reading of texts in history, science, literature, and other content areas. One of the ways you may want to introduce students to this process involves mentioning an organization that is generally thought to be benign and even nurturing or helping our environment. For example, based on the Hollywood film and the book, *A walk in the woods* by Bill Bryson (1999), Tom asks his students to mention what they think of when they encounter the U.S. Forest Service. Most mention preserving the forests, nurturing the environment, building hiking trails, and other positive contributions to our forests. As it turns out, most of the forest is indeed owned by the U.S. Forest Service. However, because the 240 million acres are designated "multiple use" mining, logging, oil and gas extraction, development of ski resorts, and other activities generally interfere with the tranquility of the forest. Indeed, the Forest Service builds a huge number of roads into the forest to support clear cutting of timber. As Bryson (1999) wryly notes, "The reason the Forest Service builds these roads, quite apart from the deep pleasure of doing noisy things in the woods with big yellow machines, is to allow private timber companies to get to previously inaccessible stands of trees." (p. 47)

If you can introduce counterintuitive meanings that jog students' thinking beyond the surface level, that is a powerful way to begin to deconstruct and dismantle misconceptions and nudge students toward a critical stance in their reading and viewing. In the strategies that follow, multiple opportunities exist to question the taken-for-granted notions that surround the disciplines.

Anticipation Guides

Throughout this text we have been using a number of prereading strategies to introduce each chapter. One of them, the *anticipation guide,* introduces each chapter in Part 1 and is an attractive way to activate your thoughts and opinions about a topic. As you are well aware by now, many of the guide statements are loaded in the sense that we want to challenge commonly held beliefs about content area literacy. Indeed, one of the major features of an anticipation guide is that it brings misconceptions about a topic to the surface. Then we can begin to modify these misconceptions through a well-formulated instructional sequence.

Since anticipation guide statements operate at the experience-based level of understanding, they elicit a response based on one's current belief system. Therefore, at the prereading stage a student may adamantly defend a response to a guide statement with little fear of failure. As the learning sequence progresses into the reading and postreading stages, a mismatch between the students' preconceptions about a topic and the information being introduced should result in a subsequent modification of their initial knowledge base.

An additional feature of the anticipation guide is its function as an informal diagnostic tool. A teacher can appraise prior knowledge at the prereading stage and evaluate the acquisition of content based on postreading responses to the guide statements. Since anticipation guides encourage a personal, experience-based response, they serve as ideal springboards for large and small group discussion. Furthermore, they seem to work equally well with print and nonprint media, including films, lectures, and field trips, and lend themselves to application in diverse subject areas such as science, art, physical education, and history.

Steps for Constructing an Anticipation Guide in Any Content Area

1. Identify the major concepts and supporting details in a print or online text selection, lecture, or film.

2. Identify students' experiences and beliefs that will be challenged and, in some cases, supported by the material.

3. Create statements reflecting your students' prereading beliefs concerning a course topic that may challenge and modify those beliefs. Include some statements that are consistent with both your students' experiential background and the concepts presented in the material or lesson. Three to five statements are usually adequate.

4. Arrange the statements on a sheet of paper or on the smart board and have the students respond positively or negatively to each statement on an individual basis. Make them record their justification for each response in writing, so they will have a reference point for discussion.

5. Engage students in a prereading discussion highlighting their current justification for responding positively or negatively to each statement.

> **Prereading Strategies**
> o Anticipation guides
> o Text appetizers

With a little practice, you will discover that anticipation guides serve to clarify your content objectives and to motivate students to approach a learning task in an active fashion. Used in conjunction with a film, they can reduce the kind of haphazard, passive processing of film concepts that often characterizes the use of media in a classroom. The following physical education anticipation guide (Figure 10.1) was developed to accompany a fitness film.

FIGURE 10.1

Anticipation Guide: Stretching

Directions: Before watching the fitness film, put a (+) by those statements with which you agree and a (−) by those with which you disagree. Jot down some notes that will help you defend your point of view in a class discussion.

Anticipation

_____ 1. Most doctors prescribe stretching for relief of tension and stress.
_____ 2. A gymnast and a football player should stretch about the same length of time.
_____ 3. Stretching is neglected because it is painful and boring.
_____ 4. Stretching with the aid of a partner can bring about greater flexibility.

In a social studies class, anticipation guides help students to appraise ideas critically in a text. For example, the following guide (Figure 10.2) was designed to accompany middle school students' reading of a US history chapter on the Constitution. One student's prereading ideas are included.

Even factual texts in US history can serve as rich sources for critical thinking when they are supplemented with an anticipation guide like this one. Students begin to see some link between their lives and the (often distant) concepts in a text. Moreover, they must adopt a critical stance toward a topic, weighing their preconceptions against the author's ideas. Indeed, many educators regard the development and evaluation of arguments as the essence of critical thinking.

As you work with anticipation guides, you may find it helpful to include an "I'm not sure," or "I don't know" response column to accommodate those students who, at the prereading stage, are really not ready to commit to a "yes" or "no" response. This reduces guessing and provides some insight into a student's background knowledge about the topic.

Anticipation guides are best used in small group or cooperative learning pairs. Students can then discuss their perceptions of the topic, which helps them see that these statements are not a test. At first, you may need to make it clear to students that these statements are designed to jog their thinking, not to serve as another true–false test of trivial facts to be memorized. In our experience, students at various levels enjoy reacting to well-constructed guide statements to narrative and expository material as well as to lectures and films.

FIGURE 10.2

ANTICIPATION GUIDE: The Constitution

Directions: Before reading pages 186 to 193, read each statement and place a "yes" by those statements with which you agree and a "no" by those statements with which you disagree under the column labeled Anticipation. Write your reasons for agreeing or disagreeing so that you can be part of a class discussion.

Anticipation

yes 1. Writers of the Constitution were everyday working class people.
Because they had to work for a living and they were not royalty.

no 2. The President, like a king, has complete power to rule the country.
Because he can be kicked out of office by the process of impeachment.

no 3. A Ford mechanic cannot become President.
Because it does not matter as long as he is the right age and is elected.

no 4. Rich and poor people have equal protection under the law.
The rich people have more influence over the law because they can bribe the law.

yes 5. Students should have the right to decide what classes they take.
After the 10th grade they should be able to, because by that time they will know what they want from life and they would take courses to prepare for their career.

ANTICIPATION GUIDE: OSPREY

Earlier in the text we mentioned a lesson development application we have been using in our classes called Blendspace at Blendspace.com. This application provides a creative platform for engaging students in anticipation guide statements followed by video clips related to the topic, text material, and a quiz. Take a look at the following link to view an example of this useful tool on the topic of Osprey in a science class: https://www.tes.com/lessons/IaMJAZO2KH7jqg/edit

Blendspace provides a wealth of YouTube and other resources and the drop and drag intuitive nature of this application allows you to type in or add preexisting text on any topic relevant to your content area. The quiz feature scores and charts students' progress as well. In our own teaching, we use this application to demonstrate engaging content and disciplinary concepts across English, music, physical education, history, mathematics, marketing, languages, and a host of other subjects.

View the website video clip showing a classroom teacher introducing a reading assignment with an anticipation guide.

Text Appetizers

Text Appetizers are teacher-created, introductory paragraphs that offer a framework for comprehending a reading selection by relating the new to the known (Bean, Readence, & Baldwin, 2012). By connecting new information in the text to their prior knowledge, students are likely to focus attention on key concepts during reading.

Steps to Develop Text Appetizers

1. **Write the introductory paragraph.** Write an interest-building paragraph based on real-life, day-to-day events that would be of interest to your students and are similar in principle to the critical target concepts in a text.

2. **Add guiding questions (optional).** Add one guiding question at each of the three levels of understanding.

3. **Read the text appetizer.** Have students read and discuss the appetizer before beginning the reading assignment. The guiding questions can be attached to the appetizer to help students focus on important information.

The text appetizer example in Figure 10.3 comes from social studies:

FIGURE 10.3

Text Appetizer: The Politics of Protest

Suppose that you like to ride a skateboard at the new skate park near your neighborhood. However, due to a small percentage of rowdy skaters taking drugs and extorting money from other kids, your City Council threatens to close down the skate park. How do you feel about this situation? What would you do about it?

The chapter you are about to read shows how groups such as small business people, workers, and farmers in the 1890s protested what they felt were unfair practices by big business, often with the support of the government. Farmers felt they were paying too much interest on equipment loans from big business banks. They banded together to protest this unfair treatment, just as you might protest lumping all teenage skaters together despite only a small minority causing problems at the skate park. Congress was viewed as a governmental body that could help the farmers with the plight, but, like many political systems, this one proved to have its flaws. As you read pages 537 to 549, try to answer the following discussion questions:

Right There on the Page
1. What was the purpose of the Sherman Antitrust Act? (p. 539, paragraph 3)

Think and Search
2. Why didn't the Sherman Antitrust Act work the way it was supposed to in 1890?

On Your Own
3. Do you think the Sherman Antitrust Act is working today?

This text appetizer and its guide questions helped students' comprehension of a potentially dull and distant topic—the farmers' efforts to gain fair treatment in the late 1800s. Having students work on the guide questions in cooperative learning pairs also helps those students who may be unaccustomed to grappling with experience-based, on-your-own issues. Text appetizers can be created for particularly problematic text reading assignments in science and other content areas. They help students approach text reading with a schema for a topic based on prior knowledge.

READING STRATEGIES

Sitting down with a print textbook or online text in the solitude of your own personal study corner is a lonely activity, devoid of the language interaction afforded by the classroom. You may well wonder what possible strategies exist to help students cope with this inherently solitary task.

Indeed, many text assignments are of the "sink-or-swim" variety. "Go home and read Chapter 13 in your text" is an all too familiar edict for many students. Unfortunately, textbooks and the idiosyncratic labyrinth of the Internet are rarely amenable to such independent reading assignments. Texts are instructional tools that require a good deal of guidance if students are to gain anything from them. In the section that follows we describe some approaches that assist students in coping with their individual text reading assignments. It is worth noting that recent efforts to better understand the particular discourse structures of disciplines like social studies, music, and mathematics are likely to yield other teaching and learning strategies not yet envisioned (Conley, 2009). In addition, if you are a highly creative teacher, you may embrace interdisciplinary learning where you combine history with art, music, and literature (Wimmer, Walker, & Bean, 2010). Each content area is unique and embedded with layers of topics and discourse structures. Nevertheless, the following approaches will help as you think about the nuances of your own content area.

> **Reading Strategies**
> o Study guides
> o Options guides
> o Analogical guides

Study Guides

The term *study guide* has been used loosely for years to describe almost any form of supplementary material that accompanies a text. Often, study guides are nothing more than a series of text-explicit questions supplied by an author at the end of a text chapter. We subscribe to a very different view of the process involved in the development of a good content area study guide. The sample study guide questions in Figure 10.4 are based on the previous chapter and contain the basic ingredients necessary to extend students' thinking beyond a mere parroting of text-explicit concepts.

FIGURE 10.4

Sample Study Guide Questions

Directions: Use the information in Chapter 9 to answer the following questions. Compare your answers to those of a colleague.

  *1. What is the second principle of comprehension advanced in the introduction to Chapter 9? (p. 210)

 **2. Why is it important for students to be able to produce a text structure in their own writing?

***3. Of the comprehension strategies introduced in Chapter 9, which one(s) do you prefer for use in your content area? Why?

   *   Text explicit

  **   Text implicit

***   Experience based

Notice that a study guide of this form asks students to react to text concepts at multiple levels of understanding. For example, the first question, which is text explicit, includes a reference to assist students in locating the answer. For some students, this form of guidance may be necessary. Indeed, some students may only be able to answer this form of question, particularly in the early stages of the course. In contrast to question one, question three asks the reader to build a bridge of text concepts and individual teaching needs. Both questions two and three offer the potential for discussion and expanded thinking. Although this study guide example has been presented after the fact, in practice, study guides typically accompany a text assignment and the reader completes the guide while reading. Thus, the guide provides a pathway to the major concepts in a content area and counters a more traditional, sink-or-swim reading assignment. A good study guide should mirror the thought process by which a reader extracts information from text. As such, a teacher-devised study guide should do the following:

1. Focus students' attention on major concepts at three levels of understanding (i.e., text explicit, text implicit, experience based);

2. Foster student reaction to the text material at each student's individual level of understanding;

3. Direct students' thought processes in extracting information from text material;

4. Serve as a basis for follow-up discussion in small groups to collaborate on the explication of text concepts and extend individual comprehension.

One might expect that students would regard study guides as an additional burden along with the text reading assignment. However, our observations of secondary students using study guides reveals that they are well received. Most felt they understood text concepts better as a result of completing and discussing guide material.

The development of a study guide involves a process of content analysis similar to the construction of an anticipation guide. Indeed, developing these two comprehension aids simultaneously with a text chapter is a good idea.

Steps to Develop a Study Guide

1. Determine the major concepts and important details in a text chapter or reading selection.

2. Develop questions that reflect these major concepts and details at multiple levels of understanding. Use vocabulary terms students can understand and, in the first few guides you develop, provide page and paragraph indicators to demonstrate the process of locating and extracting information.

3. Assign the study guide as an adjunct to independent text reading. Then, have students discuss and defend responses in small groups.

Since not all students will be able to answer the whole study guide, the discussion step gives everyone exposure to the complete array of information. This study group step is an integral part of the application of study guide material and is essential to its success as an aid to comprehension. Generally, about 10 questions per study guide should be adequate for a text chapter. The guide should look attractive in that adequate space is allowed for student answers, and information does not appear crowded on the page.

The study guide shown in Figure 10.5 was used to guide high school students' discussion in United States history. Text explicit questions are labeled "right there on the page," text implicit questions are labeled "think and search," and experience-based questions are labeled "on your own." This study guide was developed to accompany reading the Confederation and the Constitution. Students read the text and answered the study guide questions. Then, they engaged in small group discussions of their answers and a large group follow-up discussion focusing on the "on your own" items. One student's answers are included.

FIGURE 10.5

Study Guide: The Confederation and the Constitution

Right There On the Page

1. What political changes occurred in the 13 colonies as a result of the American Revolution? (pp. 119–120)

    Colonial self-rule, the recognition of minorities, new constitution, an increase in voting, and a legislature more responsive to people.

2. What social changes took place in the 13 colonies as a result of the American Revolution? (pp. 120–121)

    The separation of church and state, and the Loyalists uprooted the Anglican Church, weakening of slavery, and the development of the feminist movement.

3. What economic changes happened in the 13 colonies as a result of the American Revolution? (p. 122)

    Inventive influences, the loss of commerce because of England, high inflation, great amounts of land available, freedom of trade, a distaste for government.

Think and Search

4. Can you identify some political, social, and economic disadvantages that resulted from the American Revolution?

    We did not have many great strong leaders that we had before. We really did not have much control. We were on our own so we needed to spend money to manufacture goods and find people to buy them.

5. Why was not slavery abolished in the 1770s?

    Political fighting over slavery was avoided to preserve national unity. Too many people needed workers to make money and get their lives going again.

6. Why do you think the authors see the American Revolution as "accelerated evolution" rather than "outright revolution?"

    Because the Revolution was unknown to many people living in small, isolated villages. And, it was not as radical as other revolutions. It made future changes possible.

On Your Own

7. Would you want to travel through time back to the 1770s during the drafting of the Constitution? If so, why? If not, why not?

    Yes, so I could maybe put things in or take things out that may help the United States.

8. If you decide to travel back in time to visit the drafting of the Constitution you would be taking with you the powerful knowledge of the future! What advice could you give the writers of the Constitution?

    Be clearer in what is written. Today, interpretations of the Constitution are all different.

Study guides are particularly important in the early part of a course as students are grasping an author's writing style and dominant text structures. We have used study guides effectively even in the early grades. Study guide questions can form an effective model for student-generated questions. Indeed, study guides help model fluent, efficient text reading. Textbooks and online texts are not designed to be read word for word. Rather, they should be read selectively with an eye toward important ideas. The following activity is designed to give you further practice with the process of constructing a study guide for a content area text.

APPLICATION 10.2

Directions: The following three study guide questions pertain to the present section of Chapter 10. See if you can generate three additional study guide questions on this same material.

*** 1. Based on your own academic experience, can you think of any courses you have taken where you would have appreciated study guides with the text? Which ones? Why?

* 2. What is the second step in constructing a study guide?

** 3. How does the study guide foster the psychological principle of in-depth processing of text material?

* 4.

** 5.

*** 6.

Options Guides

An *options guide* is another form of study guide that, unlike the focused guidance provided in a traditional study guide, offers possibilities and predictions to be evaluated in subsequent reading. It asks students to function in an active, decision-making role. Unlike a study guide, which is designed to accompany a reading assignment, an options guide is discussed prior to text reading. It then serves as a guide during reading. Options guides are ideal for reading assignments in social studies texts, where students often adopt a passive role, mindlessly turning pages or trying to memorize facts.

Steps to Develop and Introduce the Options Guide

1. Carefully analyze a text reading assignment for major concepts and key sub-headings that foreshadow upcoming events. You want to identify (1) key historical figures and the specific impact they had on other groups of people; and (2) the economy, the arts, religion, and other sociocultural aspects of life.

2. Since up to the time you introduce the options guide, students' previous text reading is all they have when discussing the guide, you should construct a brief background statement that will remind students of the material they have read and studied up to this point.

3. Develop one or two central questions that ask students to consider various options open to specific groups of people within the particular historical context presented by the text.

4. When students have completed a text reading assignment up to the subheading or section of text on which your options guide is based, have them convene in small groups for about 10 to 15 minutes to discuss and complete the prereading section of the options guide. Then, when they finish reading the assignment, they should check their listed options against actual events in the text and complete the guide's postreading section. Engage students in a follow-up small-group discussion to clarify any sections of the guide that need further explanation.

The options guide shown in Figure 10.6 is designed to precede a text reading assignment in world history on the emergence of Japan. Students have read the portion of the chapter on the developing samurai warrior class. The first subheading of the new reading comprises the major heading for the guide. Subsequent subheadings were used to list various groups affected by shogun society. Representative group answers before and after reading are listed.

As you can see, in some instances students generated options that were borne out in the text. In other cases, their predictions proved far afield of what actually occurred. Options guides make potentially dull text reading assignments considerably more interesting. Indeed, using options guides in conjunction with other strategies (e.g., graphic organizers) will potentially make your lessons even more productive for students. The success of the guides hinges in large measure on the small-group discussions that precede and follow their use as reading guides. Consider using options guides for selected topics in social studies as a student-centered alternative to traditional study guides. You may want to begin with fairly detailed options guides, like the one on Japan, and slowly fade to skeletal options guides that place the responsibility on students to speculate about the impact of an event on sociocultural aspects of the economy, arts, agriculture, and so on. In our experience, your efforts to develop guide material will be richly rewarded in increased levels of student understanding and participation.

FIGURE 10.6

Options Guide: The Kamakura Shogunate (1192–1333) Began

Background: In 1156, civil war broke out between two large landowning families. Each family had a band of loyal warriors called samurai. In 1192, one samurai, named Minamoto Yoritomo, became the supreme general of all Japan. The emperor named him the shogun.

During this period of military rule, what options for political influence do you think were available to the following groups?

1. Nobles?
   1.1 Before Reading: They will be even more powerful with the strength of their loyal samurai warriors.
   1.2 After Reading: The emperor's power was less, but the local "daimyos" (nobles) became supreme rulers of their lands. They fought with other daimyos. There was no effective central government in Japan during this time. Later, in the Tokugawa Era (1603–1868), central government was strong.

2. Artists?
   2.1 Before Reading: In this military era, there probably will be no time for the arts. Artists will be forced to fight or flee. It will be a very backward time.
   2.2 After Reading: It seems strange, but the arts did flourish. Poetic "Noh" plays were created, landscape painting was prized, flower arranging, tea ceremonies, and artistic gardens were important in Japanese homes.

3. Farmers?
   3.1 Before Reading: With all the fighting, there will be no time for farming. Agriculture will suffer.
   3.2 After Reading: Farmers thrived, since the daimyos ruled to maintain peace within their own communities. But gradually, cities grew and merchants became important. The landing of the Portuguese in 1543 made the people aware of European trade possibilities.

4. The Samurai?
   4.1 Before Reading: They are soldiers, so, like all soldiers, they will have little power. They must follow orders.
   4.2 After Reading: Samurai knights were very loyal to their shogun generals. They felt a total moral obligation to do well in battle. If they did not, they would commit suicide or "harakiri." As we suspected, they did not have much power. The shoguns held the power.

5. If the Chinese try to invade Japan, how will they do?
   5.1 Before Reading: Since they are an older, more powerful people, they will win.
   5.2 After Reading: Kubla Khan invaded Japan, but his Mongol warriors were swept into a big typhoon. The Japanese called this the Kamikaze or "divine wind." As we said before reading, without this typhoon China's Mongol warriors might have defeated the samurai.

Analogical Guides

Another form of study guide has been developed for application in science classes. The *analogical guide* aims to get students to study new science concepts they are attempting to learn by thinking about the underlying properties of more familiar concepts and comparing these with new, unfamiliar ones.

We use analogies spontaneously in our everyday speech and thinking. For example, if we plan a field trip to a marine biology laboratory and the trip is successful, we may say the job went like clockwork. If our field trip plans failed, we may say they collapsed like a house of cards.

It is not unusual for scientists to use analogies to explain complex processes or theories. For example, scientists use the analogy of a giant pinwheel or disk to understand the nature of the Milky Way. Texts in biology sometimes feature analogies, but students often do not know how they can use these analogies to comprehend and recall concepts. The analogical guide is designed to make students aware of using analogies to understand concepts. Before we introduce the analogical guide on cell structure, test your knowledge of cell structure by completing Application 10.3.

APPLICATION 10.3

Your last science class may have been quite some time ago, or you may be a science teacher. In any case, we would like you to try the following activity. See if you can correctly match the six cell structure parts on the left with their related functions on the right. Simply write the letter of the correct function on the line to the left of the cell part. Good luck!

Structure		Function
1. _____ mitochondria		a. Controls heredity
2. _____ cell membrane		b. Storage
3. _____ vacuoles		c. Boundary
4. _____ nucleus		d. Intracellular transport
5. _____ endoplasmic reticulum		e. Cellular respiration
6. _____ ribosomes		f. Protein synthesis

These cell structure–function relationships comprise just a small part of a basic chapter on the cell. This material constitutes an important foundation for subsequent chapters that explore more complex aspects of the cell, such as cell division. Most biology texts contain a chart of cell parts and functions for students to study. Many students simply memorize this chart without really understanding how the different cell parts function. In your case, we gave you a small number of cell parts to match to their functions. How did you do? Our guess is that you successfully matched nucleus and cell membrane, but (unless your field is science) you flubbed the other four items. Here are the correct answers: l-e; 2-c; 3-b; 4-a; 5-d; 6-f. Now, consider students who have access to the analogical study guide in Figure 10.7 that a teacher introduces and explains. Do you think your comprehension of these six cell structure–function relations would have been better with such a guide?

Analogical Guide: Cell Structure and Function   **FIGURE 10.7**

Directions: You will be studying the parts of a cell and their functions. In some ways a cell resembles a factory, because, like a factory, it uses raw materials to manufacture a product. You will find that comparing the different parts of the cell to the parts of a factory will help you remember the functions of the various cell parts. For example, in the guide, the cell walls are compared to factory walls because both provide support and protection.

Structure	Function	Analogy (Like A)
Cell wall	Support and protection	Factory walls
Cell membrane	Boundary, gatekeeper	Security guards
Cytoplasm	Site of metabolism	The work area
Chloroplasts	Photosynthesis	Snack bar
Endoplasmic reticulum	Intracellular transport	Conveyor belts
Golgi bodies	Storage, secretion	Packaging, storing, and shipping
Lysosomes	Intracellular digestion	Cleanup crew
Mitochondria	Cellular respiration	Energy generation plant
Nucleus	Controls heredity	Boss's office and copy machine
Ribosomes	Protein synthesis	Assembly line
Vacuoles	Storage	Warehouses

The overall factory analogy provides a coherent structure for the whole guide. In a study of this guide's contribution to students' comprehension in high school biology, we found that students who were achieving low grades significantly outpaced peers in a control group when the guide was introduced as a means of studying the text. The control group simply used the cell structure–function chart provided in the text without any analogies.

1. Analyze the reading task facing students by identifying those concepts you want them to acquire (e.g., a basic understanding of cell structure and function relationships).

2. This is the most difficult and crucial step—creating appropriate analogies that will connect with students' diverse experiences. A good analogy is one that contains underlying properties similar to the target concept, but it is usually dissimilar at the surface level. For example, comparing the cell membrane to a security guard provides a familiar analogy, because the two share underlying properties of entry and exit control, even though there are no surface level similarities.

3. You need to go over the analogical guide with students, explaining how they can use the analogies on the right side of the guide to comprehend and recall the function of a particular cell structure. Some students may wish to generate their own analogies, so you can gradually transfer responsibility for this process to students.

Whenever we see a glazed look on students' faces during a classroom explanation, we spontaneously search for an appropriate analogy to provide a vivid image of the concept we are introducing. Analogical guides show students how they can effectively use analogies to link new information with prior knowledge. We recommend that you use analogical guides, when appropriate, for complex topics in science. Although such guides take some time to create, they help alleviate the sink-or-swim experience many students have as they try to fathom science texts. Their feelings are much the same as what you experienced trying to complete the cell structure–function matching activity. Unguided reading of a complex text simply produces frustration and hostility rather than comprehension and a feeling of power over the material.

In the section that follows we explore the last stage of a content reading, listening, or viewing assignment: the postreading stage.

POSTREADING STRATEGIES

Despite the intuitive and proven value of review for long-term retention of content area concepts, this activity remains the most often neglected component of a lesson structure. Important concepts are glossed over far too rapidly in an effort to cover the book and get on to new material.

Postreading Strategies
o Discussion groups
o Reaction guides
o Phony document strategy and sourcing in history
o The imposter
o Polar opposites with text and video
o Graphic organizers
o Multiple text inquiry discussion

In contrast to those who see review sessions as teacher-centered activities, we perceive the review process to be a natural outgrowth of the prereading and reading activities in a well-integrated lesson. Activities that acknowledge and, in some cases, refine students' prior knowledge of a topic also can be applied at the postreading stage. For example, the reaction guide you had been filling out at the close of each chapter in Part 1 is essentially a review activity. The graphic organizer and the study guide also lend themselves to the review process. Indeed, we regard review as more than a solitary pondering of text concepts. Review activities should involve active manipulation and collaborative discussion of information. The following are advantages in using discussion groups in a class:

1. Students are more motivated to learn when they are cooperating rather than competing individually with their peers.

2. Students display a more positive attitude toward both the class and the instructor when there are opportunities for this less teacher-centered form of learning.

3. Students in the role of the tutor and the tutee both benefit. They have to know the material in order to effectively teach it to another student.

4. Students' self-esteem is enhanced by helping one another learn content material.

5. Students display more positive perceptions of the intentions of other students. This is especially crucial in multilingual, multicultural classrooms. By working together in cooperative groups, students perceive their peers more positively than when they are isolated from each other. There is a decrease in prejudice and stereotyping.

6. There is a decrease in competitive goal structures. Students come to view other students' ideas as important to their individual learning.

7. Students become less dependent on the teacher as the only source of reliable information. They begin to take charge of problem solving in a cooperative fashion.

Using small groups entails a different style of classroom management that is, unquestionably, more of an art than orchestrating instruction from the front of the room and acting as an authority figure. Since we recommend using small groups to discuss material in the various guides introduced in this chapter, and particularly at the postreading review stage of a lesson, what are some of the features that seem to insure small groups work effectively?

Discussion Groups

GENERAL GUIDELINES. It is important to first consider the role you plan to play in guiding small group review. Analyses of effective comprehension discussion approaches emphasize the collaborative nature of productive discussion (Almasi & Garas-York, 2009): "Discussion is defined as a dialogic classroom event in which students and teachers are cognitively, socially, and affectively engaged in collaboratively constructing meaning or considering alternative interpretations of texts to arrive at new meanings." (p. 471) Indeed, this teacher stance encourages multiple and conflicting interpretations of texts that go beyond text-explicit thinking.

Alvermann, Dillon, and O'Brien (1987) also described four possible teacher roles and commented on their characteristic limitations. The first role they call "the instructor." The teacher retains the normal fountain of truth position and serves to clarify any confusion or difficulties that arise in the small groups. The disadvantage of adopting this role is that it may limit students' sense of their own responsibility for maintaining discussion and resolving problems.

A second possible role is that of "participant." The teacher becomes part of a small-group discussion. Although this sounds attractive, you may inadvertently inhibit students from participating. After all, in your normal role you are perceived as the content expert.

A third, and more appropriate role, is that of a "consultant." In this way you are free to rove about the room, responding to requests for help from various groups. It is important to restrain yourself from overassisting a group. Rather, encourage students to exhaust all their efforts in resolving problems or clarifying information before you offer to step in.

A fourth, and the most difficult role, is that of a "neutral observer" of small-group discussion. In this case, you remain silent, offering neither opinion, nor clarification, nor conflict resolution. Although this may be an ideal role to adopt, it requires a slow, methodical release of responsibility to students that may span many weeks before they are comfortable and skilled at working in small groups.

An important and often overlooked facet of using small groups effectively is the furniture and layout of your room. If students are in desks arranged by rows, they can easily work in pairs, side by side. Or, if you have circular tables, these can be ideal for groups of four to five students. In general, as group size increases, the level of individual participation decreases.

Small groups should have four to five students of mixed ability with a clear learning goal. This may range from a discussion of study guide questions or reaction guide statements to debating an issue. Students' learning should be assessed individually, with the small group receiving recognition for the success of its members. This can be accomplished by adding up individual scores to arrive at team scores for various assessments.

Developing clearly defined student roles within a group is important. One student may be chair for the week, guiding discussion of study guide questions. The group may need a recorder and a gatekeeper to maintain the flow of discussion. These roles can be exchanged periodically. It must be noted that low-ability and high-ability students both make important contributions to learning. When a small group is discussing a study guide, low-ability students often function as excellent fact finders, whereas high-ability students may see connections from text-based ideas to more global issues. Both types of students offer opportunities for creative debate, and they learn effectively from each other. There is general agreement that it is very important to compose groups that include mixed-ability students, so they can balance each other's strengths and weaknesses.

A recent study of ninth-graders engaged in peer-led discussions of the popular short story, *The Lottery* (Jackson, 1948/1982), found that while students used multiple comprehension strategies, they often skated along the surface of a topic (Berne & Clark, 2006). These authors noted that, for a rich discussion to occur, students need to be taught how to actively listen to group members' ideas and questions before darting off to another topic. In addition, they need to be introduced to comprehension strategies (e.g., graphic organizers) aimed at helping them elucidate ideas in a text or short story. Fortunately, you can ensure that small groups function productively in your content area classroom by establishing clear parameters for discussion.

Although these general guidelines for your role in guiding small-group learning and review are based on recent synthesis of research in the area of cooperative learning, you must decide how to best use small groups in your own classroom. The next section offers some specific guidelines for developing and managing small groups effectively.

SPECIFIC GUIDELINES. A good way to demonstrate clearly how you want a small group to function is to model this process. Using guide material as a focal point for the discussion, compose a small group at the front of the room and act in the role of a group chair to demonstrate the process for about 10 minutes. Keep early efforts fairly simple and focused. Remember that students are often unaccustomed to working in this cooperative fashion.

If a group is going off course, how should you respond? Unfortunately, this is not a simple issue. As we pointed out earlier, if you adopt the role of the authoritarian instructor and monitor too heavily, you may interfere with the development of independent student problem solving. On the other hand, total chaos in your classroom is equally undesirable. Fortunately, there are some solutions to this problem.

Small study groups function productively when the teacher sets the stage for the review. To prepare students, the teacher should first explain the goals and advantages of collaborating in the study process via interdependent groups. The key idea here hinges on the phrase, interdependent groups. That is, the success of the group in solving a problem is evaluated collectively, but it also depends on the contribution of the individual members. To achieve such interdependence, stress the following:

1. Explain the desired discussion behaviors that students should strive for (e.g., encouraging each other to respond; valuing each other's ideas; allowing an adequate amount of time for a group member to explain a point without dominating the discussion);

2. Explain the reward system by which you would rate group performance. These systems will vary according to the maturity and ability of the students involved.

In addition to these steps, political scientist Walter Parker (2003) offers a teaching model aimed at introducing high school students to thoughtful, deliberative small-group discussion about local or global events of interest to students. Using a discussion framework based on one used by public policy professionals, each group must do the following:

1. Identify and explain a public problem (e.g., student dress codes on campus) and related stakeholders.

2. Develop and analyze policy alternatives to include goals, consequences, and trade-offs.

3. Decide what action to take.

However, before getting to the third step, students are introduced to a deliberative process that stimulates active listening to opposing views. In groups of four,

o Students study the issue under consideration (e.g., dress codes).

o Each group breaks into pairs of two students.

o Each pair is assigned a different position on the issue and further reading to support its particular position.

o Each pair presents its arguments to the other pair.

o Each pair then reverses its perspective, taking the opposing view.

o Finally, they combine into a group of four again and, in this deliberative body, seek consensus on the issue or agree to disagree.

As a model of democratic deliberation that incorporates active listening to content area classroom discussion, this process offers teachers a step-by-step means to ensure that small groups function productively. Issues of war, international cooperation, and global politics all lend themselves to deliberative forums where students move beyond surface understanding of critical issues (Harper & Bean, 2006).

A number of other strategies can serve as jumping off points for vibrant classroom discussion in your content area. Reaction Guides, related to Anticipation Guides, center discussion on key issues.

Reaction Guides

A *reaction guide* provides a good prelude to a more intensive review when it serves as a focal point for small-group discussion. When you complete a text selection and then reassess your prereading responses to an anticipation guide, you are using a reaction guide to examine your beliefs about a topic. More than likely, you alter at least some of your prereading beliefs and can defend this change by referencing relevant portions of the text.

A reaction guide is easy to construct since it is essentially another form of the anticipation guide, and the text analysis steps are the same for both comprehension strategies. You can simply add a second column to an anticipation guide for a postreading reaction to the same statements. Although the mechanics of the guide are simple, they should not be used as individual worksheets to be completed in silence. Rather, two or three of the most important statements should be considered and discussed by small groups. For example, we might have used the following statement for Chapter 3:

Anticipation   **Reaction**

    +   –

_____   _____ Rote memorization fosters long-term retention of information.

Notice that although many students might have agreed (+) with this statement at the prereading stage, upon considering the psychological importance of deep processing and organization for retention, they would tend to disagree (–) at the postreading stage. More importantly, they would be able to defend this shift by referring to relevant portions of the text that support the respective roles of deep processing and hierarchical organization in the memory process.

Duffelmeyer and Baum (1992) have suggested an adaptation of the reaction guide that promotes students' critical reading and thinking skills as well as requires them to actively confront their potential misconceptions. This adaptation is modeled for you with the anticipation and reaction guides used in Part 1 of this text. In the beginning of each chapter of Part 1 we asked you to agree or disagree with each guide statement and then to be ready to explain your choices. At the end of each chapter of Part 1 we asked you to reconsider your responses to the guide statements. If the information you found in the chapter supported your original choice, we asked you to check the Confirmed column and then write the supporting evidence from the text in your own words in the column marked "Why my choice is confirmed." If the information did not support your original choice, you were asked to check the Disconfirmed column and then write what the text says in your own words in the column marked "Why my choice is not confirmed." Adding the writing task to the reaction guide facilitates additional interaction with the text as students are asked to justify their claims of agreement or confront their misconceptions.

Phony Document Strategy and Sourcing in History

This critical reading strategy was initially developed for history classes. Indeed, sourcing is a critical element in closely reading and evaluating historical accounts (Wineberg & Reisman, 2015). Websites related to historical events can be salacious and misleading. For example, the *Institute for Historical Review* is actually a Holocaust denial group! (Wineberg & Reisman, 2015) In order to help students learn historical reasoning and the evaluation of sources in historical documents, Wineberg and Reisman, researchers at the Stanford University History Education Group created a *Reading Like A Historian* website: sheg.stanford.edu aimed at engaging students directly in the process of close reading to interrogate the truth value and accuracy of texts.

Similarly, the *phony document* strategy is based on a teacher-authored letter that purports to be historical and authentic, commenting on a key aspect of a novel, historical event, or scientific experiment (Bean, Readence, & Baldwin, 2012). While it reads as a perfectly plausible account, it is usually embedded with errors that students must ferret out through critical reading. Indeed, the central purpose of this strategy is to engage students in a close reading of the primary source material referred to in the phony document you have written. At the outset, you let them believe in the possible authenticity of this document. However, they must, in the end, refute its authenticity and point out the untruths and flaws embedded in it.

Steps to Using the Phony Document Strategy

1. Create a phony, but plausibly written document such as a letter, critique, news article, and so on. Letters and book excerpts or introductions seem to work best.

2. Ask students to read and judge the accuracy of the document and its value as something the school or district might want to purchase for wide distribution to students. They must engage in a close reading, cross-checking information (e.g., dates, assertions, places, and so on) with other sources.

3. Conduct small-group and whole-class discussions on the document's accuracy and value.

The following phony letter from a literary scholar illustrates the use of this strategy in an American literature class with high school juniors. Students finished reading Arthur Miller's famous play, *The Crucible* (1976). This and other activities in the class prepared the students to write from the perspective of a particular character in the play and extend their thinking about key episodes and events. Students read and critiqued the following phony document:

Student Task for P. J. Pennerd's, *The Crucible Revisited*

P. J. Pennerd is the Senior Scholar in Humanities at Boston University and the Danforth Foundation Endowed Chair in Literary Criticism. He is an internationally known expert on Arthur Miller's, *The Crucible*. His work is widely quoted by other literary scholars. Our nearby university library recently purchased the complete collection of Professor Pennerd's works for student use and analysis. Copies are currently worth thousands of dollars, and our school district and English Department are interested in purchasing this collection for our English curriculum. Your opinion is important in deciding the value of these documents. Please read and comment on this introductory material.

Introduction

The Salem, Massachusetts, witch trials of 1700 resulted in the execution of 50 Salem witches and far surpassed the number of accused witches put to death in Europe during this period. The Salem girls included Abigail Williams, Ann Putnam, Jr., Mary Warren, and others.

Arthur Miller crafted his popular play around these events by creating characters who best exemplify the play's title, *The Crucible*, defined as a severe test or hard trial, or a container for melting and calcining ores.

The separation of church and state in Salem made Judge Danforth an objective judge for the trials. "Innocent until proven guilty" were his watchwords and code of conduct. The community, too, abided by this code of conduct. This is best illustrated by Abigail's willingness to co-operate in the trial's proceedings.

Judge Danforth was not worried about being hemmed in by the law. He was most concerned with seeking justice for the community.

In the pages that follow, I will show how Judge Danforth served as the most dynamic and central character of the play, riveting our attention and earning our compassion and sensitivity.

P. J. Pennerd
January 1998

There are a number of flaws in this document, and even if you have not read *The Crucible* recently, your knowledge of history will reveal some of the erroneous assertions made by the phony P. J. Pennerd! For example, at the most basic level, the date of events is wrong. The Salem witch trials occurred in 1692, and 20 accused witches were put to death, not 50. The second paragraph is okay, but in paragraph three, the presumption of innocence until proven guilty is contrary to the beliefs of this Puritan theocracy. There was no separation of church and state in legal decisions of the time. In paragraph four, Judge Danforth was so blinded by his allegiance to the law that he was unable to discern the truth. Unlike claims in the final paragraph, he is unyielding and definitely not dynamic, at least in the way Proctor and Elizabeth are portrayed by Arthur Miller in the play. Thus, students had to engage in a close reading of the play and challenge any erroneous information in this lofty document. They ultimately recommended not purchasing this material for wide student use.

As you try out the phony document strategy, be careful to make it look plausible. Of course you can only use this strategy occasionally as students will suspect something is up in subsequent, authoritative documents you circulate in class.

The Imposter

The Imposter (Curran & Smith, 2005) is another strategy that, like the phony document strategy, is aimed at getting students to critically evaluate what they read. This is particularly useful in mathematics and science text. The strategy involves including a contradictory statement, idea, or number in a science passage or mathematical problem. Students must then locate and discover the nature of the contradiction by reading closely. Thus, this strategy motivates students to focus on the text. Curran and Smith recommend the following guidelines for students:

o Find proof of the error in the text.

o Errors should be distributed throughout the text.

o The errors must be somewhat obvious and not so obscure as to be frustrating.

The following example from Curran and Smith demonstrates a quantitative error embedded in an otherwise accurate chemistry passage:

> *The pH of a solution is a quantitative assessment of the number of free protons and is measured on a negative logarithmic scale from 0 to 14. Each whole integer, then, is 10 times greater than the next highest whole integer. A pH of 5.0 then has 10 times more free protons than a pH of 6.0. Similarly, a pH of 8.0 has a thousand times more protons than a pH of 5.0. (p. 188)*

The imposter error in this passage is embedded in the last sentence where "*more free protons*" should read "a thousand times *less* free protons" (Curran & Smith, p. 188). In essence, any content area passage can lend itself to the imposter strategy with a little creative thinking. We believe that, as an extension activity, students can create their own imposter passages. To accomplish this, they must have well-grounded comprehension of the material they are reading. Therefore, we recommend carefully modeling the imposter strategy and phasing out guidance as students become more adept at detecting embedded errors.

Polar Opposites

When students have a concrete series of reaction guide statements to support or refute, they are more likely to engage in group discussion. *Polar opposites* is a strategy that also provides a concrete basis for postreading discussion. A polar opposites guide consists of descriptive adjectives such as happy versus sad that are supported or challenged by events in the text. The examples that follow include both text-related and YouTube clip examples of how to create and use a polar opposites activity with students in order to critically read print and nonprint material.

Steps to a Polar Opposites Guide

1. Develop four or five polar opposite statements and their accompanying adjectives. Place five blanks between the adjectives. For example,

    Cairo's third city is . . .

    new ____ ____ ____ ____ ____ old

2. After students have read a selection or listened to a film, have them place a check mark (✓) closest to the adjective that they feel best describes the events or character. They can also score events and characters using a five-point scale.

3. Have students defend their rating in small-group discussion or a writing activity by referring to specific examples or events in the selection.

The following example from world geography should help you develop your own polar opposites guide. The passage is from the text, *New Exploring a Changing World* (Schwartz & O'Connor, 1975, pp. 364–365).

> On the roofs of Cairo there is a third city—a town of modern roof dwellers. Tens of thousands of people live on Cairo's rooftops. In the days when you could fly a small plane over Cairo, you could clearly see its two levels of life. One is on the ground and one is in the air. . . . I have seen on a roof opposite the Continental Hotel, someone cooking under a bamboo shelter, village women washing clothes, naked children, a goat or two, and a mangy dog. These rooftop slums are mostly servants' quarters but in the old city, they are the result of overcrowding.

Cairo's third city is . . .

new	____ ____ ____ ____ ____	old
spacious	____ ____ ____ ____ ____	crowded
healthful	____ ____ ____ ____ ____	unsanitary
safe	____ ____ ____ ____ ____	hazardous
rich	____ ____ ____ ____ ____	poor
friendly	____ ____ ____ ____ ____	hostile
	5 4 3 2 1	

In this particular guide, Cairo can be viewed either positively, with a possible high rating of 30 (i.e., 5 points × 6 adjectives), negatively with a possible low rating of

6 (i.e., 1 point per item), or somewhere between these polar opposites. Indeed, some of the adjectives entail careful, critical reading to infer a response. For example, the last pair of adjectives, friendly versus hostile, usually engenders heated discussion. If you are a member of Cairo's rooftop culture, then it is undoubtedly friendly, or at least somewhat friendly. However, for the outsider unaccustomed to this overcrowded lifestyle, Cairo's rooftops may well be hostile. Thus, students can critically evaluate the author's perspective. If it seems to be overly ethnocentric, outside sources may be considered to confirm or deny information in the text. In this way, polar opposites can be used to guide students into independent projects involving library and database research.

Popular HBO commentator John Oliver's show *Last Week Tonight* takes humorous potshots at a host of topics including the Miss America Pageant (2015). The following example illustrates how you can use this strategy with various topics.

Miss America Pageant Commentary by John Oliver

Directions: Place a check mark (✓) on the line closest to how you feel about the statement after watching the YouTube clip on John Oliver's discussion of the Miss America Pageant. Be prepared to discuss your reasoning for this rating.

1. The Miss America Pageant_____women's intellectual prowess.

   Respects ____   ____   ____   ____   ____Disrespects

2. Contestants may develop_____identities as women in society.

   Positive____   ____   ____   ____   ____Negative

3. Entering beauty contests_____dieting binges.

   Discourages____   ____   ____   ____   ____Encourages

Polar opposites provides even the most reticent students with a basis for participating in discussion and writing activities. In order to defend or refute a particular rating, students must return to the text for support. Thus, it encourages critical reading in much the same way as the reaction guide.

Graphic Organizers

Although the graphic organizer was suggested as a prereading vocabulary strategy, it is an equally good review guide Graphic organizers are easy to construct. Teachers find them useful across a broad range of content areas. Research reviews on teachers' use of graphic organizers show that they lead to greater student engagement and support knowledge acquisition and transfer more effectively than simply reading text passages, writing summaries, or outlining (Nesbit & Adesope, 2006). In addition, graphic organizers are particularly helpful for students with low verbal proficiency. In the early stages of a unit, items from the graphic organizer developed by the teacher can be written on notecards or Post-it notes. Students working in small groups can attempt to reconstruct the author's conceptual organization or pattern by arranging the notecards in a logical diagram. This review activity can be conducted as a game, if desired, with points awarded for reconstructing successive portions of the unit organizer.

But students need not merely reconstruct information exactly as the teacher's schema portrayed it. Instead, they can use the top-level skeletal structure of the teacher's organizer and add on information they have acquired in text reading. Such student-constructed postreading organizers seem to contribute more to comprehension than a teacher-devised organizer. Application 10.4 illustrates the use of a skeletal graphic organizer as a review guide.

APPLICATION 10.4

Directions: Before we go on, think about the comprehension strategies you have acquired so far in Chapter 10 for each of the three stages of an integrated lesson (i.e., prereading, reading, postreading). In the organizer that follows, one strategy has been listed in each stage. Without looking back at the chapter, see if you can supply at least two additional strategies per stage.

Contemporary content-based ESL programs usually integrate the dual goals of having students work on their second language while simultaneously learning content in history, science, mathematics, and English. Without careful teacher guidance using comprehension strategies, secondary students asked to both learn a new language and to comprehend difficult content in that language will soon flounder. Indeed, visual strategies like the graphic organizer, flow charts, and Venn diagrams are particularly helpful to second language learners. In addition, modeling is essential for students to make the best use of these strategies.

Students in a junior level advanced placement American literature class might explore societal mores and gender roles through reading and discussion of Arthur Miller's play, *The Crucible* (1976), the film based on the play, a subsequent reading of *The Scarlet Letter* (Hawthorne, 1986), and Amy Tan's (1991) *The Kitchen God's Wife*. Student discussions should focus on comparing and contrasting elements in the drama, novels, and videos. Their goal would be to build rich conceptual, historical, and literary understanding of what it meant to be a woman and a citizen within the social contexts of these works. Many of the strategies introduced in this chapter can be used to take notes from multiple texts (e.g., graphic organizers), to link ideas that are similar or different across texts (e.g., Venn diagrams), and to extend students' thinking and discussion (e.g., higher-level questioning).

Multiple Text Inquiry Discussion

The use of single texts in many content classrooms is giving way to the use of multiple texts, particularly in light of the abundant resources available on the Internet (Dunkerly-Bean, & Bean, 2015; Walker, Bean, & Dillard, 2010). In addition, definitions of text are being revised to include a broad range of material. Texts can be a book, chapter, story, novel, poem, essay, biography, Internet material, and so on. But texts can also encompass videos, music, photos, a dramatic play, pantomime, and a dizzying array of other ways to communicate. If students are going to become skilled at managing the incredible diversity of information sources at our fingertips today, they need opportunities to explore this process in the content areas. As we mentioned in the previous chapter, a *multiple text inquiry discussion* is designed to generate rich discussions when students read and attempt to synthesize a diverse collection of material on a topic.

Hartman and Allison (1996) offer the following steps for creating an inquiry-based classroom: (1) assemble multiple texts on a topic (ranging from 5 to 20 sources); (2) develop questions that focus discussion on making connections across multiple sources; (3) expect the discussion to extend across many days and, possibly, weeks; (4) have students record exploratory ideas that emerge in their discussions. Topics should be broad and provocative enough to develop conceptual knowledge that is applicable to other problem-solving lessons students are likely to encounter.

Topics in science on ecological issues lend themselves to the selection of multiple texts, interviews with experts, internet searches, and conversations with other students in faraway communities. For example, the topic of water quality and population growth is one that permeates news articles throughout the country. Working with the school librarian, local community sources, internet searches, and so on, you and your students can assemble a collection of sources for multiple text inquiry discussions.

In order to guide students' small-group discussion of multiple texts, you need adequate space to lay out all the materials. Large round tables lend themselves to this process far better than individual desks, but desks pulled together in a circle can suffice. Hartman and Allison (1996) recommend sequencing questions that prompt discussions to move from those that connect information within a single text to questions that connect information across two or more texts. Finally, they suggest prompt questions that connect ideas outside the text to information in the text by tapping students' background knowledge. For example, a single text question probe for an initial discussion of *The Crucible* would be, "How were female servants like Abigail Williams treated by their employers in 1692?" A question probe designed to integrate discussion of multiple texts would be "How are Proctor's, Hester's, and Winnie Louie's situations alike or different in *The Crucible, The Scarlet Letter,* and *The Kitchen God's Wife*?" Finally, a question designed to connect ideas from outside the texts would be "How have women's roles changed since the times depicted in these three novels?"

Using butcher paper, iTouch or iPads, a smart board, or some other means of recording small-group discussion ideas will be crucial to keeping a continuous record of conceptual growth. Journals and learning logs can be used if space is a problem, or you find yourself teaching in classrooms other than your own. Culminating projects ranging from papers, plays, musical compositions, art, and so on should be a natural outgrowth of days or, in some cases, weeks devoted to exploring a multiple-text topic. Evaluation of students' projects can be accomplished through a four-point rubric focusing on the quality of their work. For example, a four-point project would display unusual creativity, care in presentation, and evidence of integration of ideas across various texts. In contrast, a one-point project would appear to be thrown together at the last minute with little evidence of connections across texts read and discussed in small groups.

Multimodal Text Sets

Multimodal text sets consist of thematically related print and nonprint resources that include multiple genres (Dunkerly-Bean & Bean, 2015). These rich, multifaceted resources help students grasp complex topics. For example, we created a multimodal text set to help students read and discuss award-winning Canadian author, Deborah Ellis's young adult novel, *Moon at Nine* (Ellis, 2014) set in the Middle East. Set in 1988 in Iran, main characters Farrin and her classmate Sadira become close in a society that views LGBT youth as targets for persecution. In order to critically address events in the novel, we created a multimodal text set using Blendspace.com:

https://www.blendspace.com/lessons/cXWlzeBxnOgLUw/moon-at-nine-exploring-human-rights-through-multimodal-literacy

We included information on human rights, a documentary, cultural elements in Iran, newscasts, magazine articles, LGBT bullying, and other resources for students. Each of the resources linked to and illustrated a specific human right: e.g., Article 2. Freedom from discrimination. Thus, when students at the postreading stage set out to create body biographies and other interpretive resources mentioned in Chapter 7, they had a rich array of powerful ideas to draw on.

POSTSCRIPT

As students become accustomed to your use of a variety of strategies in prereading, reading, or postreading, you may find that a blend of two strategies makes sense. For example, you might introduce the topic of irrational and rational numbers in a mathematics class with a few anticipation guide statements and accompany the reading and problem-solving part of the lesson with a study guide that moves students through successively more involved problems. Indeed, vocabulary strategies from Chapter 8 can be combined with the comprehension strategies in Chapter 9 and in this chapter or those in Chapter 11 on writing in the content areas. In short, do not be afraid to experiment with the strategies offered in this book. Modify them to fit your own teaching style and student needs. Field-testing the strategies will more than likely improve them. Certainly, you are in the best position to evaluate the success of these strategies in the classroom, as well as creatively construct new approaches that best fit the discourse community of your discipline.

Now go back to the comprehension vignette at the beginning of this chapter. React again to the lesson as you did before. Compare your responses with those you made before you read the chapter.

MINI PROJECTS

Using the text chapter on the website entitled, "Smoking and Smokeless Tobacco," do one or all of the following:

1. Pick one of the prereading strategies advanced in this chapter. Develop this strategy and try it out with a small group of students or your peers. Evaluate the strategy in terms of its value as a means of preparing students for a content assignment.

2. Develop a study guide, option guide, or analogical guide on smoking. Try out your guide with a small group of students or your peers. Use the follow-up discussion phase recommended in this chapter for guide material. Evaluate your guide as an independent learning aid.

3. Develop and try out one of the postreading strategies described in this chapter. Use the strategy with a small group of students or your peers. Evaluate its effectiveness in reinforcing concepts about smoking.

4. Develop an integrated unit on smoking containing one strategy from each of the three stages of instruction described in this chapter. This mini project is a synthesis of projects one through three.

RECOMMENDED WEBSITES

o Blendspace.com
  This resource is ideal for creating multimodal text sets with video clips, quizzes, and other features.
o Reading Like a Historian: sheg_stanford.edu
  This site at Stanford University is aimed at close reading and careful evaluation of historical accounts.

WEBSITE ACTIVITY

Go to the website for Chapter 5 activities.

Writing

11

VIGNETTE

Setting

Alpha Polonium's high school physics class. Students have been reading online and in their physics text about various forms of energy, including gravitational force and radiant energy. Toward the end of this class, Ms. Polonium assigns a project on alternative energy and global climate change, due in two weeks. She wants her students to meet in small groups and create YouTube video clips capturing alternative energy approaches.

The Lesson

Ms. Polonium tells students they need to research alternative energy sources such as solar energy or hydroelectric power. She gives them a few URLs for websites dealing with alternative energy, as well as names of the local university experts on this topic. She then announces that they need to write a storyboard script for their planned YouTube video clips.

Students look stressed. Ms. Polonium tries to quell their anxiety in a brief question-and-answer session just before the bell rings.

T: *"Are there any questions?"*

S: *"Ms. Polonium, we only just started on the unit on alternative energy. What if we don't know how to write a movie clip script?"*

T: *"Haven't you done those in English class?"*

S: *"No. We just read Shakespeare and other classics and talked about them. Personally, I feel lost."*

The bell rings and students enter the hallway, still conversing about the alternative energy script writing assignment and expressing their anxieties about writing in science but excited about the YouTube part of the assignment.

A week and a half later, one of the students, Kelvin Newton, struggles at home with his group's video script. He is writing about hydroelectric power, trying to organize the planned video clip around advantages and disadvantages of this gravitational energy source. Kelvin completes a first draft and decides it is good enough since only Ms. Polonium will be reading it and she already knows about hydroelectric power. He flips on the television and relaxes, secure in the knowledge that his group's video script can be put into a nice folder tomorrow night and turned in on time.

The weekend after the video scripts were due, Ms. Polonium is spending her Sunday evening bent over students' alternative energy video clip scripts with a red pen, correcting spelling and grammatical errors amid marginal comments on their many misconceptions about alternative energy. She wonders where they got these ideas.

That following Monday, students get their scripts back, riddled with corrections and Ms. Polonium's remarks about content. Students console themselves with the knowledge that writing in this class counts for only a fraction of their grade. It is not like English class.

Keeping in mind that this lesson focuses on writing about alternative energy in a physics class, jot down your thoughts on the following questions:

1. What are the good points about the lesson?

2. What are the weak points about the lesson?

3. What, if anything, would you change about the lesson?

RATIONALE

Writing is a powerful way of learning and questioning across content areas. Once the sole province of English classrooms, writing is now seen as an important bridge between students' prior knowledge and ideas expressed in science, social studies, mathematics, and other content area texts. You need to be well informed about the writing process and ways to ensure that students can write effectively in a variety of subjects. This chapter introduces you to contemporary thinking about the writing process, and shows you how to use writing successfully to help students learn and reflect on concepts in your classroom.

LEARNING OBJECTIVES

o   Understand the distinction between composing and transcribing.
o   Be familiar with various teaching strategies that help students use writing to learn and inform.
o   Be able to use various approaches to evaluate students' writing.

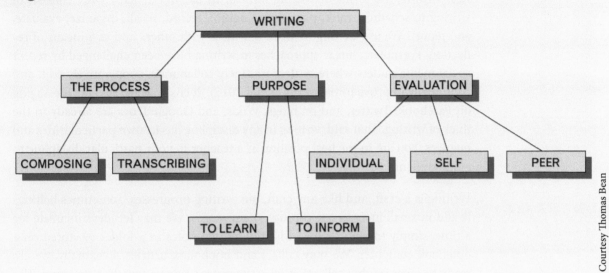

Courtesy Thomas Bean

WRITING PROCESS

Real writing, the forms of writing most of us use in our daily lives, consists of writing to schedule, rank, plan, map, inquire, record, recall, organize, evaluate, and report. We use writing to share our ideas with others and as a means of reflection. Formulaic, linear approaches to writing have been challenged by recent social media outlets where writers routinely collaborate, cooperatively edit, and continually improve initial drafts (Kelly, 2015). Teens engaged in daily messaging on Facebook, Twitter, and on blogs, Wikis, and Google Docs are already in the thick of writing. That said, writing in any discipline has its own particularities and nuances. You are in the best position as a teacher in your particular discipline to guide students' writing.

Writing is a craft, and like any craft, our writing progresses, sometimes haltingly and in small increments, through many stages. We may let ideas incubate for a time, simply tossing scraps of hastily written notes in a folder or stored on a notebook computer. We may collect and bookmark articles. Eventually, we are ready to organize this collection into categories having a tentative structure. The structure may be a narrative or one of the expository patterns introduced earlier in the text. Writing a draft, revising as we go, and sharing our draft with others eventually leads to a finished piece of writing about which we can feel good. Students need to see some of their writing evolve in this fashion. Other writing may be more exploratory, much like a diary that is not intended for public reading but may contribute to learning in your classroom. Thus, some writing in which you engage students will be designed to help inform others about a topic; other writing activities will assist their learning. Both forms of writing should take place in content classrooms. Writing remains one of the most difficult tasks students undertake. High school English teacher Kelly Gallagher (2006, p. 13) charts six pillars of writing success. Based on his experience, students need the following:

o A lot more writing practice;

o Teachers who model good writing;

o The opportunity to read and study other writers;

o Choice when it comes to writing topics;

o Authentic purposes and authentic audiences;

o Meaningful feedback from both the teacher and their peers.

Much of the pressure to fully engage students in extended, thoughtful, and well-crafted writing in argument, narrative, and informative essays comes from the National Governors Association Center for Best Practices and Council of Chief State School Officers (2010) *Common Core State Standards for English Language Arts & Literacy in History/Social Studies, Science, and Technical Subjects*. In a national study of adolescent writing in the content areas, Wilson and Jeffrey (2014) found that the amount and kinds of writing students were producing in mathematics, science, social studies, and English were largely restricted to producing little more than paragraphs. The researchers concluded that writing assignments that did not consist of extended writing in the disciplines would be unlikely to prepare students for the demands of the Common Core State Standards. This is not to say that some shorter writing is not beneficial, but these authors cautioned that "Students will need more opportunities to engage in more source-based persuasive and argumentative extended writing tasks in all subjects." (p. 174)

In this chapter we take up some of the recent research and recommendations to ensure students are engaged in writing extended essays, grounded in the particularities of the disciplines (e.g., evaluating sources in history).

In addition to using both expository and narrative forms of writing to develop content area learning in science, mathematics, history, English, and other fields, contemporary classrooms often encourage the use of multiple genres to produce digital multimedia projects (Crawley, 2015). Students use a carefully crafted blend of art, music, drama, and personal narrative to explore topics in history and other content areas. Thus, the boundaries of expository and narrative text structures are being expanded by creative teachers and students.

Before exploring specific strategies that help students use writing to learn and to inform, we want to define and consider two important aspects of the writing process: composing and transcribing.

Composing and Transcribing

Composing is the ongoing process of generating and shaping ideas before writing and as the actual writing unfolds. Composing involves thinking about ideas, weighing them, and putting them in some kind of order. Brainstorming, creating, clustering, and categorizing are some of the processes students use in composing. Out of these prewriting musings come new ways of looking at topics in content classrooms. For example, "Writer's Notebooks" consist of composing ideas that include brainstorming ideas for a manuscript or digital production (Chandler-Olcott, 2015).

As students get started composing on their laptops or iPads, or simply begin writing on a piece of paper, transcribing facilitates or inhibits the development of a finished product. *Transcribing* is a term that describes the mechanics of writing, including spelling, punctuation, capitalization, handwriting, formatting, and neatness. During the early draft stages of writing, when composing dominates students' thoughts, placing too much emphasis on the conventions of transcribing may interfere with the development of ideas. Certainly when students are engaged in reflective journal writing, which they do primarily for their own purposes, transcribing should be less of a concern than when they are preparing a final draft of a paper for a larger audience. When we look at the practice of journal writing in content classrooms, remember that composing issues are at the forefront. Personal journal writing is one of the best ways for students to explore ideas without feeling pressed to produce perfect spelling and grammar. In addition, it is a powerful way for you to carry on a dialogue about the class with individual students. Journal writing is the first writing to learn strategy that we consider.

WRITING TO LEARN

Writing-to-Learn Strategies
o Journal
o Quick Writes
o Possible Sentences
o Cubing
o Writing Roulette
o ReWrite
o Guided writing procedure

In many content classrooms, students feel that the authority for their learning resides exclusively with the teacher. Yet in classes where students write often, as much as four and five times a week, they feel like they are in the driver's seat. A number of classrooms feature blogging (weblogs) where students can comment on a topic and read other students' online comments (Kelly, 2015). Wiki writing, where students add to, edit, and modify an entry, similar to the way Wikipedia works, offers yet another powerful way to see an entry evolve. Writing becomes a powerful vehicle for guiding students' learning—a filter through which they can sift and examine concepts and see how these sometimes obscure notions that connect with their lives. With Web 2.0, student creativity through writing and composing becomes more possible than ever before. Writing-to-learn activities initiate students to various methods for using writing to explore and integrate ideas arising from a content area.

Journal Writing and Writer's Notebooks

Observational studies of classrooms reveal far too little sustained writing of a personal nature. Yet in our day-to-day world, we see teachers, business people, scientists, and artists frequently jotting down random ideas or notes in a journal for their own purposes. Journaling can be accomplished in a variety of ways including the classic paper version or by recording comments in a notebook program. Numerous notebook applications are available for laptops and notebook computers. When ideas wing briefly into short-term memory, a journal is an ideal place to pin them down for later consideration. In social studies, a student's journal may consider how the Bill of Rights might relate to students' rights in a high school environment. In science, a journal entry might wonder about gene splicing and its impact on future generations. In art, a journal comment may state how a student interprets a surrealistic painting. Or, a journal entry may have no higher purpose than to state, "I stayed up late last night. Today I'm having a lot of trouble concentrating on your lecture about the Roman Empire." In this way, *journal writing* and writer's notebooks can communicate a student's feelings and emotions, and provide you with some sense of how your lessons are progressing for individual students on various days. In our crowded classrooms, journals can serve the important need to communicate attitudes and interests beyond the typical rapid-fire charge through endless facts and concepts.

As you begin to use journal writing in your own subject area, consider the following principles (Bean, 2001):

1. Journal writing should become a regular part of your teaching. Students need to write in their journals on a daily basis.

   During the first five minutes of class, journals can be an ideal way to enter a topic or recap a previous day's lesson. For example, in a social studies classroom, on the first day of a unit students worked through an anticipation-reaction guide activity on the Bill of Rights. One of the statements reads as follows: Students should have the right to select the classes they take. At the beginning of next day's class, the teacher gives the students an opportunity to comment further in their journals on this idea. Jeff writes,

   > I think it's a good idea. But only if we pick our class schedule every other week. That way, at least some of the time we have to take classes that are good for us, even though we may not like them. Like math. Math would be okay every other week. But I know this isn't going to happen. We have to do whatever the government tells us to do. It's depressing.

   Jeff was undoubtedly reluctant to express these opinions in the large class discussion the previous day. But in the privacy of his journal, he is free to explore divergent proposals. Journals can be used to explore content area concepts from a personal perspective, so it is important for students to have opportunities to pick what they want to write about. Therefore, you may want to alternate days devoted to some commentary on previous or upcoming lessons with days devoted to reflections on general topics students choose individually. The next principle suggests how you can demonstrate the range of topics students may wish to explore in their journals.

2. You should model journal writing by keeping your own journal and sharing entries aloud with students.

   Just as sustained silent reading works best when you join in by reading a novel of your choice, journal writing takes on real importance in students' eyes when you also participate. For example, your entries may range from commentaries on how a unit is progressing to entries that chronicle your efforts to reduce your 10 kilometer running time.

3. You should look at students' journals and respond to their thoughts.

   We recognize that it is unrealistic to expect a teacher to collect endless stacks of journals every day and respond to them. Rather, collect journals randomly so that you see every student's journal a few times in the course of a semester. In order to keep some parts of the journal completely private, you may have students use a loose-leaf notebook with dividers labeled public and private. In this way you can at least respond to those sections marked public while not inhibiting opportunities for private comment. How much time should students spend each day writing in their journals?

4. Allot 5 to 10 minutes for journal writing.

These four principles do not imply that journals be used in a rigid, formulaic fashion that may become stultifying over time. Rather, we recommend that you make them a flexible and creative regular part of your teaching repertoire. You can use journals as a way to interrupt a lecture, lab, or activity in order to let students reflect on what they understand at that intermediate phase of a lesson. Using journals fosters students' enthusiasm and personal investment in the content you are trying to teach.

Dialogue journals, where you maintain an ongoing written dialogue with your students, provide a unique window to their concept understanding, confusion, concerns, and complaints (Bean & Rigoni, 2000; Werderich, 2002). In terms of concept understanding, this is a private place where students can express confusion without fear of embarrassment. The dialogue journal offers you a second chance, a chance to reteach information that may not have been understood during the first attempt. In addition, dialogue journals open the door to fluency for second language learners. Students find that dialogue journals are nonthreatening because of their uncorrected, ungraded format. Since they are written in a conversational style, dialogue journals reduce the stress of clinging to a dictionary and worrying constantly about translating to the native language. Rather, students can experiment as they would in a free writing activity. Dialogue journals offer students a sense that they do have a voice in how the class progresses. Thus, you might alter your teaching based on this written feedback from students. You can use a classroom blog in this same fashion as most students are accustomed to contributing to social media sites like Facebook and Twitter.

Other forms of journal writing allow students to respond to their reading in creative ways. For example, students can write a letter or e-mail to an author posing questions about a novel or text. Most authors have websites, and enjoy communicating with their audience. Students can take the part of a character in a novel and write a journal entry based on their reactions to a powerful episode. Journal entries can be made on e-mail and sent to students in a far-off classroom for their dialogue responses. The possibilities are endless and, increasingly, involve electronic media (Bean & Moni, 2003).

For example, students can compose and post online fanfiction writing based on popular media, books, music, and video games (Black, 2005). *Fanfiction* can be defined as original works of fiction based on popular media including television, movies, books, music, and video games. Moreover, fanfiction writing offers students a real audience for their work based on the archival website: www.fanfiction.net. Because this site offers students a real audience of peers, it provides a forum for second language students to practice language acquisition with a fan community. Along with blogging and wiki writing mentioned in Chapter 2, writing fanfiction opens the boundaries of traditional writing to include visuals and other forms of representation. The social nature of these forms of writing appeals to a variety of students including second language learners and struggling writers.

APPLICATION 11.1

Think about the most challenging group of students you have taught. Write a journal entry describing your feelings now as you think back on the impact your teaching may or may not have had on those students. Exchange your entry with a colleague in class. Discuss the teaching experience you wrote about and your views on journal writing in a content classroom.

Quick Writes

Quick Writes are an informal means of engaging students in thinking about a content topic at the prereading or postreading stages of a lesson or unit. As the name implies, they are fairly easy to integrate in an overburdened curriculum. They can be used to get an idea of students' prior knowledge at the prereading stage or to synthesize ideas after content learning. Quick Writes are typically based on teacher-generated questions. Students can jot their ideas on note cards and share them with a partner or group, or in their response journals for personal reflection. The teacher may choose to collect them occasionally as an aid to future lesson planning. The Quick Write prompts that follow give you a basic idea of how to generate both prereading and postreading prompts.

Prereading

1. Before we begin our unit on water quality, write down everything you know about this topic. You have one minute.

2. We are going to study recent efforts to achieve a Middle East peace accord. In 30 seconds, write down key political figures you think are likely to influence this effort.

Postreading

1. We have been studying cloning. Write down some of the ethical issues you think we should discuss in our next class meeting. You have one minute.

2. Today's math lesson dealt with statistical probability. Write down some examples from day-to-day life where knowing the statistical probability of an event might be important. You have three minutes.

Quick Writes are highly flexible so that you can easily adjust the response time to fit your needs. This is a great way to engage students in additional thinking about a topic when you find that some time remains in the class period.

Possible Sentences

Possible Sentences is another writing-to-learn strategy that helps students use technical vocabulary and related concepts in your content area (Semingson, 2015). This strategy places students in an active role in which they predict an author's use of language in a text and evaluate their written predictions against the actual text passage. Possible Sentences engages students in higher-order reasoning to identify examples in the text that support their prereading sentences or to revise their sentences after considering the text version. This exercise gives students a vested interest in reading the text to check their prereading possible sentence predictions.

1. List on the smartboard key terms from a chapter or reading selection. The words should be well defined by the context and pronounced several times for the students. For example:

Target Words
Pigment
Albinism
Enzymes
Melanin
Suntan
Albino
Passage

ALBINISM*

The absence of pigmentation in the skin, hair, and eyes in albinos is the result of a deficiency in the manufacture of pigment (melanin) by the body. Albinism is a metabolic disorder resulting from the absence or inactivity of a specific enzyme. Enzymes are complex compounds which act as catalytic agents or mediators of chemical changes in living forms. This enzyme is involved in the formation of melanin. The condition is not restricted to humans and it has been found in many animals: snakes, salamanders, gorillas, rats, mice, Easter bunnies, and even ravens, to name a few.

Human albinos are characterized by white translucent skin and white hair. Because of the lack of pigment in the iris, the eyes are red due to blood vessels. There is no way to overcome albinism. The necessary information to produce the right enzyme has not been inherited and will never be acquired. The specific enzyme or the melanin pigment would have to be injected continuously into each and every pigment cell of the skin, scalp, and eyes in order to produce a normally pigmented individual.

Albinos need continuous protection from sunlight, since they burn very easily. Their skin cannot develop a suntan since tans are nothing more than the accumulation of melanin as a response to an increase in the ultraviolet radiation of sunlight. They are also more susceptible to skin diseases and tend to have poor vision. They are otherwise perfectly normal people.

*Brum, G. D., Castro, P., & Quinn, R. D. *Biology and Man.* Dubuque, IA: Kendall Hunt, 1978, p. 57.

2. Individual students select any two of the words and dictate or write a sentence using them. The teacher writes the sentences on the board exactly as dictated, whether the information in them is accurate or not. For instance,

Possible Sentences
   a. Suntans come from having a lot of enzymes in your skin.
   b. An albino is a person who has no melanin.
   c. An albino can never get a suntan.
   d. Albinism is the missing of pigment in the skin.

3. After an arbitrary number of sentences have been generated, the students search through the passage to verify the sentences on the board. A twist can be added to the game by having teams generate as many sentences as possible with unique pairs of the words listed. In this example there are 15 different possible pairs of words that can be used. Once each team generates its sentences, the opposing teams challenge (with books closed, of course) the accuracy of each set of individual sentences. Points can be given for each accurate sentence. Penalty points can be deducted for inaccurate challenges.

4. The possible sentences are corrected on the board, and students are given an opportunity to enter them into their notebooks. For instance,

Revised Possible Sentences
   a. Suntans come from having a lot of melanin in your skin.
   b. An albino is a person who has no melanin.
   c. An albino can never get a suntan.
   d. Albinism is the absence of pigment in the skin.

Possible Sentences will tease out misconceptions students have about a topic. Writing sentences is generally a nonthreatening activity, even for second language learners. We have found that students enjoy Possible Sentences. They enthusiastically pursue text reading to verify their predictions.

Cubing

In order to explore a topic from various dimensions, consider using *cubing* (Tompkins, 2003). The concrete visual of a cube with its six sides serves as a starting point to consider the multiple dimensions of topics in nutrition, science, social studies, mathematics, and other content areas. To introduce cubing, start with a familiar topic and then treat more complex topics once students have a good grasp of how cubing works.

Steps for Cubing

1. Introduce the topic on the board (e.g., ice cream).

2. Have students in small groups examine the topic from the following six sides of the cube:

   o *Describe it* (including its colors, shapes, and sizes, if applicable)

   o *Compare it* (what is it similar to or different from?)

   o *Associate it* (what does it make you think of?)

FIGURE 11.1

Student Response to the Ice Cream Cube Assignment

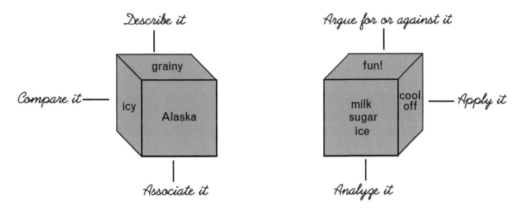

   o *Analyze it* (Tell how it is made or what it is composed of.)
   o *Apply it* (What can you do with it? How is it used?)
   o *Argue for or against it* (Take a stand and list reasons for supporting it.)

Figure 11.1 shows one student's response to the ice cream cubing assignment. This particular student *described* ice cream as grainy. She *compared* ice cream with an icy she might buy at a convenience store, and she *associated* ice cream with Alaska because it is cold and snowy. In the second half of the cube, she listed the ingredients as milk (it is actually cream or butter fat), sugar, and ice in the *analyze it* box. In the *apply it* box she said that it helps us cool off, and she naturally *argued for* ice cream because it is fun. In comparing her cube with other students, she revised the ingredients and left the other boxes the same.

Students should spend only 5–10 minutes on each side of the cube. Once they have a good grasp of the process using familiar topics like the ice cream example, you can introduce more difficult content area topics such as solar cars in science, the Bill of Rights in history, and authors in English. Initially, students should begin by using the six sides of the cube to compose descriptive paragraphs. Cubing can then form the basis for longer writing assignments including persuasive essays, letters to the editor, and extended reports treated later in this chapter.

APPLICATION 11.2

Pair up with a colleague in a class from a content area different from your own (e.g., biology and English). Select a passage from your text and guide your partner through either a Possible Sentences or a Cubing lesson.

Writing Roulette

Writing Roulette is a content area strategy that provides a platform for creative writing at the end of a unit stage in English, history, mathematics, science, and other disciplines.

Students are asked to use a simple three-part story structure for the activity so that three different students write each distinct part of the story. Second, they review content material within the framework of the story by selecting key vocabulary words from their expository reading and including these words in each section they write.

Steps for Conducting a Writing Roulette Session

1. Provide a simple structure for the story with three major elements or divisions.

   a. A setting and characters

   b. A problem or goal for the main character

   c. A resolution

2. Advise students that each section of the story must use at least two words from the lesson or unit they have been studying. These words should be underlined in the story. You can have students review their vocabulary collections, or you can simply supply a list of technical terminology from which they can choose six words.

3. Set a specific time limit for the first story section (e.g., five minutes for the setting). You can use a kitchen timer for this.

4. When time is up, have students exchange papers or collect and shuffle them so that a second author writes the problem or goal section. Advise students to read the paper they receive and continue the story. Set a time limit for this writing as well.

5. Exchange papers one last time so a third author can provide a resolution for the story. Then, have students return the story to the original author and share aloud those stories that are particularly interesting or that use content vocabulary in creative ways.

Writing Roulette is a good way for students to review important vocabulary and concepts before an essay exam or quiz. It is best introduced after students have used other strategies such as graphic organizers and semantic mapping, so that they have a good understanding of content vocabulary. The following example is a Writing Roulette story developed by three preservice content teachers. The words are taken from the glossary of our text.

Student 1

Gertrude and Susie were on their way home from school. "Gertrude," said Susie, "that *anticipation guide* we use in class was really great."

"Yeah," replied Gertrude. "And didn't you just love the *graphic organizers?* I can't wait to get home and call all our friends and let them know about our class."

Gertrude and Susie continue down the street, chatting happily.

Student 2

The big history test was rapidly approaching. Gertrude reread her graphic organizer and called Susie on the phone to discuss *study strategies.* She felt her *comprehension* had suffered because she did all of her reading in front of the television. She had never missed an episode of "American Idol" since the show's inception. Susie tried to help Gertrude fill in the blank spaces their teacher had left in the graphic organizer. They stayed on the phone for three hours in anticipation of the big *test.*

Student 3

The next day, Gertrude entered the classroom to face the test. She whispered to Susie, "I hope he gives us an anticipation guide to help us with this test."

The teacher came around and placed a cloze test on each student's desk. Gertrude took a look at it and almost died. Every other word had been deleted. Gertrude whispered to Susie, "Do you have any idea how to do this test?"

Susie said, "Sure, use your knowledge of *morphemic analysis* to *slice* the *response mode,* which will require you to have fewer pieces of information. Then the *scope of information* search will be halved.

Gertrude gave Susie a blank stare. Susie said, "Guess!"

Gertrude knew she would fail, but, fortunately for her, the teacher pulled down the overhead screen, knocking down the wall clock, and a large plastic potted fern onto his big toe. Class was immediately terminated, and Gertrude went whistling out of the classroom, knowing she had escaped a fate worse than death.

Students find Writing Roulette a pleasurable and creative approach to reviewing technical vocabulary and concepts. Since it takes a full period to conduct a Writing Roulette session, you should plan to allot this time just to the activity. Once students have completed their stories, they enjoy exchanging and reading each other's creations in the small-group setting. Writing Roulette capitalizes on a familiar narrative structure to review concepts presented in expository material.

ReWrite

ReWrite is a music strategy that combines concept learning and the creation of musical verses within a comprehensive prereading and postreading lesson framework (Bean, 2010). Music has the power to enhance abstract reasoning. Musical performance typically occurs in high-interest cooperative settings with clear, performance-based outcomes. Songwriting can be used to teach concepts in biology, mathematics, history, art, and other content areas.

You do not need to be an accomplished musician to use the ReWrite song writing strategy that follows. Using instrumental music as a foundation for a song your students write, or having a music teacher create an instrumental background piece works quite well. Karaoke, the popular sing-along activity, has spawned an endless array of tapes and videotapes of music that can be used for this activity. Or, a teacher can use alternate forms of music like rap and hip-hop, which require minimal or no musical accompaniment (Paul, 2000). The lyrics are the important ingredient in the ReWrite song writing strategy.

DAY 1

STEP ONE. As in any lesson planning, you need to do a careful task analysis of concepts and strategies needed for the reading assignment. In the example that follows, students were engaged in a science unit on entomology, or the study of insects. The insect students read about in this lesson was the crab spider, a prevalent garden pest on the Big Island of Hawaii since its arrival in 1985 (Nishida & Tenorio, 1993).

To start this ReWrite lesson, concepts that most students would have about crab spiders were incorporated in a blues song. Thus, the song contained commonsense nonscientific knowledge about crab spiders that most students living on the Big Island might know from working around their gardens. The song follows with guitar chords included.

Crab Spiders
(Key of E; Blues Shuffle)

E
Crab spiders hang their webs all over the place
I go outside to work and they just get tangled in my face
    A
Well I hit them with my rake and they stick to my hand
E
Crawling up my arm like Sherman tanks in sand
B7   A   E
I finally decided what I'm gonna do,
collect all my crab spiders and take em to school (repeat)
Well I'll let them go when my teacher isn't lookin and they'll cause
So much trouble she'll send us outside while she's searchin
      A   E
For those crab spiders, crab spiders what a waste
B7   A   E
They just lie in wait to get tangled in my face
Bridge
E
I spray em with Raid, Chlorox too but all that does is make my plants look sick and blue
A
Crab spiders, crab spiders how I hate you guys,
        E
you just exist to drive me wild
B7
Until I find a way to get rid of this strange insect
E
Maybe I'll just treat my crab spiders with more respect!

The first verse portrayed the pesky quality of these ubiquitous creatures and the next two verses implied the humor of taking them to school and letting them loose in class as a distraction for the teacher. Finally, common approaches to exterminating crab spiders are recounted. The song ends with the author ready to give up trying to fight the crab spider invasion in the yard and just be nice to these pesky, tank-like insects.

STEP TWO. Students have a copy of the song and follow along while it is played and sung by the teacher. Or, you can have a musician friend perform it and tape the performance. In this example the information in song form was designed to activate students' prior knowledge before they responded to anticipation guide statements based on a science news article about crab spiders.

STEP THREE. Following the introductory song activity, students gathered in small groups to consider and complete the five-item anticipation guide on crab spiders that included some factual and critical opinion items. You can use ReWrite without any guide material but, in this instance, we wanted to focus the discussion on some of the remarkable features of the crab spider. The anticipation guide they completed is shown in Figure 11.2.

Most students viewed the crab spider as harmful based on their experiences. They reported receiving bites that swelled up and talked about very painful bites inflicted on their younger siblings who happened to accidentally bump against one of the crab spider's thick webs. They were less sure about statements two through four and very certain number five simply ignored the facts. Fear of spiders was, in their opinion, quite justified.

FIGURE 11.2

Anticipation-Reaction Guide

Crab Spiders

Directions: Before reading, consider each statement with a partner. Write yes if you agree and no if you disagree. Write your reasons below each statement. After reading the text, go back and review each statement.

You	Author	
_____	_____	1. Crab spiders are harmless.
_____	_____	2. A crab spider's web is more deadly than other spider webs.
_____	_____	3. We have had crab spiders on our island for many years.
_____	_____	4. A crab spider's egg sac can contain more than 100 eggs.
_____	_____	5. Fear of spiders is silly.

DAY 2

STEP FOUR. Following a prereading discussion of the statements, students were assigned reading of the crab spider article in class. They then engaged in a postreading discussion of the anticipation guide statements. After reading the article they generally agreed with items two, three, and four from the guide. The more open-ended items, particularly the "fear of spiders is silly" statement, produced few changes in their initial opinions about crab spiders. Indeed, when they discovered that crab spiders were called "the land equivalent of drift net fleets at sea" and their thick, intricate community of webs termed "walls of death" for flying insects, they were impressed. Students used this text-based information to defend their general fear of all spiders.

STEP FIVE.   Students stay in their groups and write a new crab spider song by creating verses that reflect their new knowledge. In our example, each group shared their verse with the other groups by reading it aloud.

DAY 3

STEP SIX.   Students' verses were assembled and typed at home before the next class. Copies were then made of the students' song and *Crab Spider Blues* was performed at the start of the next class with each group singing its respective verse. This performance served as a review of text information and set the stage for subsequent insect study. The ReWrite version produced by students follows.

CRAB SPIDER BLUES

Crab spiders work in teams hanging walls of death
Between bushes and trees, under eaves, across a doorway or in trees
Big mama in the middle and daddy goofin off on the side
They wait for prey and take their breath away
Thelacantha bevispina down the back of my shirt
They are difficult to remove and darn they hurt
Their bite may swell up like a sting from a bee
Why do these things always happen to me?
The mothers like to lay about a hundred eggs
And when they pop out they like to bite my legs
There's no killin these bugs at all
Smash um when they're big, squash um when they're small
If you're wondering when the crab spider arrived
They've been around since 1985
The Big Island was cursed because they were the first
The answer to how they came is never the same.

Students genuinely enjoy this activity, and the ReWrite song becomes a memorable way to learn and critique content area concepts.

Guided Writing Procedure

The *Guided Writing Procedure* (GWP) gives students practice in developing a coherent written account of a topic they are studying in the text (Bean, 2001). It helps students examine their prior knowledge of a topic. They can then modify their previous knowledge based on the text reading. In contrast to the strategies we have introduced up to this point, the GWP entails editing writing for both content and form. The GWP is designed to achieve the following teaching objectives:

1. Activate and sample students' prior knowledge of a topic before they do any text reading;

2. Sample and evaluate students' written expression in a content area;

3. Improve students' written expression through guided instruction;

4. Facilitate the synthesis and retention of content area material.

GWP helps improves the quality of students' writing. They become more adept at integrating information from text and prior knowledge and produce writing that is more carefully edited and readable. The GWP usually spans three days of content instruction and involves the following steps.

DAY 1

STEP ONE. Write the topic heading you are introducing on the board and have students brainstorm words or phrases that come to mind when they think about this topic. For example, social studies students who were about to read a chapter describing conditions during the 1929 Depression generated six ideas based on their prior knowledge of this topic.

STEP TWO. Record students' ideas verbatim on the smart board or overhead. Engage students in a discussion of their ideas and ask them to explain how they are related to the topic being considered. Students produced the following list for the causes of the 1929 Depression.

No jobs	Stocks crash
No money	Everything is cheap
Poverty	Bad investments

308

STEP THREE. Guide students in constructing an outline, graphic organizer, or semantic map of these ideas with appropriate category labels. For example,

Causes and Effects of the Depression
I.   Causes
    a.   bad investments
    b.   stocks crash
II. Effects
    a.   no jobs
    b.   no money
    c.   poverty
    d.   everything is cheap

STEP FOUR. Tell students to individually write a short paragraph or two as a first draft, with the outline as a guide to content and organization. You should tell them to direct this draft to a specific audience. A reasonable audience for this information is another class member or a classmate who is absent for this lesson.

STEP FIVE. Collect students' first drafts and rapidly analyze the paragraphs, using the GWP checklist shown in Figure 11.3. You should not make any marks on their papers. The first draft that follows was written by a student based on the six ideas generated in the brainstorming on the Depression.

Causes and Effects of the Depression

The awful Depression of 1929 was caused by the stock market crash. People made bad investments and lost all their money. Some people bought too much stock on credit. They went to far into det.

When the stock market crashed people lost a lot of money. There wasn't money to pay people for work. People without jobs sunk into poverty. Everything was dirt cheap. You could probably go to a movie for a dime!

FIGURE 11.3

GWP CHECKLIST
(✓ = okay; 0 = needs revision; ? = can't tell)

Criteria

Organization of Ideas

Clear topic	✓
Supporting details/examples	0
Logical flow	✓

Comments: *Good organization of ideas. The text will give you details and examples.*

Style

Shows variety in

Word choice✓	
Sentence length	0

Comments: *Short sentences need to be balanced by some that are longer.*

Mechanics

Complete sentences	✓
Capitalization	✓
Punctuation	✓
Spelling	0

Comments: *too far (vs. to); debt (vs. det); sank (vs. sunk)*

This student constructed a first draft that has a clear topic sentence and good organization. At this prereading stage, students had only limited knowledge of the causes and effects of the Depression, so the draft is understandably brief. He made some fairly common spelling errors that the teacher simply pointed out in the mechanics section of the GWP checklist. We are now ready for day two.

DAY 2

STEP SIX. Return students' drafts and checklists. Have them make necessary edits and polish their first drafts, based on the guidelines you offered on the checklist. You can circulate among students to provide extra help. You can also use this time for individual conferences with students experiencing real difficulty with the writing process. For example, second language learners generally benefit from extra, one-on-one discussion of their writing efforts. You may want to display some sample drafts on the overhead and model the process of editing for organization of ideas, style, and mechanics.

STEP SEVEN. Have students turn in their second draft and the original GWP checklist they used to guide their editing. You can then record any comments, particularly praise, on the bottom of the original checklist.

STEP EIGHT. Assign text reading, explaining to students that the purpose of this reading is to locate additional information, especially supporting details and examples, that they can include in a final draft of their writing.

DAY 3

STEP NINE. Now that they have acquired additional knowledge about the topic (in this case, the Depression), engage students in a group discussion to revise the original outline to include this text information. Any misconceptions can be cleared up as well. Here, the text that students read added little to their basic understanding of the causes of the Depression. However, it did expand on the effects of the Depression on workers in the cities and on farmers. Thus, their new outline contained a blend of their original ideas about the Depression and the new information discussed in the text.

Causes and Effects of the Depression

I. Causes
    a. Bad investments by people and banks
    b. The stock market crash
    c. Business downturn for 10 years
II. Effects
    a. People stopped buying goods
    b. Factories closed
    c. By 1932, 13 million jobless workers (one of every four)
    d. Young people hopped trains to find work
    e. Homeless people lived on the outskirts of town in shacks called "Hoovervilles," after President Hoover
    f. Farmers had surplus corn, which they could not sell
    g. Farmers lost their farms—droughts also led to the Dust Bowl in the early 1930s
    h. Poverty was common

STEP TEN. Students should then revise and expand their compositions, based on new information from the text. You may want to have them include lecture and discussion information if the text is limited in its coverage of the topic. Students can work in pairs or small groups while you come around to help them link text and prior knowledge concepts. Then have students turn in these final drafts for a grade or give a quiz on this information. These compositions can be used as a lead-in to a unit (in this case, on the New Deal). They can also become part of the guide material you use with future classes, creating a very real audience for students' efforts. The student who wrote the original draft on the Depression produced the following final version.

> ### Causes and Effects of the Depression
>
> The awful Depression of 1929 was caused by bad investments in the stock market. People took great risks with money, stringing themselves out in debt by buying too much stock on credit. The banks also made bad investments and many had to close after the stock market crashed. The Depression that started with the stock market crash of 1929 was a business downturn that, different from the ones before it, lasted for 10 years!
>
> The effects of the Depression were many. Because people lost so much money, they stopped buying goods. The factories had to close and by 1932, 13 million people, or one in four, were out of work. Young people hopped trains to seek work in other towns. Homeless people lived on the edge of the big cities in tiny shacks called Hoovervilles, after President Hoover. Even the farms suffered. Farmers grew too much corn, which they couldn't sell. Since they couldn't sell the corn, they couldn't pay for their tractors and other equipment. They lost their farms, and droughts made things even worse. The Dust Bowl in the early 1930s wiped out even more farmers. People sank into poverty. Everything was dirt cheap. You could probably go to a movie for a dime, but I would rather live now!

This student's final version now contains supporting details from the text. Furthermore, he includes his own views about living during that era.

The GWP is an in-depth exploration of a text reading assignment. Since it is time consuming, you should plan on using it as a lead-in to a unit |so that students approach their reading with some power over the text. For example, in the Depression outline stage, students begin to see the text as a cause–effect organizational pattern, which helps them read fluently and selectively for key ideas and details to revise their original GWP compositions.

WRITING TO INFORM

Writing for an audience of peers, especially to argue a particular point of view, can help students become analytical readers. The strategies considered next emphasize both analytical reading and writing.

Argumentative Writing

The Common Core State Standards (CCSS) place a significant premium on teaching students to create cogent, well thought out and extended arguments across content areas (Newell, VanDerHeide, & Olsen, 2014). Ideally, students must become adept at creating a coherent argument, relevant claims, and evidence to support their argument. Across multiple class sessions, teachers can model the process of argument writing, use mentor texts that exemplify well-crafted argument prose, labeling key parts of a mentor text essay on the smart board, doing library research, editing drafts, and ultimately, creating a finished product for a real audience.

Argumentative writing need not be confined to print media. Rather, digital composition can aid the process with students creating compositions that include multimodal features including music, photos, illustrations, voice narration, and publishing works on the Internet (Crawley, 2015). For example, students in a middle school class developed a compelling video on "bullying" and its impact on students. They began this process by watching multimedia mentor texts.

Indeed, as a content teacher you can have fun with argumentative writing and digital compositions by starting with exemplars. For example, the following two You-Tube clips hint at the possibilities of framing arguments, the first in terms of an argument for a vegan lifestyle and the second, a satirical look at gluten-free eating.

o VeganDigitalStory@justgirl83

o "How to Become Gluten Intolerant (Funny)-Ultra Spiritual Life Episode 12" at https://www.youtube.com/watch?v=Oht9AEq1798

Students can also use Photo Story 3 and other free software applications to create 2–4 minute digital multimedia argument texts incorporating images, voice-over, narration, and music. These final projects can be shared via the Internet or with stakeholders, other classrooms, and parents (Chandler-Olcott, 2015).

In addition to providing students with mentor texts and exemplars to model and scaffold their writing in the content areas, the simple acronym PAF which stands for Purpose-Audience-Format helps guide the essay writing process (Dostal & Gabriel, 2015). Most importantly, it helps center students' thinking on the purpose of a particular form of writing as follows:

o P=Purpose (e.g., to inform, persuade, or argue a point)

o A=Audience

o F=Format (e.g., an advertisement, brochure, public service announcement, investigative report, a persuasive essay or argument

These authors note that, "Linking format to purpose and audience allows teachers to ensure that students are not just asked to follow conventions and formats for the sake of school, but they are actually using language to *do* all things in the world, besides earning a grade." (p. 15) For example, eighth-grade students wrote persuasive essays aimed at challenging a fast food advertisement that made fun of young adults who still live with their parents. As eighth-graders, these students were living in multigenerational households and were angry that a large fast food corporation mocked their lifestyle, and that of others. Students voted to write to the company's manager in the form of a business letter countering the stereotypical and offensive message in the advertisement (Dostal et al., 2015).

Autobiographies and Biographies

Writing to Inform
o Autobiographies
o Biographies
o Research papers
o I-Search papers
o Imaginative writing
   assignments

When students are asked to write an autobiography of their unique literacy histories from the earliest memories they have up to the present, this activity provides a powerful window on their experiences and feelings about reading (Bean, 2002). A *reading autobiography* charting experiences at early, middle, and later stages of reading can be shaped to focus on reading in science, mathematics, and so on. Autobiographies should be shared in class in small groups and discussed. In Application 11.3, we designed this autobiography format for English. You can modify the format to focus the autobiography on your content area and further narrow the scope of writing to encompass a particular period such as middle or high school.

APPLICATION 11.3

Reading Autobiography

Beginning with your earliest memories of reading or being read to, retrace your experiences as a reader up to and including the present time. As you think about these experiences, making notes, try to include as much of the following information as possible:

1. The kinds of books you read or that were read to you at particular ages—if you can't remember specific titles and authors, describe the plots, characters, themes, or content you can recall.

2. Your reading or lack of reading when you first became an independent reader

3. What you read or what was read to you both at school and at home during your elementary school years (Don't be embarrassed if no one read to you or if you didn't read. Just write about the lack of reading in your life.)

4. Facts and feelings about what you read as you moved through the grades up to and including senior high and beyond

5. Your present reading habits and preferences (or lack thereof)

6. The people (family members, teachers, friends, and others) who either put you off reading or encouraged you to read and why

7. Places where you acquired or now acquire books

8. The feelings and sensations you associate with reading

After you have taken notes on your experiences as a reader, write a short autobiographical sketch (three pages maximum) on your reading experiences based on the eight guidelines. Put your development in chronological order so that your autobiography shows the stages you have gone through as a reader. In the final section, review your personal history as a reader and discuss how your own experiences might influence you as a content area teacher interested in helping students cope with unfriendly textbooks and in developing in your students a desire to read for enjoyment. Be candid and honest in your writing. If you like, use an informal writing style as though you were writing in your journal. During our next class meeting, I will ask you to share these experiences with a small group.

Once students have written an autobiography, the transition to reading and writing *biographies* about an important figure in science, physical education, mathematics, history, music, or art is fairly easy. Trade book biographies offer a powerful way to enrich textbook concepts in a fashion that has human interest. In addition, women and minorities are featured in biographies in greater depth than their contributions might display in a content area textbook that surveys many topics.

Steps to Start Using Biographies in Your Content Area

1. Work with your librarian to ensure there is a good collection of biographies for your content area that encompasses women and minorities.

2. Have students self-select a biography to read and write about in some creative format. Possible project options include the following:
   a. Write about how the world in the biography you read is different from your own.
   b. Write a journal or e-mail message from the perspective of a book character.
   c. Write a movie review of the story in the book.
   d. Write and act out a historical, you-are-there scene, dressed as the character.

e. Write a biopoem. Biopoems offer students a vehicle for playing with language and taking creative risks (Cowles, 2015). The following template is useful in helping students structure their biopoems (Olson, 2003):

Structure of Biopoems

Line	1.	First name
Line	2.	Four traits that describe the character
Line	3.	Relative of
Line	4.	Lover of (3 things or people)
Line	5.	Who feels (3 items)
Line	6.	Who needs (3 things)
Line	7.	Who fears (3 things)
Line	8.	Who gives (3 things)
Line	9.	Who would like to see (3 items)
Line	10.	Resident of
Line	11.	Last name

3. Have students share their biography project with a small group or the whole class. For example, sixth-grader Kristen read a biography about a famous show dog, Duke, and wrote a biopoem about her dog, Lady Kathryn, in her middle school language arts class. Duke was Lady Kathryn's father.

Biopoem

Lady
A smart, loving, and sweet dog
Relative of Duke, a dog show champion
Lover of chewys, people, and attention
Who needs her family, chewy, and soft pillows
Who fears loud noises, new places, and new people
Who gives kisses, cute smiles, and playful attitudes
Who would like to see a huge treat, a huge stuffed animal, and other small puppies
Resident of Nevada
Kathryn

Thus, *biopoems* can take many forms and be created on virtually any topic across content areas. In science, students can write about the heart, various animals, plants, and so on. Biopoems are particularly applicable to biographies but very versatile as a creative way of writing to inform.

Biographies in music range from classical pianists to Jimi Hendrix and Shakira. With the help of your librarian, you should be able to locate biographies relevant to many content fields—physical education, agriculture, art, music, history, science, mathematics, vocational education, and so on. Searching for and selecting a biography to read and write about forms a great foundation for research paper writing. Use your imagination to create additional project options that involve writing to inform.

Research Papers

At its worst, a research paper assignment may amount to no more than students engaged in the busywork of copying facts laboriously cataloged for a teacher who knows this information in the first place. In this instance, the paper is put off as long as possible and hurriedly thrown together the night before it is due. The teacher then pays an inordinate amount of attention to the form of the paper, poison pen in hand to circle in red any grammar and spelling errors.

At its best, a research paper is the culmination of a student's efforts to become an expert in some subtopic of a field so this knowledge can be shared with an audience of peers. This may range from developing an insider's knowledge of sharks in science to an understanding of how parapsychologists explore phenomena such as poltergeists in a psychology class. You can probably recall writing papers of this sort a few times during your years in school. But notice we said "a few times." Opportunities to become actively involved in pursuing a topic of genuine personal interest are all too rare.

In this section we outline some general steps to consider as you assign research papers in your content classroom.

Steps to Assigning Research Papers

1. Selecting and narrowing in on a topic is often a difficult task for teachers and students alike. Students can form cooperative research groups for this stage of the process. A research team of two to five students with a recorder can brainstorm subtopics within the general area you suggest. For example, if the topic was earthquakes, students might narrow this to a list consisting of famous earthquakes, California earthquakes, the science of earthquakes, and so on.

2. Once the topic has been chosen, the research team can meet to plan how they are going to tackle the topic. They can brainstorm possible questions for their topic and place them on notecards. For example, if the topic were the science of earthquakes, possible questions might include the following: What causes earthquakes? Can scientists predict when they will occur? Where do they occur most often? All questions should be considered at this stage. Once all possible questions have been elicited, they should be categorized and transformed into statements that will guide the research and notetaking stage.

3. The research team should identify potential sources of information, including encyclopedias, textbooks, films, and experts who may be interviewed. If your school has access to computer databases that contain up-to-date encyclopedias, these may also be a good place to locate information. Once each research team has identified its resources for the paper, it should develop a timeline that delineates specific dates to finish each task: a date for completing the collection of information in the form of notes, another date for a paper outline, one for the first draft, and a date for the second draft. The search for information can be divided among team members so that a portion of the team reads and annotates encyclopedia information while another dyad interviews an expert on earthquakes.

4. Once information has been collected, students should regroup in their teams to categorize and consider the ideas they have. This is a good time to transform the headings that guided the information search into a tentative outline. The science of earthquakes outline might look like this:

I. Earthquake
   a. Definition
II. Cause of earthquakes
   a. Early myths
   b. Modern tectonic theory
III. Where they occur the most
   a. Pacific belt
   b. Mediterranean belt
IV. Effect of earthquakes
   a. Landslides
   b. Tsunamis
V. How they are studied
   a. Seismographs
   b. Earthquake waves

Once the outline is prepared, students can begin writing their individual reports. Be sure they realize that the outline is merely a tentative guide—it may be altered as the writing progresses and new insights develop.

5. The first draft of the paper can now be written. Once the first draft is completed, students should exchange papers and use a writing guide checklist like the one that accompanied the Guided Writing Procedure to peer-edit the papers.

6. Based on suggested edits by you and their peers, students can now complete the second and final draft. Naturally, this process takes time. Students need adequate class time to meet in their groups, and they need enough time to allow for

two drafts of the paper. Provide student groups with a form where they can list team members, the topic, categories to be explored, resources, and the timeline proposed. You then review this material for each group and sign off to indicate topic approval. Students may also need a checklist, particularly for the group recorder, that indicates the various stages of the process (e.g., brainstorming, researching, organizing, and writing), along with the substeps for each procedure (e.g., for brainstorming: generate questions, categorize the questions, and write them as statements; identify sources; and set timelines). This will help focus the group effort on the various steps in the process.

In addition to carefully describing the parameters of a writing assignment as extensive as a research paper, you may want to share with students some model papers that were completed in a previous class. Papers written by former students can become important sources of information for the present class, giving the students a functional audience for their writing aside from the usual teacher as examiner-audience. At their best, research papers should be memorable experiences for students that result in in-depth knowledge and appreciation of subtopics that might otherwise go unnoticed in a frenetic effort to cover too much content in too short a time.

I-Search Papers

The *I-Search paper* is an alternative to the more traditional research paper (Macrorie, 1988). Unlike traditional research papers where there is a tendency for students to report on a topic by reading and distilling the works of others, in I-Search papers students investigate a topic of their choosing by interviewing experts, visiting places, and telling the story of their search.

Steps to Construct an I-Search Paper

1. **Choose a topic.** Students should select topics of personal interest. For example, Jennifer, a middle school student, had been a regular visitor to the zoo for years. She was mystified by the pandas and her I-Search paper investigated how they were cared for in the city zoo. Another student, Fabio, wanted to find out more about how guitars are made. His I-Search paper took him on a journey to a local luthier.

2. **Carry out the search.** Share the topic with the class and see if anyone has some ideas about where to find an expert to interview. For example, Jennifer's interest in pandas put her in contact with the head veterinarian at the city zoo. Fabio's search sent him to a luthier. Before contacting and interviewing the veterinarian and luthier, these students did some background reading on their respective topics. Based on this background reading, they created some

interview questions on their respective topics. For example, Jennifer asked the veterinarian at the zoo, "Why are pandas on the endangered species list?" Fabio asked, "How much does a handmade koa guitar cost to build?"

3. **Conduct the interview.** Using a tape recorder to retain the information they needed for the I-Search paper, Jennifer and Fabio visited and interviewed the experts they located. They received recommendations for further reading from these experts. For example, when Fabio interviewed a luthier, the guitar maker said "read *The Guitar Handbook*" (Denyer, 1982).

4. **Write the paper.** Use the I-Search experience as a way of telling the story of how the paper evolved. Anything important in the search process should be included, and the format can follow the four categories of information listed below:
   a. *What the student knew or did not know when the topic was selected.* For example, Jennifer did not know that there are only about 1,000 pandas living in the mountains in China. The pandas depend heavily on the food source of their bamboo forests, which are vulnerable to logging and a natural life-and-death cycle.
   b. *Why the student decided to write on this topic.* In Jennifer's case, she worked as a volunteer at the zoo. She had a long-standing interest in biology and in becoming a veterinarian specializing in the care of large, endangered zoo animals. Fabio played an old koa guitar that once belonged to his grandfather, and he was interested in how it was made. He dreamed about someday making his own guitar.
   c. *The search should be described.* Fabio's paper described his visit to luthier Bob Gleason of Pegasus Guitars. Fabio commented on the old industrial warehouse where the luthier worked and how neat everything was. He spent two afternoons at the guitar maker's workshop and borrowed the book, *The Guitar Handbook,* to further research his paper.
   d. *What the student learned.* Jennifer included information on the panda's diet in the zoo (i.e., bamboo, apples, carrots, sweet potatoes, pans of slurpy ice, and mixtures of milk, eggs, and ground vegetables), sleep habits (i.e., 12 to 14 hours per day), and reproduction. In addition, she learned that in China, breeding programs are used to raise pandas in captivity to be released into the wild.

The I-Search paper should conclude with a list of sources, experts, and key people involved in supplying ideas and insights for the paper.

The I-Search paper goes well with cooperative learning. For example, rather than using individual I-Search topics, a small group or team of students can collaborate to investigate a topic of common interest. The I-Search paper is also a good alternative to the traditional research paper for multicultural topics, second language learners, and at-risk students because of its experiential nature.

Imaginative Writing Assignments

Discussing text reading and writing an in-depth research report are mainstays of content learning. But it is equally important to provide a variety of writing opportunities, especially for imaginative writing. In this section we offer some imaginative writing assignments that lend themselves to a variety of content areas. You can undoubtedly think of other possibilities.

Students can project themselves into the lives of people in historical contexts or animals in various habitats by writing a diary entry from a unique perspective. For example, have social studies students write a diary entry as if they were hobos riding the rail during the Depression. In the area of ecology, they could write a diary entry from the perspective of a whale or dolphin passing through an ocean channel near one of our polluted city harbors.

Similarly, have students write a "Who Am l?" piece in which they portray topics such as I am your heart, I am your lungs, I am President Roosevelt, I am a camera. This exercise can require researching on a topic in detail to transform what might otherwise be dull expository prose into a lively, personal account.

Imaginative writing expands students' sense of audience and encourages creativity. In business education, students can write real letters to a newspaper column or the Small Business Association, asking for advice about their business interests. They can write a business plan for a small business they wish to start, such as yard cleaning or car detailing. Some students may want to interview a small business owner and create an oral history of the trials and tribulations of business ownership.

In social studies, students can write about a historical event from the perspective of a person experiencing it. For example, what was it like to be a woman on a ranch during cattle drives, isolated from other women, responsible for a family and livestock? Students can write fictional accounts about historical events, transforming expository prose into a more lively narrative form. In mathematics, students can create a story using mathematical symbols in place of some words. In science, defending an unpopular theory, such as the notion that there is such a thing as earthquake weather, and directing this defense to a newspaper or a peer audience requires both research and imagination. In foreign language classes, acting in the role of a visiting student writing a diary entry about the first day in the United States can illuminate cultural diversity.

In music, drama, and art, writing a critical review of a concert or interviewing an artist for the newspaper helps broaden the audience for student writing. In health and physical education, keeping a sports diary that chronicles jogging or swimming progress and diet strategies demonstrates the day-to-day usefulness of writing to inform.

Students can also respond to literature or other forms of text using a variety of genres (Walker, Bean, & Dillard, 2010). *Multigenre writing* helps students experiment in imaginative ways with a host of genres including ad writing, comic strips, editorials, and so on. Consistent with other writing strategies we have introduced, it is important to model new genres for students before they attempt multigenre writing on their own. We include two excellent guides in the recommended readings that offer additional information on multigenre writing.

APPLICATION 11.4

Write a brief "I am" piece describing some aspect of your own content area. For example, in biology you could write "I am the cell." In physical education, you might write "I am a gymnast." When you have completed the description, exchange yours with a colleague from another content area.

RESPONDING TO WRITING

As students develop research papers and lengthy pieces of writing in your content area, your skill at responding to their writing becomes crucial. You may remember having a paper returned from a teacher covered with red marks attesting to your ability to produce sentences that were "awk" (i.e., awkward), and phrases that were, in the teacher's eyes, "frags" (i.e., fragments). When students receive a barrage of negative criticism for their writing efforts, they come to associate writing with frustration, depression, self-doubt, and avoidance. Furthermore, they may come to view revision as a process that involves merely making surface level changes similar to proofreading rather than a process that entails deeper structural and organizational changes. In contrast, we believe that students need to be able to risk portraying their ideas in writing without simultaneously balancing total attention to the mechanics of grammar and spelling, except in the revision stage of the second draft. You should avoid riddling a student's paper with red marks that focus on mechanical errors and consider alternate means of responding to his or her writing. This is especially important in working with second language learners who may be very intimidated by writing in English.

Valuing their writing should be at the top of your list when you confer with students. Finding value in the writing content, treating students as writers, and encouraging growth through comparisons of early and later writing make a difference. Indeed, evaluation can be defined as finding value in a piece of writing. Teachers should also display their own attempts at writing in content areas and act as colearners in the writing process. Autobiographies, journals, research papers, and imaginative writing all offer opportunities to participate with your students as writers. In our research in secondary classrooms, for example, we freewrite with students on various topics related to American literature.

Key to helping students engage in writing that matters is writing for real audiences and seeing the conventions of writing as tools for communication rather than for "correctness" (Dostal & Gabriel, 2015). "Linking format to purpose and audience allows teachers to ensure that students are not just asked to follow conventions and formats for the sake of school, but they are actually using language to do all things in the world, besides earning a grade." (Dostal et al., p. 15) For example, students in economics can write persuasive essays aimed at challenging fast food advertisements.

Developing a revision system for minilessons on writing conventions will benefit from *NIP-it* lessons (Dostal & Gabriel, 2015). NIP-it stands for Notice-Insruct-Practice and it is aimed at helping students tackle writing conventions in the context where students exhibit confusion in using writing convention. For example, a mini NIP-it lesson on commas or other writing conventions would occur as needed in the writing process. After some time, you will have a collection of NIP-it minilessons ready for use in your content area. If students' rough drafts are missing paragraph transition sentences that guide the reader from one section to the next, you can use a draft and a teacher-created example that demonstrates the value of transition sentences.

Another very useful tool to guide students' thinking about revision in your discipline is Kelly Gallagher's (2011) acronym RADAR:

o R=Replace

o A=Add

o D=Delete

o R=Reorder key sections of the essay

Phrased another way, significant revision involves rewriting something, adding something, taking something out, moving something around, or, even deleting a section of the draft and starting over.

When you write responses to a student's writing, consider the following. Begin any comments about a paper with praise. This alleviates anxiety and opens the door for revision. Second, writing marginal questions that probe areas of the paper that need revision directs the student to take responsibility for this process. Third, using an analytical checklist like the GWP checklist provides a means of guiding revision without marking up a student's paper. Fourth, individual conferences in combination with the checklist can be more productive than merely returning a paper with marginal comments. Finally, helping students use effective self-evaluation to revise their writing based on a series of generic questions lessens your paper load and encourages independence. Three response schemes are discussed in detail—individual conferences, self-evaluation, and peer evaluation.

Individual Conferences

An individual conference is a conversation between a teacher and student for the purpose of evaluating and pointing out areas for revision of a draft of a paper. These conferences can be organized with a sign-up sheet on a first-come, first-served basis, or you can circulate about the room meeting with students as needed. The conversations you have with students should be purposeful, resulting in specific ideas for revision of a draft. Having a series of generic questions in mind to guide the individual conference will help the student participate actively in these sessions rather than passively hoping you will do the revising. The following questions are recommended (Newkirk, 1986, p. 121):

1. What do you like best about this draft?

2. What do you like the least?

3. What gave you the most trouble in writing this?

4. What kind of reaction do you want your readers to have—amusement, anger, increased understanding?

5. What surprised you when you wrote this? What came out differently than you expected?

6. What is the most important thing you learned about your topic in writing this?

Sandmann (2006, p. 21) developed a questioning process to assist with revision called the *Focused Question Card* strategy. An overarching revising question guides this process:

o   Does this text say what I want it to say?

Subsequent questions home in on specific content revisions:

o   Do I have enough specific detail to make my point, or do I need to add more?

o   Did I keep the same point of view?

o   Is my writer's voice coming through? How?

Sandmann provides a list of 24 revision questions and links this process with a related rubric for evaluation of students' writing. This process can be used for peer and individual editing, particularly in the early stages of developing a sense of how to write a research paper. By modeling the use of focused question cards (on note cards), students begin to internalize the steps in revising a paper and the physical note cards can eventually be phased out.

These questions and others you devise, in combination with the GWP checklist, should emphasize the student's ideas, but there is always a tendency in teaching for the teacher to do most of the talking. Listening carefully and holding back your natural desire to grab the paper and revise in a way you think appropriate gives a student responsibility for this important process. Ideally, students need to learn effective means of self-evaluation. The individual conferences you conduct using a series of generic questions can form the basis for effective self-evaluation.

Self-Evaluation

The checklist introduced with the GWP can serve as a guide for self-evaluation. Similarly, a series of questions like the following may also focus the writer on areas needing revision:

1. What makes you happy about this writing?

2. Do you excite your reader with a good beginning?

3. Is there a clear topic sentence?

4. Do you back up your ideas with details and examples?

5. Do you use a variety of words to express your ideas?

6. Are your sentences different lengths?

7. Do you use complete sentences?

8. Did you check your writing for correct capitalization, punctuation, and spelling?

Although checklists and questions can help students detect areas needing revision, a writer's distinct style is more difficult to define. Writing that expresses each student's individual interest in his or her own unique style is often a pleasure to read. However, many of the expository texts students read seem to have had the author's voice edited out of them. If these are the only models of writing students read in a content area, their own writing may have this same bland quality. In addition to texts, students need to read trade books in science, social studies, mathematics, and business that demonstrate the author's enthusiasm for a topic and unique voice.

In addition to self-evaluation, peer evaluation can play an important role in the revision process. If you have ever tried to evaluate your own writing objectively, you know how hard this process can be. You know what you meant to say, even if the actual version you produced on paper is incoherent. A peer reader will quickly find these problem areas.

Peer Evaluation

Teams of two students can become skilled at evaluating each other's writing when they have some practice and clear guidelines for the process (Porto, 2002). We have found that students can comfortably practice peer editing by starting with some writing samples from a lower grade. They can apply the GWP checklist to these samples without feeling self-conscious about critiquing a classmate's writing. Once they are skilled at responding to these papers, they can exchange papers with a peer and collaborate to polish their first drafts.

The GWP checklist offers a good general series of composing and transcribing considerations for any content area writing. However, students should begin a peer editing session by first complimenting their partner on some aspect of the paper. The following general comments help students grasp this important first step: (1) "I thought the most interesting part of your paper was . . .," and (2) "You gave the most complete information about . . ." We suggest that students phrase any negative comments as questions. For example, "Can you tell me more about . . .?" This approach avoids engendering any defensive feelings as a peer helps in the revision process.

Another contemporary way to promote peer editing in your content area writing assignments is to use an application like Google Classroom to have students review their drafts in small groups online (Kelly, 2015). For example, in a history classroom students can become familiar with this process by initially critiquing sample essays and ultimately editing each other's essays for clarity and other issues including length, adding citations, adding examples, providing definitions, and breaking long sentences apart. Using a rubric you provide (like the GWP checklist) students can explore historical topics (e.g., problems with monopolies and the Sherman Anti-Trust Act).

In peer editing, merely finding problems in a paper is not enough. Unlike the red pen "awks" and "frags" we all remember trying to decipher and resolve, a peer reader should offer some solutions to the problems that have been identified. For example, the reader can suggest alternative organizational structures, revised sentences, correct spellings, and format changes. With the use of word processing, these changes should not be overwhelming.

Rubrics

Rubrics offer a concrete description of the qualities and criteria expected in a particular piece of writing (Bean, 2010). A good rubric tells students explicitly what is expected for maximum performance in writing. The example rubric that follows was created for a writing assignment on the development of a biography on a key figure in history from the Revolutionary War. While the actual numeric values associated with performance in writing on this rubric operate on a 4-point scale, you can have a rubric with additional items. Nevertheless, a 4-point rubric is fairly common.

Example Rubric

4 Key information about this Revolutionary War figure is presented in a coherent, carefully edited, well-organized two-page biography. Word choice, organization, grammar, and spelling make the figure described come alive for the reader. It is evident that thoughtful library research went into the final product. The writing is highly polished and enjoyable to read.

3 Most key information about this Revolutionary War figure is presented in a coherent fashion. However, greater attention to word choice, paragraph transitions, spelling, and grammar would be helpful. Overall, the paper displays reasonably thorough library research, and the writing is adequate.

2 Some key information about this Revolutionary War figure is not included, and the writing would benefit from more careful editing and polishing, particularly with respect to word choice, organization, grammar, and spelling conventions. In addition, more thorough library research is needed, and the writing is incoherent in many places.

1 Little detailed information is supplied about this Revolutionary War figure and the writing is not coherent in many places. Substantial revision is needed to correct numerous word choices, organization, grammar, and spelling problems. Overall, the paper displays a lack of attention to research and editing.

There are many different types of scoring schemes for evaluating writing, and these can be adapted for a wide array of writing assignments across various content areas.

A Final Word

Individual conferences, self-evaluation, and peer evaluation all help content teachers manage the paper load, the biggest single obstacle to writing assignments in many content classrooms. The fact that you can probably remember those content area papers you have written over the years where *you* became the class expert on some topic, whether it was sharks or the stock market, attests to the power of writing as a mode of learning and reflection. It is worth the trouble. It takes real effort to guide students through various drafts for longer papers and real restraint to resist overcorrecting writing that is intended only for the writer's eyes as a bridge to learning.

Calkins (1994) says this about writing, and we agree:

> We write to communicate, plan, petition, remember, announce, list, imagine . . . but above all, we write to hold our lives in our hands and to make something of them. There is no plot line in the bewildering complexity of our lives but that which we make for ourselves. Writing allows us to turn the chaos into something beautiful, to frame selected moments, to uncover and celebrate the organizing patterns of our existence. (p. 8)

Now go back to the writing vignette at the beginning of this chapter. React again to the lesson as you did before. Compare your responses with those you made before you read the chapter.

MINI PROJECTS

1. Visit a content area classroom for at least a week. Keep a log of writing activities you observe. Categorize these activities according to the major headings on the graphic organizer for the chapter: writing to learn, writing to inform, and responding to students' writing. Compare your findings to those of other students in your class.

2. Examine the writing activities recommended in a major student text in your content area. Using the headings from this chapter, determine what types of writing are being emphasized. Compare your findings to those of colleagues in class.

3. Using the text chapter on the website entitled "What causes weather patterns?", select one of the writing-to-learn strategies in this chapter. Conduct a lesson with a small group of students or your peers. Write a description and evaluation of this lesson and share it with colleagues in class.

4. Select one of the writing-to-inform activities and conduct a lesson with students in your content area. Respond to students' writing using the GWP checklist, and conduct at least one individual conference or peer editing session, using the guidelines in this chapter. Write a description of your experience and share it with colleagues.

RECOMMENDED WEBSITES

o ReadWriteThink: http://bit.ly/1djschu
   This site provides an example of how young adult author Paul Fleishman's essay, "My house of voices" can be used as a mentor text to model what students hear when they listen to the natural world.
o Other Mentor Texts can be found at:
   VeganDigitalStory@justgirl83 and https://www.youtube.com/watch?v=Oht9AEq1798
o Persuasive Writing Letter Generator: http://bil.ly/1QScxT2

WEBSITE ACTIVITY

Go to the website for Chapter 5 activities.

CHAPTER 12

Studying and Preparing for Examinations

VIGNETTE

Setting

Sam Valuta's tenth-grade world history class. Mr. Valuta and his students just completed a unit on the Baltic nations and their efforts to achieve independence. A unit test is scheduled for the next class, and Mr. Valuta is suggesting ways to study for this essay test.

© Lucky Business/Shutterstock.com

The Lesson

Mr. Valuta reviews material on the Baltic nations of Latvia, Estonia, and Lithuania covered in this unit. He engages students in a discussion of the cultural and linguistic differences of the three nations and problems of banding together politically in the Council of Baltic States and economically in a Baltic common market to develop a unified front in negotiations with Moscow. Mr. Valuta then highlights the general area of essay test questions he plans to ask, and he tells students about various study strategies they might use to prepare for the test. These strategies come from his own relatively recent experiences in college as a history major faced with countless essay exams.

T: *"I know you are worried about taking an essay test on this material. But if you study hard, you'll do fine. I want to tell you about some study strategies you can use. They work for me, and they should work for you too."*

S: *Students are listening more than usual and ready to take notes.*

T: *"You all know how to outline, so you might simply take the section of the text on the Baltic states and outline this information. Just writing it out, even copying it from the book, should help you memorize it."*

S: *"We do that anyway. Sometimes it works okay, sometimes it doesn't. What else can we do, Mr. Valuta? Personally, I'm really worried about this test. Is it one big question or smaller ones?"*

T: "I can't really tell you the exact question, but I can tell you that the difficulty of getting three very different groups of people like the Latvians, Estonians, and Lithuanians together for a common cause is an important part of what you need to know. As for other study strategies, I mostly rely on the outline-and-memorize approach myself, but you could try something like this. Take each subheading in the section of the text on the Baltic nations and turn it into a question. Then see if you can answer the question based on your memory from reading this section. If you can successfully get most of the information, then you'll probably do fine on the essay test."

S: "But we haven't practiced doing this at all. We've just been reading, taking notes on your lectures, talking about the book, and watching films. How do we know what to expect in an essay test?"

T: "That's the whole idea—you don't. It wouldn't be a test if you already had the question and practiced writing an essay. This way, it will be a true test of your memory, and if you do well, you can feel really good about the study strategy you used."

The bell rings, and students file out talking among themselves. They express high anxiety and a sense of powerlessness in the face of this impending essay exam.

Keeping in mind that this lesson was designed to help students prepare for an essay exam on the Baltic nations, jot down your thoughts on the following questions:

1. What are the good points about the lesson?

2. What are the weak points about the lesson?

3. What, if anything, would you change about the lesson?

 RATIONALE

Learning can be defined minimally as a cognitive process involving the transfer of information from short-term memory to long-term memory. Or, more expansively and consistent with the affordances of the Internet, learning content material in mathematics, science, English, or history may involve the creative construction of an original production (e.g., a YouTube video clip or podcast). In a much narrower sense, learning can be defined in terms of the acquisition of specific information in content areas, and the preceding chapters of this text have dealt primarily with the means by which this acquisition process can be facilitated. One focus of the present chapter is on study strategies that help students retain and retrieve information. A second focus of the chapter is on test preparation, especially as it pertains to high-stakes reading assessments (Bean, 2010; Flippo et al., 2015). Given the consequences of a school not making annual yearly progress, it is crucial that teachers in English, social studies, health, and other subject areas know how to prepare students to take and pass state reading tests.

 LEARNING OBJECTIVES

o   Justify the time required to guide students toward effective study strategies in your content area.
o   Understand the general learning principles that underlie the study strategies described in this chapter.
o   Guide students in developing study strategies that improve retention and recall of material from your content area.
o   Understand why as a content teacher you should be involved in preparing students to take and pass high-stakes reading assessments.
o   Know how to successfully prepare students for reading assessments.

 GRAPHIC ORGANIZER

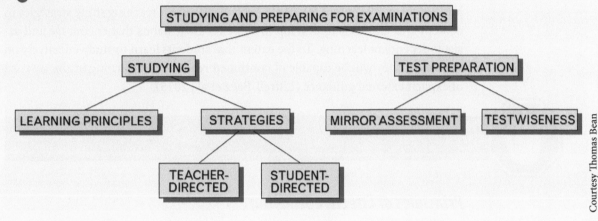

Courtesy Thomas Bean

STUDYING

Everyone has had the experience of walking into an examination, such as the SAT or GRE, only to find the answers to certain questions elusive due to memory failure. For example, the solution to a simple geometry problem may require knowing the formula for finding the circumference of a circle. (Let's see, is that πr^2, $2\pi r$, or $2\pi r^2$?) A failure to extract the necessary information from memory may result because (1) you never bothered to learn the formula in the first place; (2) you learned it but have for some reason failed to retain it in your memory; or (3) you did learn the formula and it is still locked in your memory, but you are unable to recall the formula. In any event, the net effect is the same, a wrong answer on the test. Clearly, the ability to retain and recall information is as important as the ability to learn it in the first place. For this reason, study strategies are the business of every content teacher. A second reason for teaching study strategies in content area classes is to develop in students those habits that encourage and assist independent learning. To the extent that students learn to study effectively on their own, they will be capable of continued reading and learning in the absence of explicit external guidance (Littrell-Baez et al., 2015).

Principles of Effective Studying

If I were compelled to sum up in a single word all that is embraced in the expression "a good memory," I should use the word attention. Indeed, I would define education, moral and intellectual, as attention (Aiken, 1896, p. 74).

Attention

Read through the following passage one time, and be prepared to answer a single question:

> *An empty hotel elevator stops and one person enters. The elevator goes up two floors and six people get on; up three more floors and three people get on. The elevator goes down one floor and seven people get off; down one more floor and one person gets off. The elevator then shoots up ten floors and two people get on. Now, without looking back, how many times did the elevator stop?*

The answer is six; you probably got it wrong. Why? The second word in this old joke is a distractor. The fact that the elevator is empty has no bearing on the answer to the question. However, the reader, not knowing the question in advance, guesses or assumes that keeping track of numbers of people is the pertinent task. The real rub lies in the fact that tallying the number of elevator stops is much easier than calculating how many people get on and off.

The principle in this example is that comprehension and learning/memory are not at all the same thing. It is quite possible to read with good comprehension and at the same time fail to retain the information. In most instances, the individual's active attention is a powerful factor in placing information in a durable memory store. It is a matter of common sense and common experience. Everyone remembers Miss Frock (the fourth-grade teacher) who said, "If you don't pay attention, you won't remember anything."

There is, however, another aspect of attention that has less to do with willingness or appropriateness of attention than the capacity to attend. Generally, human beings are capable of attending consciously to only one task at a time, despite all the hype about teenagers' multitasking skills. Owing to the limits of attention, many states have banned cell phone use, particularly texting, while driving, because of an overwhelming number of accidents occurring when drivers are attending to their cell phones. This principle of capacity limitation for attention will be a critical consideration in discussion of specific study strategies later in the chapter.

> **Effective Studying Principles**
> o Attention
> o Goal orientation
> o Organization
> o Rehearsal
> o Time on task
> o Depth of processing

Goal Orientation

One of the most serious and frequent impediments to learning is the counterproductive study goal. Students often read a textbook assignment for the sake of completing it, that is, to be able to tell the teacher, without fibbing, that they have in fact read the assignment. When the student's attention is focused on getting through x number of pages rather than on comprehending and retaining information, the result is almost certain to be inferior comprehension and retention. Students who fail to read the last two paragraphs of a chapter because the teacher accidentally designated reading pages 79–93 instead of 79–94 demonstrate a counterproductive study goal. They meet the letter of the assignment but not its spirit. Constructive purpose, given by the teacher and embraced by the students, is essential to effective study.

Organization

Pronounce each digit in the following number one time, and then try to recall the number from memory:

> **Mental Organization**
> o Patterns
> o Chunking
> o Mnemonics

    1248163264128
    Difficult, wasn't it? Now, try again.
    1 2 4 8 16 32 64 128

The second time should have been much easier. If you sensed the geometric progression, you should have been able to reproduce the original number sequence with minimal strain on memory. It is much easier to remember one number (in this case, 1) and one rule (in this case, digits are produced by doubling the preceding number) than it is to recall what appears to be a random series of digits. This is *organization*, the arrangement of parts of a whole in such a manner that the parts are related to each other. The analogy to study strategies is obvious; whenever information can be organized into meaningful patterns, retention and retrieval of information is facilitated.

A second type of mental organization is *chunking*. Bits of information are said to be chunked when they are transformed into one large bit of information. For example, the letters *h c r a o* can be transformed into the word "roach." The advantage in chunking is that a larger bit of information, e.g., roach, requires no more memory than a smaller bit of information, e.g., *c*. Because it permits the storage of large amounts of information without placing a corresponding strain on memory, chunking is an efficient means of organizing information.

A third type of mental organization is *mnemonics*, association devices for triggering recall. Perhaps the most familiar mnemonic device is the *acronym*. This is a process where words are formed by combining the initial letters or segments of a series of words. AWOL (absent without leave), VIP (very important person), and radar (radio detecting and ranging) are common examples of acronyms. Tying a string around your finger, remembering how to spell "piece" with the phrase "piece of pie," or improving recall of names by distorting them (e.g., "Baldwin" becomes "bald one") represent other types of mnemonic devices.

APPLICATION 12.1

Directions: Develop a set of at least 10 specific mnemonic devices that could be used to assist in the recall of specific information in your content area. Include acronyms but do not limit your devices to them.

Rehearsal

The acquisition, retention, and recall of information are all assisted by rehearsal or practice. *Rehearsal* is a natural strategy that people use to keep information in memory. In the case of short-term memory, information is repeated over and over until the immediate need for it desists. For instance, it is normal to look up a telephone number, rehearse it rapidly during the act of dialing, and then forget it as soon as the dialing has been completed.

In the case of long-term memory, recall of information is improved most through *distributed practice*, in which rehearsals are separated by some break. For example, the retention and recall of specific facts and historical trends derived from a social studies lecture will be better with frequent, spaced, and brief periods of study (rehearsal) than with a single massive study session.

Time on Task

While it is almost certainly true that the organization of practice affects retention and recall (e.g., distributed versus massed practice), it is equally true of the raw amount of time spent practicing. In fact, it has been argued that some strategies or teaching techniques appear to improve learning primarily because they result in students spending more time on learning tasks, and not because the techniques themselves are better. For example, which of the following strategies would result in the best recall: (1) reading and then outlining a textbook chapter; or (2) reading and then answering teacher-prepared questions over the content? To some degree, the answer would depend on the amount of time students spend on each technique.

Depth of Processing

Most college graduates are capable of solving an algebra problem such as (a):

$$(a)\ x - 14 = 23$$

On the other hand most college graduates probably could not solve an equation like (b), in spite of the fact that they were undoubtedly forced in high school to work problems at this level of difficulty:

$$(b)\ y = \frac{x^3 \times 5x^2 + 6x}{x+3}$$

One justification for introducing difficult material is that it helps guarantee the long-term retention of basic principles and processes. In other words, it is possible that people retain the ability to solve problem (a), not because it is easy but because they had to expend great mental energies solving problems like (b). This is the principle of *depth of processing*, which asserts that there is a greater likelihood of long-term retention and recall when (1) the mental activity demands a deeper level of thinking, (2) more schemata are committed to the task, and (3) the degree of semantic analysis is high. The depth of processing principle also explains why a new vocabulary word and its definition will be remembered longer and with greater accuracy by most people if the word is introduced with such elements as context, morphemic analysis, and an etymology. You guarantee better memory for the word and its fundamental meaning by forcing a deeper, more expansive mental processing of the word and its associations.

Specific Strategies

Strategy implies intent. A strategy is not an accident but is rather the planned means to an end. In general, it is best to plan study strategies that have the following characteristics.

Characteristics of Good Study Strategies

1. They help focus attention on important information.

2. They provide meaningful study goals.

3. They help organize information.

4. They cause students to practice.

5. They encourage deep processing of information.

The study strategies that follow are plans that teachers and students can implement cooperatively to promote the acquisition, retention, and recall of information.

Listening and Taking Notes

Notetaking during lectures and discussions is one of the most common events in the classroom, yet there is considerable confusion over the purposes and best methods of taking notes. In fact, there are many notetaking systems, but none of them have empirical documentation. In addition, given the features of contemporary smart phones where recording information is effortless, notetaking may serve as a way of organizing critical audio information recorded on a cell phone for review. Given that students are accustomed to listening to iTunes podcasts on various topics, there may be some advantages to recording lecture material in a podcast for later student review. Nevertheless, learners still need a way to approach notetaking from text and online material that organizes information for writing, for reviewing for tests, and for using in a project.

Notetaking has two presumed functions: external storage and encoding. The *external storage* (the notes themselves) of information serves as a substitute for memory and gives students an opportunity to review material that might otherwise have been forgotten. The *encoding* function presumably improves the comprehension and retention of information by forcing the notetaker to transform lecture material into personally meaningful language (depth of processing principle). The difference between external storage and encoding is often described as a contrast between taking and having notes. The validity of the encoding function is based on the assumption that during the course of a lecture students will be able to mentally transform what they are hearing. We reject this assumption on the grounds that fast presentation rates during lectures preclude the reflective thought necessary for such encoding. In fact, it is quite possible that taking any kind of notes is detrimental to learning if the material is presented too quickly. The consensus is that the external storage function in notetaking is more important than the encoding function.

In addition to the purpose notetaking, there is also disagreement regarding the best procedures for notetaking. For instance, it is customary for students to take notes in *parallel*, that is, to be writing and listening at the same time. However, *spaced* notetaking seems to improve recall of lecture material. A spaced presentation is one in which the lecture is broken into segments, followed by intervals of silence several minutes long. Students listen during each lecture segment and then make notes at the interval that follows. Why this should be an effective notetaking procedure is explained in part by the limits of human attention. If people can concentrate on only one task at a time, why should we expect students to write and listen effectively at the same time? Most notetakers probably switch back and forth; they listen for a few seconds and then write, perhaps, but do not listen during those seconds in which individual notes are recorded. The result for many notetakers is incomplete lecture information received in bits and pieces. In contrast, a spaced notetaking procedure permits students to focus their complete attention on listening to the teacher and on encoding lecture information into meaningful notes.

TEACHER STRATEGIES. It is easy to assume that the quality of students' notes is nothing more than a function of their intelligence and other attributes. However, the lecture situation is a meeting of minds, and the organization and presentation format of the lecture can affect the quality of the notes radically. Following is a list of suggestions that will make notetaking easier and more efficient for students in your lectures and class presentations.

Tips for Making Notetaking Easier

1. Do not lecture if students are expected to write down and remember everything you say. Instead, type the material and hand it out. Lectures are more interesting if they include elements of discussion.

2. Lectures typically follow the same organizational patterns found in texts, e.g., cause/effect and comparison/contrast. Point these patterns out to students while you are lecturing, and tell them about how you have organized your notes. For example, if you have three points to make under each of two headings, let students know so that they can make appropriate room in their notes.

3. Notetaking should not be a game in which the student has to guess about what is important. It is absurd to assume that novices in chemistry or political

science should, without guidance, instantly sort essential ideas from trivial details. Write important information on the board, or just tell students when to take notes and when not to.

4. Speak slowly.

5. Use a spaced notetaking procedure. Allow students to listen to your lecture for 10 minutes or so. Then give them time to write and ask you questions. This will prevent the students from having to write and listen at the same time (capacity limitation problem).

6. Give students a few minutes at the end of class to revise and/or supplement their notes, and make them do it!

7. Give students distributed practice with their notes. Encourage them to review their notes on a nightly basis or in class. You can give students frequent quizzes over lecture material, allowing them to review their notes before the quiz or even allowing an open-notebook quiz. Another review possibility is to have students create questions strictly from their notes for a class review. In general, anything you can do to get the students to modify and refer back to their notes will boost their recall and retention.

8. Have open-note, but closed-book, quizzes to give students an idea of the quality of their notes. Students who take the time to revise notes and to review them will perform better; this, in turn, will encourage others to revise and review.

STUDENT STRATEGIES. We believe that it is a good idea for students to learn to take good notes, and we define good notes as any notes, however disorganized, sloppy, or idiosyncratic, that will serve as a successful warehouse for lecture information. We know of no one best notetaking procedure for all people of all ages in all subject areas. Therefore, we recommend considerable latitude in individual notetaking systems.

VERBATIM SPLIT PAGE PROCEDURE. The notetaking procedure we recommend for students is the *verbatim split page procedure* (VSPP). VSPP is a blend of various notetaking systems and is comprised of recording and organizing notes.

1. Recording Notes. Begin teaching VSPP by having students divide their notebook paper so that 40% of each page lies to the left and 60% to the right (see Figure 12.1). Instruct students to take notes only on the left hand side during lectures. All notes should be verbatim and clipped. The idea is to expend minimum amounts of mental energy on writing in order that full attention can be focused on listening to the lecture.

FIGURE 12.1

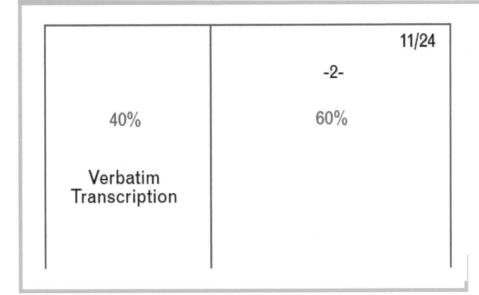

2. **Organizing Notes.** Nearly everyone has had the experience of taking abundant notes for a class, only to find those notes either unreadable or bizarre when it is time to study for the final exam. Abbreviated words, telegraphic sentences, and hasty scribbles may seem quite lucid to the notetaker at the time they are written; however, as the context in which the idiosyncratic shorthand was produced fades, notes of this sort rapidly lose meaning and integrity. For this reason, it is necessary to reorganize notes during significant pauses within the lecture or immediately following the lecture.

The right side of the page is used to reorganize and expand on the scribbles to the left. Students should be encouraged to do the following:

1. Place lecture information in an outline format;

2. Interpret notes and then encode them in their own words;

3. Expand notes to include lecture information that the student did not have time to note;

4. Write out whole words, phrases, and sentences so that notes will be clear in the future. (See Figure 12.2.)

FIGURE 12.2

Organizing Notes

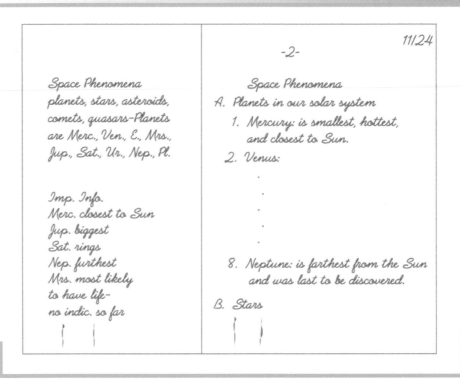

It is sometimes recommended that students take notes in an outline format. This is an extremely difficult task for two reasons. First, deciding which ideas are superordinate and which are subordinate requires attention that notetakers cannot spare as they listen. Second, lectures are hardly ever organized and presented in ways that immediately lend themselves to outline notetaking. In Figure 12.2 it is clear that the lecture on space phenomena began with an overview of superordinate concepts and then later presented subordinate bits of information. In reality, most lectures and other teacher presentations are punctuated frequently with digressions and slices of knowledge that are improperly layered within the lecture. With the help of limited verbatim notes, students should be able to rethink and reorganize the lecture material AFTER the lecture is over and when the entire presentation is fresh in their minds.

When the lecture information has been organized in the 60% column, the 40% verbatim column serves as the basis for studying the notes. Students try to recall the reorganized, expanded information using the clipped notes as a prompt.

In addition to the split-page notetaking structure, teaching students to consciously self-monitor their notetaking before a lecture begins, and after the lecture ends, can improve their notetaking performance. Based on teacher modeling of the following self-questioning routine, students should begin and end lecture notetaking with the following questions.

Before the lecture begins:

1. What is my purpose in listening to this lecture?

2. Am I interested in this topic and, if not, how will I increase interest and concentration (e.g., through an argumentative stance where I disagree with the author's point of view)?

After the lecture ends:

1. Did I achieve my purpose?

2. Did I concentrate and deal with comprehension failures?

Adding a comprehension monitoring dimension to the split-page procedure increases students' active processing and prepares them for the more advanced lecture and notetaking tasks they will encounter in college.

Go to the website and practice the VSPP using the lecture entitled, The Effects of Transfer on Learning

Metacognition

Broadly defined, *metacognition* refers to awareness of one's own mental processes, that is, knowing how you know what to do. It entails an effort to manage one's own thoughts through conscious planning. People who have good metacognitive skills understand their own behaviors, employ mental strategies that they can verbalize, and evaluate the quality of their thinking (Littrell-Baez et al, 2015). Metacognition is thinking about thinking.

Most children do not have good metacognitive skills. The most common response children give when asked why they have done something is, "I don't know." Sometimes they hide behind the "I don't know" when they do not wish to respond to parents, teachers, or other authority figures. For example,

> Dad to teenage daughter: "I told you to be home at 12 last night. Why did you come home at 3 a.m.?"

> Teenage daughter to dad: "I don't know."

Of course, the real thought of the teenage daughter is, "Jimmy and I were too busy to pay attention to your stupid rule." On the other hand, young people frequently do not understand or even attempt to monitor their own thought processes, and this is often true in the area of reading comprehension. Too many students rove mindlessly through a textbook assignment without any clearly defined purpose or conscious strategy for learning. Current research in the area of metacognition indicates that students who have good metacognitive skills are better comprehenders (Baker & Beall, 2009). Therefore, helping your students to develop their metacognitive awareness is fundamental to study strategies.

TEACHER STRATEGIES. One approach to developing metacognition in students is the think-aloud technique (Littrell-Baez, et al., 2015). The think-aloud technique is a teacher-modeling strategy in which the teacher reads aloud from a text and verbalizes whatever comes to mind in an effort to show students how to reason during reading. The teacher's verbalized thoughts may include questions, predictions, paraphrases, evaluative statements, and even text-irrelevant comments. Teacher and student think-alouds are an integral part of the next study strategy, Retrieval Practice (Littrell-Baez, et al., 2015).

Steps for Developing Think-Aloud Strategies

1. Select a passage 100 to 300 words long in your subject area. The passage should be fairly difficult so that your reasoning is actually useful to the students. If the passage is too easy the students will not see the value of what you are doing.

2. Prepare your comments for the think-aloud based on your experience. Because the material will not really be difficult for you, you need to plan an idealized set of think-aloud responses. You will be acting the part of a student with good metacognitive skills.

3. Explain to the students exactly what you are doing, e.g., "I am going to show you how I think when I read."

4. Read the passage to the class and insert your planned think-alouds as you go.

5. When you are finished, give students a chance to ask you questions about how you think or about the think-aloud procedure itself.

6. Have students practice thinking aloud with smaller segments of the text.

The paragraph below exemplifies a think-aloud for a biology text. The teacher's questions and statements are indicated by superscripts within the paragraph and referenced after the paragraph.

Amniocentesis[1] is a technique used by fetologists[2] when the parents are known or suspected to carry one of several types of genetic disease or when the woman is over age 40.[3] Older women are more likely to have a fetus with Down's syndrome.[4] The diseases specifically tested for are caused by having an extra or missing chromosome, a chromosome which has been broken,[5] or a metabolic disease such as phenylketonuria.[6] A hypodermic needle is inserted through the abdomen of the pregnant woman[7] and into the amnion.[8] A small amount of amniotic fluid, containing fetal cells,[9] is drawn into the syringe. These cells are then cultured (grown) for a period of time; when enough culture cells are available, they can be tested for many metabolic defects. Cells can also be specially stained and prepared so that the chromosomes can be seen under a microscope.

[1.] Looks like this is the topic. I better remember this word.

[2.] What is this? Someone who studies feet?

[3.] I didn't know people that old could have babies.

[4.] Okay, I know about that. A boy in our church has it.

[5.] How do you lose a chromosome or get it broken? Could it happen to me if I play football or get in an accident? How will I know?

[6.] I wonder what nerd made up this word.

[7.] Ouch!

[8.] Better ask the teacher what this is.

[9.] I get it now. Fetal refers to fetus, an unborn baby. That explains who a fetologist is, an unborn baby doctor.

[10.] Sounds cool; I'd like to see it.

View the website video clip demonstrating a think-aloud.

Steps for Retrieval Practice

The retrieval practice strategy introduces students to working without texts to recall information learned from an initial close reading of material in science, social studies, and other content areas (Littrell-Baez, et al., 2015). In addition, the strategy can be applied to make intertextual connections across multiple texts including print and nonprint material (e.g., a YouTube clip). In order to engage your students in this metacognitive process, the following steps are essential:

Day 1:

1. Have your students do a close reading of a text (e.g., a text on the hawk family bird, the osprey).

   The North American Raptor fish-eating hawk is a powerful hunter with the ability to dive from 30 to 100 feet to capture its prey under water. An osprey has a nictating membrane that protects its eyes during this maneuver. During the 1950s DDT and other chemicals threatened its survival but currently, ospreys are flourishing in waterways in North America. Indeed, its presence in our waterways is an indicator of water quality.

2. Model the process of close reading for your students by reading aloud and thinking aloud (e.g., the osprey is part of the hawk family of predators).

3. Ask your students to partner-read the next sections, pausing after each paragraph to think aloud with their partner.

A Few Days Later:

1. As a retrieval activity, ask your students to recall information about what they learned in their reading about the osprey earlier in the week.

2. Without looking back at the original text, ask students to answer a few text-based questions about the osprey (e.g., "What protects the osprey's eyes during its underwater plunge to capture a fish?").

3. Ask students to put a ✓ mark next to the answer to one of the three or four questions they are most confident about and a ✓ mark next to the answer they are least confident about.

4. Have students reread the text to check their answers and write a reflection on what they have learned during this process.

The authors of this strategy note as follows:

   This metacognitive reflection helps students to use the experience of testing their learning through retrieval practice and obtaining feedback through rereading to guide self-monitoring on their learning. Implementing retrieval practice in combination of close reading and metacognitive reflection in this way will serve to strengthen students' long-term retention of information learned from the text while also helping to improve their metacognitives skills. (p. 683)

We recommend engaging your students with this powerful approach on a regular basis across various disciplines including English, social studies, science, and other content areas. Current studies in classrooms where retrieval practice is in place show that the process increases students' long-term retention of information.

Another approach to developing metacognition in students is *embedded questions*. Embedded questions are teacher-developed questions inserted in a text at key points that are crucial to understanding the entire passage. This strategy can be used once students have been introduced to, and grasped, the modeling of the think-aloud, that is, once students understand what the teacher is demonstrating and see how reasoning occurs during reading. Thus, while think-alouds provide students the awareness and recognition of metacognitive strategies during reading, embedded questions allow them to simulate and produce metacognitive responses as they read.

Planning an embedded questions lesson begins like the think-aloud. A 100 to 300 word passage is selected, and key points in the passage are identified where students will be able to simulate the metacognitive strategies good readers would employ. Students are asked to read the passage and provide answers to the embedded questions. Following that, a substantive discussion occurs wherein comprehension of the passage is checked as well as verbalization of the metacognitive strategies used to answer the embedded questions. Though only limited to the difficulty of the passage and ability level of the students, some typical embedded questions might be as follows:

o What do you think will happen next? Why do you think so?

o What question are you thinking of at this point in the passage?

o What quality of the character (aspect of the process) do you think the author is emphasizing? Why?

o What seems to be confusing you the most at this point?

STUDENT STRATEGIES. Most of the strategies in this text improve metacognitive skills to some extent. Nevertheless, students need a guiding mental strategy for studying. PLAE (Nist, Simpson, Olejnik, & Mealey, 1991) is an acronym that stands for *P*replan, *L*ist, *A*ctivate, *E*valuate.

Preplan: Plan how to study. This may entail asking questions such as, "Should I summarize, take notes, or reread?" "What kind of a test is the instructor going to give?" "Do I want to study by myself or in a small group?"

List: The answers to such questions should result in planned behaviors rather than thoughtless or reflexive ones. The planned behaviors should be written down. For example, "I will read this chapter twice." "I will ask my teacher whether the test will be essay or multiple choice." "I will ask Marty and Beth if they want to study with me tomorrow."

Activate: This is a monitoring behavior. Basically the student needs to regularly ask, "Am I following my plan?"

Evaluate: Students assess whether or not the plan has worked. For example, "Was it worth studying with Marty and Beth?" "Would I do it again?"

PLAE is deceptively simple, so much so that you may be tempted to dismiss it as superfluous. Yet we believe that a strategy as simple as this is fundamental and not at all too obvious to bother with as you are teaching. How many times have you gotten to school or the office only to discover that you had forgotten your lunch, house keys, wallet, purse, term paper, or other important item? If the average American adult simply stopped at the front door before leaving and asked, "Do I have everything I need to take with me?" it would probably save millions in gasoline and aspirin.

APPLICATION 12.2

Select a textbook from your content area and develop a think-aloud lesson that you can demonstrate for the rest of the class.

Reading and Taking Notes

One of the content teacher's ever-present problems is how to get students to comprehend and retain information from textbook reading assignments. How does the teacher convert the passive page watcher into a reader who is actively engaged in reconstructing and evaluating the author's thoughts? Unfortunately, the best method of responding while reading—writing in the text—is not an option for most students because the books belong to the school.

Underlining main ideas, starring important terms, asking and answering questions, and making evaluative comments in the margins combine to make a highly personal and convenient response mode during reading. In the absence of this option, however, we must examine what we know about reading and taking notes and consider some alternative study strategies. Caverly, Orlando, and Mullen (2000) offer the following generalizations about reading and taking notes:

1. Students need instruction in how to take notes. While some students may spontaneously develop notetaking skills, we cannot assume that all will do so.

2. Students must be able to differentiate important material from supporting detail as well as other irrelevant information for notetaking instruction to succeed.

3. In order for students to benefit from notetaking instruction, review is essential, particularly in delayed recall situations.

TEACHER STRATEGIES. First, avoid giving assignments such as, "Okay, read pages 24–43 for Monday." Assignments like this make the completion of page 43 the objective of the assignment. A much better assignment would be "Okay, read pages 24–43. When you are finished you should be able to answer these questions . . ." or "As you are reading, write down at least 10 words, facts, procedures, or explanations you didn't understand." By the time you have finished detailing the reading assignment, your students should be able to answer the following questions:

1. What is this reading assignment about?

2. Why am I reading this?

3. What should I know when I have finished?

In fact, students have a right to this information and should be encouraged to ask for it whenever they find themselves facing purposeless reading assignments.

Second, introduce notetaking through the use of think-alouds. Select a passage for demonstration, and hand this out to your students. As you read the passage together, think aloud your reasoning processes and make your notes accordingly. The recording should occur on an overhead projector so students can visualize your recording as they hear you explain your thought processes. Do this several times until students seem to understand the process and then have them demonstrate their notetaking skills. A discussion of these demonstrations should occur. Students may also be placed in small groups to react to each other's notetaking or to produce a set of notes jointly. Joint products should be shared with the entire class. The intention of this instructional recommendation is to model the notetaking process and then have students produce their own notes.

A third teacher strategy is the use of a partial outline developed from a selected passage. The intention here is to provide students structure and guidance until they are eventually able to develop a full set of notes on their own. The first time a partial outline is used, demonstrate how to complete it in conjunction with a passage. Because the outline has a preset number of slots, attention can be drawn to the notion that only a certain amount of information is needed to complete the outline and that there is a difference between subordinate information and information that is supportive or irrelevant. Additional lessons would take the format described previously; teacher demonstrations could be followed by student ones and lessons done in small groups, always with a follow-up discussion of the thinking processes involved. The amount of structure provided in the outline as well as the amount of demonstration and instruction would be based on the ability level of the students.

STUDENT STRATEGIES. The two strategies we recommend for daily reading assignments are *f*riendliness, *l*anguage, *i*nterest, and *p*rior knowledge (FLIP) and student-generated questions.

FLIP (Schumm & Mangrum, 1991) is a textbook-previewing procedure designed to teach students how to evaluate the difficulty of daily reading assignments and allocate study time in a realistic manner. The strategy is highly personal and intentionally subjective because students need to learn how to manage reading and study assignments in ways that are consistent with their own abilities, interests, and schedules.

FLIP
o Friendliness
o Language
o Interest
o Prior knowledge

Steps for Using FLIP

1. Students record the reading assignment on the top of the FLIP chart.

2. Students skim the reading assignment and make a value judgment for each of the four FLIP categories: friendliness, language, interest, and prior knowledge. In the case of vocabulary, students read three paragraphs at random to check the level of unfamiliar vocabulary. Each of the four categories is given a rating from 1 to 5 with 1 being the most negative and 5 being the most positive.

3. Based on the FLIP ratings, students make an overall assessment of how comfortable the reading level is for them.

4. Students identify their purpose for reading, estimate how fast they should attempt to read, and then budget their reading time by dividing the assignment into as many chunks as they feel are necessary.

The FLIP procedure requires considerable metacognition on the part of students, and learning to make decisions about their own reading behaviors may be difficult for many of them at first. It is therefore recommended that teachers select an assignment and model FLIP with a think-aloud and the help of a smart board. Students can complete the FLIP chart as part of a group activity in which the students fill in the chart as the teacher completes each step of the think-aloud.

Schumm and Mangrum note that the purpose of FLIP is not to have students fill out and turn in forms. Instead they view FLIP as a set of metacognitive training wheels which helps students become aware of factors that influence their reading comprehension. Sooner or later students should learn to make FLIP decisions automatically, without the need for a chart.

In addition to the comprehension techniques presented in Chapters 9 and 10, we recommend using *student-generated questions* when they read. Questions can be used for purposes of in-class review, or they may be questions to which the student truly does not know the answer. We highly recommend teaching students how to ask questions at different levels: text explicit (reading the lines), text implicit (reading between the lines), and experience based (reading beyond the lines). Be patient; some students will have a very difficult time formulating questions that involve inferences (text implicit). There are three basic strategies for students to derive questions from reading assignments:

1. **Personal review.** Students should ask questions in order to eliminate confusion left over from their reading assignments. Each question should have a page number along with it so that you and the class can refer directly to the source of the confusion. In many cases, students with the greatest comprehension problems will be the least likely to volunteer questions. Praise these reluctant students for asking questions, even if the questions seem superfluous or oblique.

2. **Class review.** Assign students to write a set number of questions based on a reading assignment. You might, for example, assign them to create three text-explicit questions, two experience-based questions, and one text-implicit question. During the following class you can have students take turns asking and answering questions, or you might create teams for a question-and-answer showdown. In any case, praise good questions a lot, especially if they are text implicit.

3. **Stump the teacher.** Students will enjoy creating questions to test you. Again, try to get them to generate legitimate questions at a variety of levels by modeling for them the kinds of questions you might ask one of your college professors. Students may at first be inclined to ask trivial, text-explicit questions, e.g., "How many words are there on page 144?" However, with guidance from you the students should begin to ask the kinds of questions that will stimulate class discussions.

Graphic Comprehension

Graphic comprehension, or *graphic literacy*, refers to the ability to interpret charts, maps, graphs, and other visual presentations that are commonly used to supplement the prose of textbooks, nonfiction trade books, and newspapers. These visual representations of concepts in nonverbal or semi-verbal form tend to be difficult for students, yet are ignored as specific instructional objectives in basals and other school texts.

Do not assume that your students will understand even simple pie graphs. If the purpose and design of graphs have never been explained to them, many students will automatically skip graphs, an unfortunate behavior, since graphs are designed to improve comprehension—not create interference.

As a prereading activity, you should introduce graphs as you would new and important vocabulary. Have students open their texts to the graphs. Then explain the purposes of the graphs to them and demonstrate correct procedures for their interpretations, for example, how to plot points on a complex quantitative graph. We also recommend that you try the *Graphic Information Lesson* (GIL) (Reinking, 1986).

Steps for Using the Graphic Information Lesson

1. In the *introductory* stage the teacher shows the students a graph and explains the mechanics of its use. Then the teacher asks text-explicit, text-implicit, and experience-based questions designed to enlighten the students as to the relationship between the graph and the rest of the text. Students can also learn to judge whether the graph is supplemental, redundant, or complementary to the text.

2. In the *synthesizing* stage the teacher presents teacher-made *pseudographs:* graphs that are related to current text material but may or may not be accurate or believable. The students have to be able to relate the new graph to what they have learned from the text in order to judge its validity. They must also

FIGURE 12.3

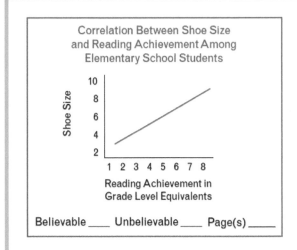

document their decision with a page number from the text. (See Figure 12.3 for examples of pseudographs.)

3. In the *application* stage students are asked to (a) develop their own pseudo-graphs to accompany the text, or (b) critique the author's use of graphic aids.

PREPARING FOR EXAMINATIONS

Test Preparation for High-Stakes Reading Assessments

There is, of course, nothing that will improve performance on state reading assessments more than improvements in your students' knowledge of American history, chemistry, English, health, and other subject areas. However, to prepare students for the format of the test, there are two general strategies you can use: mirror assessment and principles of testwiseness for multiple-choice tests.

Mirror Assessment

Mirror assessment refers to the practice of preparing classroom examinations in a format that reflects the format students will encounter on the state reading assessment. We are not suggesting that every test and quiz in every classroom should be a mirror assessment, but teachers should use some mirror assessments to guarantee the proper practice and mental readiness for the state reading assessment.

According to Figure 5.6, most of the state assessments have the following format: text passages followed by multiple-choice questions followed by a short, writing requirement (performance item). We recommend the following *mirror assessment strategy* (MAS) for subject area test development:

1. Test items should be *multiple choice* with four or five options depending on the format for your particular state. State reading assessments do not use true/false, matching, or other item formats. Items should include questions that reflect the reading standards for your state. For example, almost all states have a standard that requires students to distinguish fact from opinion, and questions reflecting this standard are common among the test items released by the various states. If your subject area lends itself easily to this standard, you may want to include such questions.

2. Include at least one performance item—*short essay*—that follows the rubric for your state.

3. The test should be *open book* so that students have an opportunity to search for information as they would in the state reading assessment.

4. The test should be *timed* so that students develop the ability to pace themselves.

5. Answers to multiple-choice items should be bubbled in on *standardized forms*.

Testwiseness

Testwiseness refers to a series of principles that can be applied to exams independent of subject area knowledge. To be testwise is to be able to (1) exploit the flaws in exams, and (2) apply logic, common sense, and good organization in test-taking situations. There is no substitute for being knowledgeable. However, testwiseness skills can help students to perform better on state reading assessments. The present discussion is limited to testwiseness in taking multiple-choice tests.

When you are preparing students for MAS tests or state assessments in reading, encourage them to do the following:

o Read all directions carefully. It is not unusual for students to get poor scores on exams simply because they fail to read and follow directions.

o Always guess if you do not know the answer. Never leave a multiple-choice question blank.

o Budget time so that you are certain to finish the test. Students sometimes spend too much time on one part of the test and then fail to finish another.

o Do not waste time on very difficult items. Take a guess and make a light mark in the test booklet—if this is permitted—and go back to the tough questions at the end of the exam. Do not leave answers blank along the way because it is easy to mark answers out of sequence on the answer sheet, which can result in devastating score reductions.

o Try to come up with the answer to the question before you look at the alternatives. By thinking of the answer first, you are less likely to be fooled by wrong choices that sound good.

o Look at all the answers before making a choice. Multiple-choice tests typically require you to select the *best* answer.

If the correct answer is not clear to you right away, try to eliminate obvious wrong or silly answers and then guess from among those that remain. For example,

The speed of sound is
  a. 3,700 feet per second
  b. 1,087 feet per second
  c. 0
  d. 186 miles per second

You should be able to eliminate answer C right away. That would give you a one third chance of guessing right instead of a one quarter chance.

Whenever two of the options are identical, both answers must be wrong. For example,

The universal donor is
  a. O–
  b. H_2O
  c. AB
  d. water

Whenever two of the options are opposites, one of them is always wrong and the other is often, but not always, right. For example,

A proton is a
  a. positively charged particle
  b. free atom
  c. negatively charged particle
  d. displaced neutron

Be aware that the answer to a question may appear in the stem of another question. For example, the answer to item I can be found in the stem of item II.

I. A *z*-score is a
   a. percentile equivalent
   b. concept in criterion referenced testing
   c. measure of standard error
   d. standardized score

II. Standardized scores such as *z*-scores and *t*-scores are based on
   a. standard deviations
   b. stanines
   c. chi squares
   d. grade equivalents

Other common testwiseness strategies for selecting the correct answer depend on flaws in test item design (e.g., when guessing, select an answer which is neither the first nor the last choice) and will not work with most state assessments because these are designed by professional test makers.

Test Preparation for Teacher-made Assessments

Evaluation tends to be an anxiety-producing situation for teachers and students. Anxiety can be reduced and learning maximized if teachers prepare students for specific examinations and if students learn how to study for and take tests intelligently (Flippo et al., 2015).

TEACHER STRATEGIES. Middle and secondary school students typically fear examinations and mistrust teachers' motivations. Many students develop a neurosis over tests because they have stereotyped teachers as a group of ogres who try to trick them with unfair questions or who purposely do not reveal what material a test will cover so that they can have the pleasure of doling out bad grades. To prove to your students that you are not a test-ogre, we suggest that you (a) give students precise information about what material an exam will cover, and (b) give students ungraded practice in taking the kinds of tests they will later have to negotiate for grades. We recommend the *Fake pop quiz* (FPQ).

Fake Pop Quiz. The FPQ is a quiz designed to reinforce rather than test recently introduced information. The purpose of the quiz format is to stimulate interest. Students are considerably more alert following, "Get your pencils ready; it's time for a fake pop quiz," than they are after hearing, "Get your pencils ready; it's time to do some review exercises." Tests are really a lot of fun once the anxiety over being externally evaluated has been neutralized. In addition, students appreciate test simulations because they know that the teacher is trying to prepare them for the true evaluation that inevitably follows.

FPQs can be brief interludes in daily lessons (placed on the board) or comprehensive reviews prepared on handouts. In either case, the quiz should be preceded by general directions, either verbal or written, along the lines of the following:

> *Today we are having a fake pop quiz on earth science vocabulary. Obviously, the score you get on this quiz will not affect your grade in the course, but it will give you some practice and an idea of how well prepared you are for a real test. When everyone has finished the quiz, you will score your own and get two points for each correct answer. Good luck! (The FPQ may be open- or closed-book depending on the teacher's objectives and the nature of the exercises.)*

Once students have finished the quiz, specific questions can serve as guides to classroom discussion. The FPQ offers a golden opportunity to focus on text implicit and experience-based kinds of questions.

STUDENT STRATEGIES. Students can acquire confidence in their own test-taking abilities if they learn how to prepare for exams and how to cope with them logically. The following information can help your students meet these objectives.

Test-taking skills refer to long-term study strategies as well as to strategies that students can use while taking exams, often referred to as testwiseness. You should be doing frequent reviews of text material, class notes, and other assigned materials. Remember, lots of short study sessions are better than a few giant cramming sessions. Students can be given the following advice for preparing for content area exams.

Tips to Students Preparing for Exams

When you hear about the test.

1. Find out as much as you can about the test itself.

2. Find out exactly when the test will be given.

3. Ask your teachers to discuss the kinds of questions that will be on the test, e.g., multiple choice, true–false, or essay.

4. If your teachers give essay tests, ask them what they look for in a good essay answer.

5. Ask your teachers to give you examples of test items and good test answers. Many will be willing to do this, but almost none will do it if you do not ask.

6. Try to guess which questions your teacher will ask.

The night before the test.

1. A light study session should be enough. Do not cram!

2. Make sure you have pencils, pens, paper, a watch, a calculator (if permissible), and any other materials you may need for the exam.

3. Get a good night's sleep.

The day of the test.

1. Eat a good breakfast.

2. Tell yourself that you will do well on the exam.

3. Make sure you have all the materials you need for the exam.

4. Do not cram right before the test. That is the worst thing you can do. Cramming can cause students to forget important information. It also causes needless test anxiety.

Tips to Students Taking Teacher-made Multiple-choice Tests

1. Read all directions carefully. It is not unusual for students to get poor grades on exams simply because they fail to read and follow directions.

2. Budget your time so that you are certain to finish the test. Students sometimes spend too much time on one part of the test and then fail to finish another. Nothing hurts a test grade worse than leaving items blank.

3. Do not waste time on very difficult items. Come back to them at the end of the exam.

4. Assume that each item has a correct answer and that you are smart enough to figure it out one way or another.

5. Always guess if you do not know the answer. Never leave a multiple-choice question blank.

6. Be alert for alternatives that do not match the stem grammatically. Teachers sometimes make this mistake. For example, the smallest unit of sound capable of making a meaning distinction in language is a
    a. morpheme
    b. allophone
    c. phoneme
    d. tagmeme

7. When alternatives seem equally good, select the one that is longest and seems to hold the most information. For example,

   In the United States, inferior intellectual development is most often caused by
   a. poor nutrition
   b. divorce
   c. the combined effects of heritability and environmental deprivation
   d. television

8. When all else fails, select an option that is not the first choice or the last. For example,

   The probability of rolling a 12 with two dice is
   a. 3 in 12
   b. 1 in 12
   c. 1 in 36
   d. 2 in 19

APPLICATION 12.3

Identify a course outside your area of expertise. Ask the instructor if you can take one of his or her multiple-choice exams to practice your test-taking strategies.

TRUE–FALSE TESTS. True–false questions are actually statements that students must decide are true or untrue. Major examinations are seldom composed entirely of true–false questions. However, many teachers like to include a section of these in their tests. True–false tests are feared by many students, who believe that teachers are trying to trick them into a lower grade. In reality most teachers are just interested in finding out how much the students know. Here are some testwise principles for true–false tests.

Tips to Students Taking True-False Tests

1. Read all directions carefully.

2. Budget your time so that you are certain to finish the test.

3. Always guess if you do not know the answer. Never leave a true–false question blank.

4. If any part of the statement is false, the correct answer for the item is "false." For example, the following item is false because the second part of the statement is false.

   The United States entered World War II after the Japanese attacked San Francisco.

5. Be alert for the words "never" and "always." These absolutes often indicate a wrong answer. For example, item A is false because it does occasionally rain in the desert. On the other hand, item B is true because the word "never" is qualified.
   a. It never rains in the Sahara Desert.
   b. It almost never rains in the Sahara Desert.

6. Long statements are somewhat more likely to be true than short statements.

   For example, A is true and B is false.
   a. In the poem "Ozymandias" Shelley uses irony to make a statement about the mortality of man.
   b. Ozymandias was a monk.

7. Assume that the teacher is asking straightforward questions. In other words, do not turn an obviously true statement into a false one by creating wild possible exceptions in your mind. For example, item A is true in spite of the fact that B, C, and D are, if you have a strong imagination, contradictions to the statement.
   a. Shoes are an important part of a businessperson's physical appearance.
   b. Business people do not wear horse shoes.
   c. Brake shoes are not part of a businessperson's appearance.
   d. If your pants are too long and cover your shoes, then the shoes will not make any difference.

ESSAY TESTS. Essay tests are among the most difficult exams because they require recall of information, good writing skills, and good organization. Here are some test-wise principles for essay tests, followed by an essay test preparation strategy.

Tips to Students Taking Essay Tests

1. Read all directions carefully. Essay tests often use in their directions key words that you must clearly understand. Here are some of the key words and their meanings:

Key Word	Meaning
Enumerate	to name one at a time
Illustrate	to explain with examples

Trace	to tell the history or development of something from the earliest to the most recent time
Compare	to point out similarities and differences
Contrast	to point out differences
Summarize	to give a brief version of the most important points
Evaluate	to judge the merit of
Justify	to give reasons for
Critique	to summarize and evaluate

Two answers (A and B) are given below for the same essay question. Answer B is a better answer because the writer followed directions and compared (noted similarities and differences) the topics under discussion.

Directions: Compare saccadic and pursuit eye movements.

Answer A: There are two basic kinds of eye movements: saccadic and pursuit. Saccadic movements are used when you go from object to object when the objects are at rest. Pursuit movements follow a moving target. During the act of reading saccadic movements allow the reader to stop on a line of print and pick up information. The word "saccade" means little jerk.

Answer B: There are two basic kinds of eye movements: saccadic and pursuit. They are the same in the sense that both of them are used to locate visual information. However, they are physically different. Saccadic movements are jumps while the pursuit movement is smooth. Another difference is that saccadic movements let the eyes go from one still object to another while pursuit movement follows a moving target.

2. Budget your time so that you are certain to finish the test. Check to see how much each essay question is worth. Spend the most time on the questions that are worth the most points.

3. Always give some kind of an answer, even if you do not understand the question.

4. Unless the directions say otherwise, never give a minimal answer. Teachers will expect you to elaborate and give full explanations on an essay. For the essay question below, responses A, B, and C technically answer the question, but only C meets the spirit of the essay exam by giving an explanation.

Question: Do you believe that American troops should fight in foreign wars?

Answer A: No.

Answer B: No. I do not think that Americans should fight in foreign wars.

Answer C: No. I think war is immoral. We should not fight unless we are attacked. Besides, when we send troops to other countries, it makes us look like fascist-capitalistic dogs.

5. Use the technical language of the course when writing an essay. Remember, the teacher wants to find out how much you know. And that includes your knowledge of the appropriate vocabulary. Compare answers A and B for the essay question below. B is a better answer because it uses more technical language.

   Question: Summarize the process of conception and the initial stage of prenatal development.

   Answer A: The male cell goes up to the egg and digs its way inside. Once this happens, the genetic material from the man and the woman mix to form the genetic pattern for the baby. After this happens, the cell begins to split up again and again as the fertilized egg works its way down to the uterus where it will attach itself to the woman's body.

   Answer B: The male sperm cell digs its way into the ovum, and the egg is fertilized. Once this happens, the chromosomes from the sperm cell and the chromosomes from the ovum mix to form the genetic pattern for the baby. After this happens, the fertilized ovum begins to reproduce itself through a process called mitosis. As this process continues, the fertilized egg, now called a zygote, works its way down the fallopian tube to the uterus where it will attach itself to the wall of the uterus.

6. Pay attention to capitalization, punctuation, spelling, grammar, and neatness. Proof for these things as you reread your answers. Remember, the grading of essays is largely subjective. A careless presentation of your answer can only reduce your grade.

PORPE: An Essay Writing Strategy

PORPE
- Predicting
- Organizing
- Rehearsing
- Practicing
- Evaluating

In addition to general student strategies for essay preparation, Simpson (2007) developed and validated a powerful integrated study strategy under the acronym *PORPE* which stands for (a) *p*redict; (b) *o*rganize; (c) *r*ehearse; (d) *p*ractice; and, (e) *e*valuate. PORPE involves students in the following sequence of activities:

1. *Predicting* potential essay questions;

2. *Organizing* key ideas using their own words;

3. *Rehearsing* the key ideas;

4. *Practicing* the recall of the key ideas in a self-assigned writing task that requires analytical thinking, and

5. *Evaluating* the completeness, accuracy, and appropriateness of the essay in terms of the self-predicted essay question.

Unlike many sink-or-swim essay exam experiences students have, PORPE does not assume that students readily grasp the preparatory and analytical steps involved in writing a strong essay question response. Rather, it offers a step-by-step process to guide students' independent studying for an essay test. Each of the five steps is elaborated in the following section along with a student-predicted essay question from physical education and a student's response.

STEP ONE: PREDICT. Once students have finished a reading assignment in a unit or lesson where an essay test will be given, have them create potential essay questions, particularly those eliciting higher-order thinking through analysis, comparison, and critique. Simpson cautions that you should not assume students grasp the language of essay questions. Rather, she recommends conducting a short session on the language of essay questions, including such common requests as explain, criticize, compare, and contrast. In addition, she recommends teacher modeling of the question prediction step. Following this teacher-directed assistance, ask students to create their own predicted essay questions and share these in small groups.

STEP TWO: ORGANIZE. In preparation for the predicted essay question, students should outline, map, or use a graphic organizer to organize the information they plan to use in their written response. Initial teacher modeling and small-group sharing of outlines or graphic organizers are also helpful in this step.

STEP THREE: REHEARSE. The idea in this step is to develop a long-term memory for the information in the outline or graphic organizer that needs to be easily retrieved at the time of essay question response. Simpson recommends self-testing by reciting the overall organizational structure of the outline or graphic organizer and writing it out from memory.

STEP FOUR: PRACTICE. This is a key step as students are asked to write the answer to their predicted essay question from recall. However, prior to actually writing, they should sketch the outline or graphic organizer of their rehearsed response to guide the structure and content of their essays.

STEP FIVE: EVALUATE. An important final step involves having students evaluate their practice essay answers. You may wish to provide students with a checklist that reiterates the criteria for a good essay response. Simpson recommends including a checklist like the one in Figure 12.4.

FIGURE 12.4   *PORPE Checklist*

	BELOW AVERAGE	AVERAGE	ABOVE AVERAGE
1. The writer answered the question directly.	1	2	3
2. There was an introductory sentence that restated the essay question or took a position on the question.	1	2	3
3. The essay was organized with major points or ideas that were made obvious to the reader.	1	2	3
4. The essay had relevant details or examples to prove and clarify each point.	1	2	3
5. The writer used transitions to cue the reader.	1	2	3
6. The writer had knowledge of the content and made sense.	1	2	3

In the example that follows, Ardis, a student in physical education, carried out the various steps of PORPE to answer her predicted essay question in preparation for a test. The test was on the topic, Prosocial Skills for Human Movement, and the teacher indicated that there would be a series of short essay questions.

STEP ONE: PREDICT. Ardis predicted that the teacher would ask her to explain how games reflect culture, based on a subheading in the text chapter on Multicultural Considerations in Physical Education.

STEP TWO: ORGANIZE. Next, Ardis developed a graphic organizer (see Step Three) showing how games reflect culture based on the information in this section of the text.

STEP THREE: REHEARSE. Ardis then studied, recited, and tested herself on her memory for these key ideas in preparation for writing an essay response.

STEP FOUR: PRACTICE. In this most difficult step, Ardis composes a practice answer to her essay question by using the graphic organizer she created as a guide for writing her response.

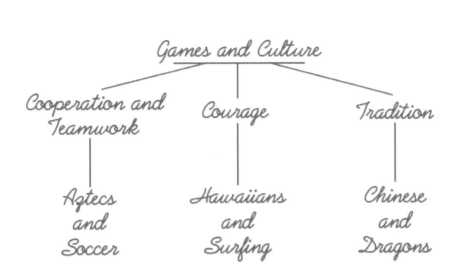

Games and Culture

Cooperation and Teamwork — *Courage* — *Tradition*

Aztecs and Soccer — *Hawaiians and Surfing* — *Chinese and Dragons*

Ardis'S Practice Essay

Games reflect culture because they represent the values of a cultural group. For example, cooperation and teamwork are highly valued by Native American Indians. The game of soccer we play in P. E. that needs careful teamwork was played by the ancient Aztecs in Mexico. Another example is the Hawaiian value of courage or "koa." The ancient Hawaiian royalty fearlessly surfed large waves on heavy koa boards. They tried to ride with a smooth casual style that is now a crucial skill in modern longboarding. And the Chinese value tradition. Their New Year's celebrations maintain the ancient traditions by featuring the dragon, which symbolizes prosperity, authority, and royalty. Each of these games, soccer, surfing, and the folk dance of the Chinese dragon, display the cultural values of their respective cultural groups.

STEP FIVE: EVALUATE. Applying the checklist to Ardis's essay response, she has clearly written a very coherent and carefully planned answer.

	BELOW AVERAGE	AVERAGE	ABOVE AVERAGE
1. The writer answered the question directly.	1	2	③
2. There was an introductory sentence that restated the essay question or took a position on the question.	1	2	③
3. The essay was organized with major points or ideas that were made obvious to the reader.	1	②	3
4. The essay had relevant details or examples to prove and clarify each point.	1	2	③
5. The writer used transitions to cue the reader.	1	②	3
6. The writer had knowledge of the content and made sense.	1	2	③

It is not surprising that Ardis's essay meets each of these criteria. She applied the steps involved in PORPE and was fully prepared for the essay question. Indeed, Simpson points out that students using this strategy outpace students using a more traditional read and answer chapter questions approach. Although PORPE takes time to use with students, it develops a studying approach that serves students well as they advance into more difficult text material in college. Moreover, the movement away from multiple-choice assessment and the increasing interest in essay questions that tap critical thinking make PORPE an ideal strategy to share with your students.

Go to the website and apply the PORPE strategy to the lecture entitled Our Crazy Spelling System and How It Got to Be This Way.

NOW go back to the studying vignette at the beginning of the chapter. React to the lesson as you did before. Compare your responses with those you made before you read the chapter.

MINI PROJECTS

1. Draw an "unbelievable" pseudograph suitable for your content area. Describe the pseudograph and explain how you might use it with a class of students.

2. Try the VSPP notetaking procedure for a lecture in a class you are presently attending. Prepare a written evaluation of the method.

3. Interview a small group of college students to determine the test-taking strategies they use. List the different strategies they report and then provide a written evaluation indicating the quality of their metacognitive skills in test-taking.

4. Develop and administer a mirror assessment for your content area. The assessment should be consistent with evaluation rubrics for reading assessments in your state and should include all of the principles in the MAS.

WEBSITES

o Kahoot.com
This free application allows you to create questions to quiz your students in a game-based platform. In addition, students can create their own quizzes for partner learning and keeping a tally of their scores. This is ideal as a review tool.

o www.jeopardyrocks
This site offers a platform for creating your own online review categories and questions in your content area.

WEBSITE ACTIVITY

Go to the website for Chapter 5 activities.

Glossary

Academic Vocabulary: academic vocabulary includes the array of general and technical terms students encounter in the disciplines.

Academic Word List: this list of 570 words encompasses those general words students encounter across the disciplines (e.g. "principle").

Accommodation: the process of adjusting one's existing cognitive structure to accept new information.

Acronym: a word that is formed by combining the initial letters or segments of a series of words.

Adolescent Literacy: moving literacy beyond the notion of school and textbook-based definitions of literacy to one which acknowledges not only that there are multiple literacies and multiple texts but also that texts transcend the adult-sanctioned notions of text forms to include CD-ROM, the Internet, popular music, television, magazines, etc.

Aiming Toward Content: teaching that focuses on content acquisition with no consideration for how to acquire that information.

Analogical Guide: a form of study guide in which students use familiar concepts to learn and retain new information.

Annual Yearly Progress: the improvements a school must make each year in state reading and mathematics test scores, graduation rates, and other measures of performance as defined by *No Child Left Behind.*

Anticipation Guide: a prereading strategy that activates students' ideas about a topic by asking them to react to a series of guide statements related to that topic.

App: an abbreviation for application but with specific reference to software programs for hand-held communication technologies.

Argumentative writing: the written development of a cogent argument on a content area topic.

Assimilation: the process whereby new information is simply added to one's existing cognitive structure.

Attitudes: those feelings that cause a reader to approach or avoid a reading situation.

Biographies: reading and writing about an important figure in any content area.

Biopoem: a creative poetry framework for writing about virtually any major figure or topic in the content areas.

Blog: an online weblog that can be circulated but not edited by anyone other than the original blog author unless the author uses collaborative software like Googledocs and others.

Body Biographies: a multimedia interpretation of a character in a novel or short story or a major figure in any content area.

Book Clubs: small groups of students meeting to discuss a common reading.

Bound Morpheme: a meaningful language unit that occurs only as an attachment to words or other morphemes, e.g., tele-.

Byte: the amount of space necessary to store one character such as a number or letter.

Capacity Limitation: refers to the theory that human beings are capable of attending consciously to only one task at a time.

Cause-Effect: a pattern of text organization linking reasons with results.

CD-ROM: computer hardware that reads data from a laser disk and is capable of storing large amounts of data.

Censorship: the indirect supervision of morality by regulating films, books, magazines, music, and other information to which people may have access.

Central Questions: a prereading strategy that places students in a problem-solving role.

Chunking: a type of mental organization in which related bits of information are processed as a single unit.

Close reading: making connections across multiple texts through careful, thoughtful interpretive reading.

Clues and Questions: vocabulary review procedure that centers on student-generated questions and answers.

Cognitive Structure: the interrelated network of our experiences, organized in memory through a system of categories.

Common Core Standards: these standards aim to specify content students should acquire, as well as contemporary reading tasks involving integrating ideas across multiple texts in the content areas.

Comparison-Contrast: a pattern of text organization that demonstrates likenesses and differences between things or ideas.

Composing: the process of generating and shaping ideas before writing begins and as the actual writing unfolds.

Connotation: subtle shades of meaning that define a word; there can also be specific grammatical and semantic conditions that delimit a word's appropriate usage.

Content Area Literacy: the level of reading and writing still necessary to read, comprehend, and react to appropriate instructional materials in a given content area.

Content Reading Inventory: a teacher-made and text-based test designed to assess students' ability to effectively read and learn from the text.

Context Clues: a decoding technique that consists of utilizing surrounding words and their meaning to identify unfamiliar words.

Contextual: refers to the connotative meaning of words in context.

Contextual Redefinition: a vocabulary strategy in which the teacher places new vocabulary in selfdefining or high-utility contexts.

Creativity: the production of something that is novel and engaging.

Criterion: a relative standard, or score, that implies adequate achievement without reference to the performance of others.

Criterion-Referenced Test: a test of specific content, measuring individual performances without comparison to the entire group.

Critical Literacy: asks readers to carefully examine power relations in texts in terms of social justice dimensions and is an especially powerful way to consider novels as social constructions that position characters, sometimes in stereotypical ways, to be deconstructed and critiqued.

Critical Literacy Discussion: a strategy that asks students to consider power relations in a novel with a particular focus on which characters have a voice and how race, class, and gender are constructed.

Critical Media Literacy: lesson designed to use the popular media as a forum for discussion and critique.

Cubing: writing strategy that allows students to consider the multiple dimensions of topics; students examine topics by describing, comparing, associating, analyzing, applying, and arguing.

Culturally sustaining pedagogy: engaging students in critical research around cultural issues (e.g., linking contemporary hip-hop to poetry).

Culture: a collection of values, beliefs, and standards which influences how students think, feel, and behave in various social settings.

Cyberbullying: online messages that threaten or use profane language to call out a person or persons (note that these messages do not enjoy First Amendment Rights).

Cybrary: a blend of the words cyber and library, referring to a collection of websites accessible from a single site and dedicated to a specific subject area.

Debriefing: feedback by students in the form of self-reports, introspection, and hindsight.

Decoding: any process whereby a coded message is converted back into thought.

Definitional: refers to the denotative meaning of words.

Denotation: the broad meanings of words.

Depth of Processing: a memory principle that asserts that the likelihood of long-term retention and recall is greater when a mental activity involves close semantic analysis and cognitive attention.

Developmental Bilingual Education: similar to transitional bilingual education without a specified phase-out of the native language.

Diagnostic Test: a test employed to determine specific skill strengths and weaknesses of students.

Dialogue Journals: journals in which the teacher maintains an ongoing written dialogue with students.

Digital media: nonlinear, fluid visual embellishments aimed at meaning making.

Dinner Party: a strategy based on the idea that you could invite characters from a young adult novel or any other form of text to your home for dinner and conversation.

Directed Reading-Thinking Activity: a selfquestioning process that encourages students to predict oncoming information in text and sets purposes for reading that are personally interesting.

Disciplinary literacy: understanding the various discourse communities within disciplines like history, the sciences, mathematics, and other disciplines.

Distributed Practice: rehearsals separated by breaks.

Diversity: the varied student characteristics of language, culture, and learning differences.

DVD: a Digital Video Disk; a device capable of storing 6 gigabytes of electronic data.

Electronic Books: complete works of fiction and nonfiction that have been digitized for reading on computer or on portable eBook readers.

Embedded Questions: a series of teacher-developed questions inserted in a text at key points that are crucial to metacognitive awareness and understanding the entire passage.

Encoding: any process whereby thought or meaning is converted into a code.

English as additional language: providing extra support for students learning both English as an additional language and content area academic vocabulary.

English as a Second Language: structured lessons in English while maintaining facility in the native language.

Etymology: study of the history of words and their origins.

Experience-Based: thinking that requires drawing an inference that is not derivable from the text, but rather from one's existing schemata; i.e., reading beyond the lines.

Expressive Vocabulary: words that a person can use properly when speaking or writing.

Extension Activities: pencil and paper exercises designed to reinforce and expand the schemata of newly acquired content area vocabulary.

External Reference: any source of information outside the passage being read.

External Storage: in notetaking, a written substitute for memory.

Facebook: an Internet-based social networking service.

Fake Pop Quiz: a quiz designed to reinforce, rather than test, recently introduced information.

Fanfiction: original works of fiction based on popular media, including television, movies, books, music, and video games.

Feature Analysis: an instructional strategy in which sets of new concepts or vocabulary are defined and discriminated by identifying the unique characteristics of each member of the set.

FLIP: friendliness, language, interest, prior knowledge; a technique for helping students preview a reading assignment.

Focused Question Card Strategy: use of targeted questions on note cards to assist students in revising their writing.

Formal Tests: standardized, norm-referenced tests used to monitor student progress.

Free Morpheme: a morpheme that can stand by itself as a word, e.g., boy.

General Vocabulary: words that are not specifically associated with any one teaching area and are assimilated into existing schemata.

Global Literature: a growing array of young adult novels that chronicle life in the Middle East and other important international regions.

Glossary: an alphabetized list of technical words and their definitions used in a textbook or other work.

Goldfish bowl: a discussion strategy using concentric circles where the inner circle shares ideas on a topic (e.g., racism) and an outer circle of students observes, takes notes, and comments.

Graphic Information Lesson: strategy designed to teach students how to interpret graphs.

Graphic Literacy: ability to interpret graphs and other visual presentations in text.

Graphic Organizer: a visual aid that defines hierarchical relationships among concepts and that lends itself to the teaching of technical vocabulary.

Group Test: a test administered in a group situation.

Guided Listening Procedure: a comprehension strategy employed on a listening level; the purpose is to enhance recall and organization of text information as well as to promote student self-inquiry.

Guided Writing Procedure: an integrated lesson approach that serves as an alternative to the guided reading procedure by capitalizing on writing as a means to commit information to long-term memory.

Hypermedia: hypertext with sounds and pictures.

Hypertext: large and easily programmed linked visual and text databases.

Immersion Bilingual Education: all instruction is in the second language.

Index: an alphabetized list of important terms and topics and the page numbers on which they occur in the text.

Individualization: incorporating the gamut of grouping procedures—whole group, small group, and individual—within the confines of a well-developed instructional plan utilizing the textbook and with the teacher acting as facilitator of learning.

Individual Test: a test that may be administered on only an individual basis.

Informal Tests: teacher-made or published tests that employ a criterion to monitor student progress.

Information Index: a device used to structure the information search by keying students into the location of important concepts.

Inquiry Charts: strategy for nurturing critical reading in content classrooms by having students examine multiple sources of information and charting their findings.

Integrated Thematic Units: teams of teachers from various subject areas collaborate to create units and lessons with a central theme.

Interests: what students like to read about.

Internet: a highly complex, interlinked system of computers forming a worldwide communication network.

Internet Workshop: a set of teacher-directed activities designed to show students how to navigate the Internet and utilize its resources.

Intertextuality: meanings based on reading a particular text and making connections to other texts, including media-based and digital texts.

I-Search Paper: an alternative to the traditional research paper such that students investigate topics of their choosing by interviewing experts, visiting places, and telling the story of their search in a written report.

Journal Writing: writing to explore ideas freely without worrying unduly about mechanics.

Jump Drive: a small device for storing and transferring files and data, sometimes called a flash drive.

Knowledge Rating: strategy for establishing what students already know about a topic by having them rate how well they know the vocabulary words.

K-W-L: a three-step integrated strategy designed to encourage active reading of expository text; K = what we know before reading, W = what we want to find out during reading, L = what we learned after reading.

Learning: a change that occurs in an organism at a particular time as a function of experience.

Lesson Planning: teacher planning that includes learning objectives, set induction, content outline, activities, lesson closure, resources and materials, evaluation, and student assignments.

Levels of Text Understanding: the differing levels of thinking involved in reading text material; e.g., text explicit, text implicit, experience-based.

Lexiles: these reader and text scores are based on an indication of material that a student can read that is predicated on a measure of word frequency and sentence length. Both materials and standardized tests now include Lexile scores (e.g., L800).

Library Power: strategies designed to expand the reading horizons of children by introducing them to the wealth of books in the school library.

Listen-Read-Discuss: an integrated strategy involving students in a guided lecture, independent reading, and summary discussion to ensure in-depth comprehension.

Listening Guide: used to guide listening to an oral presentation; a skeletal outline of the important concepts arranged in the order and relationship in which they occur to aid students as they listen and fill in the appropriate information.

Literate: being able to read and write.

Literature Circles: a collaborative approach to instruction that integrates the reading of a book with discussion of themes and background information related to it.

Literature Response Journals: journals where students reflect and write their thoughts so they can share their views with the teacher, peers, or parents.

Long-Term Memory: an organized store of information based on a person's cumulative experiences.

Mean: the arithmetic average of a set of numbers.

Metacognition: awareness of one's own mental processes.

Metadiscourse: text intrusions in which the author talks directly to the reader about the information in the text.

Mirror Assessment: a test preparation technique in which classroom exams are designed in a format that is as close as possible to a specific standardized reading assessment.

Miscues: observed responses to printed text that do not conform exactly to the print and may preserve (e.g., auto for car) or disrupt meaning (e.g., cat for car).

Mnemonic: a strategy for remembering one thing by associating it with something else.

Mobile learning: learning across multiple contexts using personal devices (e.g., cell phones).

Modeling: a report by an individual of the mental operations involved in his or her comprehension process to illustrate its logical steps to others.

Morpheme: the smallest unit of language that has an associated meaning.

Morphemic Analysis: the analysis of affixes and roots to decode unknown words.

Multicultural Literature: literature by and about people who represent groups often on the fringes of the socio-political mainstream.

Multigenre Writing: imaginative writing using a variety of genres, including ad writing, comic strips, and editorials.

Multimedia: refers to technological combinations of audio, video, text, graphics, and animation.

Multimodal text sets: collections of print and nonprint texts related to a central theme or topic.

Multiple Literacies: the expansion of the meaning of the word *literacy* to include multimedia, the Internet, and other electronic or even non-text mediums for exchanging information.

Multiple Text Inquiry Discussion: students read across various sources to synthesize and discuss a topic.

Multiple Texts: teaching in the content areas using various texts, including traditional textbooks, magazines, newspaper articles, young adult novels, video, and a host of other multimedia digital texts available from the Internet and other sources, whose aim is to guide students toward the independent use on multiple sources on topics in science, math, English, social studies, and other subject area domains.

MySpace: an Internet-based social networking service.

NetGeners: this term refers to the generation growing up with digital tools that are second nature to them (i.e., native users of technology).

New Literacies: newer forms of texts, including Internet-based texts, instant messaging (IMing), blogging, e-zines, and various websites where visual elements, in addition to print elements, carry meaning.

No Child Left Behind: the 2002 revision of the Elementary and Secondary Education Act (ESEA) of 1965.

Norm-Referenced: an assessment in which the performance of an individual is defined relative to the performances of a group of individuals who have taken the same test.

Normal Curve: a symmetrical distribution of scores.

Norms: a set of scores against which the test performance of others may be compared.

Novel Journal: having students write in their journals about their reactions to events occurring in the novels they are reading.

Objectives: the specific learning expectations a teacher plans for a lesson, including students' performance, products, learning conditions, and criteria for successful performance.

Online literature circles: using a blog application to discuss a work of literature (e.g., Edmodo, Word Press, and others).

Options Guide: a form of study guide in which students predict, discuss, and evaluate options available to key political and historical figures.

Organization: the arrangements of parts of a whole in such a manner that the parts are related to each other.

Parallel Notetaking: listening and taking notes at the same time.

Passage Dependent: in an assessment of reading, it refers to a test question that can be answered only if the text has been read with comprehension.

Passage Independent: in an assessment of reading, it refers to a test question that can be answered without reference to the text.

Passive Failure: a term describing students who are resigned to fail and believe they do not have the ability to succeed in their learning.

PDA: refers to Personal Digital Assistants that now combine the features of cell phones and the Internet to offer remote connectivity.

Percentile Rank: the position of a score in relation to the entire group of scores.

Performance Items: in reading assessments, this refers to test items that require written responses.

Personal Glossary: a strategy to aid students' longterm memory of words that are novel or with which they have had difficulty.

Petaflop: a measure of computer processing speed equal to 1,000 trillion (1,000,000,000,000,000) calculations per second.

Phony Document: a critical reading strategy where students read, research, and authenticate information in a letter or other document.

PLAE: guidance strategy for studying that consists of preplanning, listing, activating, and evaluating.

Podcasts: these audio (and sometimes video) commentaries can involve young adult novel critiques created with various software programs (e.g., Garageband) and archived for an audience of listeners (e.g., on iTunes).

Polar Opposites: a teaching strategy using contrasting words to critique a reading selection.

PORPE: essay writing study strategy consisting of predicting, organizing, rehearsing, practicing, and evaluating.

Port folios: systematic collections of students' work in the classroom used for ongoing diagnosis of their abilities.

Possible Sentences: a vocabulary teaching strategy in which students use new vocabulary to create sentences for verification when reading.

Prediction Guide: a means of assessing students' prior knowledge about a topic through a series of factbased statements that students determine are true or false before reading.

Presenting Content and Processes Concurrently: teaching that provides direct instruction in the processes necessary to acquire content as well as in what content is to be acquired.

Presenting Isolated Skills: teaching that consists of the direct teaching of skills with no consideration for content.

Prior Knowledge: an individual's background experience.

Problem-Solution: a pattern of text organization exemplified by an interaction of a problem and a potential answer to that problem.

Proficiency: an arbitrarily established level of skill in reading or mathematics sufficient to meet societal demands as defined by parents, a school district, the state, or the federal government.

Pseudographs: studentor teacher-made graphs that may not be an accurate representation of text material.

Qualitative Factors of Readability: nonmeasurable variables of text selection that include prior knowledge, text organization, and interest, among others.

Quantitative Factors of Readability: language variables of word length and sentence length as counted and measured in readability estimates.

Questioning the Author: designed to help struggling readers to approach segmented text passages with an active mind and critical stance; the use of embedded questions in the form of queries helps guide readers' thinking.

Quick Writes: a brief prereading or postreading written student response to a prompt question about a content area topic.

RADAR: an acronym for revising writing that stands for replace, add, delete, and reorder items in an essay.

Raw Score: the number of items answered correctly on a test.

Raygor Readability Estimate: a readability formula based on word and sentence length; noted for ease of administration and reduced potential for error.

Reaction Guide: a postreading strategy used to stimulate review of a selection by asking students to react to a series of guide statements related to the selection.

Readability: a measure of the extent to which a reader finds a given text comprehensible.

Readability Formulas: mathematically derived indices of text difficulty based on an analysis of linguistic variables, the two most common being word length and sentence length.

Readers Theater: students read aloud in a dramatic fashion to present key text concepts.

Readiness Principle: refers to the mental state in which an individual is prepared to derive maximum meaning from a learning situation with a minimum of frustration.

Reading Autobiography: a personalized account of early, middle, and recent reading experiences.

Reading Preferences: the material students might like to read.

Receptive Vocabulary: words that can be read and comprehended in print or heard and understood in spoken context.

Rehearsal: the repeating of information for the purpose of retaining the information in memory.

Reliability: the degree to which a test gives consistent results when administered repeatedly.

ReQuest: a reciprocal questioning procedure that helps students adopt an active, questioning approach to text reading.

Response Bias: writing down what one believes an examiner wants rather than what the examinee really believes.

Response Mode: the type of response required by students' assigned questions; e.g., recall vs. recognition.

Retrieval practice: a close reading strategy that emphasizes thinking aloud about key concepts in a content area text.

ReWrite: a music strategy involving the writing of music verses about content area concepts.

Rubric: a concrete description of the qualities and criteria expected in a particular piece of writing; usually assigns numeric values to a description of a writing task, ranging from a high-quality piece of writing and its related dimensions to a low-quality piece of writing.

Scaffolded Reading Experience: comprehensive lesson framework designed to provide students with guidance and support with difficult text.

Scaffolding: refers to the degree of support and guidance a teacher needs to provide to help students engage text that would be too difficult, left to their own devices.

Schema Theory: describes the process by which we add to (assimilate) or adjust (accommodate) our existing cognitive structure in the face of new or discordant information.

Schemata: a category system of the mind containing information about the surrounding environment; the plural of schema.

Scope of Information Search: the number of concepts for which students are held responsible in a given reading assignment.

Second Life: an extensive virtual world owned by Linden Lab.

Self-Concept: how one views oneself.

Semantic Map: a diagram that groups related concepts.

Short-Term Memory: the "working memory" that holds incoming information temporarily until a decision is made to include this information in long-term memory.

Signal Words: the key words that cue a particular pattern of text organization.

Slicing: simplifying the complexity of learning tasks by reexamining those that are required and recasting them to ease the demands placed on students.

Sociolinguistics: the study of language in a cultural context.

Software: refers to applications that run on computers, including word processing applications, games, encyclopedias, and so on.

Sourcing: carefully judging the authenticity of information in a text particularly in history.

Spaced Notetaking: taking notes during intervals of silence between segments of a lecture.

Spam: originally an acronym standing for *Selected Parts All Meat*, it now refers to Internet junk mail.

Standard Deviation: a measure of dispersion or variability of a group of scores.

Standard Error of Measurement: the variation, or built-in error, in standardized test scores.

Standardized Scores: general term for describing a variety of transformed raw scores that can be compared across other individuals.

Standardized Test: a formal test instrument utilizing norms as a basis for student comparison of achievement.

Standards: a means of delineating what students should know and should be able to do as a result of what they learn in school, with their aim being to make sure all students develop the skills necessary for success in school and in their future careers in the workplace.

Stanines: standardized score with a mean of five and a standard deviation of two.

Strategy: the planned means to an end.

Student-Generated Questions: questions students derive on their own from their reading assignments.

Study Guide: a strategy that focuses students' attention on the major ideas of a selection at three levels of comprehension.

Study Strategies: the specific strategies that focus on locating, retaining, and recalling information.

Survey Test: usually a standardized test that measures global areas of achievement, such as vocabulary or comprehension.

Survey the Text: a prereading strategy that involves some form of preliminary look at a reading selection before more intensive reading is undertaken.

Sustained Silent Reading: a systematic program that establishes regular reading times for students to practice their reading skills on pleasurable and selfselected content-related materials.

Talking Drawings: a prereading and postreading strategy that helps students visualize their knowledge of a topic.

Technical Vocabulary: words uniquely related to particular academic disciplines; the words are accommodated by modifying old schemata or creating new schemata.

Test Ceiling: the upper limit placed on an individual's performance at a particular grade level on a standardized test.

Test Floor: the lower limit placed on an individual's performance at a particular grade level on a standardized test.

Testwiseness: a series of principles that can be applied to exams independently of subject area knowledge.

Text Appetizer: a teacher-devised introductory passage that provides a detailed framework for comprehending a reading selection.

Text Explicit: thinking that requires only getting facts as literally stated by an author; i.e., reading the lines.

Text Implicit: thinking that requires an inference from the text to derive an answer to a question; i.e., reading between the lines.

Text Structure: the various organizational patterns writers and readers use to encode and decode thoughts.

Textbook Adaptations: study guides, graphic organizers, and other guide material a teacher provides to aid student learning of the content material.

Textbook Aids: elements included in a textbook to help students with new vocabulary, e.g., a glossary.

The Imposter: critical reading strategy that challenges students to read mathematics and science passages where intentional errors have been embedded in the material.

Thematic Unit: a series of lessons developed around a theme.

Think-Aloud: a teacher modeling strategy whereby one's thoughts about how a text is comprehended are verbalized for students.

Time Order: a pattern of text organization exemplifying a sequential relationship between ideas or events over the passage of time.

TOAST: a strategy for independently studying vocabulary using the acronym derived from the procedural steps—test, organize, anchor, say, and test.

Tradebooks: literature that is found in bookstores.

Transcribing: refers to the mechanics of writing, including spelling, punctuation, capitalization, handwriting, formatting, and neatness.

Transitional Bilingual Education: content area instruction in a native language while a student receives second language instruction for a three-year period with the native language slowly phased out.

Transnationalism: written language practices that move beyond national borders via the Internet where students may communicate with family members in distant countries.

Twitter: an Internet-based social networking and microblogging service.

Two-Way Bilingual Education: both native English and non-native English speakers learn each other's language while they do the bulk of their content learning in the strong, native language.

Unit Blueprint: a unit planning structure that includes the unit topic, goals and objectives, content outline, learning activities, resources and materials, and evaluation plan.

Unit of Instruction: a related series of lessons lasting from 1 to 6 weeks.

Unit Plan: a plan of instruction in which students explore and respond to a selected topic through their interaction with a variety of integrated activities designed to enhance their knowledge and attitude.

Validity: the degree of accuracy with which a test measures what it is intended to measure.

Verbal and Visual Word Association Strategy: a mnemonic strategy in which students associate a word they are trying to learn with personal examples or a concrete drawing.

Verbatim Split Page Procedure: a comprehensive method of taking notes during lectures.

Virtual Reality: an artificially created, electronic environment that extends the sensory abilities of the user and creates the illusion of intimate interaction with the environment.

Virtual World: a computer-generated, threedimensional environment in which participants interact with each other in the form of avatars.

Vocabulary: a corpus of many thousands of words and their associated meanings.

Vocabulary Self-Collection Strategy: a vocabulary acquisition technique designed to teach students how to select the most important vocabulary from reading assignments.

WebQuest: an inquiry-oriented activity in which some or all of the information acquired from the activity comes directly from the student's interaction with the Internet.

Wiki: software that supports an open editing environment and named after the Hawaiian word for fast.

Word: a pattern of auditory or visual symbols that represent schemata, or concepts.

Word Analogies: exercises requiring students to draw inferences and expose subtle word associations.

Word Map: a visual representation of a definition.

World Wide Web: an extensive collection of text and multimedia documents interlinked and accessible through the Internet.

Writing Roulette: a strategy in which students create a simple story containing some of the technical vocabulary they are learning.

Young Adult Literature: selections of interest to readers ages 12 to 20.

Bibliography

CHAPTER 1, CONTENT AREA LITERACY: DEVELOPING CONTEMPORARY LEARNERS

Recommended Readings

Adolescent literacy: A position statement of the International Literacy Association (2012). Newark, DE: International Literacy Association.

This statement makes clear the key ingredients for promoting contemporary literacy practices in the content areas. The position statement is very applicable to professional development initiatives in the schools.

Alvermann, D. E., & Mojje, E. B. (2013). Adolescent literacy instruction and the discourse of "Every teacher a teacher of reading." In D. E. Alvermann, N. J. Unrau, & R. B. Ruddell (Eds.), *Theoretical models and processes of reading* (6th ed., pp. 1072–1103). Newark, DE: International Reading Association.

The authors argue for a more nuanced model of what it means to actualize teaching practices in particular content area disciplines and the need to move away from blanket, "one size fits all" generic strategies applied across disciplines.

Bean, T. W. (2016). Digital media and cosmopolitan critical literacy: Research and practice. In B. Guzzetti & M. Lesley (Eds.), *Handbook of research on the societal impact of digital media* (pp. 46–68). Hershey, PA: IGI Global.

This chapter examines global youth communication across nation-state boundaries via the Internet with a particular look at how we can develop an informed and critical citizenry.

References

Banks, J. A. (2015). *Cultural diversity and education* (6th ed.). Boston: Pearson.

Bean, T. W. (2016). Digital media and cosmopolitan critical literacy: Research and practice. In B. Guzzetti & M. Lesley (Eds.), *Handbook of research on the societal impact of digital media* (pp. 46–68). Heshey, PA: IGI Global.

Bean, T. W., & Dunkerly-Bean, J. M. (2015). *Beyond the debate: Towards a critical approach to content area and disciplinary literacies.* Paper presented at the American Educational Research Association Annual Conference, Chicago, IL.

Common Core State Standards Initiative. (2010). Retrieved September 17, 2010, Website: http:www.corestandards.org/

Harrison, R. (2011). *License to pawn: Deals, steals, and my life at the gold and silver.* New York: Hatchette Books.

Kaestle, C. F. (1991). *Literacy in the United States.* New Haven: Yale University Press.

Noddings, N. (2013). *Education and democracy in the 21st Century.* New York: Columbia University.

Pew Research Center. (2014, August). *Digital life in 2025: AI, robotics, and the future of jobs.* Available: http://www.pewinternet.org/2014/08/06futureofjobs/

Sartre, J. (1948). *The emotions: Outline of a theory.* New York: Book Sales.

CHAPTER 2, TECHNOLOGY AND CHANGING LITERACIES

Recommended Readings

Bean, T. W., & Dunkerly-Bean, J. (2016). At the intersection of creativity and engagement: Adolescents' literacies in action. *Journal of Adolescent & Adult Literacy.* 60, (3), 247-253.

The authors of this commentary define and discuss teaching for creativity and highlight civic engagement projects where this effort is underway.

Kaku, M. (2014). *The future of the mind.* New York: Doubleday.

Award winning physicist, Dr. Michio Kaku interviewed hundreds of scientists to understand the contributions and relative limitations of artificial intelligence.

Williamson, B. (2013). *The future of the curriculum: School knowledge in the digital age.* Cambridge, MA: The MIT Press.

This author argues that no single model of the curriculum, particularly top-down mandates, will produce learners who are creative, collaborative and skilled in problem solving.

References

Bean, T. W. (2016). *Digital media and cosmopolitan critical literacy: Research and practice.* Hershey, PA: IGI Global.

Bean, T. W., & Dunkerly-Bean, J. (2016). At the intersection of creativity and engagement: Adolescents' literacies in action. *Journal of Adolescent & Adult Literacy.*

Cook, D. L. (1962). The atomization of Socrates. *Theory into Practice, 1,* 9–19.

Cuban, L. (1986). *Teachers and machines. The classroom use of technology since 1920.* New York: Teachers College Press.

Cuban, L. (2003). *Oversold and underused: Computers in the classroom.* Cambridge, MA: Harvard University Press.

Dobler, E. (2015). E-textbooks: A personalized learning experience or a digital distraction? *Journal of Adolescent & Adult Literacy, 58*(6), 482–491.

Jacobs, T. (2010). *Teen cyberbullying investigated.* Minneapolis, MN: Free Spirit Publishing.

Kaku, M. (2014). *The future of the mind.* New York: Doubleday.

Leu, D. J., & Leu, D. D. (2000). *Teaching with the Internet: Lessons from the classroom* (3rd ed.). Norwood, MA: Christopher-Gordon.

Nettrekker. (2006). Retrieved October 28, 2006, Website: http://www.nettrekker.com/home/index.html

Oppenheimer, T. (1997). The computer delusion. *The Atlantic Monthly, 280*(1), 45–62.

Oppenheimer, T. (2003). *The flickering mind: The false promise of technology in the classroom and how learning can be saved.* New York: Random House.

Postman, N. (1999). *Building a bridge to the 18th century: How the past can improve our future.* New York: Knopf.

Ronson, J. (2015). *So you've been publicly shamed.* New York: Penguin.

Williamson, B. (2013). *The future of the curriculum: School knowledge in the digital age.* Cambridge, MA: The MIT Press.

CHAPTER 3, LANGUAGE AND DIVERSITY IN THE DISCIPLINES

Recommended Readings

Harper, H. J., & Bean, T. W. (2007). Literacy education in democratic life: The promise of adolescent literacy. In J. Lewis & G. Moorman (Eds.), *Adolescent literacy instruction: Policies, programs, and promising classroom practices.* Newark, DE: International Reading Association.

The authors review useful theories, projects, and strategies aimed at developing students' critical literacy with a focus on social justice issues. These strategies include Structured Academic Controversy and Resident Critic, among others.

Jimenez, R. T., Smith, P. H., & Teague, B. L. (2009). Transnational and community literacies for teachers. *Journal of Adolescent & Adult Literacy, 53,* 16–26.

This article offers teachers specific approaches using community resources (e.g., billboards) to engage

ELL students in working with the target language using community resources they know.

Moje, E. B. (2008). Foregrounding the disciplines in secondary literacy teaching and learning: A call for change. *Journal of Adolescent & Adult Literacy, 52,* 96–107.

This article argues for the primacy of the disciplines and the special features of each content area's academic vocabulary and ways of knowing. Becoming an "insider" in math, science, social studies, or English requires immersing students in how professionals operate in these contexts.

Stevens, L. P., & Bean, T. W. (2007). *Critical literacy: Context, research, and practice in K–12 classrooms.* Thousand Oaks, CA: SAGE.

This book introduces recent work in critical literacy with an array of classroom examples to help teachers implement these practices in various content area classrooms, including science, social studies, mathematics, and English.

Townsend, D. (2015). Who's using the language? Supporting middle school students with content area academic language. *Journal of Adolescent & Adult Literacy, 58*(5), 376–387.

This article recommends that teachers integrate morphemic analysis, disciplinary language development, and debating the subtle nuances of word meanings to help student develop in-depth ownership of content area vocabulary.

References

Au, K. H. (2000). A multicultural perspective on policies for improving literacy achievement: Equity and excellence. In M. L. Kamil, P. B. Mosenthal, P. D. Pearson, & R. Barr (Eds.), *Handbook of reading research: Volume III* (pp. 835–851). Mahwah, NJ: Erlbaum.

Au, K. H. (2006). *Multicultural issues and reading achievement.* Mahwah, NJ: Erlbaum.

Au, K. H., & Kaomea, J. (2009). Reading comprehension and diversity in historical perspective. In S. E. Israel & G. G. Duffy (Eds.), *Handbook of research on reading comprehension* (pp. 571–586). New York: Routledge.

Bean, T. W. (2008). The localization of young adult fiction in contemporary Hawai'i. *The ALAN Review, 35*(2), 27–35.

Bean, T. W. (2010). *Multimodal learning for the 21st century adolescent.* Huntington Beach, CA: Shell Education.

Bean, T.W., & Dunkerly-Bean, J. M. (2015). Expanding conceptions of adolescent literacy research and practice: Cosmopolitan theory in educational contexts. *Australian Journal of Language and Literacy, 38,* (1), 46-54.

Bean, T. W., & Harper, H. J. (2011). The context of English language arts learning: The high school years. In D. Fisher & D. Lapp (Eds.), *Handbook of research on teaching the English Language Arts* (3rd ed.). Mahwah, NJ: Lawrence Erlbaum.

Beck, U., & Sznaider, N. (2010). Unpacking cosmopolitanism for the social sciences: A research agenda. *The British Journal of Sociology, 61,* 381–403.

Bergknut, L. L. (1997). Stink eye. In A. Von Alemann & M. Kunz (Eds.), *Kanilehua* (pp. 32–33). Hilo: University of Hawaii at Hilo/Hawaii Community College Board of Student Publications.

Cervetti, G., Damico, J. S., & Pardeles, M. J. (2001). A tale of differences: Comparing the traditions, perspectives, and educational goals of critical reading and critical Literacy. *Reading Online.* Available: http://www.reading.org

Cummins, J. (2009). Literacy and English-language learners: A shifting landscape for students, teachers, researchers, and policy makers. *Educational Researcher, 38,* 382–384.

Dunkerly-Bean, J. M., Bean, T. W., & Alnajjar, K. (2014). Seeking asylum: Adolescents explore the crossroads of human rights education and cosmopolitan critical literacy. *Journal of Adolescent & Adult Literacy, 58*(3), 230–241.

Dunkerly-Bean, J. M., & Crompton, H. (2016). The role of mobile learning in promoting global literacy and human rights for women and girls. In B. Guzzetti, & M. Lesley (Eds.), *Handbook of research on the societal impact of digital media* (pp. 582-609). Hershey, PA: IGI Global.

Gallo, D. R. (2007). *First crossing: Stories about teen immigrants.* Somerville, MA: Candlewick Press.

Garcia, G. E., & Godina, H. (2004). Addressing the literacy needs of adolescent English Language learners. In T. L. Jetton, & J. A. Dole (Eds.), *Adolescent literacy research and practice* (pp. 304-320). New York: Guilford.

Harper, H., & Bean, T. W. (2007). Literacy education in democratic life: The promise of adolescent literacy. In J. Lewis & G. Moorman (Eds.), *Adolescent literacy instruction: Policies, programs, and promising classroom practices.* Newark, DE: International Reading Association.

Hartman, D. K., Morsink, P. M., & Zheng, J. (2010). From print to pixels: The evolution of cognitive conceptions of reading comprehension. In E. A. Baker (Ed.), *The new literacies: Multiple perspectives on research and practice* (pp. 131–164). New York: The Guilford Press.

Hudelson, S. (2001). Working with second language learners. In L. W. Searfoss, J. E. Readence, & M. H. Mallette (Eds.), *Helping children learn to read: Creating a classroom literacy environment* (4th ed., pp. 366–393). Boston: Allyn & Bacon.

Janks, H. (2014). *Doing critical literacy: Texts and activities for students and teachers.* New York: Routledge.

Jimenez, R. T., Smith, P. H., & Teague, B. L. (2009). Transitional and community literacies for teachers. *Journal of Adolescent & Adult Literacy, 53,* 16–26.

Kieffer, M. J., & Lesaux, N. K. (2010). Morphing into adolescents: Active word learning for English language learners and their classmates in middle school. *Journal of Adolescent & Adult Literacy, 54,* 47–56.

Kinney, G. (1993). *W.K. Kellogg transcultural education grant.* Hilo: Department of Baccalaureate Nursing, University of Hawaii at Hilo.

Kist, W. (2010). *The socially networked classroom.* Thousand Oaks, CA: Corwin Press.

Kress, G. (2003). *Literacy in the new media age.* London: Routledge.

Laird, D. M., & Jossen, C. (1983). *Wili Wai Kula and the three mongooses.* Honolulu, HI: Barbaby Books.

Lesko, N. (2001). *Act your age! A cultural construction of adolescence.* New York: Routledge Falmer.

Maaka, M. (2001). Foreword to S. Florio-Ruane, *Teacher education and the cultural imagination.* Mahwah, NJ: Erlbaum.

McCarthey, S. J., & Dressman, M. (2000). How will diversity affect literacy in the next millennium? *Reading Research Quarterly, 35,* 548–552.

Moje, E. B. (2002). Re-framing adolescent literacy research for New Times: Studying youth as a resource. *Reading Research and Instruction, 41,* 211–228.

Moje, E. B. (2008). Foregrounding the disciplines in secondary literacy teaching and learning: A call for change. *Journal of Adolescent & Adult Literacy, 52,* 96–107.

Moje, E. B., & Dillon, D. R. (2006). Adolescent identities as demanded by science classroom discourse communities. In D. A. Alvermann, K. A. Hinchman, D. W. Moore, S. F. Phelps, & D. R. Waff (Eds.), *Reconceptualizing the literacies in adolescents' lives* (2nd ed., pp. 85–106). Mahwah, NJ: Erlbaum.

Morrell, E. (2009). Critical research and the future of literacy education. *Journal of Adolescent & Adult Literacy, 53,* 96–104.

Murillo, L. A., & Smith, P. H. (2008). Cultural diversity: Why is matters in school and what teachers need to know. In Y. A. Freeman, D. E. Freeman, & R. Ramirez (Eds.), *Diverse learners in the mainstream classroom* (pp. 3–30). Portsmouth, NH: Heinemann.

Nagy, W., & Townsend, D. (2012). Words as tools: Learning academic vocabulary as language acquisition. *Reading Research Quarterly, 47,* 91–108.

Nieto, S. (2004). *Affirming diversity: The sociopolitical context of multicultural education, MyLabSchool Edition* (4th).
Boston, MA: Allyn & Bacon.

O'Brien, D. G., & Stewart, R. A. (2007). Resistance to content area reading instruction: Dimensions and solutions. In T. W. Bean, J. E. Readence, & R. S. Baldwin (Eds.), *Content area literacy digital supplement.* Dubuque, IA: Kendall Hunt. Note this article should be deleted and it's no longer in the website

Pearson, P. D. (2009). The roots of reading comprehension instruction. In S. E. Israel, & G. G. Duffy (Eds.), *Handbook of research on reading comprehension* (pp. 3–31). New York: Routledge.

Paris, D. (2011). *Language across difference: Ethnicity, communication, and youth identities in changing urban schools.*
Cambridge, England: Cambridge University Press.

Pitre, A. (2007). Critical pedagogy and multicultural education. In T. W. Bean, J. E. Readence, & R. S. Baldwin (Eds.), *Content area literacy digital supplement.* Dubuque, IA: Kendall Hunt.

Sattouf, R. (2015). *The Arab of the future: A childhood in the Middle East, 1978-1984: A graphic memoir*. New York: Metropolitan Books.

Skerrett, A. (2015). *Teaching transnational youth: Literacy and education in a changing world*. New York: Teachers College Press.

Stevens, L. P., & Bean, T. W. (2007). *Critical literacy: Context, research, and practice in K–12 classrooms*. Thousand Oaks, CA: SAGE.

Townsend, D. (2015). Who's using the language? Supporting middle school students with content area academic language. *58*(5), 376–387.

Walker, N. T., Bean, T. W., & Dillard, B. R. (2010). *When textbooks fall short: New ways, new texts, new sources of information in the content areas*. Portsmouth, NH: Heinemann.

Warner, L. S. (1993). *From slave to abolitionist: The life of William Wells Brown*. New York: Dial Books.

Zwiers, J. (2008). *Building academic language: Essential practices for content classrooms, grades 5-12*. San Francisco, CA: Jossey-Bass.

CHAPTER 4, SELECTING TEXTBOOKS AND MULTIMEDIA MATERIALS

Recommended Readings

Dunkerly-Bean, J., & Bean, T. W. (2015). Exploring human rights and cosmopolitan critical literacy with global young adult literature multimodal text sets. *New England Reading Association Journal*, *50*(2), 1–7.

The authors provide an example of how to construct a multimodal text set to accompany reading and discussion of a young adult novel.

Hinchman, K. A., & Moore, D. W. (2013). Close reading: A cautionary interpretation. *Journal of Adolescent & Adult Literacy*, *56*(6), 441–450.

The authors review the history and underpinning of close reading and provide support for engaging students in reading and rereading complex, multiple texts in the disciplines.

References

Bean, T. W., Dunkerly-Bean, J., & Harper, H. J. (2014). *Teaching young adult literature: Developing students as world citizens*. Thousand Oaks, CA: SAGE.

Dunkerly-Bean, J., & Bean, T. W. (2015). Exploring human rights and cosmopolitan critical literacy with global young: Adult literature and multimodal text sets. The *New England Reading Association Journal*, *50*(2), 1–7.

Leonard, W. H., & Penick, J. E. (1993). What's important in selecting a biology textbook? *The American Biology Teacher*, 55, (1), 14-19.

Loewen, J. W. (2007). *Lies my teacher told me: Everything your American history textbook got wrong*. New York: The New Press.

Norman, D. A. (2004). *Emotional design: Why we love (or hate) everyday things*. New York: Basic Books.

Raygor, A. L. (1977). The Raygor readability estimate: A quick and easy way to determine difficulty. In P. D. Pearson (Ed.), *Reading: Theory, research, and practice* (pp. 259–263). Twenty-sixth yearbook of the National Reading Conference. Clemson, SC: National Reading Conference.

Singer, H. (2007). Friendly texts: Description and criteria. In T. W. Bean, J. E. Readence, & R. S. Baldwin (Eds.), Content area literacy digital supplement. Dubuque, IA: Kendall/Hunt.

CHAPTER 5, ASSESSMENT

Recommended Readings

Darling-Hammond, L. (2010). *The flat world and education*. New York: Teachers College Press.

This analysis argues for a shift away from narrow, high-stakes assessments and movement toward extensive writing, critical thinking, and problem solving in the classroom. Darling-Hammond includes extensive global data to support this proposal.

Gillis, V., & Van Wig, A. (2015). Disciplinary literacy assessment: A neglected responsibility. *Journal of Adolescent & Adult Literacy*, *58*(6), 455–460.

The authors provide examples of how to conduct a literacy assessment in your content area with models from English, science, and social studies.

National Governors Association, Council of State
School Officers and Achieve Inc. (2010). *Common
core state standards initiative*. Washington, DC:
National Governors Association.

The creation of national standards bodes well for
a move toward higher-order thinking skills in
teaching and the adoption of 21st century problem
solving curriculum in the content areas. Additional
information can be found on the website: (http://
www.corestandards.org/).

Wagner, T. (2010). *The global achievement gap*. New
York: Basic Books.

The author challenges our current, narrow accountability agenda that fails to meet the standards
for work, college, and citizenship in a global 21st
century.

References

Blachowicz, C. L. Z. (1991). Vocabulary instruction in
content classes for special needs learners: Why and
how? *Reading, Writing, and Learning Disabilities, 7*,
297–308.

Darling-Hammond, L. (2010). *The flat world and education*. New York: Teachers College Press.

Gillis, V., & Van Wig, A. (2015). Disciplinary literacy
assessment: A neglected responsibility. *Journal of
Adolescent & Adult Literacy, 58*(6), 455–460.

National Governors Association, Council of State
School Officers and Achieve Inc. (2010). *Common
core state standards initiative*. Washington, DC:
National Governors Association.

Tierney, R. J. (2009). The agency and artistry of
meaning makers within and across digital spaces.
In S. E. Israel & G. G. Duffy (Eds.), *Handbook of
reading comprehension* (pp. 261–288). New York:
Routledge.

Wagner, T. (2010). *The global achievement gap*. New
York: Basic Books.

Webster, B. (1984, December 12). Science sheds light on
bats. *The Register*.

CHAPTER 6, UNIT AND LESSON PLANNING

Recommended Readings

Bean, T. W. (2010). *Multimodal learning for the 21st
century adolescent*. Huntington Beach, CA: Shell
Education.

This professional development book includes
a wealth of lesson and unit planning Internet
resources.

Britzman, D. (2003). *Practice makes practice: A critical
study of learning to teach* (2nd ed.). Albany, NY:
State University of New York Press.

The update of this now classic book offers a
critical examination of the complex social practice
elements of teaching. Britzman views teaching and
learning as much more than a matter of method.
The meanings learners and teachers ascribe to their
classroom experiences are crucial in any complex
analysis of teaching and learning.

Kist, W. (2010). *The socially networked classroom:
Teaching in the new media age*. Thousand Oaks,
CA: Corwin/SAGE.

This book features numerous examples of units and
lessons tapping into the creative potential of the
digitial media.

Kist, W. (2015). *Getting started with blended learning:
How do I integrate online and face-to-face instruction?* Alexandria, VA: ASCD.

This book offers examples of how to create in class
and out-of-class assignments that tap into inquiry
via conventional class meetings and Internet discussions (e.g. blogs), virtual field trips, online scav-
enger hunts, and a host of other digital resources.

Lesson Plan sites online:

There are numerous sites, some developed by publishers, to support teachers' lesson planning. To gain
an idea of the richness of these sites, see the omnibus
site at: http://www.internet4classrooms.com/lesson.
htm. Also see ReadWriteThink for an array of lesson
and unit plans in English Language Arts.

The omnibus site features multiple links to other
lesson and unit planning resources. It spans 8 pages
and is divided by grade level.

References

Bean, T. W. (2010). *Multimodal learning for the 21st century adolescent*. Huntington Beach, CA: Shell Education.

Britzman, D. (2003). *Practice makes practice: A critical study of learning to teach* (2nd ed.). Albany, NY: State University of New York Press.

Kist, W. (2015). Getting started with blended learning: How do I integrate online and face-to-face instruction? Alexandria, VA: ASCD.

Gaut, B. (2014). Educating for creativity. In E.S. Paul & S.B. Kaufman (Eds.). *The philosophy of creativity: New essays*. New York: Oxford University Press.

Hunt, L. C., Jr., & Sheldon, W. D. (1950). Characteristics of the reading of a group of ninth-grade pupils. *School Review, 58*, 348–353.

Kist, W. (2010). *The socially networked classroom: Teaching in the new media age*. Thousand Oaks, CA: Corwin/SAGE.

Walker, N. T., Bean, T. W., & Dillard, B. R. (2010). *When textbooks fall short: New ways, new texts, new sources of information in the content areas*. Portsmouth, NH: Heinemann.

CHAPTER 7, LITERATURE

Recommended Readings

Baer, A. L., & Glasgow, J. N. (2010). Negotiating understanding through the young adult literature of Muslim cultures. *Journal of Adolescent & Adult Literacy, 54*, 23–32.

This article offers a good list of young adult books within a global literacy framework that would be particularly useful in social studies.

Bean, T.W., Dunkerly-Bean, J., & Harper, H. J. (2014). *Teaching young adult literature: Developing students as world citizens.*. Thousand Oaks, CA: SAGE.

This young adult literature methods text includes extensive lists of books, both fiction and non-fiction, as well as graphic novels and other genres related to the content areas.

Bean, T. W., & Harper, H. J. (2006). Exploring notions of freedom in and through young adult literature. *Journal of Adolescent & Adult Literacy, 50*, 96–104.

This article guides the reader through a critical literacy questioning approach with examples from contemporary young adult literature set in international sites of global conflict. Also, see Harper and Bean (2006) in the reference list for a book chapter centered on democracy and citizenship discussions based on young adult literature.

Bean, T. W., & Harper, H. J. (2007). Reading men differently: Alternative portrayals of masculinity in contemporary young adult fiction. *Reading Psychology, 28*(1), 11–30.

This article reviews recent research on masculinity and its importance for working with boys and reading. In particular, through an analysis of contemporary young adult books aimed at examining spaces for masculinity to be multifaceted, the article provides student discussion options and examples.

Bean, T. W., & Moni, K. (2003). Developing students' critical literacy: Exploring identity construction in young adult fiction. *Journal of Adolescent & Adult Literacy, 46*, 638–648.

This article walks the reader through a classroom example of how to employ critical literacy in the reading and discussion of contemporary young adult fiction.

Blackburn, M. V., & Buckley, J. F. (2005). Teaching queer-inclusive English language arts. *Journal of Adolescent & Adult Literacy, 49*, 202–212.

The authors offer a comprehensive discussion of gay, lesbian, and transgender young adult literature, along with useful websites and classroom examples incorporating powerful literature and an understanding of difference.

Boyd, F. B. (2003). Experiencing things not seen: Educative events centered on a study of *Shabanu*. *Journal of Adolescent & Adult Literacy, 46*, 460–474.

This article guides the reader through the use of multicultural literature and various literature response strategies, including journaling, body biographies, and the integration of technology.

Brozo, W. G. (2010). *To be a boy, to be a reader: Engaging teen and preteen boys in active literacy* (2nd ed.). Newark, DE: International Reading Association.

This book offers concrete recommendations and resources for influencing adolescent males' reading engagement.

Buscher, K., & Manning, M. L. (2006). *Young adult literature: Exploration, evaluation, and appreciation.* Upper Saddle River, NJ: Pearson.
This contemporary young adult literature text includes resources for linking books to films and offers a chapter on comic books, graphic novels, and magazines. Numerous websites offer teachers additional resources.

Fisher, D. (2004). Setting the "opportunity to read" standard: Resuscitating the SSR program in an urban high school. *Journal of Adolescent & Adult Literacy, 48,* 138–150.
This report of an action research study in a large, urban high school shows in very concrete ways how to turn around an SSR program that is not operating according to key principles. If SSR is to realize its potential to impact students' reading attitudes, interests, and achievement, they must find SSR an engaging and worthwhile time rather than a time to simply rest and recuperate from other text reading.

Hadaway, N.L., & McKenna, M.J. (Eds.). (2007). *Breaking boundaries with global literature: Celebrating diversity in K–12 classrooms.* Newark, DE: International Reading Association.
This edited volume features extensive lists of young adult literature that can be used in social studies and other content areas.

Johnson, D. (2010). Teaching with author's blogs: Connections, collaboration, creativity. *Journal of Adolescent & Adult Literacy, 54,* 172–180.
Most young adult authors have their own blogs in support of their writing. This article offers advice and a process for integrating this resource in the English classroom.

Landt, S. M. (2006). Multicultural literature and young adolescents: A kaleidoscope of opportunity. *Journal of Adolescent & Young Adult Literature, 49,* 690–697.
The author explores the concept of cultural authenticity and includes a list of award winning multicultural young adult literature and useful websites.

Larson, L. (2009). e-reading and e-responding: New tools for the next generation of readers. *Journal of Adolescent & Adult Literacy, 53,* 255–258.
The author describes a classroom where students read a young adult novel in electronic form, offering response features including mark-ups and annotation notes.

Rozema, R. (2007). The book report, version 2.0: Podcasting on young adult novels. *English Journal, 97*(1), 31–36.
The author demonstrates how to integrate podcasting in the classroom where students are responding to young adult literature via an audio commentary that can be archived and shared with an audience.

Smith, M. W., & Wilhelm, J. D. (2002). *"Reading don't fix no Chevys": Literacy in the lives of young men.* Portsmouth, NH: Heinemann.
This book, based on extensive interviews with middle and high school young men, provides innovative solutions to the well-documented disconnection between students' in and out-of-school literature.

Smith, M. W., & Wilhelm, J. D. (2006). *Going with the flow: How to engage boys (and girls) in their literacy learning.* Portsmouth, NH: Heinemann.
By centering discussion on essential questions, often from a wide-angle lens perspective, the authors offer an alternative to narrow discussions of literature and other text forms. They include dramatic action strategies and other visual support approaches students find engaging.

Vasquez, V., Tate, S.L., & Harste, J. (2013). *Negotiating critical literacies with teachers: Theoretical foundations and pedagogical resources for pre-service and in-service contexts.* New York: Routledge.
This book provides a wealth of examples of critical literacy practices in action, along with a strong theoretical foundation aimed at developing an astute justice oriented citizenry.

References

Abdek-fattah, R. (2008). *Does my head look big in this?* New York: Scholastic Paperbacks.

Achebe, C. (1958). *Things fall apart.* Portsmouth, NH: Heinemann.

Albright, L. K. (2002). Bringing the Ice Maiden to life: Engaging adolescents in learning through picture book read-alouds in content areas. *Journal of Adolescent & Adult Literacy, 48,* 418–428.

Alexie, S. (2007). *The absolutely true diary of a part-time Indian*. New York: Little, Brown.

Al-Windawi, T. (2004). *Thura's diary*. London, England: Penguin.

Anaya, R. (1972). *Bless me Ultima*. San Francisco, CA: Tonatiuh Press.

Aoki, E. M. (1993). Turning the page: Asian-Pacific American children's literature. In V. J. Harris (Ed.), *Teaching multicultural literature in grades K–8* (pp. 109–135). Norwood, MA: Christopher-Gordon.

Baer, A. L., & Glasgow, J. N. (2010). Negotiating understanding through the young adult literature of Muslim cultures. *Journal of Adolescent & Adult Literacy, 54*, 23–32.

Baldwin, R. S., & Leavell, A. G. (2007). When was the last time you read a textbook just for kicks? In T. W. Bean, J. E. Readence, & R. S. Baldwin (Eds.), *Content area literacy digital supplement*. Dubuque, IA: Kendall Hunt.

Balliett, B. (2005). *Chasing Vermeer*. New York: Scholastic.

Bean, T. W. (2000). Reading in the content areas: Social constructivist dimensions. In M. L. Kamil, P. D. Mosenthal, P. D. Pearson, & R. Barr (Eds.), *Handbook of reading research: Volume III* (pp. 629–644). Mahwah, NJ: Erlbaum.

Bean, T. W. (2002). Making reading relevant for adolescents. *Educational Leadership, 60* (3), 34–37.

Bean, T. W., & Harper, H. J. (2004). Teacher education and adolescent literacy. In T. L. Jetton & J. A. Dole (Eds.), *Adolescent literacy research and practice* (pp. 392–411). New York: Guilford Press.

Bean, T. W., & Harper, H. J. (2011). *Teaching young adult literature in new times*. Thousand Oaks, CA: Sage.

Bean, T. W., & Harper, H. J. (2006). Exploring notions of freedom in and through young adult literature. *Journal of Adolescent & Adult Literacy, 50*, 96–104.

Bean, T. W., & Harper, H. J. (2007). Reading men differently: Alternative portrayals of masculinity in contemporary young adult fiction. *Reading Psychology*, 11–21.

Bean, T. W., & Moni, K. (2003). Developing students' critical literacy: Exploring identity construction in young adult fiction. *Journal of Adolescent & Adult Literacy, 46*, 638–648.

Bean, T. W., & Rigoni, N. (2000, May). *Exploring the intergenerational dialogue journal discussion of a multicultural young adult novel*. Paper presented at the annual meeting of the International Reading Association, Indianapolis, IN.

Bean, T. W., Valerio, P. C., Money Senior, H., & White, F. (1999). Secondary English students' engagement in reading and writing about a multicultural novel. *Journal of Educational Research, 93*, 32–37.

Blackburn, M. V., & Buckley, J. F. (2005). Teaching queer-inclusive English language Arts. *Journal of Adolescent & Adult Literacy, 49*, 202–212.

Blackburn, M., Clark, C. T., Nemeth, E. A. (2015). Examining queer elements and ideologies in LGBT-themed literature: What queer literature can offer young adult readers. *Journal of Literacy Research, 47* (1), 11–48.

Boyd, F. B. (2003). Experiencing things not seen: Educative events centered on a study of *Shabanu*. *Journal of Adolescent & Adult Literacy, 46*, 460–474.

Brozo, W. G. (2010). *To be a boy, to be a reader: Engaging teen and preteen boys in active literacy* (2nd ed.). Newark, DE: International Reading Association.

Brozo, W. G., Valerio, P. C., & Salazar, M. M. (1996). A walk through Gracie's garden: Literacy and cultural explorations in a Mexican-American junior high school. *Journal of Adolescent & Adult Literacy, 40*, 2–8.

Brozo, W. G., Walter, P., & Placker, T. (2002). "I know the difference between a real man and a TV man": A critical exploration of violence and masculinity through literature in a junior high school in the hood. *Journal of Adolescent & Adult Literacy, 45*, 530–538.

Bruchac, J. (2006). *Geronimo*. New York: Scholastic.

Conradi, K., Jang, B.G., Bryant, C., Craft, A., & McKenna, M. (2013). Measuring adolescents attitudes towards reading. *Journal of Adolescent & Adult Literacy, 56*, (7), 565-576.

Cooney, C. B. (2005). *Code orange*. New York: Delacorte.

Crew, L. (1989). *Children of the river*. New York: Dell.

Csikszentmihalyi, M. (2002). Do students care about learning? A conversation with Mihaly Csikszentmihalyi. *Educational Leadership, 60*(1), 12–17.

de la Pena, M. (2008). *Mexican white boy*. New York: Delacorte.

Deuker, C. (2007). *Gym candy*. Boston: Houghton, Mifflin, Harcourt.

Donelson, K. L., & Nilsen, A. P. (2008). *Literature for today's young adults* (8th ed.). Boston: Allyn & Bacon.

Ellis, D. (2000). *The breadwinner*. Toronto, Ontario: Groundwood.

Ellis, D. (2014). *Moon at nine*. Toronto, Ontario, Canada: Pajama Press.

Fisher, D. (2004). Setting the "opportunity to read" standard: Resuscitating the SSR program in an urban high school. *Journal of Adolescent & Adult Literacy, 48,* 138–150.

Flake, S. (2001). *Money hungry*. New York: Hyperion.

Fleischman, P. (1990). *Saturnalia*. New York: HarperCollins.

Franzak, J., & Noll, E. (2006). Monstrous acts: Problematizing violence in young adult literature. *Journal of Adolescent & Adult Literature, 49,* 662–672.

Galda, L., Ash, G. E., & Cullinan, B. E. (2000). Children's literature. In M. L. Kamil, P. B. Mosenthal, P. D. Pearson, & R. Barr (Eds.), *Handbook of reading research: Volume III* (pp. 361–379). Mahwah, NJ: Erlbaum.

Gallo, D. R. (2007). *First crossings: Stories about teen immigrants*. New York: Candlewood Press.

Godina, H. (1996). The canonical debate-implementing multicultural literature and perspectives. *Journal of Adolescent & Adult Literacy, 39,* 544–545.

Gonzalez, G. (2009). *A so-called vacation*. Houston, TX: Pinata Books.

Gray, A. (2003). Conversations with transformative encounters. In G. Gay (Ed.), *Becoming multicultural educators* (pp. 67–90). San Francisco, CA: Jossey-Bass.

Guthrie, J. T., & Wigfield, A. (2000). Engagement and motivation in reading. In M. L. Kamil, P. D. Mosenthal, P. D. Pearson, & R. Barr (Eds.), *Handbook of reading research: Volume III* (pp. 403–422). Mahwah, NJ: Erlbaum.

Gwynne, P. (1998). *Deadly unna?* Victoria, Australia: Penguin Books.

Gwynne, P. (2000). *Nukkin ya*. Victoria, Australia: Penguin Books.

Hadaway, N., & McKenna, M. (2007). *Breaking boundaries with global literature: Celebrating diversity in k-12 classrooms*. Newark, DE: International Reading Association.

Harper, H. J. (2000). *Wild words dangerous desires*. New York: Peter Lang.

Harper, H. J., & Bean, T. W. (2006). Fallen angels: Finding adolescents and adolescent literacy in a renewed project of democratic citizenship. In D. E. Alvermann, K. A. Hinchman, D. W. Moore, S. F. Phelps, & D. R. Waff (Eds.), *Reconceptualizing the literacies in adolescents' lives* (2nd ed., pp. 147–160). Mahwah, NJ: Erlbaum.

Hinton, S. E. (1967). *The outsiders*. New York: Viking.

Houston, J. (2012). *Farewell to Manzanar*. Portland, OR: Ember Publishing.

Ivey, G., & Broaddus, K. (2001). "Just plain reading:" A survey of what makes students want to read in middle school classrooms. *Reading Research Quarterly, 36,* 350–377.

Kincaid, J. (1988). *A small place*. New York: Penguin.

Janks, H. (2013). Doing critical literacy: *Texts and activities for students and teachers*. New York: Routledge.

Johnson, D. (2010). Teaching with author's blogs: Connections, collaboration, creativity. *Journal of Adolescent & Adult Literacy, 54,* 172–180.

Klass, D. (1994). *California blue*. New York: Scholastic.

Klass, D. (1996). *Danger zone*. New York: Scholastic.

Koss, M. D., & Teale, W. H. (2009). What's happening in young adult literature? Trends in books for adolescents. *Journal of Adolescent & Adult Literacy, 52,* 563–572.

Larson, L. (2009). e-reading and e-responding: New tools for the next generation of readers. *Journal of Adolescent & Adult Literacy, 53,* 255–258.

Lee, M. (1997). *Necessary roughness*. New York: HarperCollins.

Lloyd, S. (2010). *The carbon diaries 2017*. New York: Holiday House.

Love, K. (2002). Mapping online discussion in senior English. *Journal of Adolescent & Adult Literacy, 45,* 382–396.

Lyons, M. E. (1992). *Letter from a slave girl: The story of Harriet Jacobs*. New York: Charles Scribner's Sons.

McClean, C. A. (2010). A space called home: An immigrant adolescent's digital literacy practices. *Journal of Adolescent & Adult Literacy, 54,* 13–22.

McKenna, M. C., Kear, D. J., & Ellsworth, R. A. (1995). Children's attitudes toward reading: A national survey. *Reading Research Quarterly, 30,* 934–956.

McMahon, S. I., & Raphael, T. E. (1997). *The book club connection.* New York: Teachers College Press.

Miller, D. E. (1993). The literature project: Using literature to improve the self-concept of at-risk adolescent females. *Journal of Reading, 36,* 442–446.

Moje, E. (2000). "To be part of the story:" The literacy practices of gangsta adolescents. *Teachers College Record, 102,* 651–690.

Monaghan, A. (2013). *A girl named digit.* Boston, MA: HMH Books for Young Readers.

Myers, W. D. (1988). *Fallen angels.* New York: Scholastic.

Myers, W. D. (1999). *Monster.* New York: HarperCollins.

Myers, W. D. (2008). *Sunrise over Fallujah.* New York: Scholastic.

Naidoo, B. (2000). *The other side of truth.* New York: HarperCollins.

Nieto, S. (2003). *Affirming diversity: The sociopolitical context of multicultural education* (4th ed.). New York: Longman.

Palmer, R. G., & Stewart, R. A. (1997). Nonfiction trade books in content area instruction: Realities and potential. *Journal of Adolescent & Adult Literacy, 40,* 630–641.

Perez, A. H. (2015). *Out of darkness.* Minneapolis, MN: Carolrhoda/Lerner Books.

Petrone, R., Sarigianides, S. T., & Lewis, M. A. (2015). The youth lens: Analyzing adolescents/ce in literary texts. *Journal of Literacy Research, 64,* (4), 506-533.

Rosenblatt, L. M. (1978). *The reader, the text, the poem.* Carbondale, IL: Southern Illinois University Press.

Rozema, R. (2007). The book report, version 2.0: Podcasting on young adult novels. *English Journal, 97*(1), 31–36.

Savage, J. F. (1994). *Teaching reading using literature.* Dubuque, IA: WCB Brown & Benchmark.

Serafini, F. (2015). *Reading workshop 2.0: Supporting readers in the digital age.* Portsmouth, NH: Heinemann.

Smagorinsky, P., & O'Donnell-Allen, C. (1998). Reading as mediated and mediating action: Composing meaning for literature through multimedia interpretive texts. *Reading Research Quarterly, 33,* 198–226.

Smith, M. W., & Wilhelm, J. D. (2002). *"Reading don't fix no Chevys:" Literacy in the lives of young men.* Portsmouth, NH: Heinemann.

Smith, M. W., & Wilhelm, J. D. (2006). *Going with the flow: How to engage boys (and girls) in their literacy learning.* Portsmouth, NH: Heinemann.

Smith, R. (2005). *Cryptid hunters.* New York: Hyperion.

Soto, G. (1997). *Buried onions.* New York: Scholastic.

Soto, G. (2003). *The afterlife.* New York: Harcourt.

Stevens, L. P., & Bean, T. W. (2007). *Critical literacy: Context, research, and practice in the K–12 classroom.* Thousand Oaks, CA: SAGE.

Stover, L. T., & Tway, E. (1992). Cultural diversity and the young adult novel. In V. R. Monseau & G. M. Salvner (Eds.), *Reading their world: The young adult novel in the classroom* (pp. 132–153). Portsmouth, NH: Boynton/Cook.

Tatum, A. (2015). Writing through the labyrinth of fears: The legacy of Walter Dean Myers. *Journal of Adolescent & Adult Literacy, 58*(7), 536–540.

Vasquez, V., Tate, S.L., & Harste, J. (2013). *Negotiating critical literacies with teachers: Theoretical foundations and pedagogical resources for pre-service and in-service contexts.* New York: Routledge.

Ventresca, Y. (2014). *Pandemic.* New York: Sky Pony Press.

Vogt, M. (2002). Active learning: Dramatic play in the content areas. In M. McLaughlin & M. Vogt (Eds.), *Creativity and innovation in content area teaching* (pp. 73–90). Norwood, MA: Christopher-Gordon.

Walker, A. (1983). *The color purple.* New York: Harcourt, Brace, Jovanovich.

Warner, L. S. (1976). *From slave to abolitionist: The life of William Wells Brown.* New York: Dial.

Wein, E. (2015). *Black dove, white raven.* New York: Disney-Hyperion.

Wendeberg, A. (2014). *The climate fiction saga.* CreateSpace Independent Publishing Platform.

Werlin, N. (2004). *Double helix.* New York: Penguin.

Winkler, K. J. (1994, January 12). An African writer at a crossroads. *The Chronicle of Higher Education,* A9.

Woodson, J. (2002). *Hush.* New York: G. P. Putnam's Son.

Worthy, J., Patterson, E., Salas, R., Prater, W., & Turner, M. (2002). More than just reading: The human factor in reaching resistant readers. *Reading Research and Instruction, 41,* 177–202.

Xu, S. H., Perkins, R. S., & Zunich, L. O. (2005). *Trading cards to comic strips: Popular culture texts and literacy learning in grades K–8.* Newark, DE: International Reading Association.

Young, T. A., & Vardell, S. (1993). Weaving readers' theater and nonfiction into the curriculum. *The Reading Teacher, 46,* 396–406.

CHAPTER 8, VOCABULARY

Recommended Readings

Baumann, J. F., & Graves, M. F. (2010). What is academic vocabulary? *Journal of Adolescent & Adult Literacy, 54*(1), 4–12.
This article differentiates various categories of academic vocabulary and provides guidelines for teaching based on a classification system.

Bean, T. W. (2010). *Multimodal learning for the 21st century adolescent.* Huntington Beach, CA: Shell Education.
Chapter 2 of this professional development book provides a number of websites aimed at helping students develop ownership of academic vocabulary.

Coxhead, A. (2000). A new academic word list. *TESOL Quarterly, 34*(2), 213–238. Available from: http://www.nottingham.ac.uk/~alzsh3/acvocab/index.htm
The Academic Word List provides the most common general academic words (e.g., "principle"), as opposed to technical vocabulary. These are often words that have specific meanings within disciplines and give students difficulty.

Kieffer, M. J., & Lesaux, N. K. (2010). Morphing into adolescents: Active word Learning for English Language Learners and their classmates in middle school. *Journal of Adolescent & Adult Literacy, 54*(1), 47–56.
This article offers a process for teaching students how to independently unlock words using morphemic analysis principles and word form charts.

Mountain, L. (2015). Recurrent prefixes, roots, and suffixes: A morphemic approach to disciplinary literacy. *Journal of Adolescent & Adult Literacy, 58*(7), 561–567.
This is an excellent resource for introducing students to key morphemes across the disciplines with examples from mathematics, science, and the social sciences.

Templeton, S., Bear, D. R., Invernizzi, M., Johnston, F., Flanigan, K., Townsend, D. R., Helman, L., & Hayes, L. (2015). *Vocabulary their way: Word study with middle and secondary students* (2nd ed.). Boston: Pearson.
This is another tremendous resource that includes English Learners, Language Arts, social studies, mathematics, science, and art, music, physical education, and career and technical education.

Townsend, D. (2009). Building academic vocabulary in after school settings: Games for growth with middle school English Language Learners. *Journal of Adolescent & Adult Literacy, 53*(3), 242–251.
This article, based on the Academic Word List, illustrates the use of various engaging vocabulary games in the classroom. These include: Picture Puzzlers, Matching Games, Action Jeopardy, and others.

References

Baumann, J. F., & Graves, M. F. (2010). What is academic vocabulary? *Journal of Adolescent & Adult Literacy, 54*(1), 4–12.

Bean, T. W. (2010). *Multimodal learning for the 21st century adolescent.* Huntington Beach, CA: Shell Education.

Bean, T. W., Readence, J. E., & Baldwin, R. S. (2012). *Content-area literacy: Reaching and teaching the 21st Century adolescent.* Huntington Beach, CA: Shell Education.

Butcher, J., & Raminez, M. (2007). Vocabulary development for English Language Learners. In T. W. Bean, J. E. Readence, & R. S. Baldwin, *Content area literacy digital supplement.* Dubuque, IA: Kendall Hunt.

Coxhead, A. (2000). A new academic word list. *TESOL Quarterly, 34*(2), 213–238.

Cunningham, P. M. (1992). Content area vocabulary: Building and connecting meaning. In T. W. Bean, J. E. Readence, & R. S. Baldwin (Eds.), *Content area literacy digital supplement.* Dubuque, IA: Kendall Hunt.

Dana, C., & Rodriguez, M. (1992). TOAST: A system to study vocabulary. *Reading Research and Instruction, 31*, 78–84.

Ebner, R.J., & Ehri, L.C. (2013). Vocabulary learning on the Internet: Using a structured think-aloud procedure. *Journal of Adolescent & Adult Literacy, 56*(6), 480–489.

Ford,-Connors, E., & Paratore, J.R. (2015). Vocabulary instruction in fifth grade and beyond: Source of word learning and productive contexts for development. *Review of Educational Research, 58*(1), 50–91.

Funk, C. E. (1950). *Thereby hangs a tale: Stories of curious word origins*. New York: Harper & Brothers.

Kieffer, M. J., & Lesaux, N. K. (2010). Morphing into adolescents: Active word learning for English Language Learners and their classmates in middle school. *Journal of Adolescent & Adult Literacy, 54*(1) 47–56.

Maurer, D. W. (1955). Whiz mob. *Publication of the American Dialect Society*, No. 24.

Mountain, L. (2015). Recurrent prefixes, roots, and suffixes: A morphemic approach to disciplinary literacy. *Journal of Adolescent & Adult Literacy, 58*(7), 561–567.

Ruddell, M. R., & Shearer, B. A. (2002). "Extraordinary," "tremendous," "exhilarating," "magnificent": Middle school at-risk students become avid word learners with the Vocabulary Self-Collection Strategy (VSS). *Journal of Adolescent & Adult Literacy, 45*, 352–363.

Templeton, S., Bear, D. R., Invernizzi, M., Johnston, F., Flanigan, K., Townsend, D. R., Helman, L., & Hayes, L. (2015). *Vocabulary their way: Word study with middle and secondary students* (2nd ed.). Boston: Pearson.

Tierney, R. J., & Readence, J. E. (2005). *Reading strategies and practices: A compendium* (6th ed.). Boston, MA: Pearson.

Townsend, D. (2009). Building academic vocabulary in after school settings: Games for growth with middle school English Language Learners. *Journal of Adolescent & Adult Literacy, 53*(3), 242–251.

CHAPTER 9, COMPREHENSION: PRINCIPLES AND INTEGRATED APPROACHES

Recommended Readings

Cervetti, G., Damico, J. S., & Pardeles, M. J. (2001). A tale of differences: Comparing the traditions, perspectives, and educational goals of critical reading and critical literacy. *Reading Online.* Online journal of the Inter-national Reading Association. Available: http://www.reading.org

This article does an excellent job of clarifying the differences between critical reading and critical literacy. Both are important elements in a comprehensive effort to enhance students' guided and independent comprehension, but they arise from very different philosophical foundations.

Dunkerly-Bean, J., Bean, T., & Alnajjar, K. (2014). Seeking asylum: Adolescents explore the crossroads of human rights education and cosmopolitan critical literacy. *Journal of Adolescent & Adult Literacy, 58*(3), 230–241.

In this article the authors describe a year long research project where middle school students created art work, music, and an iMovie on immigration in an urban school site.

Morrell, E., Duenas, R., Garcia, V., & Lopez, J. (2013). *Critical media pedagogy: Teaching for achievement in city schools*. New York: Teachers College Press.

This important volume includes a wealth of classroom examples aimed at engaging students in critical media literacy lessons across various content areas.

Stevens, L .P., & Bean, T. W. (2007). *Critical literacy: Context, research, and practice in the K–12 classroom*. Thousand Oaks, CA: SAGE.

This book offers an array of classroom examples exploring critical literacy and critical media literacy. Specific strategies such as Resident Critic guide students toward a predisposition to deconstruct and reconstruct multiple forms of texts including traditional textbook accounts, advertisements, media, and Internet sites.

Sturtevant, E. G., Boyd, F. B., Brozo, W. G., Hinchman, K. A., Moore, D. W., & Alvermann, D. E. (2006). *Principled practices for adolescent literacy: A framework for instruction and policy.* Mahwah, NJ: Erlbaum.

This collection of classroom examples gleaned from a Carnegie project aimed at chronicling outstanding teaching in the content areas provides specific principles and examples of teaching with multiple texts in science, mathematics, English, and other content areas.

Tierney, R. J. (2009). The agency and artistry of meaning makers within and across digital spaces. In S.E. Israel & G.G. Duffy (Eds.), *Handbook of research on reading comprehension* (pp. 261–288). New York: Routledge.

This volume and the article spotlighted here span print and digital text forms with an eye toward the changing nature of what counts as "text."

Tierney, R. J., & Readence, J. E. (2005). *Reading strategies and practices: A compendium* (6th ed.). Boston: Allyn & Bacon.

Units 7 and 12 describe numerous comprehension strategies.

Walker, N. T., Bean, T. W., & Dillard, B. R. (2010). *When textbooks fall short: New ways, new texts, new sources of information in the content areas.* Portsmouth, NH: Heinemann.

Based on over eight years of research exploring content area teachers' use of multiple texts and digital texts in English, physics, economics, history, and other content areas, this book examines how creative teachers design engaging curriculum in the content areas.

References

Bean, T. W. (2000). Music in the content areas. In M. McLaughlin & M.E. Vogt (Eds.), *Creativity and innovation in content area teaching* (pp. 91–103). Norwood, MA: Christopher-Gordon.

Bean, T. W. (2010). *Multimodal learning for the 21st Century adolescent.* Huntington Beach, CA: Shell Education.

Bean, T. W. (2016). Digital medias and cosmopolitan critical literacy: Research and practice. In B. Guzzetti, & M. Lesley (Eds.), Handbook of research on the impact of digital media (pp. 46–67). Hershey, PA: IGI Global.

Bean, T., Baldwin, S., & Readence, J. (2012). *Content-area literacy: Reaching and teaching the 21st century adolescen*t. Huntington Beach, CA: Shell Education.

Behrman, E. H. (2003). Reconciling content literacy with adolescent literacy: Expanding literacy opportunities in a community-focused biology class. *Reading Research and Instruction, 43,* 1–30.

Budiansky, S. (1997). *The nature of horses: Exploring equine evolution, intelligence, and behavior.* New York: Free Press.

Dunkerly-Bean, J., Bean, T., & Alnajjar, K. (2014). Seeking asylum: Adolescents explore the crossroads of human rights education and cosmopolitan critical literacy. *Journal of Adolescent & Adult Literacy, 58*(3), 230–241.

Draper, R. J., Broomhead, P., Jensen, A. P., Nokes, J. D., & Siebert, D. (Eds.). (2010). *(Re) Imagining content area literacy instruction.* New York: Teachers College Press.

Finders, M., & Balcerzak, P. (2013). It's time to revise K-W-L. *Journal of Adolescent & Adult Literacy, 56*(6), 460.

Ford-Connors, E., Dougherty, S., Robertson, D. A., & Paratore, J. R. (2015). Mediating complex texts in the upper grades. *Journal of Adolescent & Adult Literacy, 58,* (8), 650-659.

Hoffman, J. V. (1992). Critical reading/thinking across the curriculum: Using I-charts to support learning. *Language Arts, 69,* 121–127.

Jumanji. (1995). [Film]. Columbia/Tristar Pictures.

Manzo, A. V., Casale, U., & Thomas, M. M. (2004). *Content area literacy: Strategic thinking for strategic learning* (4th ed.). New York: Wiley.

Martin, T. (1999). *Essential surrealists.* Bath, England: Parragon.

Morrell, E., Duenas, R., Garcia, V., & Lopez, J. (2013). *Critical media pedagogy: Teaching for achievement in city schools.* New York: Teachers College Press.

Raphael, T. E., Highfield, K., & Au, K. H. (2006). *QAR now: A powerful and practical framework that develops comprehension and higher-level thinking in all students.* New York: Scholastic.

Shanahan, C. (2004). Teaching science through literacy. In T. Jetton & J. A. Dole (Eds.), *Adolescent literacy research and practice* (pp. 75–93). New York: Guilford Press.

Stahl, S. A., & Shanahan, C. (2004). Learning to think like a historian: Disciplinary knowledge through critical analysis of multiple documents. In T. Jetton, & J. A. Dole (Eds.), *Adolescent literacy research and practice* (pp. 94–115). New York: Guilford Press.

Stevens, L. P. (2001). *South Park* and society: Instructional and curricular implications of popular culture in the classroom. *Journal of Adolescent & Adult Literacy*, 44, 548-555.

Stevens, L. P., & Bean, T. W. (2007). *Critical literacy: Context, research, and practice in the K–12 classroom.* Thousand Oaks, CA: SAGE.

Sturtevant, E. G., Boyd, F. B., Brozo, W. G., Hinchman, K. A., Moore, D. W., & Alvermann, D. E. (2006). *Principled practices for adolescent literacy: A framework for instruction and policy.* Mahwah, NJ: Erlbaum.

Tierney, R. J. (2009). The agency and artistry of meaning makers within and across digital spaces In S. E. Israel & G. G. Duffy (Eds.), *Handbook of research on reading comprehension* (pp. 261–288). New York: Routledge.

Tierney, R. J., & Readence, J. E. (2005). *Reading strategies and practices: A compendium* (6th ed.). Boston: Allyn & Bacon.

Walker, N. T., Bean, T. W., & Dillard, B. R. (2010). *When textbooks fall short: New ways, new texts, new sources of information in the content areas.* Portsmouth, NH: Heinemann.

CHAPTER 10, COMPREHENSION: GUIDING CONTENT LITERACY

Recommended Readings

Almasi, J. F., & Garas-York, K. (2009). Comprehension and discussion of text. In S. E. Israel & G. G. Duffy (Eds.), *Handbook of research on reading comprehension* (pp. 470–509). New York: Routledge.

The authors review key studies on discussion and point to those that increase students' higher-order thinking through collaborative approaches.

Bean, T. W., Readence, J. E., & Baldwin, R. S. (20112). *Improving reading for the 21st century adolescent.* Huntington Beach, CA: Shell Education.

This book offers a succinct array of strategies designed for middle and secondary teacher professional development inservices and workshops.

Berne, J. L., & Clark, K. F. (2006). Comprehension strategy use during peer-led discussion of text: Ninth graders tackle "The Lottery." *Journal of Adolescent & Adult Literacy, 49*, 674–686.

These authors offer a number of concrete recommendations for guiding students toward productive discussions in English and other content areas. Their work is based on classroom research with adolescents in English.

Dunkerly-Bean, J., & Bean, T. W. (2015). Exploring human rights and cosmopolitan critical literacy with global young adult literature multimodal text sets. *New England Reading Association Journal, 50*(2), 1–7.

This feature article explores how to construct and use multimodal text sets with a young adult novel.

Parker, W. C. (2003). *Teaching democracy: Unity and diversity in public life.* New York: Teachers College Press.

This book provides an excellent discussion of democratic processes along with specific strategies and materials teachers in social studies and other content areas can use to help students develop deliberative discussions.

References

Almasi, J. F., & Garas-York, K. (2009). Comprehension and discussion of text. In S. E. Israel & G. G. Duffy (Eds.), *Handbook of research on reading comprehension* (pp. 470–509). New York: Routledge.

Alvermann, D. E., Dillon, D. R., & O'Brien, D. G. (1987). *Using discussion to promote reading comprehension.* Newark, DE: International Reading Association.

Alvermann, D. E., O'Brien, D. G., & Dillon, D. R. (1990). What teachers do when they say they're having discussions of content area reading assignments: A qualitative analysis. *Reading Research Quarterly, 25*, 296–322.

Bean, T. W., Readence, J. E., & Baldwin, R. S. (2012). *Improving reading for the 21st century adolescent.* Huntington Beach, CA: Shell Education.

Berne, J. L., & Clark, K. F. (2006). Comprehension strategy use during peer-led discussion of text: Ninth graders tackle "The Lottery." *Journal of Adolescent & Adult Literacy, 49,* 674–686.

Bryson, B. (1999). *A walk in the woods: Rediscovering America on the Appalachian trail.* New York: Broadway Books.

Conley, M. W. (2009). Improving adolescent comprehension: Developing comprehension strategies in the content areas. In S. E. Israel & G. G. Duffy (Eds.), *Handbook of Research on reading comprehension* (pp. 531–550). New York: Routledge.

Curran, M. J., & Smith, E. C. (2005). The Imposter: A motivational strategy to encourage reading in mathematics. *Journal of Adolescent & Adult Literacy, 49,* 186–190.

Dunkerly-Bean, J., & Bean, T. W. (2015). Exploring human rights and cosmopolitan critical literacy with global young adult literature multimodal text sets. *New England Reading Association Journal, 50*(2), 1–7.

Dunkerly-Bean, J., & Bean, T. W. (2016). Missing the savoir for the connaissance: Disciplinary and content area literacy as regimes of truth. *Journal of Literacy Research.*

Duffelmeyer, F. A., & Baum, D. D. (1992). The extended anticipation guide revisited. *Journal of Reading, 35,* 654–656.

Ellis, D. (2014). *Moon at nine.* Toronto, Ontario, Canada: Pajama Press.

Harper, H. J., & Bean, T. W. (2006). Fallen Angels: Finding adolescents and adolescent literacy in a renewed project of democratic citizenship. In D. E. Alvermann, K. A. Hinchman, D. W. Moore, S. F. Phelps, & D. R. Waff (Eds.), *Reconceptualizing the literacies in adolescents' lives* (2nd ed., pp. 147–160). Mahwah, NJ: Erlbaum.

Hartman, D. K., & Allison, J. (1996). Promoting inquiry-oriented discussions using multiple texts. In L. B. Gambrell & J. F. Almasi (Eds.), *Lively discussions! Fostering engaged reading* (pp. 106–133). Newark, DE: International Reading Association.

Hawthorne, N. (1986). *The scarlet letter.* New York: Penguin. (Original work published 1850.)

Jackson, S. (1982). The lottery. In *The lottery and other stories* (pp. 291–301). New York: Farrar, Strauss and Giroux. (Original work published 1948.)

Jimenez, R. T. (1997). The strategic reading abilities and potential of five low-literacy Latina/o readers in middle school. *Reading Research Quarterly, 32,* 224–243.

Miller, A. (1976). *The crucible.* New York: Penguin.

Nesbit, J. C., & Adesope, O. O. (2006). Learning with concept and knowledge maps: A meta-analysis. *Review of Educational Research, 76,* 423–448.

Oliver, J. (2014). *Miss America Pageant: Last Week Tonight.* HBO: YouTube.

Parker, W. C. (2003). *Teaching democracy: Unity and diversity in public life.* New York: Teachers College Press.

Schwartz, M., & O'Connor, J. R. (1975). *New exploring a changing world.* New York: Globe Book.

Tan, A. (1991). *The kitchen god's wife.* New York: Ballantine.

Tierney, R. J., & Readence, J. E. (2005). *Reading strategies and practices: A compendium* (6th ed.). Boston: Allyn & Bacon.

Walker, N. T., Bean, T. W., & Dillard, B. R. (2010). *When text-books fall short: New ways, new texts, new sources of information in the content areas.* Portsmouth, NH: Heinemann.

Wimmer, J. J., Walker, N. T., & Bean, T. W. (2010). Exploring two content area teachers' creativity and use of multiliteracies in science and history. In R. T. Jimenez, V. J. Risko, M. K. Hundley, & D. W. Rowe (Eds.), *59th Yearbook of the National Reading Conference* (pp. 329–339). Oak Creek, WI: National Reading Conference.

Wineberg, S., & Reisman, A. (2015). Disciplinary literacy in history: A toolkit for digital citizenship. *Journal of Adolescent & Adult Literacy, 58*(8), 636–630.

CHAPTER 11, WRITING

Recommended Readings

Gallagher, K. (2006). *Teaching adolescent writers.* Portland, ME: Stenhouse.
Veteran English teacher Kelly Gallagher offers a powerful array of insights and approaches to engage reluctant writers in honing their compositions.

Kelly, L.B. (2015). "You can't just write an essay in an hour": Supporting middle schoolers' peer feedback and revision process through online writing groups. *Voices from the Middle, 23*(2), 81–86. This article demonstrates how to use an online peer editing application that helps small groups of students comment on each other's essays. The whole issue of this particular journal is full of good ideas about the teaching of writing.

Stephens, L. C., & Ballast, K. H. (2011). *Using technology to improve adolescent writing.* Boston: Pearson. The authors provide examples and guidelines for engaging students in wiki writing, blogging, and other Web 2.0 collaborative composition.

References

Bean, T. W. (2001). Writing across the curriculum. In L.W. Searfoss, J.E. Readence, & M.H. Mallette (Eds.), *Helping children learn to read* (5th ed., pp. 277–309). Boston: Allyn & Bacon.

Bean, T. W. (2002). Literacy autobiography. In B. J. Guzzetti (Ed.), *Literacy in America: An encyclopedia of history, theory, and practice* (pp. 308–310). Santa Barbara, CA: ABC-CLIO.

Bean, T. W. (2010). *Multimodal learning for the 21st century adolescent.* Huntington Beach, CA: Shell Education.

Bean, T. W., & Moni, K. (2003). Developing students' critical literacy: Exploring identity construction in young adult fiction. *Journal of Adolescent & Adult Literacy, 46,* 638–648.

Bean, T. W., & Rigoni, N. (2000, May). *Exploring the intergenerational dialogue journal discussion of a multicultural young adult novel.* Paper presented at the annual meeting of the International Reading Association, Indianapolis, IN.

Black, R. W. (2005). Access and affiliation: The literacy and composition practices of English-language learners in an online fanfiction community. *Journal of Adolescent & Adult Literacy, 49,* 118–128.

Calkins, L. M. (1994). *The art of teaching writing* (2nd ed.). Portsmouth, NH: Heinemann.

Chandler-Olcott, K. (2015). Using writers' notebooks to support inquiry and digital composing. *Voices from the Middle, 23*(2), 56–61.

Cowles, S. (2015). My absolutely crummy first draft: The trials and triumphs of motivating the adolescent writer. *Voices from the Middle, 23*(2), 74–80.

Crawley, S.A. (2015). Beyond digital stories: Crafting digital compositions for opinion writing. *Voices from the Middle, 23*(2), 49–55.

Denyer, R. (1982). *The guitar handbook.* New York: Knopf.

Dostal, H., & Gabriel, R. (2015). Designing writing instruction that matters. *Voices from the Middle, 23*(2), 14–20.

Gallagher, K. (2006). *Teaching adolescent writers.* Portland, ME: Stenhouse.

Gillespie, J. (2005). "It would be fun to do again": Multi-genre responses to literature. *Journal of Adolescent & Adult Literacy, 48,* 678–684.

Kelly, L.B. (2015). "You can't just write an essay in an hour": Supporting middle schoolers' peer feedback and revision process through online writing groups. *Voices from the Middle, 23*(2), 81–86.

Macrorie, K. (1988). *The I-search paper.* Portsmouth, NH: Heinemann.

Moore, D. W., Moore, S. A., Cunningham, P. M., & Cunningham, J. W. (2010). *Developing readers and writers in the content areas, K–12* (6th ed.). Boston: Allyn & Bacon.

National Governors Association Center for Best Practices & Council of Chief State School Officers. (2010). *Common Core State Standards for English Language Arts, & literacy in history/social studies, science, and technical subjects.* Washington, DC.

Newell, G. E., VanDerHeide, J., & Olsen, A. W. (2014). High school English Language Arts teachers' argumentative epistemologies for teaching writing. *Research in the Teaching of English, 49*(2), 95–119.

Newkirk, T. (1986). Time for questions: Responding to writing. In T. Newkirk (Ed.), *To compose* (pp. 121–124). Portsmouth, NH: Heinemann.

Nishida, G. A., & Tenorio, J. M. (1993). *What bit me? Identifying Hawaii's stinging and biting insects and their kin.* Honolulu: University of Hawaii Press.

Olson, C. B. (2003). *The reading/writing connection: Strategies for teaching and learning in the secondary classroom.* Boston: Allyn & Bacon.

Paul, D. G. (2000). Rap and orality: Critical media literacy, pedagogy, and cultural synchronization. *Journal of Adolescent & Adult Literacy, 44,* 246–251.

Porto, M. (2002). Implementing cooperative writing response groups and self-evaluation in South America: Struggle and survival. *Journal of Adolescent & Adult Literacy, 45,* 684–691.

Sandmann, A. (2006). Nurturing thoughtful revision using the Focused Question Card strategy. *Journal of Adolescent & Adult Literacy, 50*, 20–28.

Semingson, P. (2015). Meeting of the minds. *Journal of Adolescent & Adult Literacy, 59*(1), 6.

Stephens, L. C., & Ballast, K. H. (2011). *Using technology to improve adolescent writing.* Boston: Pearson.

Tompkins, G. E. (2003). *Teaching writing: Balancing process and product* (4th ed.). Columbus, OH: Merrill.

Walker, N. T., Bean, T. W., & Dillard, B. R. (2010). *When text-books fall short: New ways, new texts, new sources of information in the content areas.* Portsmouth, NH: Heinemann.

Werderich, D. E. (2002). Individualized responses: Using journal letters as a vehicle for differentiated reading instruction. *Journal of Adolescent & Adult Literacy, 45*, 746–754.

Wilson, K. C., & Jeffrey, J. V. (2014). Adolescents' writing in the content areas: National study results. *Research in the Teaching of English, 49*(2), 168–176.

CHAPTER 12, STUDYING AND PREPARING FOR EXAMINATIONS

Recommended Readings

Bean, T. W. (2010). *Multimodal learning for the 21st century adolescent.* Huntington Beach, CA: Shell Education.

Chapter 4 includes study strategies specific to online reading and studying, as well as other approaches for reading across multiple texts.

Flippo, R. (2015). *Studying and learning in a high-stakes world: Making tests work for teachers.* New York: Rowman & Littlefield.

This comprehensive book provides an array of test taking strategies and practices designed to help students succeed on high stakes tests including multiple choice and short answer formats. The book also offers tips on coping with test anxiety.

Littrell-Baez, M. K., Friend, A., Cacccamise, D., & Okochi, C. (2015). Using retrieval practice and metacognitive skills to improve content learning. *Journal of Adolescent & Adult Literacy, 58*(8), 682–689.

The article provides a detailed look at how to implement retrieval practice along with think-alouds and examples from science and social studies material.

References

Aiken, C. (1896). *Methods of mind training.* New York: Harper.

BakerL., & Beall, L. C. (2009). Metacognitive processes and reading comprehension. In S. E. Israel, & G. G. Duffy (Eds), *Handbook of research on reading comprehension* (pp. 373-388). New York: Routledge.

Bean, T. W. (2010). *Multimodal learning for the 21st century adolescent.* Huntington Beach, CA: Shell Education.

Flippo, R. F., Gaines, R., Rockwell, K. C., Cook, K., & Melia, D. (2015). *Studying and learning in a high-stakes world: Making tests work for teachers.* New York: Rowman & Littlefield.

Caverly, D. C., Orlando, V. P., & Mullen, J. L. (2000). Textbook study reading. In R. F. Flippo, & D. C. Caverly (Eds.), *Handbook of college reading and study strategy research* (pp. 105-147). Mahwah, NJ: Erlbaum.

Littrell-Baez, M. K., Friend, A., Cacccamise, D., & Okochi, C. (2015). Using retrieval practice and metacognitive skills to improve content learning. *Journal of Adolescent & Adult Literacy, 58*(8), 682–689.

Nist, S. L., Simpson, M. L., Olejnik, S., & Mealey, D. L. (1991). The relationship between self-selected study processes and test performance. *American Educational Research Journal, 28*, 849–874.

Reinking, D. (1986). Integrating graphic aids into content area instruction: The graphic information lesson. *Journal of Reading, 30*, 146–151.

Schumm, J. S., & Mangrum, C. T. (1991). FLIP: A framework for content area reading. *Journal of Reading, 35*, 120–124.

Simpson, M. L. (2007). PORPE: A study strategy for learning in the content areas. In T. W. Bean, J. E. Readence, & R. S. Baldwin (Eds.), *Content area literacy digital supplement.* Dubuque, IA: Kendall Hunt.

Wade, S. E., & Reynolds, R. E. (1989). Developing metacognitive awareness. *Journal of Reading, 33*, 6–14.

Author Index

Subject Index

Note: Page numbers followed by *f* indicate figures; those followed by *t* indicate tables.

E

Economic change, 97
Edu-blogs, 170
Electronic Numerical Integrator and Computer (ENIAC), 19
Embedded questions, 347
Encoding, 338
English as second language, 39
English Journal, 182
Enthusiastic model, of vocabulary, 203
Essay tests, preparation, 361–363
Etymologies, 211–213
Evaluating relevance, 239
Evaluation of textbooks
    checklist, 84*f*, 86*f*
    guidelines, 83–85
    qualitative factors, 79–83
Evaluations, 135–138
    by peer, 326–327
    by self, 325–326
Examination preparation, 334–366, 354–366
    essay tests, 361–363
    high stakes reading assessments, 354–357
    mirror assessment, 354–355
    multiple choice, 354
    PORPE: essay writing strategy, 363–366
        evaluation, 363, 364, 366
        organization, 363, 364
        PORPE checklist, 365*f*
        practice, 363, 364, 365–366
        prediction, 363, 364
        rehearsing, 363, 364, 365
    teacher-made assessments, 357–363
        student strategies, 358–360
        teacher strategies, 357–358
    testwiseness, 355–357
    tips for students, 358–360
    true-false tests, 360–361
Experience-based comprehension, 230, 231, 232
Explications, 232
    text structure, 236–237
Expressive vocabulary, 194
Extension activities, 223–225
    analogies, 223–224
    crossword puzzles, 225
    hidden-word puzzles, 224
    scrambled words activity, 224, 225*f*
External references, 196, 200–202
External storage, 338

F

Failure, passive, 142
Fake pop quiz, 357–358
Fallacy of grade-level reporting, 104
    standardized testing, 104
Fallen Angels, 160
False assumptions, content teachers, 8*t*
Fanfiction, 297
Farewell to Manzanar, 171
Feedback, 128
First Crossings: Stories about Teen Immigrants, 38, 166, 168
FLIP procedure, 350, 351*f*
    class review, 352
    personal review, 352
    steps for using, 350–352
    stumping teacher, 352
Focused question cards, 324
Focusing of attention, 10
Formal tests, 99–100
Formulas, readability, 77
Forward inferencing, 239
Free morpheme, 196
From Slave to Abolitionist: The Life of William Wells Brown, 161

G

General interest inventory, 158*f*
General vocabulary, 194
Geronimo, 165, 167
A Girl Named Digit, 162
Global literature, 166
Glossary, 200
    for vocabulary instruction, 208
Goal orientation, in studying, 335
Grade-level reporting, fallacy of, 104

M

multiple text inquiry discussion, 285–286

phony document strategy and sourcing in
history, 278–280

polar opposites, 281–283

reaction guides, 277–278

Prediction guides, prior knowledge assessment,
117–118, 118*f*

Preferences, reading, 157

Preparation for tests, 334–366, 354–366

essay tests, 361–363

essay writing strategy, 363–366

evaluation, 363, 364, 366

organization, 363, 364

PORPE checklist, 365*f*

practice, 363, 364, 365–366

prediction, 363, 364

rehearsing, 363, 364, 365

high stakes reading assessments, 354–357

mirror assessment, 354–355

teacher-made assessments, 357–363

student strategies, 358–360

teacher strategies, 357–358

testwiseness, 355–357

tips for students, 358–360

true-false tests, 360–361

Prereading phase modifications, 128, 144–145

Prereading strategies, 258–263

anticipation guides, 258–261, 260*f*, 261*f*

constructing, 258–261

text appetizers, 262–263, 262*f*

developing, 262–263

guiding questions, 262

introductory paragraph, 262

Presentation of content, concurrent, 11–12

Presenting content, processes concurrently, 11–12

Previewing text, 86–89, 87–89*f*

Prior knowledge, 51–65, 230

activating, 10

assessment, 116–118

knowledge rating, 116–117, 117*f*

prediction guides, 117–118, 118*f*

classroom social context, 62–65

cognitive structure, 51

concept learning, 53–54

digital literacies, 61–62

long-term memory, 57–59

memory, 56

motivation to learn, 54–55

organization in memory, 51–65

classroom social context, 62–65

cognitive structure, 51

concept learning, 53–54

digital literacies, 61–62

long-term memory, 57–59

memory, 56

motivation to learn, 54–55

reader interest, prior knowledge, 54

schema theory, 52

short-term memory, 56–57

student language, 60–61

text structure, 61–62

textual language, 59–60

topic, prior knowledge, 54

reader interest, prior knowledge, 54

schema theory, 52

short-term memory, 56–57

effect on literacy, 56–57

standardized testing, 103

student language, 60–61

text structure, 61–62

digital literacies, 61–62

textual language, 59–60

topic, prior knowledge, 54

Problems with Internet, 28–30

Problem/solution, 237

Process of writing, 292–294

composing and transcribing, 293–294

Processes

concurrent presentation, 11–12

content, concurrent presentation, 128

Pseudographs, 353, 354*f*

Public schools, high-stakes assessment, 107

Purposes of

economic change, 97

political change, 97

program evaluation, 97–98

student diagnosis, 98

testing, 95–98

I-Search papers, 319–320
    interview, 320
    search, 319–320
    topic selection, 319
    writing paper, 320
imaginative writing assignments, 321–322
multigenre writing, 322
research papers, 317–319
    assigning, 317–319
Writing-to-learn activities, 294–312, 306*f*, 310*f*
    cubing, 300–302
    Guided Writing Procedure, 308–312
    journal writing, 294–297
    Possible Sentences, 298
        creating sentences lesson, 298–300
    Quick Writes, 297–298
        postreading, 298
        prereading, 298

ReWrite, 304–308
student responses, 301*f*
writer's notebooks, 294–297
Writing Roulette, 302–304
    session, 302–304

Y

Young Adult Choices, 182
Young adult literature, 158–162
    for American history units, 158–162
    annotated list of, 158–162
    developing, 162–163
    multicultural, 163–166
    sources of, 182–183